REQUIREMENTS
ENGINEERING

REQUIREMENTS ENGINEERING
FRAMEWORKS FOR UNDERSTANDING

R. J. Wieringa

Faculty of Mathematics and Computer Science
Vrije Universiteit, Amsterdam

JOHN WILEY & SONS
Chichester · New York · Brisbane · Toronto · Singapore

Copyright © 1996 by   John Wiley & Sons Ltd.
Baffins Lane, Chichester,
West Sussex PO19 1UD, England

National   01243 779777
International   (+44) 1243 779777

Reprinted August 1996

Other Wiley Editorial Offices

John Wiley & Sons, Inc., 605 Third Avenue,
New York, NY 10158-0012, USA

Jacaranda Wiley Ltd, 33 Park Road, Milton,
Queensland 4064, Australia

John Wiley & Sons (Canada) Ltd, 22 Worcester Road,
Rexdale, Ontario M9W 1L1, Canada

John Wiley & Sons (Asia) Pte Ltd, 2 Clementi Loop #02-01,
Jin Xing Distripark, Singapore 0512

Library of Congress Cataloging in Publication Data

Wieringa, Roel.
   Requirements engineering: Frameworks for understanding / R. J.
  Wieringa
     p. cm.
  Includes bibliographical references and index.
  ISBN 0 471 95884 0 (alk. paper)
  1. Systems engineering. 2. System analysis. 1. Title.
 TA 168. W458 1995
 004.2' 1 – dc20   95 25014
                                       CIP

British Library Cataloguing in Publication Data

A catalogue record for this book is available from the British Library

ISBN 0 471 95884 0

Produced from camera-ready copy supplied by the author using LaTeX.
Printed and bound in Great Britain by Bookcraft (Bath) Ltd.
This book is printed on acid-free paper responsibly manufactured from sustainable forestation,
for which at least two trees are planted for each one used for paper production.

Contents

Preface

This book is about methods for determining computer system requirements. It is written primarily as an introduction to requirements engineering methods for computer science students, but the text has been organized in such a way that it can also be used by practitioners who want to place their work in a wider context.

Over the past 30 years, a jungle of methods and techniques has grown that can be used at different stages of development, from requirements determination to implementation and maintenance. This jungle is ill-structured in appearance, and students as well as practitioners are at a loss where to look for useful methodological advice. One may wonder if it is worthwhile to hack the methodological jungle at all. The goal of the book is to show that there is a structure in this jungle. The book starts in part I with the definition of a methodological framework that can be used to compare methods. In part II it then analyzes five methods for requirements determination, using this framework, and it ends in part III by collecting the results of these analyses into an integrated framework for requirements engineering methods. The text has the following features.

- Several frameworks for methods are defined. In part I, frameworks for system development and for requirements specifications are defined. In part III, the development framework is extended to a framework for development strategies.

- The development of computer-based systems is viewed as a species of industrial product development. Consequently, the frameworks are borrowed partly from the methodology of industrial product development.

- An engineering approach to system development is emphasized. Features of such an approach are the separation of specification from implementation, rational search for alternatives, and simulation of a solution before implementing it.

- The book focuses on methods for requirements engineering. These methods bridge the often informal world of human desires with the formal world of symbol manipulation. Mistakes are easily made in this task, it is hard to discover them, and the later they are discovered, the harder it is to repair them.

- The chapters on the five methods are written for computer science students without any knowledge of development methods. They present methods to the level of detail needed to do practical work with them, without getting buried in a mass of syntactic details. The chapters include two running case studies and each chapter finishes with exercises. Appendix A contains answers to selected exercises.

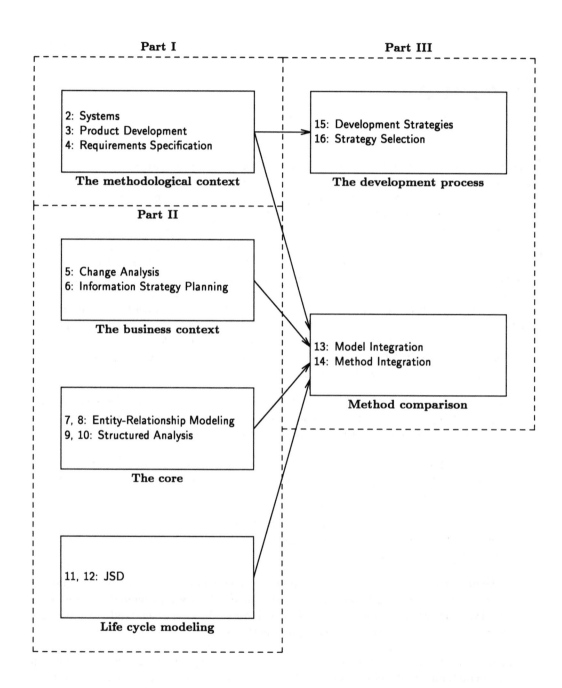

- There is an index containing all keywords and defined terms. The number of the page where a term is defined, is printed in boldface.

- As indicated in the figure, the substance of the chapters on the five methods can be read without knowing about the methodological frameworks of part I. The chapters are structured according to these frameworks, but it is not necessary to know these frameworks in order to read the chapters.

- Each chapter about a method ends with a methodological analysis of the method that presupposes the methodological frameworks of part I. This methodological discussion culminates in part III with an indication where and how the discussed methods can be integrated.

- The choice of methods has been very conservative. The methods included in part II are either widely used or they illustrate an interesting methodological point. One premise of this book is that every method contains at least one good idea and that there is no method that contains only good ideas. The approach has been to emphasize the good ideas. For reasons of space, only a fragment of some methods is explained.

It should be clear that this book advocates an eclectic approach to methods. The frameworks defined in this book can be viewed as empty toolboxes, to be filled with tools taken from different methods. These tools are conceptual. Their user should understand their possibilities and limitations, and should know which ones can be combined and which are mutually exclusive alternatives. It is one of the hallmarks of the engineer that he or she keeps an open mind about possibilities and does not choose a particular design too soon. This also applies to the choice of tools: even tools that have been invented long ago and are regarded as "outdated" may be useful.

Object-oriented methods are conspicuously absent from this book. The reason for this is that in order to achieve progress in the field of methods, we should understand and consolidate older methods before we advance to newer methods. A sequence of revolutions in which every revolution obliterates all memory of what has gone before, does not constitute progress. The book accordingly tries to consolidate the good ideas in structured methods. A companion volume currently in preparation (*Requirements Engineering: Semantic, Real-Time and Object-Oriented Methods*), uses the frameworks developed in this book to analyze advanced requirements modeling methods.

Chapters 1 through 14 and the practical work that goes with it can be covered in a one-semester course of 5 credit points (5 full-time weeks of student work) that includes practical work. Chapters 15 and 16 complete the methodological analysis begun in chapter 3 and can be reserved for a consolidation of these ideas in a follow-up course on process issues.

To understand methods, one should practice them. The chapters on the five methods should be accompanied with laboratory work in which students do case studies with these methods. A workbench that can be used to draw the diagrams of the different methods is available for academic and research purposes without fee at ftp site `ftp.cs.vu.nl` in directory `pub/tcm`. The workbench runs on Unix systems. For precise system requirements, refer to the file `README.TCM`.

As illustrated in the figure, the book has been structured in such a way that teachers can choose to omit some chapters.

- After the introductory chapter, chapters 7 to 10 form an introduction to the classical **core** of requirements specification, viz. ER modeling and Structured Analysis.

- To embed the core in its **methodological context**, part I can be used to discuss (software) product development and the framework for development methods used in this book. Each method chapter in part II ends with a methodological analysis, that presupposes knowledge of part I. By skipping these methodological analyses, the methods of part II can be treated without treating part I first.

- To explain the relation between requirements specification and the **business context**, the core can be extended with chapters 5 and 6 on Change Analysis and Information Strategy Planning.

- Jointly, chapters 1 to 10 give a fairly standard introduction to requirements specification. Chapters 11 to 14 treat JSD and method integration. These chapters are more difficult and can be used as part of an optional, more advanced course that focuses on **life cycle modeling** and on **method comparison**.

- Chapters 15 and 16 discuss strategies for the **development process** and can be used in any course that has covered part I of the book.

Parts of chapter 13 have been published in the *Computer Journal*, volume 38, number 1, by Oxford University Press. Thanks are due to five generations of students who, every year, patiently plodded through a version of this manuscript and took everything seriously that was written in it. Their problems with the text have taught me a lot. This book contains some of the fruits of many stimulating and enjoyable discussions with John-Jules Meyer, Frank Dignum and Hans Weigand about the formalization of system constraints, and with Wiebren de Jonge about the methodology of entity classification and identification. The book also benefited from discussions with and critical comments from Frank Dehne, Marcel Franckson, Remco Feenstra, Hanna Luden, Gunter Saake, Jeroen Scheerder and John Simons. Gaynor Redvers-Mutton of John Wiley & Sons, Inc. showed me how to rephrase my prose as natural language. Ameen Abu-Hanna provided some stimulating and useful comments on the first chapters of the book. Jan Broersen read the entire manuscript and prevented many typos and errors from going into print. Any remaining errors are to be blamed upon me.

Writing this book has been made bearable by the unseizing efforts of Mieke Poelman who, despite a busy career of her own, managed to find the time to keep me from my work. Her unconditional support has given me both the freedom and the strength to finish this project. I dedicate this book to her.

Bilthoven and Amsterdam, December 1995
RJW

1

Introduction

1.1 Computer-based Systems

This book is about methods to specify requirements for computer-based systems. To focus thoughts, it is useful to identify three groups of computer-based systems: automated information systems, communication systems and control systems. These groups are not disjoint, but each group has particular characteristics. In this section, I give a number of examples of systems in each group and in the next, we turn to methods to develop these systems.

The characterizing feature of computer-based **information systems** is that they store and manipulate large amounts of data.

- A system that registers the current store of items held by an outlet of a supermarket chain is an information system. For each kind of item sold by the outlet, the information system contains, say, a record containing information about the price, the number of items still in store, the supplier of the item, etc. These records are updated when goods are delivered and when the goods are moved from the store to the shop. The system may be connected to point-of-sale terminals with bar code readers, that read the kind and number of products when they are sold and transmit this information to the information system.

- A reservation system for airline tickets is an information system. The system may be distributed over many different travel agencies, that all have concurrent access to the services of the system in real time. The business transactions processed by the reservation system are reservations of flights made by air transport companies.

- A system that helps managers to analyze market trends and to predict possible effects of changes in strategy or of different ways to implement a chosen strategy is an information system. The system collects data from corporate databases, summarizes this into aggregate data, plots trends, and uses econometric models to compute alternative future scenarios.

The point-of-sale system and the reservation system are called *transaction processing systems*, because their main function consists in registering or performing business transactions.

The management support system is an example of a *decision support system*, because it supports management in making strategic decisions. If these systems are used by senior executives, they are also called *executive information system*. In this book, we view all of these systems as examples of information systems.

The characteristic feature of **communication systems** is that they involve heavy communication traffic between nodes that are located at geographically different places. As can be seen from the examples above, some information systems can be classified as communication systems as well. Other examples of communication systems include the following.

- An *electronic data interchange system* (EDI system) is a system that connects information systems of different companies with each other. The EDI system can be set up in such a way that the information systems of all outlets of a supermarket chain can be connected, through an EDI network, with the order processing system of a supplier of dairy products. For example, every Friday before noon, the information systems in the supermarket chain outlets determine the current stock of dairy products, compute or retrieve the expected buying pattern for the next week, and place an order for dairy products at the supplier over the EDI network, to be delivered on Monday morning.

- The INTIS network in the port of Rotterdam connects information systems of transport companies, shipping agents, docks, ship brokers, insurance companies, the Dutch postal services and customs. Movement of goods into and out of the harbor is accompanied by an exchange of messages over this network, that replaces a labor-intensive and error-prone flow of manually written documents.

- Weapons systems typically involve intensive communication between a command center, ground stations, satellites, and remote systems such as aircraft, in a highly distributed environment in which systems must respond in real time.

The characteristic feature of **control systems** is that they respond to events in their environment by sending control messages to the environment. Some communication systems may be classified as control systems as well. Usually, control systems have interfaces to hardware other than computers, they control the behavior of some of this hardware, they must function in real time and there are strict limits on the response time of the system. For this reason, control systems are also called *real-time systems* or *embedded systems*. We will not use these terms, for any system must operate in real time and is embedded in an environment. For example, most administrative systems must perform certain actions before certain hard deadlines, such as the end of the month (salary payment) or the end of the year (financial reporting). All information and communication systems are embedded in a social system, and many must communicate with hardware, just as control systems do. Examples of control systems include the following.

- A computer-based system that controls the barriers at the gate of a parking garage is a control system. The system must be able to sense that a car wants to enter the building, check that the car has permission, raise the barrier, sense that the car has passed and lower the barrier before another car can enter. The system must monitor the number of cars in the building and refuse entry of a car as long as the building is full.

- Another example is an elevator control system that monitors requests for elevator service and directs the elevator cage to the appropriate floors.

- A computer integrated manufacturing control system that monitors the movement of material through a number of machines is an example of a control system.

Having given an idea of the kind of systems that we are interested in, we now turn to the topic of the book, methods to develop these systems.

1.2 System Development Methods

Since, at the end of the 1960s, the idea arose that computer-based systems must be developed in a methodical way, the field of system development methods has been in a state of flux. In the 1960s, system development was mainly concerned with implementation, viewed narrowly as programming. Wider issues such as requirements analysis and system specification were ignored. In the 1970s, a number of methods were introduced that in one way or another left the computer programming level and took these wider issues into account. Several methods for structured analysis and requirements specification came into being, culminating in methods for the structured specification of real-time systems in the mid-1980s. In parallel to this, methods were proposed to specify the meaning of data, such as entity-relationship modeling and these evolved into so-called semantic modeling methods in the early 1980s. By the end of the 1980s, the structured and semantic approaches were followed by an ever growing crop of object-oriented analysis and design methods. The bibliographical remarks in section 1.5 lists references to 26 methods for requirements specification, illustrative for each of the groups just mentioned: structured, semantic and object-oriented methods. This is not an exhaustive list: the actual number of methods in use by practitioners or proposed by researchers runs in the hundreds, if not thousands, if counted world-wide. Clearly, this multitude of methods poses problems for the novice as well as for the experienced practitioner.

- A problem for the novice is that it is not clear which of these methods one should learn, if any. Do the new, object-oriented (OO) methods make other methods obsolete? Can we save time by ignoring the older methods and limit our reading only to the object-oriented methods? Is it possible to understand object-oriented methods without knowing anything about the older methods? Conversely, is it possible to understand current practice after having read only about object-oriented methods?

- The practitioner too wonders what the relation between new object-oriented methods and the older structured ones is. How can methods be evaluated on their effectiveness and efficiency in developing the system that the user really wants? Supposing it is worthwhile to move to a new method, how can this transition best be accomplished? Which method is "best", according to a set of criteria chosen by management, for a given development project? Is there a way in which a customized method can be built for a development project, using components from existing methods?

These questions revolve around the underlying problem of what the relationships between the different methods — new and old — are. It is the aim of this book to provide analytic frameworks with which to understand current and future methods, and to apply these frameworks to a number of important current methods.

1.3   The Structure of the Book

Although some of the frameworks given in this book apply to the entire development process, we focus on methods for *requirements specification.* The reason for this is that requirements specification is an identifiable and important activity within system development. Requirements specification is an identifiable activity for which many methods have been proposed. Indeed, it is arguable that all development methods listed in section 1.2 deal with requirements at some level of aggregation, and ignore other important topics like system decomposition, integration and testing. The focus on requirements specification can be justified because errors made in requirements become increasingly costly to repair the later we are in development, and are extremely costly to repair after delivery of the system — if they can be repaired at all in that stage.

In order to understand requirements specification methods, we look in part I at the wider context of product development. In chapter 2, we define **systems** as parts of the world that have an observable behavior and an internal structure, and **products** as artificial systems constructed to provide a function to users. In chapter 3, we look at product development, the product life cycle, product evolution and product engineering. Chapter 3 ends with the definition of a framework for product development methods, which allows us to identify the place of requirements specification in product development. The framework also shows what the logical structure of the requirements specification activity is. In chapter 4 we focus on the result of the requirements specification process, and give a framework that tells us what the logical structure of requirements specifications is. The two frameworks are used in part II to analyze five methods for requirements specification.

- In chapter 5, we look at Change Analysis and Activity Study, which are part of the ISAC method for developing information systems.

- In chapter 6, we look at Information Strategy Planning (ISP), which is part of Information Engineering.

- In chapters 7 and 8, we look at the Entity-Relationship (ER) method and at the structure of the specifications produced by this method.

- In chapters 9 and 10, we look at Structured Analysis (SA) and at the structure of the specifications produced by this method.

- In chapters 11 and 12, we look at a part of the Jackson System Development (JSD) method and at the structure of the specifications produced by this method.

In part III, we gather the results of our analyses and fill out the two frameworks. In chapter 13, we compare the structure of software requirements specifications produced by ER modeling, SA, and JSD by placing them in the framework developed in chapter 4. In chapter 14, we summarize the results about finding and evaluating requirements specifications by placing them in the framework developed in chapter 3.

The focus of the two frameworks is on the *logical* structure of requirements specifications and of methods to find and evaluate such specifications. In chapters 15 and 16 we extend our framework to incorporate the temporal dimension. This allows us to define alternative development **strategies** in chapter 15. These are all compatible with the logical framework for development defined in chapter 3, but choose different paths through the logical tasks.

In chapter 16, we conclude the book by discussing the spiral method and Euromethod as ways to select an appropriate strategy for a particular development process.

1.4 Methods, Techniques, Heuristics, Notations and Methodologies

As can be seen from the short overview above, a major element in the approach of this book is the distinction between methods and methodology. Part II of this book is a description of methods, parts I and III contain a methodological analysis of methods. In this section, we define some terms that are used throughout the book.

A **method** is a systematic way of working by which one can obtain a desired result. The desired result may be the specification of a more cost-effective way of operating a business, a specification of product requirements, a specification of the decomposition of a system, a specification of a marketing plan, a specification of a production process, an implemented product, an installed product, etc.

A **technique** is a *recipe* for obtaining a certain result. Since a recipe is a systematic way to obtain a certain result, all techniques are methods. However, not all methods are techniques. Usually, techniques prescribe a way of working in detail, whereas methods need not contain detailed instructions. There are techniques to serve a volleyball, to perform a dance, to bake a pancake, and to write a structured program. Many methods contain techniques to perform particular tasks. Examples of techniques treated in this book are the diagonalization technique of Information Engineering and the technique of transforming an ER model into a relational database schema. Techniques can often be practiced to perfection and in many cases can be automated. When applied to the right problem in the right context, they are guaranteed to deliver the desired result. However, applied outside their proper context, they lead to garbage.

Most methods additionally provide heuristics to help the developer find or evaluate a system specification. A **heuristic** is a problem-solving advice that has proved to lead to a good solution in many cases. Application of a heuristic is not guaranteed to lead to the desired result. Heuristics given by Polya [263] to solve mathematics problems are to look at related problems, to try a more accessible related problem first, to go back to definitions, etc. Examples of heuristics to find a system specification are to analyze natural language descriptions of system behavior, to look at possible use scenarios, to list the events to which the system must respond, etc.

A **notation** is a systematic way to *represent* something. Notations may be linguistic, consisting of textual symbols, or graphical, consisting of diagrams. All methods discussed in this book use diagrams as part of their notation to represent a system. Examples are ER diagrams, data flow diagrams, Jackson process structure diagrams, etc. Most methods supplement the diagram notation with textual notation, in the form of a data dictionary, annotations to diagrams, narrative text, etc.

Methodology is the study of methods. For example, the methodology of empirical science is the study of methods used to discover laws of nature; the methodology of mathematics is the study of methods used to find and prove mathematical truths; and the methodology of engineering is the study of methods used to produce useful artifacts. This book is an example of engineering methodology, in particular of the methodology of building computer-based systems.

1.5   Bibliographical Remarks

Computer-based systems. The engineering of computer-based systems (ECBS) was the subject of a workshop held in Neve-Ilan, Israel in May 1990 [189]. This workshop led to the institution of an IEEE Computer Society task force on ECBS [360], which summarized the state of the practice in this area and identified topics for research. In Europe, the ATMOSPHERE project was launched in 1990, partly funded as an Esprit II technology integration project [245]. Its aim was to contribute to the state of the art in the engineering of computer-based systems. An overview of methodological results of the ATMOSPHERE project is given by Thomé [345].

Introductions to particular kinds of computer-based systems are Davis and Olson [82] and Kendall and Kendall [174] for information systems, and Keen and Scott Morton [171] for decision support systems. Good introductions to control systems are given by Ward and Mellor [354, 355, 227], Hatley and Pirbhay [141] and by Goldsmith [118]. These references include some discussion of distribution and communication aspects.

System development methods. Examples of information system development methods developed in the 1970s and 1980s are ISAC [204], SSADM [14, 91], Information Engineering [217], ETHICS [235] and Multiview [16], which is built from components of other methods. Examples of conceptual modeling methods that have their roots in the 1970s are ER modeling [65], Structured Analysis [84, 108] and SADT [210]. Two methods with their roots in the 1970s, but which were published in the 1980s, are NIAM [244] and JSD [57, 56, 158]. Another development in the 1980s is the advent of semantic modeling methods, such as the Event Model [179, 180], SDM [135], TAXIS [46], and ACM/PCM [52]. Important methods for the development of control systems (real time and embedded) are the Ward-Mellor extension of SA [354, 355, 227] and the Hatley-Pirbhai extension [141]. Goldsmith [118] develops the Ward-Mellor method further and Shumate and Keller [313] integrate the Hatley-Pirbhai method with elements of the Ward-Mellor method. Gomaa developed a family of structured methods for control systems called DARTS, ADARTS and CODARTS [119, 120, 122]. These methods contain useful advice on structuring criteria for control systems. Examples of methods composed of elements of other methods are Information Engineering [213], SSADM [14, 91, 98], and Multiview [16].

In the 1990s, object-oriented methods became the focus of interest. Examples are the Booch method [45], OMT [296], the Shlaer-Mellor method [308, 309], the Coad-Yourdon [68, 377], the Martin-Odell [218], Objectory [163] and the ROOM method [307]. The FUSION method [71] is built from components of other methods, notably OMT and some elements of formal specification. An important part of research in object-oriented methods is concerned with the question whether object-oriented methods can be integrated with older, well-known methods like SA and ER modeling and whether semantic modeling can be made part of object-oriented modeling [6, 19, 304, 353, 363].

Part I

An Analysis of Product Development

2

Systems

2.1 Introduction

The concept of a system is a crucial tool in understanding system development methods. Unfortunately, different authors use different definitions of this concept. Some view a system as an organized collection of components, others view the concept of a state space as central to the system concept and still others take purposive behavior as the defining characteristic of a system. In section 2.2, we start from a minimal concept of a system that is common to all different approaches, viz. that of a system as an observable part of the world. In section 2.3, we introduce the familiar concept of a system as an organized collection of related elements. In section 2.4, we add the perspective of observable system behavior, which allows us to define the important concept of state space. In section 2.5, we look at systems from the perspective of their function for their environment, which allows us to introduce the concept of system objective. This falls short of the idea of purposive behavior mentioned above, but it suffices for our purpose. The distinctions between function, behavior and structure are summarized in section 2.6. In section 2.7, we look at a concept that is characteristic for data-manipulating systems such as computers, the universe of discourse.

2.2 System Boundary

2.2.1 The observability of systems

It is possible to speak of the system of natural numbers, a system of law, a software system, a system of logical inference rules and the solar system. For our purpose, a system concept that would encompass all these different uses of the word "system" would be too general to be useful. We will therefore restrict the use of the term to **observable** systems, where the concept of observation is left unexplained. If pressed for an explanation, I would say that an observation is always an interaction of a system with its environment, where the interaction may be initiated by the system or by its environment. Conversely, any interaction of a system with its environment is viewed in this book as an observation of the system by its environment. (Depending upon one's point of view, it can also be viewed as an observation of the environment by the system). This reduces one unexplained concept (observation) to another (interaction) and vice versa. Perhaps this is typical for starting points.

In what follows, I treat **observation** as synonymous with **interaction** between systems. To make the situation more vivid, I will often treat the environment of a system as an *observer* who observes the system by interacting with it. Each interaction can be viewed as an experiment in which the observer learns something about the system.

Given this, a **system** is defined as any actual or possible part of reality that, if it exists, can be observed. We illustrate this definition with some examples, non-examples and borderline cases of systems:

- Physical objects like cars, stones, trees, elevators and airplanes are systems. Observations of these systems include observations of their color, weight, speed, and location. To make observations, we perform an interaction with the system, and when we interact with these systems, we make observations.

- Intangible objects like operating systems, database management systems, information systems and organizations are systems. From the point of view of physics, these objects are not observable. Nevertheless, they can interact with other systems and from our point of view therefore, they are observable. If we were to restrict ourselves to observations allowed in physics, organizations would be invisible, but since we allow observations allowed in social science and psychology, organizations are observable. Observations of these systems include observations of responses to commands, queries, requests, statements, of the time it takes to produce these responses, of resource usage during the production of the responses, etc.

- Abstract entities like numbers, truth values and letters are not systems. The number 3 cannot interact with other numbers or with anything else. It does stand in mathematical relations to other numbers, but this is different from engaging in interactions with those numbers. The mathematical relations are not events occurring in time. Similarly, the letter denoted by the symbol "a" cannot interact with other systems. By contrast, a *symbol* that represents the number 3 or the letter "a" can interact with other systems. It can be written, read and erased, for example.

- The "system" of Peano axioms for the natural numbers is not a system in our sense, for it cannot interact with other systems. It just has some logical relations to other axiom "systems" and to propositions about the natural numbers.

- Physicists define a "closed system" as something that cannot interact with its environment. For example, a closed container of gas is an idealized body that has no interaction with its environment. "Closed systems" are useful fictions for doing thought experiments and for approximating the behavior of real systems, but they do not exist in reality. They are not systems as we define the term here.

- A system of law is a system in our sense. It has a period of existence and may interact with other systems of law as well as with events occurring in the society ruled by the system of law. Nevertheless, it also shares some properties with the "system" of natural numbers. A system of law has for example logical relations to other systems of law and to propositions about the real world. It is therefore a borderline case of our concept of a system.

As pointed out above, many entities that we talk about are social constructs that have no physical existence. In one way or another, employees, committees, organizations, bank accounts, and budgets are socially constructed entities that are physically invisible. All we can observe physically are human bodies, buildings, symbols written on pieces of paper, symbols printed on screens, and sounds produced by people. Nevertheless, these socially constructed entities always include observation procedures in their definition. Observable properties of an employee include his or her employee number, role in the organization, and salary; observable properties of a committee are its name, function and composition; observable properties of a bank account are its number, owner and balance. These social constructs exist because we agreed upon ways to observe them. If no observation procedures were agreed upon, the salary of an employee, the composition of a committee and the balance of a bank account would not exist.

From a physical point of view, making these observations always consists of interacting with *something else*. Often, this something else is a system that *is* physically observable, such as a written or printed record. For example, we observe the balance of a bank account by observing a paper-based or computer-based administration. In this book, we view these physical interactions as *implementations* of abstract interactions with these social constructs. In the physical interactions, we observe properties of these social constructs.

Of course, ocassionally, there may be conflicts about the observable properties of social constructs; but then there are procedures agreed upon to resolve those conflicts. For example, when there is disagreement about the actual balance on of a bank account, we turn to recorded statements to resolve the disagreement; if there is disagreement about what is recorded, we resort to procedures to reach an irrefutable verdict about what the balance is; and if this verdict contradicts some written records, then the verdict states the fact of the matter and the written records are overruled. This means that observation of the balance is not the same thing as observation of what is recorded. Reading what is recorded is a way to *implement* the observation, but this implementation may be wrong and we may turn to other implementations.

Our definition of systems has three important consequences. First, define the **environment** of a system as that part of the world with which it can interact. It then follows from the definition that each system has an environment; and that the environment of a system is a system itself too. The choice to call it an environment merely indicates our focus.

A second consequence is that systems may be actual or possible. We define a system to **exist** if it is capable of interacting with other existing systems. This is a circular definition, for the concept of an existing system is used to define the concept of an existing system. However, this circularity is harmless. The definition just says that to exist is to be able to interact, i.e. to be able to initiate or suffer interactions. For example, a symbol stored on disk exists, because it can be operated upon: it can be read or erased. According to this concept of existence, abstract entities like numbers and truth values do not exist, because they cannot interact with existing systems. By contrast, a symbol written on paper that represents a number exists, because it can be manipulated.

The third consequence of the definition is that systems are **dynamic**. This is because systems can *interact* with other systems and interactions occur in time. Systems therefore exist in time. Going through the list of examples and nonexamples of systems above, we see that each of the examples can be said to exist in time and each of the nonexamples stands outside time.

- Each system should have an underlying **system idea** that describes its coherence.
- Interaction among system components (**cohesion**) is higher than interaction between the system and its environment (**coupling**).
- Changes within a system should cause minimal changes outside the system.
- There are more relations between system components than between system components and the environment.
- More energy is needed to transfer something across the system boundary than to transfer something within the system boundary.
- Each system boundary should "divide nature at its joints".
- The system boundary should be chosen in such a way that the number of regularities in the behavior of the system is higher than with any other choice of system boundary.
- The system boundary should be chosen in such a way that system behavior is simpler than with any other choice of system boundary.

Figure 2.1: Modularity guidelines.

2.2.2   System boundary and modularity

We call the set of *all possible* interactions of a system its **interface** or **boundary**. Some interactions in a system's interface may never occur, others may occur frequently. The interface of a candy store contains interactions like *sell chocolate bar*, which may occur frequently, and *sell 100 bars of chocolate*, which may never actually occur.

The choice of where to put a system boundary is up to us, the observers of the system. Of course, some choices are better than others. Suppose that we define a system S as consisting of a coffee machine *excluding* the buttons to operate it. Since S is an observable part of the world, it is a system according to our definition. However, the observable behavior of S is harder to understand than it would be if we had included the buttons in the system. In both cases, we can observe interactions like *insert coin* and *emit cup*, but without the buttons, we cannot observe interactions like *push coffee button*. This makes system behavior unnecessarily hard to understand, because the machine seems to emit cups without reason. If we had included the behavior of the buttons in the system boundary, then observable behavior would have been easy to understand. Apparently, there are good and bad choices of a system boundary.

There is in general one guideline for defining a system boundary: define it such that the system is **modular**. This means, vaguely, that the system must act as a more or less independent unit and that the separation between the system and its environment is "larger" than the separation of the components of the system. Figure 2.1 lists some criteria for modularity. These are still vague, but nevertheless should convey a message. The underlying **idea** of a system is its concept of operation, the rationale of its behavior. When a system has a single underlying idea, it is likely to be coherent and should therefore be modular. For example, the idea of a solar system is that a number of bodies revolve around the sun, and the idea of a coffee machine is that it dispenses coffee upon request. From this idea of a coffee machine, it follows that there should be some device that allows the user to make a request for coffee. Consequently, the system boundary should be chosen in such a way that this device, say a button, is included.

2.3 System Structure

2.3.1 Subsystems and aspect systems

Any observable part of the world, except the smallest particle (if it exists), consists of components that themselves are observable and hence are systems. These components are called **subsystems**. For example, an organization consists of departments, a software system consists of modules, a house consists of rooms, etc. We will say that a system is **implemented** in its subsystems. The behavior of a system is realized by means of the behavior of its subsystems, including their interactions with each other and with the environment. This means that a system is a collection of subsystems *acting as a whole*. An arbitrary collection of mechanical parts is not usefully regarded as a system; a collection of parts put together to form a car is usefully regarded as a system. The system behaves as it does, not only because each of its parts behaves as it does, but because the parts interact in a way such that the total system behavior is realized. A system is thus an *organized* collection of interacting subsystems. As expressed by the modularity heuristics, there is a cohesion between the subsystems.

Subsystem boundaries should be chosen in such a way that the subsystems are modular. The entire system is then said to have a **modular architecture**.

We define an **aspect** of a system as a subset of all possible interactions of the system. If we observe all subsystems of a system S but restrict our observations to some of the interactions between them, then we observe an **aspect system** of S. For example, the financial aspect system of an organization consists of all departments of the organization, together with their financial interactions. An information system may be viewed as a *subsystem* of an organization, consisting of hardware, software, users, user procedures and the data manipulated by them. Alternatively, we may view it as an *aspect system* of the organization, consisting of all departments of the organization and the flows of information among them.

We call interactions in which only subsystems of a system S participate **internal** to S, and interactions in which at least one external system of S participates **external**. Figure 2.2 shows a library L and an environment consisting of a single user U, and some subsystems of L, viz. a database D, a circulation desk C and a store room S. Interactions are represented by lines. The interactions *available?*, *availability* and *get_book* are invisible for the environment U and hence internal to L. The interactions *borrow_request*, *give_book* and *not_available* are observable by U, and hence external. Note that in real life, the clerk may search the database and go to the store room in full sight of the user. However, these observations are not relevant interactions with the user and they have not been modeled in figure 2.2. As far as this model is concerned, they are invisible to the user.

Engineers usually try to hide internal interactions from view by the users. Thus, a protective cover is placed around the internals of a coffee machine to hide implementation behavior that is irrelevant for the user of the coffee machine. In a business viewed as a system, such a protective cover may take the form of procedures for interacting with customers, layout of offices, rules for restricting the disseminating information, etc., all of

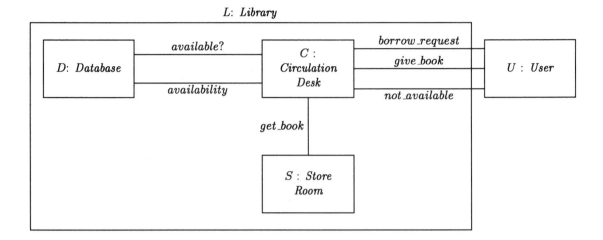

Figure 2.2: Some subsystems and interactions of a library.

which serve to hide internal interactions from external view. Interestingly, there are also internal interactions in a business that need no protective cover to be hidden: gossip at the coffee machine, secret agreements, etc. Indeed, the protective cover of these internal interactions is itself invisible. People can hide some of their interactions by pretending that they never took place. Unlike the metal plate covering the internals of a coffee machine, the cover-up of secret interactions between people can itself be made invisible. This is something the information analyst will have to deal with when he or she tries to model some of the internal business interactions.

2.3.2   A hierarchy of system levels

The world can be divided into levels such that systems that exist at any level are decomposed into systems at the next lower level. We call this the **aggregation** or **implementation hierarchy** in this book. At each level of aggregation, we view the world as a collection of interacting systems. The behavior of a system is the result of the interactions among its subsystems and between its subsystems and its environment. For example, figure 2.2 shows the interactions between the subsystems of a library and its environment that realize the *borrow* interaction between the library and a user. The behavior of the system is sometimes said to **emerge** from the behavior and interaction of the subsystems. The concept of emergence indicates that the behavior of the subsystems itself is not sufficient to explain the behavior of the compound system. To explain the compound behavior, one must additionally take into account the way in which the subsystems interact.

Any partitioning of the world into hierarchical levels is a simplification. For example, the library database may be part of a national network of library databases in which the clerk can search through the normal database interface. Are these other databases subsystems of the library? Is the library a subsystem of this network? Any answer to these questions leaves out an aspect of reality. Nevertheless, hierarchical decomposition is the major tool of the human mind for complexity reduction. We use it precisely with the purpose of simplifying

Level	Examples
Social system	An organization, a company division, a set of organizations
Computer-based system	An information system, an elevator system, an EDI network, a flight simulator
Software system	A database system, an elevator control system, a network communication software system
Software subsystem	An error recovery module, an authentication subsystem, a scheduler

Figure 2.3: A useful aggregation hierarchy from the software engineer's point of view.

our model of reality. As long as we do not forget that we are dealing with a simplification, hierarchical decomposition allows us to focus on the systems of interest within an otherwise bewildering complexity of systems within systems.

In this book, we will use the system hierarchy shown in figure 2.3. We explain the hierarchy level by level.

- Any system that we build for human use interacts with a human environment. The top level of the hierarchy is therefore that of **social systems**. The social system into which our product is embedded may be a human-machine system consisting of one user and one machine, or it may be an organization, or a group of organizations. For example, a word processing package is used by an individual, an information system is used by an organization, and an EDI system is used by a group of organizations.

- Taking the archetypical case of a system developed for use in an organization, the next lower level of aggregation is that of a **computer-based system**. Examples of computer-based systems are automated information systems, EDI systems, elevator systems and flight simulators. Of course, many of these systems may be implemented without using computers — paper-based information systems, electromagnetic elevator control systems, etc. Figure 2.3 takes a software engineer's point of view and focuses on computer-based systems.

- In the cases of interest for us, the computer-based system is composed, at the next lower level, of hardware and **software** systems (and possibly other kinds of systems). For example, an information system, viewed as a subsystem of an organization, is composed of hardware, software, users, procedures followed by users, and data manipulated by the people and the software. If the computer-based system is composed of hardware and software only, such as an elevator system, then it is customary to call it simply *the system* and to call the software *embedded*. Figure 2.3 takes a software engineer's point of view and shows only software systems below the computer-based system level. There are other relevant kinds of systems at this level of aggregation, such as hardware systems, users, and operators. The software engineer must interact with developers specialized in these other subsystems.

- Software systems are in turn composed of **software subsystems**, which may be called *packages*, *modules*, *classes*, or whatever.

If we develop a system at some level in this hierarchy, then we must determine *what* that system must do and *how* the system is going to do this. A specification of *what* the system must do at that level of aggregation is usually called a *requirements specification*. This is contrasted with *how* the system is realized internally at the next lower level of aggregation, which is called its *implementation*. The hierarchy of figure 2.3 shows that these distinctions are meaningless if we do not indicate to which level of the hierarchy we refer. A specification of the *implementation* of a computer-based system contains a specification of the *requirements* for its software subsystems, for example. This is not different from the fact that in an apartment building, one person's floor is another person's ceiling [76] — but it is more confusing, because the distinctions we make in system engineering are cast in concepts rather than in concrete.

To resolve the ambiguity between the *what* and the *how*, we should replace the distinction between *what* a system does and *how* it does it with the distinction between

- an indication of the level of aggregation we want to refer to, and

- an indication of the observer looking at that level of aggregation.

For example, at the level of libraries, a library user can observe such interactions as *borrow* a document (figure 2.2). At the same level of aggregation, a publisher can observe other interactions, such as *buy document*. These two observers (user and publisher) see different observable behavior of the library but they observe the library at the same level of aggregation. Descending one level of aggregation, the very same observers will see different behavior too. At the level of library subsystems, the library user can observe interactions such as *borrow_request*, *give_book* and *not_available* and the publisher observes such interactions as *order document*, *send invoice* and *pay for invoice*.

2.4 System Behavior

2.4.1 System state

Systems engage in observable behavior by engaging in interactions with their environment. Any system with interesting behavior has a *memory* of past interactions such that its behavior in a current interaction depends upon this memory. The memory of a system is called the system **state**, and the set of all its possible states is called its **state space**. A system is called **discrete** when its state space is a discrete set. Skipping the formal definitions, a state space is discrete when all states in it can be numbered using the natural numbers. For many purposes, organizations can be modeled as discrete systems. Information systems and many communication systems are also usually specified as discrete systems.

A system is called **continuous** when state information cannot be encoded by the natural numbers but we need real numbers to represent the possible states. In a **hybrid** system, part, but not all of a state can be encoded by the natural numbers. An example of a hybrid system is a computer-controlled audio system. The computer control itself is discrete, but it must interface with continuous systems such as potentiometers and speakers, so that the total system is hybrid.

The concept of a state is linked to those of the aggregation level and the observer of a system. For example, the state of the library is the sum of the states of each of its subsystems; in turn, each of these subsystem states is the sum of the states of *its* subsystems, etc. We can decompose the state of the library down to any level of decomposition we want. However, for the library user, it is only useful to observe some of the states at the highest level of aggregation. A library user can observe whether or not a document is available for borrowing — e.g. by trying to borrow the document. What this means for the state of the store room and the database system is not important to the user. For the circulation desk clerk, on the other hand, these internal states *are* important. In other words, at any level of aggregation, and with respect to an observer or class of observers at that level of aggregation, part of the state space of a system is *observable*.

As a consequence, there is no such thing as "the" state space of a system. We must define a state space with respect to a level of aggregation and with respect to an observer of system states at that level of aggregation. This determines which states are observable and at what level of detail they are observable.

2.4.2 System transactions

In this subsection, we restrict the discussion to observable system states. At the start of an interaction, a system is in a certain (observable) state and at the end of the interaction (assuming the interaction has an end), it is again in in a state. Let us call these states the *initial* and *final* states, respectively. Any state of the system after the initial state of the interaction and before the final state of the interaction is called an *intermediary* state of the interaction. An interaction is called a **transaction** if it is has no observable intermediary states. We say that transactions are **atomic**. Transactions have the atomicity property that at any moment in time, either the transaction has occurred or it has not occurred; there is no observable intermediary state in which the transaction has started to occur but has not yet finished. For example, at the library level of aggregation and with respect to library users, *borrow* is a transaction that either occurs or does not occur. At the next lower level of aggregation, and again for library users, transactions like *borrow_request* and *give_book* can be observed. These lower level transactions implement the higher level *borrow* transaction (figure 2.2).

According to Gray [126], the concept of transaction has its roots in contract law. In making a contract, two or more parties negotiate for a while and then make a deal. The deal is made binding by some ceremony, like signing a contract or even a simple handshake or nod. The function of this ceremony is to mark a discrete point in time, before which the contract did not exist and after which the contract exists; as far as the observers of the negotiations are concerned, there are no intermediary states between non-existence and existence of the contract. Important observers of the negotiations are the parties to the contract themselves and, possibly, the judge if there is disagreement about the contract.

Just like the concept of observable state, a transaction is defined at a particular level of aggregation and with respect to a particular observer, or class of observers. The crucial characteristic of a transaction is that, at that level of aggregation and with respect to those observers, it has no observable intermediary states. To implement this, the next lower level of aggregation must offer a **rollback** mechanism to undo an unsuccessful transaction attempt, and a **commitment** mechanism by which a successful transaction attempt is turned into a transaction. For example, during the negotiations for the sale of a house, either party can withdraw, after which the transaction attempt has been rolled back and no transaction is said to have taken place. However, after the sales contract is signed, the transaction has been committed and rollback is not possible.

Figure 2.4: Payment by giro as a complex transaction. The role of postal services has been ignored here.

Deciding when a transaction has been committed may be a case to be ruled in court. For example, making a payment by giro involves a process involving in general two banks, a clearing house and two customers (figure 2.4). High court in the Netherlands has ruled that the payment transaction takes place at the moment when the receiver of the payment gets the legal power over the transferred amount [125, page 270]. For a payment by giro, this happens at the moment that the receiver's bank credits the receiver's bank account, i.e. when *BANK 2* credits the account of the payee.

After a transaction has been committed, we may try to undo some of its results, by means of a **compensating transaction**. For example, after we bought a house, we may want to undo this transaction by reselling the house to the original owner. After borrowing a document, we may change our mind and return the document. These compensating transactions do *not* roll back the original transaction, but try to undo some of its effects. The difference with a rollback is that once a transaction has been committed, it is part of the observable history of the system. By contrast, when a transaction attempt is rolled back, the transaction never took place and it is not part of the observable history of the system. This is often expressed by saying that the result of a committed transaction is available to other transactions. This means that later transactions can use results of earlier transactions that occurred in the observable history of the system to that point.

We may compose transactions synchronously with other transactions and preserve atomicity. For example, suppose you reserve a document with the library and borrow it later. This borrowing transaction may be viewed as a synchronous occurrence of two transactions: one in which a reservation is terminated, and another one, occurring at the same time, in which a document loan is started. The resulting transaction is composed of two other transactions but is still atomic, because it has no observable intermediary state.

What is atomic at one level of aggregation may be a process at the next lower level. For example, the *borrow* transaction is atomic at the level of social systems, since it is an atomic interaction between a library and a customer, but it is a process at the level of computer-based systems, since it involves a dialog betweena circulation desk employee, the customer and the circulation desk information system.

Due to the atomicity requirement, some would-be "transactions" are not transactions according to the above definition. A famous example in this respect is a holiday booking [126]. At the highest level of aggregation this is a single transaction between a customer and a travel agency in which the agency books a holiday for the customer and the customer pays for this service. The trouble is that this "transaction" would take place *before* it is known whether it can be performed. The holiday booking "transaction" consists of other transactions like *reserve flight*, *book hotel room*, *take out a travel insurance*, etc. Some of these transactions occur after the contract between the customer and the travel agency is signed and all of them must occur if the holiday booking is to occur. But some of these transactions may fail and any failure causes an attempt to roll back the holiday booking "transaction". However, other transactions may already have been committed, so that the holiday booking "transaction" cannot be rolled back. But this leaves the *holiday booking* "transaction" in a state where it cannot be committed and cannot be rolled back, and so it does not satisfy the criteria for atomicity of a transaction.

This dilemma can be resolved if we realize that the holiday booking contract is a *promise* by the travel agency to book a holiday and a *promise* by the customer to pay for the holiday once the preconditions for the booking are satisfied. This mutual promise is a transaction in our sense of the term that can be rolled back as long as it is not committed, and that, once committed, cannot be rolled back. After this mutual promise is made, a number of other transactions are performed in fulfillment of this promise. When all required transactions have taken place, the actual holiday booking transaction can take place. All these transactions take place at the same aggregation level.

2.4.3   System behavior

The **behavior** of a system is the way in which the system interacts with its environment over time. Here are some examples of system behavior of a discrete system, a hybrid system, and a continuous system:

- When you buy furniture in a furniture store, a certain protocol is executed, which consists of viewing different pieces of furniture, requesting information, selecting a piece, ordering it, making a down payment, etc. There is a certain temporal structure to this process that goes beyond a mere listing of the set of interactions that take place. It is for example impossible to make a down payment before having selected a piece. The detailed structure of organization behavior depends among others on company policy.

- A system that controls barriers at the entrance of a parking garage interacts with the systems that it controls following a certain protocol. First a car arrival is sensed, then it is checked whether the garage is full, then whether this car is permitted to enter, then the barrier is opened or the car is given a message that it cannot enter, etc. Again, there is a protocol in this behavior that is not visible from merely giving the set of interactions.

- When a sailing boat with its sails up catches wind, it responds by moving forward. The direction of movement depends upon the position of the rudder, the direction and force of the flow in the water, and certain properties of the boat.

Part of the behavior of discrete systems can conveniently be represented by transition diagrams such as the one shown in figure 2.5. A small arrow points to the initial state of the behavior, the arrows represent transactions and the nodes represent states. Transition diagrams can be used to represent **properties** of system behavior. For example, the book transition diagram in figure 2.5 represents regularities that can be observed in the occurrence of system transactions. Some properties represented by figure 2.5 are that a *lose* can only occur after at least one *borrow* occurred, and that after *lose*, nothing else can happen to the book.

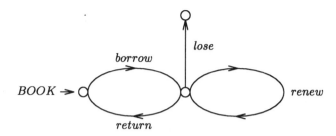

Figure 2.5: A simple book transition diagram.

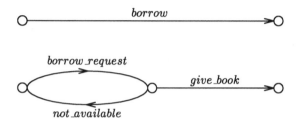

Figure 2.6: Implementation of the *borrow* transaction.

Transition diagrams can also be used to represent the implementation of a transaction at the next lower level of aggregation. For example, figure 2.6 shows the implementation of the *borrow* transaction into the three lower level transactions of figure 2.2.

Transition diagrams are not always the best kind of notation for behavior representation of discrete systems. For continuous systems they are totally inadequate and we should use other kinds of notation systems. For example, in order to represent the observable continuous behavior of a ship, we may draw a graph of the speed of the ship as a function of the speed and direction of wind, or we may draw a stylized diagram of its rudder and include a vector diagram of the effect of the forces exerted on it, etc. It is one of the challenges of engineering to find ways to communicate system behavior to other engineers, to designers, to users and to customers.

2.4.4 System properties

A **system property** is an aspect of system behavior. Stated more abstractly, a property of a system is the contents of any true proposition about observable system behavior. In software engineering, software product properties are often called *attributes* or *quality attributes*. We will not use this terminology, because the term "attribute" is used in Entity-Relationship models to indicate properties of a restricted class of entities, viz. entities represented by a software system, rather than properties of the software system itself. Note that system properties are always aspects of system *behavior*. Here are two examples.

- An industrial product may be required to have a certain size, color, strength, stiffness etc. All these properties summarize an aspect of product behavior. They tell us something about the behavior of the product in certain circumstances. When the size is measured, we should observe a certain value, when light is applied to the product, we should observe a certain color, etc.

- A tree can be tall, old, wide, straight, etc. Again, the meaning of these properties is that, when certain operations are applied, certain observations will follow.

This view of properties implies that all properties of a system are, at least in principle, observable. A "property" that does not make an observational difference is not, in our terminology, a property.

Often, it is difficult to indicate an experiment in which we can observe a property. For example, software products may be required, among others, to be user-friendly, reliable, portable, flexible and maintainable. All of these properties summarize some aspect of software product behavior, but which aspects do they summarize exactly? Is a product user-friendly if novices learn to use it in a short time, or, alternatively, if there are few help requests? Is it portable if it can be easily ported to many kinds of systems? What is the appropriate measure of easiness here? Is a software product maintainable if it is well-documented or if it is modular? Are there unambiguous measures of modularity?

We will say that a property is **specified behaviorally** if an experiment has been specified that will tell us unambiguously whether a system has the property. If no such experiment has been specified, then the property is specified **nonbehaviorally**. If a property is specified behaviorally, then it is always possible to define a *transaction* in which the property is observed. This transaction is just the successful completion of the experiment in which the property is observed. But then each behavioral property specification indicates some kind of transaction that the system should be able to perform. For example, if we want a system to be fast, we can specify that the average response time per day should be 0.1 seconds and never exceed 2 seconds, etc. Often, the experiment/transaction in which a property P is observed requires the observation of a set of other transactions. Observation of these other transactions is then a *precondition* of the observation of P.

In software engineering, behaviorally specified properties are often called **functional properties**, and properties for which no observation procedure has been specified are called **nonfunctional properties**. This terminology is misleading, for it transfers a distinction of *specifications* of properties to the properties themselves. We have just seen that all *properties* are behavioral, for they all summarize an aspect of system behavior. However, a property *specification* may be nonbehavioral, because we cannot define an observation procedure for the property.

Nonbehavioral property specifications give information about a system, because groups of people may agree on the presence or absence of these properties without using experimental evidence that unambiguously settles the question whether a system has the property. There is agreement among large groups of people about the beauty of Beethoven's sonatas, the quality of Rembrandt's paintings, or the user-friendliness of some software product interfaces. Typically, there are other groups of people that vehemently disagree about the presence of these qualities in these products. There is nothing wrong about this. It just shows that the market for these products is not homogeneous. During the development of a product, nonbehavioral specification of some important properties gives important marketing information, and it can motivate developers to build certain useful properties into the product.

If a behavioral specification of a property cannot be found, it may be useful to give behavioral specifications of *different* properties, whose presence indicates the presence of the nonbehaviorally specified property, but which are not equal to it. These different properties are then treated as **proxies** of the intended property. For example, proxies of user-friendliness are "easy to learn" and "easy to use", which can be specified behaviorally in terms of, say, average time needed for training and average number of help requests. The term *proxy* is used to indicate that the behaviorally specified properties are a substitute for the intended property, and that they approximate the intended property but are not equal to it.

2.5   System Function

So far, we have said that any system has a boundary that separates its internal structure from its externally observable behavior. In this section we turn to an aspect of system behavior present in some but not all systems: the function that a system can have for its environment. A system **function** is here defined as a *service* provided by the system to its environment. Here are some examples of systems that have a function for another system.

- The function of the liver for a vertebrate is to transform certain substances in the blood; the organism needs this for its sustained existence.

- The function of an elevator for its users is to transport them from floor to floor; the reason for the existence of elevators is that people do not like walking the stairs.

- The function of an information system for an organization is to provide members of an organization with useful data; they need this data to be able to communicate with each other effectively. The reason that information systems exist is that organizations cannot continue to exist for long without a properly functioning (manual or automatic) information system.

We will use the term "function" also in the derivative sense of *useful behavior*. The determination of required product functions is then the determination of useful product behavior.

A system that has a function for its environment provides for a *need* or *desire* in its environment. The liver answers a need of its environment, and the elevator answers a desire of its users. The needs of people may differ from the desires of people: managers may desire an information system, but perhaps what is really needed is a change in organizational procedures. In product development, the developer and the client should reach agreement about the client's needs such that what the developer perceives to be the client's needs is indeed what the client desires. In this book, we therefore define a **need** as the lack of something *desirable*.

If a system has a function, then there is always some system in its environment whose needs (desires) are answered by interacting with the system. We call this system the **user** of the system. The function of a system is thus always relative to a user and a need is for us always a **user need**. The same system can have different functions for different users because these have different needs. If we take away all users, then the system does not have any function.

2.5.1   Products

Outside the realm of biology, most natural systems have no function in the above sense. For example there is no environment that has a need which is fulfilled by the planet Jupiter.

In the universe of physics, things just exist and behave. In the universe of social systems, however, some natural systems occur in contexts where they have a certain function for man. For example, the sun provides light and warmth to living beings on earth, and a mountain can provide aesthetic pleasure to tourists. In the realm of biology, we find many cases in which one system (e.g. an organ) has a function for another (e.g. an organism).

In system development, we are not interested in natural systems with a function, but in artificial systems with a function. We call these systems **products**. A product has two properties:

- it is manufactured, built, developed, or otherwise created by man, and

- it is created in order to provide a function to its user.

Thus, like the liver, the reason for existence of a product is the provision of a service to its environment; but unlike the liver, it is manufactured by man in order to provide this service. According to this definition, a coffee machine is a product built to provide its users with coffee, and an information system is a product built to provide an organization with useful data.

We call the most general function of the product the **product idea**. For example, the product idea of an elevator is that

> upon request, it should transport people from floor to floor.

The statement of a product idea should be succinct and clear. Generally, a clear product idea leads to well-defined system boundaries and hence to modular systems (figure 2.1).

If any system created by man to provide a service to its environment is a product, then a business is a product, too. The users of the business are called *customers* and the function of the product is called the **mission** of the business. The mission statement of a business says "who we are and what business we are in". For example, the mission of a hospital is

> the care and treatment of the ill.

Mission statements, like product ideas, should be succinct. Like products, implementing an organization according to a simple coherent underlying idea enhances the modularity of the organization and increases the regularity and simplicity of its behavior.

A product idea or business mission can be decomposed into **objectives** that the product or business must realize. Each business is managed in such a way that these objectives are reached (or so one hopes). Each business therefore displays the purposive behavior that some people take to be characteristic of systems in general. In this book, we take a more general view of systems. Thus, products like information systems or coffee machines do not engage in purposive behavior but nevertheless are viewed as systems. Note that the realization of product objectives is the task of designers and maintenance personnel.

2.5.2 Functions of computer-based systems

Because computers are data manipulation systems, computer-based systems provide functions in which data manipulation plays an essential role:

- **Computation**. Computer-based systems can perform complex computations faster and with less errors than we do. This is useful for us.

- **Registration**. Computer-based systems often register data. This is useful for us because we need an external memory to supplement our own fallible memories. More-over, law often prescribes that we keep external records of business transactions.

- **Communication**. Because a computer-based system allows us to read data that has been written earlier, it allows asynchronous communication between people at the same location at different times (information systems). This can be extended to synchronous or asynchronous communication between nodes at geographically different locations (EDI systems).

- **Control**. Embedded systems often send commands to machines in their environment, to make them behave in a certain way that is useful for us.

Traditionally, computer-based systems are classified as oriented towards one of these functions. In **computing-intensive** systems, computation outweighs registration and control. An example is a simple pocket calculator. Another example is a decision-support system that performs linear programming or other optimization tasks, or that contains an econometric model to be used for computing what-if scenarios. In **data-intensive** systems, large amounts of data are registered and relatively simple computation and control functions are performed. Classical examples are database systems and transaction-processing systems. In **communication-intensive systems**, a set of nodes performing relatively simple computations and having little memory is connected by a network with heavy traffic. An example is a telephone system. In **control-intensive** systems, part of the environment is controlled but relatively simple computations are performed and few data are stored. Examples are control software for an elevator system, a cruise control system, or a chemical processing plant.

With the advent of telematics systems, EDI systems and integrated manufacturing systems, the borders between these systems disappear. All these systems have more control functions than classical data-intensive systems, manipulate more data than classical control-intensive systems, and contain more communication than the other kinds of systems.

2.6   The Why, the What and the How

A specification of observable product behavior is a specification of *what* the product does, a specification of the product function is a specification of *why* it does this, and a specification of its implementation is a specification of *how* it does this. The major concern in these three specifications is that of utility. **Utility** is a relation between something that has a use and something else that benefits from this use. There are two utility relations to be considered (figure 2.7).

- The **service** that a product delivers to its environment is the benefit that the environment has from the product. Service is a relation between the behavior of the product and the needs of the user.

- The **correctness** of the implementation is the degree to which the implementation actually realizes the required behavior of the product. Correctness is a relation between a specification of observable behavior and an implementation.

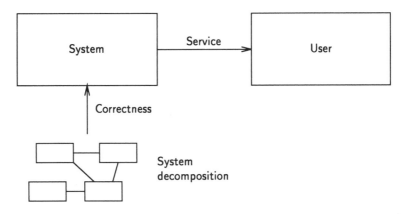

Figure 2.7: Correctness and service.

If we consider the function, behavior and implementation of a product, then behavior is central in this triad. Looking at figure 2.3, if we start at any level of aggregation and ask *what* the product does at that level, we ask for the behavior of the product and if we ask *why* the product behaves as it does, then we move upwards in the hierarchy. If we ask *how* the product behaves as it does, then we move downwards in the hierarchy. For example, the mission of a business may be to provide its customers with a certain product. The function of an information system in this business is then to provide the data required to fulfill this business mission, and the function of a database system within this information system is then to accept updates and queries required to fulfill this information system function. Moving further downwards, the function of database programs is to fetch and store data on disk as needed to fulfill the database system function, etc.

A consequence of this is that the *reason* for certain behavior becomes visible when we move up and becomes invisible when we move down in the aggregation hierarchy, and that the *implementation* of a behavior becomes invisible when we move up and becomes visible when we move down. Of course, invisibility does not means absence. The highest level function to which the behavior of a low-level system component contributes is still very much present. This presence makes itself felt when someone asks whether the utility of a low-level component is still justified by the cost of maintaining the component. If in our daily work, we are concerned mostly with building and repairing these low-level components, then such a question disrupts our unquestioning acceptance of what we are familiar with and forces us to travel in the *why*-direction of the aggregation hierarchy, i.e. upwards. Conversely, the lowest-level components that implement a high-level function are present even though they are invisible to system users. This presence makes itself felt when a low-level component breaks down and our high-level user is confronted with low-level error messages and other incomprehensible system behavior. Such behavior disrupts the unquestioning acceptance of the normal flow of events for the user. Fixing erroneous system behavior always requires traveling in the *how* direction of the aggregation hierarchy, i.e. downwards.

To show that an implemented product is useful, we must show that the two utility relations are present. Thus, we should show that the behavior of the product is useful for its users and that the implementation of this behavior is correct. If an argument for the quality of the product ignores one of these two relations, then this argument does not prove its claim. In order to produce such an argument, it is important that links are maintained between related specifications at all levels in the hierarchy such that each specification is linked to specifications (at higher levels) that justify it and to specifications of components (at lower levels) that implement it. A set of specifications for which these links are maintained is called **traceable**. (Although *traced* would be more appropriate, we follow accepted terminology here.) Behavior specifications should be traceable to specifications of user needs and system objectives on the one hand and to specifications of subsystems on the other. **Forward traceability** of a specification is the property that each part of the specification can be traced to specifications of lower-level components that implement it. Forward traceability requires maintenance of links in the *how*-direction, which is down the aggregation hierarchy. **Backward traceability** of a specification is the property that for each part of the specification, it is clear why it is included. This is the maintenance of links in the *why*-direction, which is up the aggregation hierarchy. Backward traceability ensures that the impact of changing a component of a specification can be traced to changes in product behavior and in the service that the product delivers to its user. The realization of traceability is particularly important when user needs, product objectives, behavior specifications or system decompositions are changed and the impact of such a change must be estimated.

2.7 The Universe of Discourse of Computer-based Systems

Computer-based systems contain software systems, and software manipulates *data*. Now, the essence of data is that they *mean* something. Data items are symbols that, for their readers and writers, refer to something. The part of the world to which the manipulated data refers is called the **universe of discourse** (UoD) of the system. The UoD of a system is sometimes called the *domain* of the system, but we will not use that term in this way. We give some examples of computer-based systems and their UoD.

- The universe of discourse of an order administration system contains suppliers, ordered material, orders, deliveries, etc.

- The universe of discourse of an elevator control system consists of buttons, requests for service, elevators and their movement, lights that can be told to switch on and off, doors that can be told to open and close, etc.

- The universe of discourse of an EDI system connecting different businesses in a harbor consists of cargo to be moved, container shipments, insurances, payment obligations, etc.

- The UoD of a pocket calculator is the abstract, mathematical world of arithmetic. The pocket calculator registers no events that occur in its UoD, nor does it send control signals to its UoD, because nothing happens in its UoD. Its function is to indicate relations between elements of its UoD.

- A decision support system is an information system that registers events in its UoD, and that contains an econometric model of the UoD. It registers no events but com-

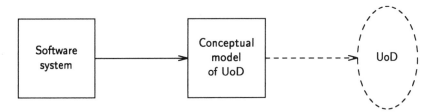

Figure 2.8: The UoD and its conceptual model.

putes a number of relations that exist in this abstract, mathematical model. For example, it can compute possible futures according to this model,

In order to achieve a shared understanding of the meaning of data manipulated by a computer-based system, users, developers and builders of the system must have a shared model of the UoD of that system. The function of this model is to act as the semantic structure in which the manipulated data are interpreted by all relevant people. The model must be understood by the users of the system, because they would otherwise misunderstand the meaning of the data, and it must be understood by the developers and builders of the system, because they must know what are the meaningful data manipulations that they have to make the system perform. In addition, to avoid misunderstandings about the meaning of the data manipulations of the system, users and developers must have the *same* understanding of the model of the UoD. To emphasize the important role of the model in the understanding of the behavior of a data manipulating system, we call it a **conceptual model** of the UoD of the system. A conceptual model of the UoD is an abstract representation of the behavior of the UoD, understandable and understood in the same way by the users and developers of the system. The term "conceptual" refers to the fact that the model consists of concepts by means of which users and developers interpret and observe the UoD. Put more prosaically, a conceptual model of a UoD is a pair of spectacles by which people can observe the UoD. Figure 2.8 illustrates the situation.

Later, we will also look at conceptual models of the system under development (SuD). The hallmark of conceptual models is that they are conceptual structures used as framework for communication between people. The communication may be about a UoD, a computer-based system, a software system or any other kind of system.

2.8 Summary

In the systems approach, the world consists of building blocks called *systems*. Any actual or possible observable part of the world is a system. Any observation of the system is an interaction between the system and its environment, and conversely any interaction with the system is an observation of that system. The system *interface* or *boundary* is the set of all possible interactions of the system and the *environment* of the system is the part of the world it interacts with. Each system has a *state space*, where a *state* is the memory the system has of past behavior. A system is *discrete* if its state space is a discrete set and *continuous* if its state space is a continuous set. It is *hybrid* if a projection of its state space is a discrete set and another projection is a continuous set. A *transaction* is a smallest interaction between a system and its environment, i.e. an interaction that has no intermediary states. Whether or not an interaction is considered to have intermediary states is a matter of choosing a level in the aggregation hierarchy at which to observe the system.

A system is called *modular* if its boundary has been chosen in such a way that there would be less regularities in its behavior, and more complexity, with any other choice of boundary. In addition, there should be much cohesion within the system but loose coupling between systems.

The *structure* of a system is the way it is composed of subsystems and the *behavior* of a system is the way it interacts with its environment. Often, some of this can be represented by transition diagrams, but in most cases, other kinds of notations must be used additionally. A *property* summarizes an aspect of system behavior. All properties are observable, but some properties may be hard to specify behaviorally. For these properties, it may be useful to specify *proxies* for which behavioral specifications can be given.

A *function* of a system for another system is a service that the first system delivers to the second. System developers develop *products*, which are systems that are built to provide a service to their environment. The reason for existence of a product is (or should be) that it has a function for another system. The basic function of a product should be describable as a *product idea*.

Computer-based systems have at least one of the functions of computation, registration, communication, and control. The traditional division of computation-intensive, data-intensive, communication-intensive and control-intensive systems tends to be blurred when we move to EDI, telematics and manufacturing control systems.

System structure, behavior and function cover the *how*, *what* and *why* perspectives from which we can view a system. There are two utility relations between these views: system structure must be *correct* with respect to required system behavior, and the behavior itself must deliver a *service* to the users. A collection of system specifications at different levels of aggregation is called *traceable* if each part of each specification is linked to specifications of the components that implement it (*forward traceability*) and to the justification for including this part in the specification (*backward traceability*).

Each computer-based system manipulates data that have meaning in a *universe of discourse* (UoD). A *conceptual model* of the UoD represents the shared interpretation that users and developers should have of this data.

2.9   Exercises

1. A coffee grinder is connected to a power plug, has a reservoir for coffee beans, an on/off switch, and a light that indicates its on/of status.

   (a) What is the function of the grinder?

   (b) Describe the interface of the grinder, including the systems with which it interfaces.

   (c) Is the grinder a discrete, continuous or hybrid system?

2. The interface between a grocery store and its customers can be described at several levels of aggregation. At the highest level, there is a simple interface with only one transaction, *sell grocery*.

(a) Decompose this high level transaction into lower level transactions and decompose one of lower level transactions again into still lower level transactions.

(b) At each of the three levels of aggregation, the grocery store has another interface. Some observers are interested only in the highest level, some in the next lower level, etc. For each level, give an observer who is interested in observing the system at that level.

3. An observable system state may be an equivalence class of internal system states whose difference is not observable. For each of the following systems and observers, give an example of an internal system state that is not observable by the observer. State the reason why you think that the internal state is not observable.

(a) A coffee machine and its user.

(b) A text editor and its user.

(c) A fashion store and a potential buyer.

(d) A database system for the library circulation desk, and its user.

(e) A database system for the library circulation desk, and a library user.

4. Figure 2.4 shows a series of communications between systems that occurs when a giro payment is made.

(a) the communication between the banks and their customers takes place through the postal services, and the communications between the banks and the clearing house takes place through a special transport company specialized in armed transports. Add these systems to the communication diagram.

(b) Describe the process that a payment goes through by means of a transition diagram. First, draw the diagram of the normal process and next, at each stage, add abnormal events by which the *pay by giro* transactions may go wrong. For example, the payment order may get lost in the post, etc. Finally, take care that the whole payment process implements the *pay by giro* transaction by adding, where necessary, rollback actions.

5. Suppose an artist uses a hammer as part of a piece of art. Is the hammer then still a product?

6. We can represent finite state machines by a transition diagram, but also by a regular expression. For example, $a.(c.b+c.d)$ is a regular expression in which the dot represents sequence and the plus represents choice.

(a) Draw the transition diagram corresponding to this expression.

(b) Draw the transition diagram of $a.c.(b + d)$.

(c) Do both diagrams represent the same behavior? Explain your answer.

2.10   Bibliographical Remarks

The systems approach.   Two important roots of the systems approach lie in biology and in engineering. In the 1920s, the biologist Von Bertalannfy argued that an explanation of the functioning of biological organisms required a level of explanation above that of physical and chemical processes because biological organisms persist for some time under sometimes adverse circumstances [32]. According to Von Bertalannfy, this goes counter to the second principle of thermodynamics, which says that any state change in a closed system decreases the energy available for work in the system. He maintained that biological organisms must be seen as systems that interact with their environment with the purpose of extracting energy from the environment to sustain themselves. The concept of a system is thus connected to the idea of purposive behavior.

In the 1940s, the mathematician Norbert Wiener studied goal-seeking mechanisms that could be used to improve automatic radar, and this led to the idea of feed-back loops to implement purposive behavior in machines [144]. Wiener termed the study of goal-directed systems *cybernetics* and published a book about this in 1948 [361]. In engineering, too, the concept of a system has been connected with the idea of purposive behavior. The connection of systems theory with feedback loops and purposive behavior has been ignored in this chapter because it is not necessary to understand the structure of product development. Checkland [63] gives a grand vision of the history of the systems approach.

The systems approach in computer science.   An important application of the systems approach in computer science, especially of the idea of modularity, is the method of *structured analysis and structured design* [84, 378]. Structured analysis is discussed in chapter 10. General systems ideas in this approach go back to work by G.M. Weinberg [357], C.W. Churchman [67] and Ross and Schoman [294]. Another important application of the system approach is Checkland's *soft systems methodology* [63, 62].

Automata theory.   The classical definition of the concept of a state of a deterministic finite-state system is given by Minsky [233, pp. 13 ff.]. A state concept that is useful in the context of communicating systems is given by Milner [231, 232]. Milner defines various notions of equivalence on transition diagrams, such that two equivalent diagrams represent the same observable behavior. Another good survey of equivalence notions can be found in Baeten and Weijland [18].

Modularity and complexity reduction.   The building blocks view of the world which pervades systems theory is primarily a method of complexity reduction. Descartes had already advocated this method in the seventeenth century. To understand an object, he said, we must decompose it into its parts and repeat this process until we reach a clear understanding of the simplest building blocks. Then we recompose to achieve an understanding of the whole [85, pages 15–20].

In addition to being indispensable as a method to *understand* a complex system, reduction to simpler subsystems is advocated by Simon [314] as the only way we can *build* a complex system. By reducing a complex system to simpler subsystems, we can define intermediary products that have a stability of their own and can be used in several ways at higher levels. *Structured programming* uses the same idea [75] to reduce the complexity of a program to manageable chunks, and, as said before, *structured design* [378] and *structured analysis* [84] took these ideas to earlier stages in the system development process. The same idea is central in structured computer organization [337] and the leveling of computer systems in general.

Modularity heuristics. The requirement that a system must have an underlying idea that defines its coherence is common in industrial product development [289]. Lawson [190] emphasizes the importance of an underlying product idea for successful software system design. Tully [348, pages 57–60] expresses the same idea. The close cohesion and loose coupling heuristics are well-known from Structured Design [251, 378]. The heuristic that a change inside a system should cause a minimal change outside the system is given by Page-Jones [252]. Parnas' [253] heuristic that each module should hide a design decision (so that changing the decision will not affect other modules) is special case of this.

System behavior and properties. The concept of a transaction is well-known in database research. A readable introduction, which puts the concept in historical perspective, is given by Gray [126]. A practical introduction to the specification of required system properties is given by Gilb [115], who stresses observability of the properties in experiments. Gause and Weinberg [111] is a treasure island full of insights and heuristics in the specification of required system properties. "Nonfunctional properties" are treated extensively by Vincent, Waters and Sinclair [350]. A brief introduction is given by Ould [250]. Other useful sources are Davis [77] and Yeh [374].

System levels. The idea of system leveling is central in general systems theory. Boulding [49] and Checkland [63] published two influential hierarchies. The idea of leveling is coupled with complexity reduction and modularity, as well as with the concept of emergent behavior [346]. According to this idea, system behavior cannot be explained merely by the behavior of its components, but must be explained by referring to the way in which these components are put together. It is also the key to the disentanglement of the confusion about the difference between requirements and implementation. Davis [77, pages 17–18] gives a very clear explanation of this. Hatley and Pirbhai [141] use it as a basis for their structured requirements specification and system decomposition method.

System function. The definition of system function as service for the environment is taken from In't Veld [349]. A very good introduction to system concepts, including that of function, is given in the first few chapters of Katz and Kahn [170].

The UoD. The concept of UoD was introduced by the 19th century logician De Morgan to stand for the whole of some definite category of things under discussion [181]. It is central in the ISO report *Concepts and Terminology for the Conceptual Schema and the Information Base* [127] and to the NIAM method [244].

Conceptual models. The term "conceptual model" is often defined vaguely as a set of concepts from a given reality that can be used to describe a set of data and manipulations to operate on those data [25, pages 6, 26]. In this meaning, the Entity-Relationship (ER) approach to data modeling is a conceptual model. Sometimes, conceptual models are identified with ER-like models. We will not follow this usage in this book. Loucopoulos and Karakostas [198] define conceptual models as cognitive structures used for the purposes of understanding and communicating aspects of the physical and social world around us. This usage of the term arose in the field of data modeling but has a wider applicability than just ER modeling [51]. In this book, we use the term in this sense.

3

Product Development

3.1 Introduction

In this chapter, we define product development as a rational problem solving process. The problem to be solved by product development is that there is a need to be met; the solution delivered is a specification of a product that would meet this need. Section 3.2 distinguishes client-oriented development from market-oriented development and identifies the tasks in these two kinds of development. Once a product is used, the needs of its users evolve and hence a point may be reached where the product must be adapted to meet these changed needs. In section 3.3, we identify product evolution as a nonterminating alternation between product (re)development and product use. An important characteristic of product evolution is that the effects of a product on the satisfaction of the client or consumer are evaluated *after* the product is built and delivered. In section 3.4, we contrast this with product engineering, in which design choices are made based on an evaluation of likely effects of alternative product designs *before* any of the specified designs is implemented.

In chapter 2, we saw that computer-based systems manipulate data that has a meaning in a UoD. During the development of a computer-based system, developers must make a descriptive model of the UoD. The method to find such model is the empirical cycle, discussed in section 3.5. The empirical cycle is an application of the rational problem solving method to find an appropriate model of the world. This is the mirror image of the engineering cycle, which is an application of the rational problem solving method to find a proper intervention in the world.

In section 3.6, we combine the engineering cycle with the hierarchy of system levels identified in the previous chapter to yield a simple framework within which we can place the requirements engineering methods reviewed in part II.

3.2 Client-oriented and Market-oriented Development

Product development is a process in which a specification is delivered of a product that would satisfy an identified need (figure 3.1). For example, the development of a new kind of car ends in a specification of a car design that would satisfy the needs of a certain niche in the market. *Implementation* of the product specification lies outside the development

Figure 3.1: The essence of development is the transformation of a need into a solution that is expected to satisfy this need.

process so in a way, product development would more appropriately be called product *specification* development. However, we will stick to the shorter expression. We will use the terms "system development" and "product development" as synonyms, because in this book, all system specifications are product specifications.

The starting point of a development process is a need in the environment of the future product. This need can exist in an individual user or in a market. In the first case, we call the development process **client-oriented** and in the second case, we call it **market-oriented**. The **client** has a desire for a product and as we will see below, the client may also pay for development, or pay for the product, or use the product, or all of these at the same time. Examples of client-oriented development are designing a suit for a client, designing a kitchen to be installed in a house on assignment of the inhabitant, specifying an information system for a business, and specifying control software for a nuclear reactor system. Examples of market-oriented development are designing a new type of vacuum cleaner, developing a new type of printing equipment, developing a new version of a word processing package and developing control software for a type of elevator system. Client-oriented and market-oriented development are distinguishable from each other in a number of ways.

- In client-oriented development, the need that starts the development process is *experienced by the client*. Because the client experiences it to exist, it exists. In market-oriented development the need is perceived by marketing specialists. There is always room for debate whether the perceived need really exists in the market.

- In market-oriented development, a specification of a product *type* is delivered, such as a type of vacuum cleaner, a type of printer, or a software package. Product development results in a description of a mass production process by which a series of instances of the type is produced. Client-oriented development on the other hand delivers an individual solution, such as the drawings for a tailor-made suit, the plans for a house, or a specification of an information system. Only one instance of an implementation is produced.

- In client-oriented development, not only the product, but also the client itself is an individual. This creates room for the client to change his or her mind during development and to demand a high degree of satisfaction of his or her needs. In market-oriented development, on the other hand, the variability of needs is much less, because these are not subject to individual whims. Consumers do not expect as high a degree of satisfaction as clients do.

There are borderline cases that can be classified in both classes. A project in which a block of houses is built is client-oriented in as far as there is a client who commissions the project, but market-oriented in as far as the client intends to sell the houses in the block on the

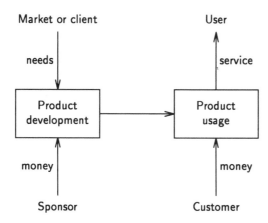

Figure 3.2: Different stakeholders in product development and usage.

market. Consequently, the need for the block is felt by an individual (the client) and is also perceived to exist in the market. Similarly, the delivered product is an individual (a block of houses) as well as a type (a blueprint used to build several houses).

There are a number of **stakeholders** that have an interest in the processes of product development and usage. We identify a number of important stakeholders in figure 3.2. Note that one person or organization can play the role of several stakeholders at once.

- The **development organization** is the organization (or person) that performs the development process. The development organization of a new car model would contain, among others, the engineers, industrial designers, ergonomists, project managers and supporting personnel who participate in the design of the car. The development organization of an information system would consist of the information analysts, software engineers, system designers, programmers, project managers and supporting personnel.

- The **sponsor** of the development process is the person or organization that pays for the development organization and its process. In the development of a new car model, the sponsor would be the company that commissions the development process. In information system development, the sponsor is the organization that pays the developers to produce an information system.

- The **customer** of the developed product is the person or organization that pays for the delivered product. In the development of a new type of car, the customer is the person who buys an individual car. In information system development, the customer is the sponsor that pays for the development process, because the sponsor owns the result of development. In general, in client-oriented development, the customer and sponsor are identical.

- The **user** of the product is the person or organization that actually uses the product. In the development of a new type of car, the users of the individual cars probably include the customer who bought the car, but most probably his or her spouse and possibly some of their children as well, if they all drive the car. In the development of an information system, the users of the system are the employees who actually initiate the transactions of the information system.

If we include more stages of a product life cycle, we can identify more stakeholders. Examples are marketing, manufacturing, sales, distribution, and maintenance personnel, and of course operational, tactical and strategic management.

In software development, the sponsor is often called the *user* and the people actually using the software are called *end-users*, but we will not follow this terminology.

Note that in client-oriented development, the roles of sponsor and customer are identical: he or she that pays for the development (sponsor) also pays for the delivered product (customer). In turn, both are often identical to the person or organization that experiences the need for the product (client). However, there may be client-oriented developments where the customer/sponsor differs from the client who feels the need for development. An example is the development of a scheduling system for a government-owned public transport system. The client is the public that uses of the transport system, the customer/sponsor of the scheduling project is the government.

3.3   The Product Life Cycle

3.3.1   Product development

The life of a product can be partitioned into a number of stages, which are slightly different for market-oriented and client-oriented products. The stages are shown in figures 3.3 and 3.4, respectively. Market-oriented development typically follows a **strategic product planning** task, in which innovative new products or renovations of existing products are planned. Strategic product planning includes the management of the product evolution process discussed later. Using the results of strategic product planning, the market-oriented development process consists of the following tasks:

- **Needs analysis**: analyze the needs of the market and determine the objectives that the solution must satisfy.

- **Marketing**: describe the market segments to which the product is targeted and the distribution channels and outlets for the product.

- **Product specification**: describe the product to be implemented. There are two subtasks in product specification:

  - **Behavior specification**: specify observable product behavior.
  - **Decomposition specification**: specify a decomposition of the product into parts.

- **Production specification**: describe the process by which instances of the product are produced.

Each of these tasks produces deliverables, often with the same name as the task. For example, the development of a new bicycle model would result in a specification of the objectives that the bicycle should fulfill, a specification of a marketing and distribution

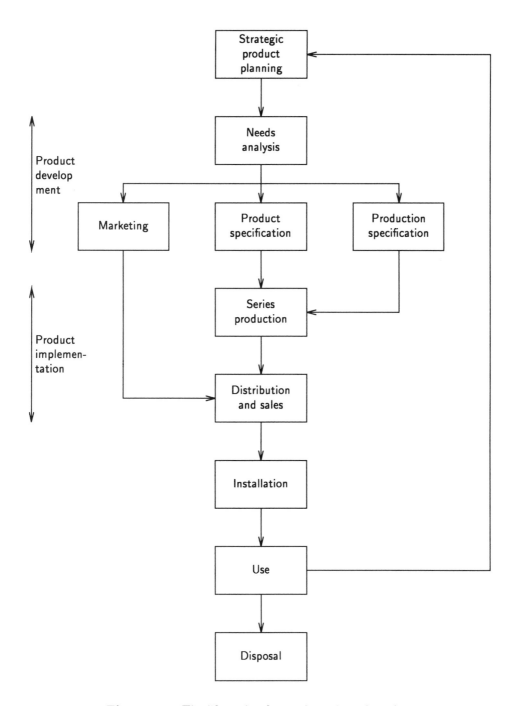

Figure 3.3: The life cycle of a market-oriented product.

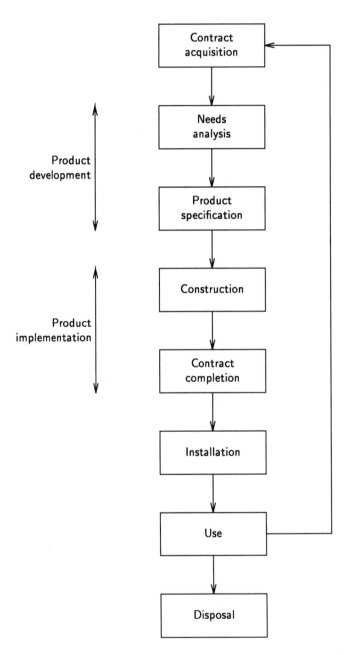

Figure 3.4: The life cycle of a client-oriented product. Contract completion can lie anywhere between development to use of the product.

plan, a specification of the observable behavior of the bicycle in different circumstances, a specification of the decomposition into parts, and a specification of the production process that describes how the parts can be assembled along a production line. The specification of observable bicycle behavior would include such things as how the product looks and feels, its performance characteristics, its color, size and weight, etc.

Market-oriented *software* development is exceptional because production specification is nearly absent or extremely trivial compared to other kinds of market-oriented product development. Unlike other kinds of products, software can be duplicated indefinitely with very little effort. The major problem of software production for a market is the realization of portability of the software product across differend hardware and software platforms. However, the solution of this problem does not require a specification of a production process, but of platform-independent interfaces of the product. There is thus no production specification to speak of for software produced for a market.

A borderline case of market-driven and client-oriented software development is the development of parametrized software, such as packages for order-processing, sales administration, personnel administration, etc. These packages are developed for a market but they have parameters that can be set to meet the individual customer's needs. Development of parametrized software should therefore include a software product specification as well as a specification of the production process in which the software is customized for an individual customer.

Turning to client-oriented development, we see in figure 3.4 that this typically follows **contract acquisition**, in which an agreement is made with a customer to produce a product. Depending upon the contents of the contract, **contract completion** can lie anywhere between development and use of the product. Figure 3.4 shows contract completion after construction and before installation of the product. Client-oriented development consists of the following tasks:

- **Needs analysis**: analyze the needs of the client and determine the objectives that the solution must satisfy.

- **Product specification**. As before, this consists of two tasks:

    - **Behavior specification**: specify observable product behavior.
    - **Decomposition specification**: specify a decomposition of the product into parts.

This yields three deliverables: a specification of product objectives, a specification of required product behavior and a specification of the product decomposition. For example, a tailor will specify the objectives to be reached by the suit he or she will make (make the person look taller, give a distinguished look, etc.) specify the observable behavior of the suit (color, look and feel, size etc.) and the decomposition of the suit into parts (material, form of the parts, etc.).

3.3.2 Product implementation

Implementation of a product developed for a *market* consists of acquiring resources for production, setting up a production facility, producing the product in series, and distributing the product according to the marketing plan. The production process consists of integrating the parts of the product into a whole according to the decomposition specification, so that the whole behaves as required by the behavior specification. Implementing a product developed for a *client* consists similarly of integrating the parts of the product into a whole that behaves as required of the product. Depending upon the contract, implementation of a product developed for a client may also include installation of the product. For example, information systems are usually installed in an organization as part of the contract.

Products developed for a client are often implemented and installed by the development organization, although different people within that organization may perform the development, implementation and installation tasks. For example, a kitchen may be specified by a designer, and then implemented and installed by carpenters, plumbers and electricians, all working for the organization that sold the kitchen.

Software product implementation is special, because *the specification of the decomposition into parts is already part of the implementation of the software*. Software is text that is executable by a computer and this makes it possible to write a specification in an executable language. The smallest parts into which the software product is decomposed may be programming language statements, or routines from a software library, or other reusable components that are executable by computer. As a consequence, software product implementation consists of specification of a decomposition of the product into executable parts and then of integrating these parts into an executable whole. Software product development and implementation therefore overlap and software engineers usually consider integration of the software components to be part of the development task. The result of software development is then an implemented software product, not a software product specification. Contrast this with the development of a piece of custom-made hardware such as a house: the specification of the product decomposition is still a piece of text and diagrams, and implementation is a separate task in which the parts are constructed and assembled into a whole. The overlap of software development with software implementation may lead to linguistic confusion when software engineers talk with hardware engineers.

3.3.3   Product evolution

Almost any development process starts because some disatisfaction exists with the current version of an existing product. Here are some examples:

- When a new type of bicycle is developed, there is experience with current bicycles. It is this experience that goes into the strategic product planning process and that leads to novel product ideas.

- Any company has a current information system, be it an automated system, a paper-based system or even a system implemented in the memory of the employees. It is experience with this information system that leads to the needs which are analyzed in the development process.

- Any elevator system has a control system, that may be implemented as a system of electromechanical relays or as software. Experience with this control system is analyzed when a new control system is specified.

In all these cases, there is a gap, small or large, between the existing system and existing needs, and over time this gap is likely to increase. There are several causes of the increase of the gap between an existing product and existing needs:

- By using the product, the user discovers new possibilities and thereby acquires new desires, that cannot be satisfied by the current version of the product.

- The environment of the product may change. For example, new laws may impose more stringent safety requirements, competitors may have introduced a more successful product, new technology may create new possibilities, etc.

- In client-oriented development, evolution may be even more dynamic than in market-oriented development, because clients tend to change their needs *as a result of the development process* (even before the product is delivered and used). When we interview someone about his or her desires, these desires are refined and new desires are discovered by the very process of talking about them. The process of change continues after we finished the interview, and by the time we return to verify our notes, the notes may have become out of date. We call this phenomenon **requirements uncertainty**.

Whatever the cause, after a sufficiently long period of time, the gap between product and needs is sufficiently large to justify the start of a new development process, oriented at reducing the size of the gap. This has been represented in figures 3.3 and 3.4 by an arrow from the use of a product to strategic product planning or contract acquisition for redevelopment.

We call the iteration through improvements of a product on the bases of experience in actual use **product evolution**. In software engineering, this process is called **adaptive maintenance** and in market-oriented product development, it is called **product innovation**. We saw that product innovation, and hence product evolution, are part of the strategic product planning process. The essence of the evolution process is that a new development is started due to an increase in the gap between existing needs and the existing version of the product.

3.3.4   The regulatory cycle

We may try to influence the course of product evolution by interventions that aim to steer the process in a certain direction. If we do this, the evolution process is subjected to a **regulation process**. The logical structure of the regulation process is that of the **regulatory cycle**, which is shown in figure 3.5. Note that the regulatory cycle is nothing else but a cyclic process of feedback control. It is followed by anyone who wants to achieve a desired effect by his or her actions. Managers control the primary process of an organization by observing the performance of this process, evaluating this and taking action to steer the process towards the intended business objectives. A physician analyzes the state of his or her patient, evaluates possible remedies, chooses one and prescribes it, and then observes the result.

The regulatory cycle can be used to steer the product evolution processes in a desired direction. Product specification is the planning part of the regulatory cycle. After implementation, the customer, user or marketing department evaluates the product in real use, and this may lead to an action ranging from a change request of the current product to an idea for a product innovation that is implemented in a new development process. (In this context, not doing anything is also an action.)

The important feature of the regulatory cycle is that we evaluate the effects of an action *after* the action is performed. We choose a next action to perform on the basis of an

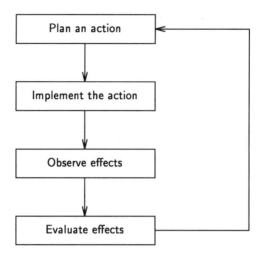

Figure 3.5: The regulatory cycle of action.

evaluation of the experience with the actual implementation. The regulatory cycle is to be contrasted with the engineering cycle, discussed next.

3.4   Product Engineering

3.4.1   The engineering cycle

In this book, we view product engineering as a species of rational problem solving. A simple model of the rational problem solving cycle is the following one:

- Analyze the problem to determine what the current situation is and what the objectives are.

- Generate some possible solutions.

- Estimate the expected effects of the generated solutions.

- Evaluate the expected effects with respect to the objectives.

- Choose a solution or go back to analysis or to solution generation.

Applying this rational method to the problem of finding a product specification, we get the **engineering cycle** shown in figure 3.6. After a needs analysis, we generate alternative product specifications, which are then simulated to discover their likely effects. These effects are evaluated and one of them is then chosen, or we return to the generation process to generate additional product alternatives. We may even return to the needs analysis task in order to learn more about the objectives of the engineering process. Note that needs analysis occurs in both the product life cycles of figures 3.3 and 3.4. The rest of the engineering cycle corresponds to the task of finding a product specification. Looking at it in another way, product specification is *solution* specification.

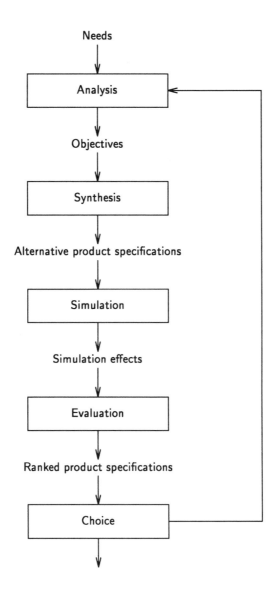

Figure 3.6: The engineering cycle.

The essence of the engineering process is that we estimate the likely effects of a possible solution, and evaluate the likely effects of implementing the solution, *before* the solution is implemented. This contrasts with the regulatory cycle, where we observe and evaluate the effects of an action *after* they have occurred. Thus, where the regulatory cycle is the logical structure of a feedback control loop, the engineering cycle is the logical structure of a feedforward control loop.

Engineering as well as regulation presuppose the existence of *regularities* in the problem domain, so that it is at least meaningful to speak of the effects of an action. Without regularities, there would be no effects but only random phenomena; and if actions would have no effects, we could not rationally choose among actions on the basis of expected effects, nor could we evaluate performed actions on their effects. The presence of regularities guarantees the existence of repeatable cause-effect relationships.

Engineering additionally requires *knowledge* of these regularities by the problem solver, so that the likely effects of intervention and non-intervention can be estimated. In the case of regulation, this kind of knowledge is not necessary, because we can perform an action and observe what its effects are without being able to predict these effects. In the case of engineering, we need this knowledge to perform *simulation* of alternative solutions before they are implemented. We take a wide view of simulation here, including simulation with scale models, by analytical computations, by deduction, by numerical approximations using difference equations, by rules-of-thumb, by observing the results of actions performed elsewhere, etc. For example, nuclear engineers who want a quick and dirty estimate of the amount of energy a power plant will generate use the rule of thumb that one gram of uranium gives one megawatt day of energy, and mechanical engineers estimate the point of failure of a wide variety of materials by the rule of thumb that the yield strength of a material is equal to a 0.02% offset on the stress-strain curve [182]. This is validated knowledge, even if the underlying physical processes may not be fully understood. Using this knowledge to estimate likely effects counts as simulation of the likely effects.

To summarize, the essence of engineering thus contains two elements:

- Separation of specification from implementation of an action.

- The prediction of the likely effects of the action from the specification, before the action is implemented.

There are domains where it is an open question whether engineering is possible, either because there are no regularities in the domain or because we have insufficient knowledge of the regularities that exist. For example, the stock market is a domain that sometimes behaves so chaotically that no regularities exist. The stock broker may try to predict the effect of buying or selling stock beforehand, but these predictions have a large margin of uncertainty. This margin is rumored to be so big that in the long run, stock market specialists perform on the average just as good or bad as random generators.

As another example, management scientists and consultants have amassed a large body of theories about aspects of organizational behavior. If these theories are true, they represent regularities in the organizational domain and they can be used as a basis for rational action. Management would then become a social engineering process, in which the manager estimates the likely effects of alternative actions and chooses an action based on an evaluation of the estimated effect of each alternative action. As a matter of fact, the estimated effects of an action often differ from their real effects and managers must decide what to do next on the basis of an evaluation of an effect after it has occurred, rather than on the basis of an estimated effect. To the extent that this happens, organization development is an evolutionary process rather than an engineering process. Terms like "business process reengineering" must therefore be taken with an appropriate grain of salt.

Software engineering too strives for the status of an engineering discipline. This requires the ability to predict how a software system will behave *before* it is implemented. In practice, we content ourselves with observing the behavior of a software system *after* it is implemented and fiddling around with the system until it behaves as required. Most software development is *evolutionary development*, where part of the evolution takes place after construction but before installation (i.e. as testing) and part of the evolution takes place as adaptive maintenance. We return to evolutionary development in the final part of this book.

3.4.2   Example of an application of the engineering cycle

It is interesting to follow the engineering cycle through a few iterations in a case study of industrial product development given by Roozenburg and Eekels [289, pages 325–339].

TANA Nederland (henceforth TANA) produces shoe polish sold to consumers in glass jars and is a market leader in the Netherlands in this area. The problem that triggered the development process is that TANA's sales of shoe polish are stagnating. Competitors produce shoe polish with the same range of colors and TANA sees its market share decreasing.

1. According to marketing management theories, there are three possible actions to be taken in this case:

   - search for new markets with the current products,

   - develop a new product for the same market, or

   - adjust the marketing mix.

   TANA management chose the second of these options for implementation. It was decided to develop a new kind of packaging for existing kinds of shoe polish.

2. A number of product ideas were generated for the packaging by combining different product and market characteristics.

   Figure 3.7 shows the alternative product-market combinations that were considered [289, page 238, figure A]. To make the alternatives more vivid for TANA management, a typical example of each alternative was sketched with pencil on paper. The alternatives were discussed with management and evaluated on a number of criteria derived from the chosen marketing strategy. Product idea marked with an X was selected for further development.

3. The product idea was analyzed by following the product through its life cycle, from production to distribution, use and disposal. For each stage in the life cycle, requirements were determined. This resulted in twenty-nine design objectives, three of which are reproduced here.

   - Subassembly of parts of the packaging should be done by current suppliers of TANA.

   - The cost to store the packaging, including its contents (polish) and its bulk packaging, should not be larger than Dfl 0.95 per packaging.

   - It should be impossible that the polish leaks through the packaging.

   - The packaging should be transparent, so that the color of its contents can be seen by the consumer.

Product types	Product functions				
	Storing Closing	Storing Closing Measuring dosage	Storing Closing Measuring dosage Applying spreading	Storing Closing Measuring dosage Applying Spreading Rubbing	Storing Closing Measuring dosage Applying Spreading Rubbing Cleaning
Single use	.				
Refillable packaging					
Multiple use, dispose when empty			X		

Figure 3.7: Matrix for generating product ideas [289]. Reproduced with permission from Lemma B.V., 1991.

Next, twenty different usage concepts and twenty different implementation mechanisms were generated. A usage concept is a way in which the consumer could perform the desired product functions. Examples of the generated usage concepts are:

- application of the package to the shoe as a marker pen,
- application of the packaging as a deodorant stick, etc.

The implementation mechanisms were generated by looking at the way products with a similar function are implemented. Examples of the mechanisms that were considered are:

- a twister mechanism,
- a starlock mechanism, etc.

From the 400 possible combinations of usage concepts and implementation mechanisms, six combinations were evaluated by the developer by scoring them on the objectives. In a further evaluation by management, three combinations were selected for further development. The first selection was a package in the shape of a bulb, the second one had the shape of a flacon, and the third one was a jar with a special kind of lid with which the polish could be applied.

4. The selected packages were analyzed and three prototypes were built on the basis of this analysis. These were evaluated by presenting them to a group of consumers as far as possible in the form in which they would be marketed, and conducting qualitative interviews with these consumers. On the basis of these interviews, the third design (jar with lid) was selected by the consumers. In parallel with this consumer evaluation, the three designs were evaluated on their consumer price, cost of assembly, investment in a new production line, and some other criteria. This parallel evaluation led to the selection of the jar design too.

5. The chosen design was worked out by adding all technical details and making experimental moulds for the product, to be tested in a trial series production.

There are a number of interesting observations to be made about this example.

- The case consists of five iterations through the engineering cycle. In the first iteration, it is the *business* that is developed. In the other four iterations, a product is developed.

- In all iterations, simulation of some possible actions is performed in order to estimate what the likely effects of the action would be. For example, in the first iteration, this simulation was done by the managers by thinking through the best response to a business problem using their knowledge of the business and its market.

- Each iteration through the product engineering cycle produces a product specification of increasing explicitness. The first product engineering iteration (the second of the five iterations in the example) produces a **product idea** consisting of a combination of product type and product function. As explained in chapter 2, a product idea is the underlying idea of what the product is. Having a product idea increases the coherence and modularity of the product. The final iteration produces a technical product specification and the initial version of a production specification.

- Explicit design objectives to be satisfied by the product are only produced in the second of the product engineering iterations. They are stated in such a way that their achievement or nonachievement by a product is observable. In other words, they are stated in behavioral, operational, measurable terms.

- A final point to notice, which may be of interest to software developers, is that in the second iteration through the product engineering cycle (the third of the five iterations in the example), decisions about the decomposition of the product into components are made in *parallel* with decisions about observable behavior (the "usage concepts").

Of course, there are some obvious differences between developing a computer-based system and developing a new kind of packaging for shoe polish. First of all, software is a major part of computer-based systems. Software is intangible and many people conclude from this that software is very flexible. By contrast, industrial products are tangible and, once they are produced, everyone can see that they are not very flexible. The problem of changing requirements, which often occurs in client-oriented development, is therefore even more widespread in the development of computer-based systems. If requirements changes become too frequent or too erratic, then the development cycle will never stop or, if it stops, it will deliver a product that does not meet client needs. This makes the management of software development considerably more complex than the management of industrial product development.

Second, computer-based systems are often closely interwoven with organizational infrastructures. For example, as observed in chapter 2, an information system can be viewed as an *aspect system* of a business. All business units interact by exchanging information with other business units and with the business environment. Viewed in this way, the information system is inextricably bound to the organizational infrastructure. The interweaving between organizational infrastructure and computer-based systems becomes even tighter with EDI systems, which require standardization of business procedures of the connected businesses. This means that the development of those systems is integrated with business development, and this in turn makes the complexity of managing the development of a computer-based system larger than the management of industrial product development.

Despite these differences, an engineer developing a computer-based system iterates through the same engineering method as an industrial designer developing a manufacturing product. The rational method of engineering in both kinds of development is the same, even though process attributes like complexity and flexibility differ. Especially noteworthy is the interleaving of the specification of observable product behavior at one level of aggregation, and the specification of the decomposition of the product into parts at a lower level of aggregation. Above, we saw that this interleaving takes place in the development of such humble systems as a packaging for shoe polish.

One last lesson to be learned from the shoe polish packaging example is that rational product development *is* possible. The engineering cycle is a rational process that does not deal with mistakes, personnel changes, budget cuts, departmental politics and changing requirements other than by iterating through the problem solving cycle. As explained in chapter 15, these phenomena are dealt with by process management methods. We will argue there that the engineering cycle is useful as the target structure for a *rational reconstruction* of the development process, by which the results of development can be justified to others. Here, it is important to realize that the engineering cycle is the *logical* structure of development, not the *temporal* structure. Its purpose is to allow us to classify tasks in different development methods, i.e. to act as a framework for understanding development methods.

3.5   System Modeling

3.5.1   Current system modeling and UoD modeling

There are two tasks in the development of computer-based systems where the developer has to make a descriptive model of some system. First, in many cases of computer-based system development we must make a model of the observable behavior of an *existing* system. For example, in the development of a new version of an information system, we may at some time have to model that part of the behavior of the current one that must be preserved by the new one. Current system modeling is often called **reverse engineering** in computer science. This is a curious but accurate term, for we will see below that current system modeling is the exact opposite of engineering. Reverse engineering is often part of a larger process called **reengineering**, in which a current system must be reimplemented with largely the same functionality. This is an important development heuristic recommended by classical structured analysis (chapter 10).

There is a second situation in which the developer must make a model of an existing system. We have seen in chapter 2 that computer-based systems have a UoD in which their data is interpreted. Developers of computer-based systems must therefore build conceptual models of the UoD that can be understood by stakeholders such as implementors and users of the system.

Finding an accurate and useful conceptual model of the UoD requires expertise of the UoD. In some cases, this expertise is shallow enough to be learned by the system developers that are not specialists in the UoD. For example, the UoD of a library administration is simple enough to be learned by system developers themselves — but even here they may bump into surprises. Even simpler, the UoD of a pocket calculator requires knowledge of arithmetic at the primary school level and some simple mathematics at the secondary school level extended with knowledge of finite arithmetic, knowledge which any developer of pocket calculators can be expected to have. At the other extreme, a decision support system uses a model of its UoD that requires econometric expertise to build and understand. Building such a model is a profession in its own right and may take a lifetime. The development of decision support systems must therefore involve specialists that have the required econometric expertise, as well as software engineers who can cooperate with econometrists in building a decision support system.

3.5.2   The empirical cycle

Whenever a descriptive model of a currently existing system or of a UoD must be made, we should follow the **empirical cycle of discovery**. Once again, this is a species of the rational problem solving cycle. Figure 3.8 shows the structure of the empirical cycle. The similarity with the engineering cycle arises from the fact that both are specializations of the rational problem solving method. The difference with the engineering cycle arises from the fact that in engineering we aim at finding a product specification, which is a *prescriptive* model of a product, whereas in the empirical cycle we aim at finding a *descriptive* model of an existing part of the world.

Following the empirical cycle, we start from observations and generate one or more models that explain the observed phenomena in something called an induction step. These models are evaluated by deducing observable consequences from them and testing these in experiments. As a result of these tests, we choose a model or we generate additional models that explain the phenomena. We may even return to the observation task to collect more data.

Induction is a reasoning form in which, from a finite number of observations, a model is specified that accounts for these and infinitely many other phenomena. For example, from repeated observation that a physical object expands when heated, we may induce that *any* object expands when heated. Induction is logically unsound because it may lead from true premises to a false conclusion. In daily life as well as in science, we must continuously jump to conclusions by inducing general models from particular observations.

The unsoundness of induction is a consequence of the fact that any finite set of observations can always be explained by an infinite set of possible models of those observations. Some of these models are true, but most of them are false. For example, if objects a, b and c are observed to expand when heated, we can induce any of the following models:

- All objects expand when heated.

- Most objects expand when heated.

- Some objects expand when heated; others burn immediately.

- Until today, all objects expand when heated, but from tomorrow onwards they will contract when heated.

- Objects a, b and c expand when heated but all other objects contract when heated.

- Here, all objects will expand when heated; elsewhere, the same objects would contract when heated.

We could go on indefinitely. Each of these models is a **hypothesis** that must be tested by deducing observable consequences from it, and by testing these consequences in experiments. This leads to confirmations or falsifications. There is an asymmetry between confirmation

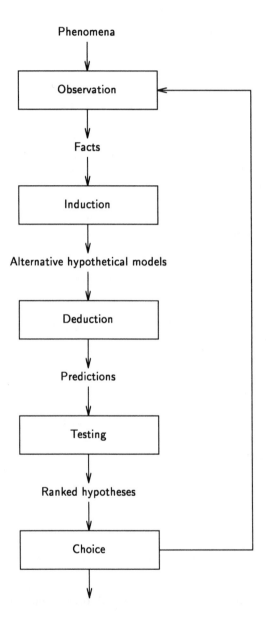

Figure 3.8: The empirical cycle.

and falsification that follows from the structure of deduction. Suppose that from hypothesis H we deduce observable consequences O and we do not observe O but something else. Then we have falsified H. The reason is that if $H \rightarrow O$, then it logically follows that $\neg O \rightarrow \neg H$ (here we represent logical implication by $\rightarrow$ and negation by $\neg$). On the other hand, if we do observe that O takes place, then we have not confirmed the truth of H. O follows from indefinitely other hypotheses as well, and among these other hypotheses there may very well be better explanations of the phenomena than H.

In practice, confirmation and falsification are not so far apart as suggested here. If the consequences of H are observed frequently by different people in different circumstances, then our belief in H tends to become very strong. If we strongly believe in H and once in a while one of H's consequences is falsified, then we attribute this to unknown disturbances, measurement errors or other secondary causes, and forget about the falsification. In general, no model can be completely verified or completely falsified by experiments, and we end up with a ranking of models in order of plausibility, just as in the engineering cycle we end up with a ranking of product specifications in order of utility.

The following classical example of an application of the empirical cycle is taken from Kemeny [173].

Example of the empirical cycle. In the beginning of the 19th century, Newtonian mechanics was a well-established body of theory, that had been validated in numerous physical experiments and astronomical observations. Observations made in the 1820s of the orbit of the then-known outermost planet, Uranus, revealed a discrepancy between the predictions made by Newton's theory and the actual orbit of Uranus. There were several alternatives to explain this discrepancy. For example, Newton's theory could be considered refuted, or the observations unreliable. The first option is very unattractive and the second could be shown to be very implausible. Astronomers therefore generated another hypothesis, namely that Uranus is not the outermost planet, but that there is a planet beyond it. The French mathematician Leverrier showed that a planet with a certain size, position and orbit could account for the aberration between the observed and predicted orbit of Uranus. Using the mathematical techniques available at that time, this was a considerable feat. In addition, he could predict the position of this hypothesized planet in the sky. Having deduced these observable consequences, it was relatively easy for Berlin Observatory to observe the hypothesized planet in the real world, and Neptune was discovered.

Just as the engineering cycle represents the logical structure of product specification, so the empirical cycle represents the logical structure of model building. It does *not* represent what actually happens during discovery, nor does it represent how scientists think. In these processes, competition between research groups, budget cuts, personnel turnover, mistakes, blunders, blind spots and prejudices all play a role. The study of what happens during discovery is part of the sociology and history of science, and the study of how scientists think is part of psychology. The empirical cycle does however show how the resulting models must be *justified*. Scientific publications must present their results as if the empirical cycle were followed, so that others can reproduce these results, following the same cycle. In chapter 15, we refer to this as a *rational reconstruction* of the modeling process. The purpose of the empirical cycle for us is to act as a framework to understand methods for making a model of a UoD, not to help the research manager deal with such problems as budget cuts and personnel turnover. Note the analogy with the engineering cycle, which can be used to justify a product specification and to understand engineering methods, but does not represent the temporal sequence of engineering tasks.

3.5.3   Comparison of the empirical and engineering cycles

The empirical and engineering cycles are closely related, because both are specializations of the rational problem solving method. There are also a number of important differences between the two cycles, which all stem from the fact that in engineering we search for a specification of *useful behavior*, whereas in modeling we search for a specification of *true knowledge*. Of course, it is possible that the engineering cycle leads to new knowledge and the empirical cycle leads to new technology, but these are secondary products that do not alter the primary aim of following these cycles.

One consequence of this difference is that in the engineering cycle, we are searching for a *prescriptive* model, the product specification, whereas in the empirical cycle we are searching for a *descriptive* model. The difference is that in case of a mismatch between a prescriptive model and the modeled product, the product is wrong and the prescription is right. In case of a mismatch between a descriptive model and the modeled part of reality, the model is wrong and modeled reality is right.

Another important consequence of this is that the engineering cycle has a *normative* orientation where the empirical cycle has a *normatively neutral* orientation. The norms by which the results of engineering cycle are evaluated are instrumental, i.e. they are norms that tells us that a particular user need is to be satisfied. The justification of a product always has the form "because this human desire must be satisfied". However, it is always meaningful to ask whether this justification itself is *morally* sound. Some human desires may be immoral in some contexts; and even if they are moral, the means by which they are fulfilled may be immoral. The desire to observe people without being observed is moral in some contexts and immoral others; and the production of cheap products by means of child labor is immoral in all contexts. Engineering cannot be separated from moral problems.

By contrast, the only norm in the empirical cycle is the norm that true models be found. Even if morally reprehensible behavior is modeled, then the norms by which this behavior is rejected do not play a role in evaluating the outcome of empirical research, which is a descriptive model. A descriptive model is true or false, not morally good or bad. The empirical researcher should *not* try to improve the behavior he or she is studying. By contrast, the engineer does try to improve the product on which he or she is working.

The empirical researcher must keep a *distance* from his or her subject in order not to disturb the behavior he or she is modeling. The engineer, on the other hand, is *engaged* in his or her subject and is committed to improving it in a shared value judgement with the client. This creates normative problems which may become moral problems. As a result, professional societies usually set up codes of conduct, which include guidelines for professional and moral behavior.

3.6   A Framework for Product Development Methods

A **framework** for product development methods is a conceptual structure which provides us with points of reference in an analysis of development methods. Viewing the set of all development methods as the terrain, a framework for development methods provides a grid to be laid upon the terrain. The grid defines reference points that tell us where we are

	Needs analysis	Behavior specification			
		Synthesis	Simulation	Evaluation	Choice
Social system					
Computer-based system					
Software system					
Software subsystem					

Figure 3.9: A framework for development methods.

and where we might go to and, importantly, allows us to communicate our current location and destination to others. Frameworks for development methods usually have a number of dimensions that represent the orthogonal conceptual substructures out of which the framework is built. As the number of dimensions *increases*, the ease with which the framework can be understood *decreases* but the accuracy with which methods can be mapped by the framework *increases*. We must therefore search for an optimum between understandability and accuracy of the framework. Most frameworks have two or three dimensions, something which may be related to our limited mental capacity for understanding multidimensional spaces as well as with the ease with which two-dimensional diagrams can be drawn on paper. In this section, we start with a two-dimensional framework, but we indicate how this can be extended to a four-dimensional one — without trying to draw this more complicated framework.

3.6.1 The specification of needs, product behavior and product decomposition

If we apply the engineering cycle at every level of the aggregation hierarchy presented in chapter 2, then we get the two-dimensional framework for product development methods shown in figure 3.9. The vertical dimension of the framework indicates the *aggregation level* at which the engineering cycle is applied and the horizontal dimension indicates the *logical tasks* to be performed in the engineering cycle. There are three groups of tasks identified by the framework:

- In **needs analysis**, the function that the system must have for its users is determined. Needs analysis establishes *why* a system should exist. It is the problem analysis task of the engineering cycle. It is oriented to the environment of the product, i.e. to the client or to the market. It produces a specification of the **objectives** that the system must satisfy.

- The **behavior specification** activity corresponds to the rest of the engineering cycle at the same level of aggregation. Behavior specification establishes *what* a system should do. It produces a specification of the observable behavior of a system that would satisfy the stated objectives. If performed according to the engineering cycle, the behavior specification task consists of generating a number of alternative specifications, simulation of their likely effects, evaluation of these effects against the objectives, and a choice of one specification. Behavior specification is the interface between client/market needs on the one hand and product decomposition on the other. To write a behavior specification, the engineer should be able to switch between the viewpoints of the client or user and that of the designer. This requires social and communicative skills as well as technical knowledge.

- **System decomposition** moves down in the aggregation hierarchy and results in a specification of the internal structure of the system. System decomposition establishes *how* a system shall be structured. This task too can be performed following the engineering cycle, by generating alternative decompositions, simulating their effects, evaluating these against the behavior specification and the system objectives, and choosing one. This application of the engineering cycle is not shown in figure 3.9.

These three tasks correspond to the three views of a system identified in chapter 2: the function, behavior and implementation view, respectively. In the product life cycles shown in figures 3.3 and 3.4, needs analysis is explicitly shown. Behavior specification and the specification of product decomposition are jointly called *product specification* in those life cycles.

A behavior specification is rarely found in one iteration through the engineering cycle, and generally we iterate through the cycle at one level of aggregation several times before we settle upon a specification. This leads to a specification of product behavior at different levels of refinemert that are at the same level of aggregation. Three useful levels of refinement are the following.

- The **product idea** is the most abstract concept of what the product should do. It is comparable in abstraction to a mission statement of an organization.

- A **function specification** is a description of the functions that the product should offer its users.

- A **transaction specification** is a list of transactions of the product with its users. As explained in chapter 2, each transaction is an interaction with the environment considered to be atomic.

The product objectives specify a *problem* to be solved; a specification of product objectives is always a specification of user needs. The specifications of the product idea, product functions and product transactions describe a *solution* of the problem at increasing levels of refinement. As illustrated in figure 3.10, solution specifications at different refinement levels describe a product at the same level of aggregation. We call the table in figure 3.10 the **magic square**.

The movement from left to right in the magic square represents an act of **refinement** of an initial product idea by becoming more specific about the observable behavior of the solution. Even then, later discoveries can cause us to perform some more iterations. In the shoe polish packaging example, the developers first delivered a product idea to management, and refined this in several iterations through the engineering cycle until there was a product specification. During refinement, we move from the *why* to the *what*. Refinement reduces the uncertainty about a problem situation because we select a solution to a set of design objectives. The movement from right to left in the magic square decreases the level of

Figure 3.10: The magic square.

refinement and increases the level of **abstraction**. During abstraction, we move from the *what* to the *why* at the same level of aggregation, i.e. from behavior to function. Because refinement is a decomposition of functions into more detailed functions, it is also called **function decomposition**. It is important not to confuse this with system decomposition, discussed next.

The movements in the vertical dimension are **system decomposition** moving down and **system integration** moving up. System decomposition moves from the *what* at one aggregation level to the *how* of that level (which is the *what* of the next lower level). Just as refinement resolves uncertainty about the behavior that would satisfy system objectives, system decomposition resolves uncertainty about which decomposition would satisfy system objectives.

It is worth repeating that the system decomposition dimension is orthogonal to the function refinement dimension. There is an important tradition in system design in which these dimensions are mapped to each other. This is the tradition of **functional system decomposition**, in which we decompose a system into subsystems that each implement a system function in such a way that different subsystems implement different functions (at the same level of refinement). In functional system decomposition, the levels of decomposition correspond to levels of refinement. There are however other ways to decompose a system and in general, system decomposition is orthogonal to function refinement.

Comparing the magic square with figure 3.9, we see that in a rational development process, a move from a lower to a higher level of refinement (left to right in the square) takes place according to the engineering cycle. In an actual development process, development may proceed in a less rational way. In general, at any point in the development process, decisions may be made at any level of aggregation and at any level of refinement. For example, a particular development process may contain a sequence of decisions as shown in figure 3.11. Each square indicates a level of aggregation and a level of refinement at which a decision was made. A number in a square represents the fact that a decision has been made at that level of aggregation and refinement, and higher numbers represent later decisions. Occurrences of the number 0 represent the decisions already made before development started. As illustrated by the placement of numbers in figure 3.11, the progression of

	System objec-tives	System idea	System functions	System transac-tions
Social system	1	2,5	3,5,7	4,5,7
Computer-based system	2,5	6	0	7
Software system		0	3	
Software subsystem		3		0

Figure 3.11: A possible sequence of design decisions.

decisions is not necessarily in the direction of increasing behavior refinement or towards lower levels of system decomposition. The figure contains only one example and other development processes may contain other decision sequences. We return to strategies for ordering the tasks in a development process in chapter 15.

3.6.2 Disentangling requirements and other ambiguities

The framework is helpful in disentangling a number of ambiguities in a number of important terms used in product development. First, let us define **requirements engineering** as the process consisting of needs analysis and behavior specification, and **product specification** as the activity of producing a behavior specification and a decomposition specification. As shown in figure 3.12, these activities overlap. To relate these concepts to others introduced earlier in this chapter: product specification occurs in market-oriented as well as in client-oriented development. In market-oriented development, the two additional tasks of product development are writing a marketing plan and a production specification. Requirements engineering and product specification jointly form the development activity. *Implementation* is separate from development, except in software development, where we can decompose a product into components whose specifications are executable. In software development, decomposition *is* implementation. Depending upon the aggregation level, decomposition/implementation of software is called **global design**, **detailed design** or **coding**.

Figure 3.13 relates the results of development with each other. Results are also called **deliverables**. The deliverables of requirements engineering are called a **requirements specification** and the deliverables of product specification are, due to the process-product ambiguity in the word "specification", called a **product specification**. A requirements specification includes everything except the product decomposition; a product specification includes everything except product objectives.

An important ambiguity introduced by the above definitions is that specifications of objectives, behavior and decomposition can be produced at any level of the aggregation hierarchy. Thus, what is a specification of an objective at one level of aggregation is "really" a system decomposition when viewed from a higher level of aggregation. As a result, arguments about whether we are specifying system objectives or a system decomposition

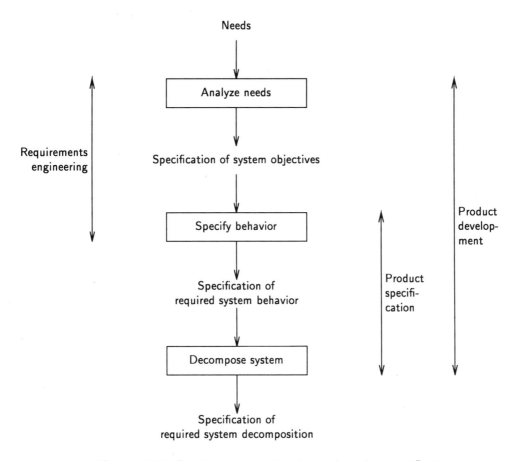

Figure 3.12: Requirements engineering and product specification.

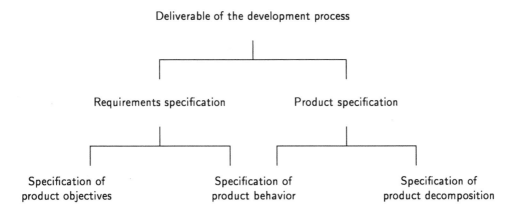

Figure 3.13: Classification of different kinds of deliverables of development.

may be interminable. The answer to both sides in the argument is usually "Yes". The resolution of the argument simply lies in the identification of the aggregation level at which we observe a system: a *system* decomposition gives us *subsystem* objectives.

Note that this ambiguity is analogous to the ambiguity in the concept of transaction. Arguments about whether a certain interaction is a transaction or not are interminable for the same reason. As we found in subsection 2.4.2, these arguments must be resolved by identifying the aggregation level at which we consider the interactions.

The term **requirement** is perhaps the most overloaded term of all. Are system objectives requirements, or are requirements really behavior specifications? But a system decomposition also gives us requirements. Add to this the ambiguity in the word "specification", and it becomes clear that the expression "requirements specification" by itself is virtually meaningless. Whenever we use the term, it refers to a deliverable of development consisting of a specification of product objectives and of required product behavior. Where necessary, we will disambiguate the term by indicating the level of aggregation to which we refer.

The term **implementation** is subject to all of the ambiguities identified so far, and some more. Just as "specification", "implementation" can refer to a process as well as the product of that process; and just as with "specification", this ambiguity is harmless, because it is always removed by the context of the term. More seriously, for one person, an "implementation" is an organizational subsystem that implements the information supply infrastructure, where for another person it is a piece of code that implements an algorithm. Again, the resolution of many of these ambiguities lies in the identification of the aggregation level.

Figure 3.14 presents a grand picture of the cycle of product evolution. The arrows indicate direction of influence. The reader may want to identify the place of requirements engineering and product specification in product evolution, and check the meaning of the bidirectional arrows in the diagram.

3.6.3   Other framework dimensions

So far, our framework has only two dimensions, aggregation level and logic. This is sufficient for an analysis of development *methods*. If we want to analyze the development *process*, we must include *time* as the third dimension of out framework. This will allow us to represent different ways of ordering the tasks of development in time. The distinction between the logical and the temporal dimension of the framework is that the logical dimension represents the process as it would take place in a rational world — which is not the one we live in — and that the temporal dimension represents the process as it can be planned to take place in the actual world. We turn to strategies for *planning* the temporal sequence of tasks of the development process in chapters 15 and 16. We defer the addition of the temporal dimension to those chapters.

A fourth dimension that it is useful to add is that of *aspect*. In section 2.3, an aspect of a system is defined as a subset of the interactions of a system. Each system has potentially infinitely different aspects such as the financial aspect, the technical aspect, the social aspect, the organizational aspect, the economic aspect, the legal aspect, the ergonomic aspect, etc. Most information system development methods focus on the technical aspect of computer-based systems but there are some methods that include organizational or social aspects. For example, ISAC and Information Engineering (part II) include the organizational aspect

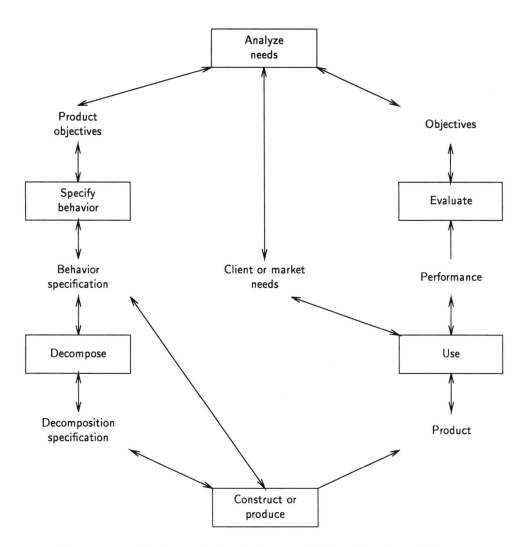

Figure 3.14: Product evolution. The arrows indicate direction of influence.

	ISAC	Information Engineering	Entity-Relationship modeling	Structured analysis/Structured design	Jackson System Development
Social system	**Change analysis**	**Information strategy planning**			
Computer-based system	**Activity study**	Business area analysis			
Software system	Information analysis	Business system design	**Entity-Relationship modeling**	**Structured analysis**	**UoD modeling, function specification**
Software subsystem	Implementation	Technical design and construction		Structured design	Implementation

Figure 3.15: Application of the framework to five requirements specification methods.

in their method, and ETHICS (appendix C) includes the social aspect.

Because all these aspects are relevant, the engineer will have to cooperate with specialists from different professions. This puts a high premium on the communicative skills of the engineer. Contrast this with the communicative skills required of a scientist who is trained to communicate his or her discoveries to other specialists in the *same* science, all of whom can be assumed to have a similar training and to use the same vocabulary. The engineer will always work in an interdisciplinary context and will have to communicate with people who use another language, geared to the description of other system aspects.

3.6.4   Application of the framework

The tasks in the methods described in part II of this book can be mapped to different aggregation levels as shown in figure 3.15. In part II, we only discuss in-depth the tasks printed in boldface. The figure only maps tasks to aggregation levels and does not show the internal structure of the tasks in terms of the engineering cycle. The internal structure will be analyzed after we discussed the methods in some detail.

All methods are *requirements engineering methods*, i.e. they produce a statement of objectives and/or a specification of required system behavior. Entity-relationship modeling, Structured Analysis and Jackson System Development can be applied to the level of computer-based systems as well as of software systems, but they are more at home in the specification of software systems.

One methodological question asked in this book about the methods is

- How can we map the tasks recommended by the methods to the engineering cycle?

Because all studied methods are methods for specifying the behavior of computer-based systems, and these systems have a UoD, there is an additional question to be answered:

- How does the method mix UoD modeling with the specification of required system functions?

It will be shown that Entity-Relationship modeling is primarily a method for finding a conceptual model of the UoD, whereas Structured Analysis does not distinguish a conceptual model of the UoD from a system model. Jackson System Development is unique in making a clear distinction between conceptual model of the UoD and a specification of required system behavior.

The two questions above are about the tasks to be performed in requirements specification process. Two other important questions to be asked concern the structure of the specifications produced when the methods are followed:

- What is the structure of system specifications produced by the methods?

- Can the specifications produced by different methods be integrated?

We will answer these questions in detail for the software system specification methods. As a preparation, we look at the structure of product specifications in general in the next chapter.

3.7   Summary

Product development is a process that, given a need, delivers a specification of a solution that is expected to satisfy this need. In *client-oriented* development, the need is felt by a single client, in *market-oriented* development, the need is identified to exist in a market. Client-oriented development produces a specification of an an individual product, whereas market-oriented development produces a marketing plan, a product specification and a production specification. In both cases, we can identify a number of *stakeholders* in the development process. The *development organization* is the person or organization performing the development process. The *sponsor* pays for the development process, the *customer* buys the delivered product, and the *user* uses the product. In client-oriented development, the sponsor and customer are identical. The client may be the sponsor, customer or user of the product.

All products *evolve*, because when they are used, the needs of the user change and the environment of uses changes as well. In client-oriented development, the needs of the client may even change because of the determination of objectives. This is called *requirements uncertainty*. The characteristic feature of product evolution is that an evaluation of experience of the product *after* it is developed, leads to a (re)development of the product. The logical structure of product evolution is the same as the logical structure of feedback control, viz. the *regulatory cycle*.

In *product engineering*, a product specification is produced by means of a rational problem solving process. The essence of this process is that the effects of alternative specifications are simulated and evaluated *before* the specification is implemented. This evaluation may lead to a new iteration through the engineering process until the desired effects are found.

The *empirical cycle* is a rational problem solving process in which a true model of observed phenomena is sought. The essence of this process is the experimental evaluation of alternative models of the phenomena. The empirical cycle is a useful method for current system modeling as well as for conceptual modeling.

The engineering and empirical cycles are applications of the rational problem solving cycle and are not methods for planning the development or modeling process. They can however be used as targets for a rational reconstruction of the process after the fact, used for justifying the results of the processes.

The empirical and engineering cycles are closely parallel in their form, but they have a few fundamental differences. The empirical cycle is a search for knowledge, but the engineering cycle is a search for the satisfaction of requirements. The empirical cycle is therefore value-free in the sense that it does not pass judgement on the subject of study. The engineering cycle is normative in the sense that the engineer continually passes value judgements on the subject of study, viz. how well the behavior satisfies the objectives of the development process. Related to this difference is the fact that the empirical scientist is an observer with a detached attitude with respect to his or her subject of study, but that the engineer is involved in his or her subject. The engineer is an actor in the world, not an observer of the world. As a consequence, the engineer may be engaged in situations that raise moral questions. There are codes of conduct that provide guidelines for professional and moral behavior.

If we combine the levels of aggregation identified in the previous chapter with the engineering cycle, we get a framework that can be used to classify development methods. In this framework, *requirements engineering* consists of two tasks, *needs analysis* and *behavior specification*. *Product specification* is the partly overlapping task consisting of behavior specification and product decomposition. Market-oriented development consists of needs analysis, product specification, production specification and marketing; client-oriented development consists of needs analysis and product specification.

The development framework is not a strategy to plan the development process. *Time* would be a third dimension of the framework, orthogonal to the partitioning in aggregation levels and to the logical tasks of product development. A fourth dimension would be *aspect*. Important system aspects that may have to be subject of development include the organizational, social, ergonomic, and legal aspects.

3.8   Exercises

1. For each of the following development processes, identify the client(s), sponsor(s), customer(s), and user(s).

   (a) The development of air traffic control software which, by law, must be installed on board of airplanes by the aircraft builder.

   (b) The development of a new version of a database management system (DBMS) by a vendor of database software.

   (c) The development of parametrized software for the administration of document circulations.

   (d) The development of software to register military conscripts.

2. This question is about the TANA case study.

   (a) What kind of simulations are performed in each of the iterations through the engineering cycle?

   (b) How are the evaluations of the simulation results performed?

3. Loucopoulos and Karakostas [198] define requirements engineering as the transformation of business concerns into software system requirements. They present a framework in which requirements engineering is decomposed into the following three interacting processes, that are performed in parallel with each other:

   - **Requirements elicitation**: reaching an understanding of the problem. Sources of requirements knowledge are identified and their relevance and significance estimated.

   - **Requirements specification**: describing the problem. In this process, the acquired knowledge is analyzed and organized into a coherent requirements model. A series of conceptual models is produced that represent the problem domain. The conceptual models in the series become increasingly refined, and increasingly represent the software domain instead of the problem domain.

   - **Requirements validation**: ensure that the requirements model agrees with the user's expectations. In this process, experiments are prepared, performed and the results of experiments evaluated.

   Compare these tasks with the framework for development of figure 3.9.

4. Nadler [238] observed the problem solving processes of an engineer, a commercial artist, an architect, a physician and a lawyer and found following common structure:

   (a) Determine the function of the required system.

   (b) Develop a number of very high level versions of the required system. Evaluate them and select one.

   (c) Gather information necessary to continue the design.

   (d) Generate alternative systems on the basis of the abstract ideal and the information gathered.

   (e) Select the feasible solution.

   (f) Specify the chosen solution.

   (g) Subject the selected solution to internal and external review.

   (h) Test the system design.

   (i) Install the system.

   (j) Measure the performance of the system.

   Map this process to the regulatory cycle.

5. Verification by testing cannot show the correctness of an implementation, but can show its incorrectness. Compare this with the fact that experiments can falsify a hypothesis but cannot prove it to be true.

6. In the discovery of Neptune, one induction step took place. Identify this step.

7. Dewey [86, pages 107-115] defines what he calls *the process of reflective thinking* as follows:

   (a) *Suggestions* of alternatives for action. This is the first moment at which we become aware of a problem. Direct, unreflective action is inhibited and the hesitation and delay necessary for reflective thinking arises.

   (b) *Intellectualization* of the situation, in which the conditions that constitute the trouble and cause the stoppage of action are investigated.

   (c) A *hypothesis* about what to do "springs up" to the mind and is formulated.

   (d) *Reasoning* about the possible consequences of the hypothesis.

   (e) *Testing* the hypothesis by action.

   Compare this with the method of rational problem solving discussed in this chapter by correlating each task in Dewey's method with task(s) in the rational problem solving cycle. In addition, indicate a relationship with the regulatory cycle.

8. Kolb and Frohman [184] define the process of planned change, to be followed by organization consultants, as follows.

   (a) Scouting: the consultant and the organization explore a potential relationship with the other.

   (b) Entry: Negotiate a contract.

   (c) Diagnosis: The consultant analyses the problem of the client, the objectives of the client, the resources of the client and the resource of the consultant.

   (d) Planning: Generate alternative solutions or change strategies and simulate the consequences of each plan.

   (e) Action: Implement the best action.

   (f) Evaluation: Evaluate the results of the change efforts.

   (g) Termination: Terminate the contract between the consultant and the client organization.

   Compare this with the engineering method discussed in this chapter by correlating each task in Kolb and Frohman's method with task(s) in the engineering cycle. Is there also a similarity with the regulatory cycle?

9. The arrows in figure 3.14 indicate direction of influence. For each arrow, give an example of a case where influence goes in the indicated direction(s).

3.9 Bibliographical Remarks

Rational problem solving The model of rational problem solving used in this chapter goes back to a proposal by Dewey [86, pages 107-115], used in exercise 7 above. A simplified version of Dewey's proposal was adopted by Simon [315, 316]. This model has been very influential in artificial intelligence, where it took the shape of means-ends analysis [318] and was implemented in the General Problem Solver (GPS) [97].

The rational problem solving method has been recognized to be useful by management scientists and consultants too. For example, in a famous descriptive study of 25 strategic decision processes in organizations, Mintzberg, Raisinghani and Théorêt [234] found that the rational problem solving method serves as a useful framework to understand what managers do. Managers do not blindly follow through this process step by step, but choose a path through it that may skip tasks that are easy or for which there is no time, and that may iterate over tasks that are important for the problem at hand.

As a second example, Kolb and Frohman [184] define the process of planned change, to be followed by organization consultants, as a rational problem solving cycle (see exercise 8 above).

Against this prevalence of rational problem solving methods one can observe that often the time to generate all alternatives, or the information to investigate their consequences, are not available. Simon [315] proposed the model of *bounded rationality*, in which only some alternatives are investigated, using the resources available. Secondly, March and Olsen [211] remark that rational problem solving in organizations presupposes that different people have the same preferences and that these preferences can be specified before the choice is made. Both presuppositions are often not satisfied. As an alternative model for organizational decision making they propose the *garbage can model of organizational choice*, in which an organization is viewed as a sea in which problems, solutions and people float around and occasionally meet each other. When the three meet and the organization is expected to behave in a way that is called "making a choice", some people that happen to be around connect solutions that happen to be available with problems they find themselves confronted with. This model is not suitable to use as a basis for planning product development, but it may help the manager of the development process to understand some of the things going on inside and around the development process.

The engineering cycle. The engineering cycle used in this chapter is based upon a model of the decision cycle in engineering design given by Roozenburg and Eekels [289] and by Hall [131]. Additional explanations of the engineering cycle are given by Asimov [15], Jones [169] and Archer [13]. Pugh [276] shows how these ideas can be implemented in a process for integrated product engineering. Archer [11] shows how the product development process is embedded in the larger process of product innovation (viewed in this chapter as a species of product evolution). The example of the development of a new kind of packaging for shoe polish is taken from Roozenburg and Eekels [289].

Software engineering. Peters [257] uses some of the insights from industrial design to define a framework for software engineering methods. Jensen and Tonies [165] analyze the software engineering process from a general engineering standpoint as a problem solving process and come up with a model of the engineering cycle similar to the one presented in this chapter.

The view that software engineering should be an *engineering* discipline is supported by D.M. Berry in a report for the Software Engineering Institute [30]. However, Berry ignores or at least underplays the role of simulation in engineering before implementation. He quotes Koen [183] in defining engineering as the strategy for causing the best change in a poorly understood situation with the available resources, and he then quotes an unpublished definition of Mary Shaw and Watts Humphrey that software engineering is "that form of engineering that applies computer science and mathematics to achieving cost-effective solutions to software problems". In this definition, software engineering is problem solving, but the use of simulation and evaluation before the software product is implemented, is not mentioned. Baber [17] takes the same view of engineering as we do and emphasizes the use of scientific knowledge and principles in the computation of product properties before the product is actually built. Consequently, he doubts whether software engineering currently is really an engineering discipline.

Although software engineering, if it is to fulfill the promise of its name, can learn from product engineering, there are nevertheless some fundamental differences between software engineering and product engineering. In a famous position paper published in 1985, Parnas [254] argues that due to discrete state-changing behavior and complexity, software is inherently unreliable. Software engineering, formal methods and artificial intelligence techniques may provide some help to master the complexity of software, but will do so only in small increments. In an equally famous paper that appeared two years later, Brooks [53] lists four essential differences between industrial product development and software development, that make the engineering of software essentially hard: the complexity, invisibility, and changeability of software when compared to other products, and the intertwining of software with other products. Because of this intertwining, software must conform to a large number of requirements imposed upon it by these other products. In a reaction to these papers, Harel [138] provides a more optimistic view by arguing that system modeling, visual languages and model execution may provide the means to tackle some of these problems. We may observe that modeling a system before it is built and executing the model to evaluate it, both proposed by Harel, are part of the essence of the engineering method as defined in this chapter.

Empirical cycle. The empirical cycle is described in any introductory textbook on the philosophy of science. Classic statements are given by Kemeny [173] and Nagel [239]. The observation that hypotheses can only be falsified, not verified, comes from Popper [264]. Popper's falsification theory corresponds with Dijkstra's [87] famous observation that tests can only show the presence of bugs in a program, not their absence. The comparison of the engineering cycle and empirical cycle is based on an analysis of the logic of social action given by van Strien [329] and on a comparison of the two cycles by Roozenburg and Eekels [289].

Codes of conduct. Codes of conduct relevant for engineering computer-based systems are the *ACM Code of Professional Conduct* [2] and the *IEEE Code of Ethics* [154]. Anderson *et al.* [9] illustrate the use of the ACM code in decision making. There are now several books on ethical aspects of decision making in computer-based system development, including Johnson [167], Ermann, Williams and Guttierez [96] and Forester and Morrison [106].

Needs analysis. Needs analysis is the most difficult task in the entire development process. Mistakes made here have the most expensive consequences. The problem to be solved at this stage is not to find a solution to the requirements; it is to find out what the objectives of the product are [12], and this is a **wicked problem**. According to Rittel and

Webber [279], wicked problems have no definitive formulation, and the solution is determined to a large extent by the formulation of the problem. Wicked problems do not have a solution space that can be enumerated or even described, and once we start analyzing them, we always find they are symptoms of other problems. There is no criterion to determine the quality of solutions and the problem solving process has no stopping rule. Whatever we accept as a solution is not true or false, it is good or bad. Wicked problems are unique, and they are so urgent that the problem solver cannot afford to be wrong. There is no occasion to try a solution first and implement it later; every trial solution counts as an irreversible step in real life. In other words, a wicked problem is a *real* problem.

Given this predicament, one may wonder what to do. In a delightful little book, Gause and Weinberg [112] give a number of important hints on how to go about solving real problems. In a more extensive treatment [111], they give numerous practical methods and techniques by which to tackle problems in needs analysis. Gause and Weinberg argue that we can never know what the client's *needs* are and that requirements determination is all about determining the client's *desires*. As defined in chapter 2, user needs are user desires, so in the terminology of this book, needs analysis is the determination of the client's desires. A survey of experimental techniques for needs analysis is given by Gutierrez [129]. Byrd, Cossick and Zmud [55] give a synthesis of techniques for needs analysis and knowledge acquisition. Jones [168] gives a very interesting survey of techniques for different stages in product development, including needs analysis.

Requirements uncertainty. The principle of requirements uncertainty has been called the *uncertainty principle of data processing* by James Martin and Clive Finkelstein [217] and by McCracken and Jackson [221] and *Heisenberg-like uncertainty* by Lehman [191]. The essence of this uncertainty is that by installing and using a product, needs tend to change so that the product tends to become obsolete by being used.

Behavior specification. An early survey of behavior specification techniques (also called *requirements* specification techniques) was given by Taggart and Tharp [336]. In the same year, Ross and Schoman [294] published a classic paper on the specification of required system behavior, that is full of insights in the requirements engineering process. The distinction between function, observable behavior and structure (why, what and how), which is one of the structuring themes of this book, is already made in this paper.

Davis [77] gives a survey of techniques which uses roughly the same classification of techniques as we do here, viz. problem analysis (called objectives determination here) and requirements specification (called behavior specification here). However, Entity-Relationship modeling, Data Flow modeling and Jackson System Development are treated as problem analysis methods by Davis and as behavior specification methods in this book. This is explained by the fact that we focus on computer-based systems, whereas Davis focuses on software systems, which is one level lower in the aggregation hierarchy. What is behavior specification for a computer-based system is objectives determination, and hence problem analysis, for a software system.

Requirements engineering. There are a number of good surveys of issues in requirements engineering. Curtis, Krasner and Iscoe [74] report on an empirical study of software product development processes that the major problems in these processes are the thin spread of application knowledge, changing and conflicting requirements, and communication and coordination breakdowns. The first two of these problems concern the requirements engineering task. Dorfman [89] gives a brief introduction to requirements engineering at the level of computer-based systems and of software systems and shows how requirements flow down from one level to the next. Stokes [326] gives a survey of the problems with requirements engineering, possible solutions to these problems, and methods and techniques for the specification of required system behavior. Brackett [50] gives an interesting survey of the subfields of requirements engineering in the form of a curriculum outline and an extensive annotated bibliography. Yeh and Ng [373] give a brief survey of methods and techniques for specifying requirements. They emphasize the need for specifying the environment of the product in addition to specifying the properties required of the product. In an interesting study by Lubars, Potts and Richter [199] of requirements engineering in ten organizations, it was found that most problems of requirements engineering in practice are organizational, and that organizational solutions to technical problems were sought. Examples of problems that exist in practice are poor interactions between developers and users, lack of guidance in finding a product specification, problems in specifying product objectives, and changing requirements. Hsia, Davis and Kung [149] suggest a number of research directions to tackle these issues, such as animation of specifications, computer-aided requirements engineering and method integration.

It is clear that interest in requirements engineering is rapidly rising. In 1991, a special issue of the *IEEE Transactions on Software Engineering* was devoted to requirements engineering [79] and in 1993 a two-yearly conference on requirements engineering [102] was started. The March 1994 issue of IEEE Software includes some papers from the first conference in this series [80]. Starting from 1996, Springer will publish the *Requirements Engineering Journal*. In addition to Davis' book [77] on software requirements specifications, there is now a textbook by Loucopoulos and Karakostas on requirements engineering [198]. This book gives a useful survey of techniques and heuristics for elicitation, modeling, and validation of system requirements.

Frameworks.   There are numerous framework for system development. The framework defined in figure 3.9 has two dimensions, *logic* and *aggregation level*. In an influential paper, Hall [132] defines a framework with three dimensions: *logic* (problem solving procedure), *time* (problem solving process) and *aspect* (kind of knowledge of the developed system). The logic dimension is virtually the same as the logic dimension of our framework. Hall's time dimension is introduced in chapter 15, when we look at strategies to perform the actual system development process. A two-dimensional logic-time framework, corresponding to two of Hall's three dimensions, is now well-accepted in software engineering [222, 287, 240], but to my knowledge, no reference is made in the software engineering literature to Hall's framework. The term "magic square" comes from Harel and Pnueli [140], but they do not mention the particular levels of refinement and decomposition that I use. They give a clear argument for the importance of the magic square in understanding system development.

Roman, Stucki, Ball and Gillett [286] define a framework for system development that uses an aggregation hierarchy too. At each level of the hierarchy, a sequence of tasks is defined that can be construed as a division of requirements determination and conceptual modeling into subtasks, and a merging of the resulting steps.

Davis [76] gives a framework that resembles the one used in this book. Davis' framework consists of an aggregation dimension and a logical dimension. However, he focuses on one aggregation level only, that of software product development, and he does not use the engineering cycle as a logical task structure at each level of aggregation. Rather, he distinguishes user needs analysis, solution space definition, external behavior definition and preliminary design as logical tasks at one level. In terms of our framework, these would be the result of successive iterations through the engineering cycle at one level of aggregation.

The frameworks discussed so far are *method-oriented*. They try to classify tasks in the development process. Some frameworks are *specification-oriented*, i.e. they are based on a classification of the intermediary or final specifications produced. An example is Blum's [34] framework, which distinguishes problem oriented from product oriented specifications along one dimension, and semi-formal and formal representations on the other. Pohl [259] distinguishes three specification dimensions: (in)completeness of the specification, (in)formality of the specification and (dis)agreement about the specification.

When we turn to frameworks for information system development methods, we find a wide variety, most of them oriented towards what aspect of the UoD is represented. Many of these are published in the proceedings of the conferences on Comparative Research in Information Systems (CRIS) [248, 247, 249]. These frameworks can best be understood as frameworks for UoD models, and should be compared with the modeling framework discussed in chapter 13.

4

Requirements Specifications

4.1 Introduction

A requirements specification consists of a specification of product objectives and a specification of required product behavior. In this chapter, we discuss the structure of a specification of product objectives (section 4.2), classify different kinds of behavior specifications (section 4.3) and give a simple framework for the structure of behavior specifications (section 4.4). In section 4.5, we list a number of desirable properties of requirements specifications.

4.2 Product Objectives

The generic objective of any product is to answer needs that exist in its environment. Any development process starts with a statement of product objectives and produces behavior specifications and product decompositions along the way. As explained in chapter 3, what is a decomposition from one point of view is part of the objectives at the next lower level of aggregation. It is therefore useful to distinguish the top level objectives identified as the result of a needs analysis from lower level objectives. Figure 4.1 clarifies the situation. At each level below that of the top level objectives, the behavior specification and decomposition specification are the objectives for systems at the next lower level of aggregation.

An example top level objective in the TANA case study (chapter 3) was to maintain TANA's market share. The output of the first iteration through the engineering cycle in that example was the decision to develop a new product for the current market of TANA. This output then became the objective to be realized in the ensuing development process (figure 4.1). The product specification was then written in a number of iterations that stayed at the same level of aggregation. For example, in the second iteration, a product idea was delivered as initial product specification. This became the objective of the third iteration through the engineering cycle, in which a concept of operation was produced, etc.

Example top level objectives identified in the library case study of ISAC change analysis in chapter 5 are the improvement of acquisition procedures and the improvement of return procedures of the library. In all cases, top level objectives are the translation of client or market needs into objectives to be achieved by the product under development.

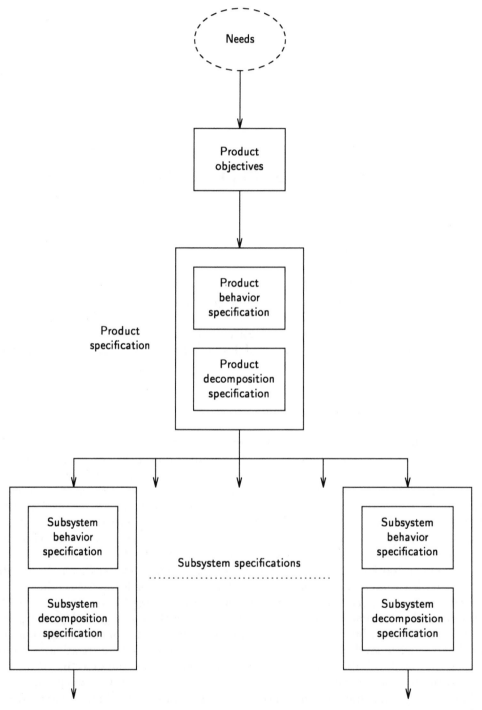

Figure 4.1: The role of objectives in the development process. Each product specification is a statement of objectives for its subsystems.

It is common to distinguish objectives from **constraints** that the product must satisfy. The difference between objectives and constraints is however more in the eye of the beholder than in the objectives or constraints themselves. Both are norms that the product must satisfy. The difference seems to be that limitations on the solution space, imposed from the outside, are experienced by some developers as constraints on their design freedom. By contrast, goals worth striving for, peaks of achievement to be realized by the choices that the developer makes, are viewed by those developers as objectives. This distinction is wholly subjective, and in what follows the term "constraint" is used as a stylistic variant of "objective".

4.3 Behavior and Property Specifications

We can specify product behavior at different levels of refinement. We saw in subsection 3.6 that the following three levels are useful in practice:

- The **product idea** is the most abstract specification of what the product should do.

- A **function specification** is a description of the functions that the product should offer its users.

- A **transaction specification** is a list of transactions of the product with its users.

In subsection 2.4.4, we saw that aspects of product behavior can be summarized by product *properties*. At the level of abstraction of the product idea or that of required system functions, it is often not possible to specify properties behaviorally. Once we are able to specify required product transactions, we should also be able to specify most required product properties in a behavioral way. For properties for which we cannot find a behavioral specification, we should try to find *proxies*, whose presence can be behaviorally specified and that suggest the presence of the desired property. Indeed, decreasing the abstraction level from product idea to product transaction, we often replace a high level desired product property by lower level proxies for that property.

A behavioral specification of a property describes an experiment in which evidence is given for the presence or absence of the property. This experiment can be described at various levels of detail. For example, we can represent user-friendliness by the proxies that the average initial training time needed by all users must be short and that the number of help requests about the system must be low. These observation procedures must be made more precise by indicating how users are sampled, or over which period they are observed, what is the size of the user population over which we average help requests, etc. To keep the main flow of ideas in a specification clear, we should write a global specification of the property first and add measuring procedures later as footnotes [111, page 172].

There are a number of checklists of kinds of properties that a software system can have. Figure 4.2 gives one such list. *Correctness* is a meta-property, for it indicates the degree to which the product satisfies its (other) properties. *Security* is an example of a **negative** property, because it is about something that should *not* be observed. An example of a security property is the property that unauthorized access cannot occur. Other examples of negative properties are absence of deadlock, absence of collisions in a robot control system and, more generally, absence of unsafe behavior. Examples of **positive** properties are that a system should cost less than Dfl 10 to the customer and that it should have a response time

- Correctness: The extent to which the product satisfies the objectives.
- Reliability: The extent to which the product behaves as specified in different circumstances.
- Efficiency: The amount of resources needed by the product.
- Security: The extent to which unauthorized use of the product can be prevented.
- User-friendliness: The ease of use of the product.
- Maintainability: The ease with which product malfunction can be repaired.
- Testability: The ease with which the product can be ascertained to conform to its specification.
- Flexibility: The ease with which the product can be modified after delivery, so that it conforms to a changed specification.
- Portability: The ease with which the product can be ported from one hardware and software environment to another.
- Reusability: The ease with which components of the product can be used in other products.
- Interoperability: The ease with which the product can interface to other products.

Figure 4.2: Kinds of software product properties.

of less than 2 seconds. It is much harder to specify an observation procedure for negative properties than for positive properties. Experimental verification that a product satisfies a negative property would require observation of the product throughout its complete lifetime. Obviously, such an experiment is too expensive and is useless — we would like to verify the property before the product is used, not after it is disposed of. A convincing verification of the presence of a negative property in a product must take the form of a mathematical or logical proof that the unwanted behavior *cannot* occur.

Different required properties may conflict with each other. In case of conflict, the engineer must perform trade-off studies, and to perform these studies, it is desirable that required properties be specified in the form of **preferences** for certain properties above others. A minimal indication of preferences is a distinction between **essential** properties that the product must have, and **desired** properties that it would be nice to have. A more refined specification would give an ordering of all possible property values in order of preference. For example, preferences of the market for washing machines may be such that a noise level of 0 dB has the highest preference and 9 dB the lowest. A noise level of 0 dB may be achievable at a very high price by using expensive state-of-the-art anti-noise technology, and the market also happens to have a preference for cheap washing machines. As a result, the marketing department adjusts its preferences and settles on an acceptable combination of noise level and price. Of course, preferences depend upon the objectives to be realized by the product. Should the washing machine be targeted for the expensive but small high end of the market or for the mass consumer market? This determines the preferences used in the trade-off between high technology and low price.

	Static dimension		Dynamic dimension	
	States	Static constraints	Transitions	Dynamic constraints
UoD	ER	ER	JSD	JSD
SuD	ER	ER	SA JSD	JSD

Figure 4.3: A framework for behavior specifications.

4.4   A Framework for Behavior Specifications

The methods reviewed in part II all lead to the specification of required product behavior. ISAC change analysis and IE information strategy planning additionally lead to the specification of product objectives. In part III, we will show how to integrate behavior specifications produced by the different methods. We will use a simple framework for behavior specifications, based upon the following two dimensions.

- **Static dimension of behavior**: each behavior specification specifies the set of all possible observable system **states**. There is a small set of techniques and notations for the specification of a system state space, converging on the specification of entities, relationships, and properties. Constraints on the state space are called **static constraints**. Important classes of constraints on the state space are existence constraints and cardinality constraints.

- **Dynamic dimension of behavior**: each behavior specification specifies the set of all possible observable **state transitions** in the state space. Observable state transitions are the transactions of the system. There is a large set of techniques and notations used to specify these transitions. Examples of techniques are decision trees, decision tables, and state transition diagrams. In addition to specifying individual state transitions, most techniques allow the specification of constraints on those transitions, such as constraints on sequencing, delay and response time. Constraints on state transitions are called **dynamic constraints**.

Because computer-based systems manipulate data, there are two systems we can specify: the computer-based system and its UoD. In a development process, the computer-based system is also called the **system under development** or SuD. The specifications of the SuD and UoD are **conceptual models**, because they embody our shared understanding of these systems and are used to facilitate communication between people about the UoD or SuD. The conceptual model of the SuD is prescriptive, the conceptual model of the UoD is descriptive.

Figure 4.3 indicates the coverage of the behavior specification methods reviewed in part II.

- The ER method (chapters 7 and 8) can be used to write a specification of the state space of a data manipulation system and of some of the static constraints on the states in this space. It is neutral with respect to modeling the SuD and modeling the UoD of the system. That is, by looking at the specification itself, we cannot discover whether it is a system model or a UoD model.

- The Structured Analysis method (chapters 9 and 10) can be used to write a specification of the transactions of the SuD. It produces a model of a data manipulation system and not of the UoD of such a system. It focuses on the specification of transactions.

- The JSD method (chapters 11 and 12) can be used to write a specification of the transactions of the SuD and of sequencing constraints on those transactions. It distinguishes a model of the UoD of the system from a model of the system functions itself.

A glance at figure 4.3 shows that jointly, the three methods have a good coverage of the different aspects of system behavior. In chapters 13 and 14, we use the framework of figure 4.3 to analyze the possibilities to combine and integrate these behavior specification methods.

4.5   Desirable Properties of a Requirements Specification

Product specifications should themselves have a number of properties, that follow from the purpose for which they are written. The purpose of a specification is to specify all and only the behavior required of a product, so that customers and sponsors know what they get and constructors know what to build (or buy). The requirements specification should be fulfill this purpose during construction or production as well as during product evolution. In order to fulfill this purpose, product specifications should be communicable, true, complete, feasible, verifiable, and maintainable. Figure 4.4 defines these properties and gives a number of aspects of each property.

The most important property of a specification is that it should be communicable. If it is to have any use for the sponsor, developer, client or marketing department, it must be able to use it as a channel of communication between them. Communicability is a presupposition of the other properties of a specification. For example, truth and completeness cannot be verified if the specification is not communicable. Communicability means, first, that the specification must be *understandable* by all stakeholders, and second, that the stakeholders must have the *same* understanding of the specification. In other words, the specification must be unambiguous. Understandability and unambiguity are sometimes at odds with each other. For example, mathematical expressions are unambiguous but are not understandable for many people. Nevertheless, without understandability and unambiguity, validation of a specification with stakeholders is problematic. Gause and Weinberg [111] single out unambiguity as the most important desirable attribute of specifications.

The requirement that a product specification be **true** does not mean that it describes the product accurately, but that it specifies the requirements on the product accurately. This is also called **validity** of the specification. This means, among others, that the specification should not specify the decomposition of the system, nor make any other implementation decisions. Of course, implementation constraints may be part of the product objectives, but this should not be a decision on the part of the writer of the specification.

- **Communicability**: The specification should serve as a channel of communication about the product among all stakeholders.
  - Understandability
  - Unambiguity
- **Truth**: The specification should describe requirements and nothing else.
  - Validity
  - Implementation-independence
- **Completeness**: The specification should describe all requirements and not less.
  - Validated
  - Preferences included
- **Feasibility**: The specification should describe behavior that can be realized in a product.
  - Consistency
  - Cost-effectiveness
- **Verifiability**: It should be possible to observe whether a product satisfies the specification.
  - Observation procedures
- **Maintainability**: The specification must be maintainable when requirements change after delivery of the product.
  - Traceability
  - Modifyability

Figure 4.4: Properties that a product specification should have.

Completeness of a specification entails that no requirement has been omitted from the specification. In practice, this means that the requirements have been validated with the sponsor and that the sponsor agrees that there are no other requirements to be satisfied. Completeness entails that where possible, constraints have been annotated with preferences.

Feasibility of a specification means, minimally, that the specification is *consistent*. By this we mean that a product that satisfies the specification can exist. A specification that requires a response time to be less than 3 seconds and greater than 5 seconds cannot be satisfied and is therefore inconsistent. Beyond this minimal requirement, a specification should be *cost-effective*. This means that the cost of implementing the product is justified by the benefit that accrues from implementing it.

A specification is **verifiable** if there is a cost-effective procedure for ascertaining whether a product satisfies the specification. This means that all properties must be specified in a measurable way. The observation procedure is the experiment by which the property can be observed, and it can serve as an acceptance test when the product is handed over to the customer.

A specification is **maintainable** if changes in client or market needs that arise after delivery of the product, can be easily incorporated in the specification. If product evolution is done in a controlled way, changed needs lead to a (re)development process that starts with an update of the product specification. Product evolution by updating the product specification requires at least modifyability of the specification itself, but in addition, it requires traceability of the specification in the forward and backwards directions.

4.6   Summary

A requirements specification at any level of the aggregation hierarchy consists of a specification of product objectives and a specification of observable product behavior. The top level objectives of the product link a product specification to the needs of the client or market. At any aggregation level, the behavior specification and decomposition specification of a product jointly form the objectives of the lower level product components.

A behavior specification can be as abstract as a product idea, or it can be a more concrete specification of required product functions or even atomic transactions. At each abstraction level, properties capture an aspect of product behavior. All properties should be specified in a measurable way, but there may be properties for which only nonbehavioral specifications can be found. For these properties, proxies should be given that can be behaviorally specified. Properties can be classified under the headings of correctness, reliability, efficiency, security, user-friendliness, maintainability, testability, flexibility, portability, reusability and interoperability. For *positive* properties, a finite experiment should be specified in which the property can be observed, but for *negative* properties, which require a certain behavior to be absent, specifying such a procedure is difficult, if not impossible. Presence of a negative property in a product can only be verified by mathematical or logical proof.

Where possible, preferences should be indicated for different values of a property. A minimal preference specification is a classification of properties into *essential* and *desirable* properties.

A simple framework for behavior specifications distinguishes a *static dimension*, in which states and static constraints are specified, from a *dynamic dimension*, in which transitions and dynamic constraints are specified.

A product specification must itself satisfy certain requirements. In particular it must be true, complete, feasible, verifiable and maintainable. Secondary features, which derive from these primary ones, include implementation-independence, consistency, cost-effectiveness, modifyability and forward and backward traceability. A very important requirement is the communicability of the specification, for without this, it could not satisfy any of its other properties. Two important aspects of communicability are understandability and unambiguity.

4.7   Exercises

1. A certain university faculty sells a lecture notes series to its students. For most courses, there is a volume of lecture notes that students can buy. In order to give these notes a more visible presence on the bookshelves of the students, the faculty decides to design a new style for the cover of the volumes in the series. You are to write a product specification for the new cover.

   (a) Identify the stakeholders of this project.
   (b) Write down the list of functions that the product should have.
   (c) Write down a list of properties that the functions should have. Use the list of figure 4.2 as a checklist to see if you have forgotten any properties.
   (d) List three alternative decomposition specifications that would satisfy the properties and evaluate them with respect to the properties.

2. Consider the TANA case study of chapter 3.

   (a) The first iteration through the engineering cycle produced a deliverable containing, as components, a description of the objectives of that iteration, simulations of the alternatives considered and the evaluation of their effects. Describe the contents of the objectives and alternatives. How do you think the evaluations were recorded?
   (b) In the second iteration, a deliverable was produced that contains, as components, a description of the generated alternatives and their simulations and evaluations. Describe the contents of these deliverable components.

3. Look up the IEEE/ANSI standard for requirements specifications [156, 90] and classify the sections in this standard under one of the following headings:

   • Top level objectives.
   • Product behavior. Classify this as a specification of the product idea, a function specification, or a transaction specification.
   • Properties, classified according to the list in figure 4.2.

4.8   Bibliographical Remarks

Product objectives and properties.   Gladden [116] maintains that the specification of product objectives is a critical success factor in product development. Combined with vivid simulation of expected product properties, it will, according to Gladden, lead to a successful product. Although this is probably an overstatement, it is clear that the specification of product objectives plays an important unifying and regulatory role in product development.

Two very useful discussion of the specification of product objectives and properties are given by Gause and Weinberg [111] and Gilb [114]. The observation that the difference between objectives and constraints is more in the eye of the beholder than in the requirements themselves was made by Simon [317]. The list of kinds of software product properties given in figure 4.2 is based on a similar list given by Vincent, Waters and Sinclair [350, page 12], who base themselves upon a report by McCall, Richards and Walters [220] and on a discussion by Davis [77]. Yeh et al. [374] also give a list of the kinds of "nonfunctional" properties that a software product can have. Keller, Kahn and Panara [172] describe procedures to make software product properties observable by defining metrics.

Requirements specification.   Davis [77] gives a thorough survey of requirements specification techniques and discusses several standards for requirements specifications. Dorfman and Thayer [90] contains a large number of requirements specification standards, and Thayer and Dorfman [343] contains a number of useful papers on requirements specification. Surveys of the desirable characteristics of requirements specifications are given by Boehm [38], Davis [77] and Lindland *et al.* [194]. Davis convincingly shows that there are trade-offs among the desirable properties, such that increased satisfaction of one property implies decreased satisfaction of another.

Backward traceability of a specification to reasons is discussed by Potts and Bruns [265]. However, Potts and Bruns use a more elaborate argumentation theory than the simple listing of alternatives, simulations and evaluations proposed here. Backwards traceability to sources is proposed by Gotel and Finkelstein [124].

Part II

Requirements Engineering Methods

5

ISAC Change Analysis and Activity Study

5.1 Introduction

ISAC (Information Systems Work and Analysis of Changes) was developed in the 1970s at the *Institute for Development of Activities in Organizations* in Stockholm, Sweden, under the direction of Mats Lundeberg. ISAC is a method for client-oriented development of information systems. It is not well-suited to the development of control systems. ISAC was developed in order to ensure that the business gets the information system it needs. To reach this goal, ISAC starts with an organizational problem analysis that tries to find real solutions to real problems. If a solution involves the development of an information system, then ISAC continues developing this system by starting a detailed study of the business activities to be supported by the system. To increase the fit between the delivered system and the business needs, both the problem analysis and the activity study are characterized by a high degree of participation and cooperation of users, developers and sponsors of the information system. The role of developers in these stages is to facilitate the process by which users and sponsors analyze their problems and perform an activity study. This means that developers call meetings, conduct meetings, handle conflicts, identify prejudices, negotiate differences, take care that notes are taken and distributed, present results, etc.

ISAC consists of four stages, which concentrate on user and management questions as shown in figure 5.1. Figure 5.2 shows how ISAC answers these questions. During **Change Analysis**, current business problems are analyzed, different possible solutions are investigated and one solution is chosen. ISAC specifies an activity model for the chosen solution, which is, roughly, a high level specification of the desired business situation in terms of its activities. Change Analysis is a general problem solving method and is not particularly oriented towards defining information system requirements. However, if the solution involves building one or more information systems, then **Activity Study** determines the required information system properties. In addition, the important decision whether or not to automate one or more information systems is made. For each system to be automated, an **Information Analysis** is performed, which results in a behavior specification for each automated system. The term "information analysis" is misleading, for this is used

83

---

1. **Change Analysis**.

   - What does the organization want?
   - How flexible is the organization with respect to changes?

2. **Activity Study**.

   - Which activities should we regroup into information systems?
   - Which priorities do the information systems have?

3. **Information Analysis**.

   - Which inputs and outputs do each information system have?
   - What are the quantitative requirements on each information system?

4. **Implementation**.

   - Which technology (information carriers, hardware, software) do we use for the information systems?
   - Which activities of each information system are manual, which automated?

Figure 5.1: Lead questions in each stage of ISAC.

in most other methods for the initial stage of information system development, information needs analysis. The final stage of ISAC is an **Implementation** of the specified information system behavior. Change Analysis is discussed in section 5.2 and Activity Study in section 5.3. The library case of appendix B is used as an example. We will not look at behavior specification or implementation of ISAC. Section 5.4 contains an analysis of ISAC from a methodological point of view.

5.2   Change Analysis

The purpose of Change Analysis is to ensure that the business problems to be solved are identified and that these problems are diagnosed correctly. To this end, we make lists of current problems and problem owners, and correlate these lists with each other. Facilitated by the developer, the problem owners then search for solutions to the problems. Promising alternatives are specified by making a model of business activities as they are performed in the new situation. The alternatives are then evaluated on their problem solving power, and one of them is chosen for implementation. If the chosen solution involves the development of an information system, ISAC continues with information system development. However, ISAC stresses that a solution may have been chosen that does not involve a change to an information system at all. If such a solution is chosen, the rest of ISAC is not followed.

5.2.1   Make a list of problems

The purpose of this task is to reach agreement among problem owners, developers and the sponsors of the development process what the problems are that the development process

1. Change Analysis.

- List problems.
- List problem owners.
- Analyze problems.
- Make current activity model.
- Analyze goals.
- Define change needs.
- Generate change alternatives.
- Make activity model of desired situations.
- Evaluate alternatives.
- Choose activity model.

2. Activity Study.

- Decompose chosen activity model into information subsystems.

  — Elaborate chosen activity model.

  — Identify information subsystems.

  — Analyze suitability for automation.

  — Elaborate activity models until each information system is one activity.

- Analyze each information system:

  — Analyze contribution of each information system to change objectives.

  — Generate ambition levels for information system.

  — Test the feasibility of ambition levels.

  — Perform cost/benefit analysis of ambition levels.

  — Choose ambition level.

- Coordinate information systems.

  — Define interfaces between information systems.

  — Assign a priority to each information system.

3. Information analysis. For each information system:

- Specify input/output relations for information system.
- Specify data structures for information system.
- Specify process structures for information system.

4. Implementation.

Figure 5.2: The ISAC method.

should solve. A **problem** is a dissatisfaction with the current situation, for which a possibility of improvement exists. A **problem owner** is a person, group or institution that is dissatisfied with the current situation. Problem owners are called **interest groups** in ISAC. This term is more general, because it also includes groups that have an interest in *not* solving the problems, groups that cause the problems, etc. Analyzing interest groups is relevant and interesting for project management, but ISAC is restricted to analyzing problems and solving them for the problem owners. We therefore use the term "problem owner" instead of "interest group".

We illustrate Change Analysis by applying it to the library example of appendix B. The sequence of case study descriptions that follows tries to mimic the historical sequence of decisions and discoveries as they could have occurred in a development process. This is *not* what a presentation of the deliverables of development would look like. The deliverables do not contain revisions but the result of revisions; they are a rational reconstruction of the development process as if no errors and false starts ever occurred.

Case study. In an initial meeting with the sponsor of the development process, the developer learns about a number of problems, which he writes down as follows.

1. Too many documents are lost or stolen.
2. Documents are kept too long by library members.
3. There are too many reservations in proportion to borrowings.
4. There are no reliable use statistics.
5. The budget will probably shrink over the next few years.
6. The current budget is overspent.
7. The dollar rate is fluctuating unpredictably, which causes unpredictable rises in the costs of journal subscriptions.

Each of these problems in one way or another prevents the library from fulfilling its mission satisfactorily. The list is merely a first version and below we will find more problems, unnoted here.

Each problem in the initial list of problems is now screened to determine whether it is worth devoting a development process to solving it. There are two reasons why we would remove a problem from the list. One reason is that the problem is so easy to solve that it is not worth the trouble of setting up a development project to solve it. The other reason is that a problem is so hard to solve that a development project cannot solve it. The reason for listing these problems first and then eliminating them is that this gives an occasion for people to become aware of the problems, talk about them, and reach an agreement that at least in this development project they should ignore them.

Case study. Two examples of hard problems in the problem list are problem (7), the fluctuating dollar rate, and problem (5), shrinking budgets. Both of these are beyond the control of any development process taking place in the university library, so they had better be seen as facts of nature. We eliminate them from the problem list.

5.2.2   List problem owners

Now that we have identified the problems to be solved by ISAC, we can identify the groups of people for whom these problems exist. Representatives from each of these groups should

	Faculties	Library members	Librarian	Treasurer	Circulation desk clerks
1. Too many documents are lost or stolen.		X	X	X	
2. Documents are kept too long by library members.		X	X		
3. There are too many reservations in proportion to borrowings.		X			
4. There are no reliable use statistics.			X	X	
5. The current budget is overspent.	X		X	X	

Figure 5.3: Initial matrix of problems against problem owners.

participate in Change Analysis. In order to get a clear understanding of the situation, ISAC recommends making a matrix of problems against problem owners. Identifying the problem owners requires social skills and insight, because some groups may be interested in suppressing the interests of others. The matrix connecting the problems with problem owners is constructed by the problem owners themselves, facilitated by the developer.

Case study. After some discussion, we find that there are five groups of problem owners, who can be correlated with the problems as shown in figure 5.3. The library members have interest in solving the problem of lost and stolen books. Interestingly, they are also the cause of this problem, but this is not represented by the matrix. The librarian and treasurer also have an interest in solving this problem, because they are responsible for the property of the library and for the way the library spends its money, respectively.

Keeping a document too long is likewise a problem *caused by* the library members as well as a phenomenon *causing* a problem for the library members. Each library member is a problem owner on his own, against all other members, because each library member plays a zero-sum game against all other members as far as borrowing books is concerned.

The first three problems may also be considered to be problems for circulation desk personnel, because they will have to provide a less satisfactory service to the library members because of these problems. After some discussion, it is decided that they will not be listed as problem owners with respect to these problems, because they have at most a derived interest in the solution of these problems.

5.2.3 Analyze the problems

The problems identified so far are now subjected to a **cause-effect analysis**. There are three reasons to do this. First, a difficulty in drawing up a problem list is that people tend to describe problems in terms of their solutions. Sometimes, a problem is not perceived until a solution is perceived and then the problem is formulated in terms of the absence of the perceived solution, such as "there is no magnetic labeling of documents." The purpose of problem analysis is to eliminate solution-oriented problems as much as possible and get to the underlying problems. This makes room for alternative solutions. Second, problem analysis is another way to reduce the problem list in size, in addition to the elimination of easy and hard problems. Problem analysis allows us to limit ourselves to the underlying problems only. Third, problem analysis helps us preparing an effective action, because the rest of the Change Analysis can then concentrate on the underlying causes and ignore derived problems.

Cause-effect analysis is performed by **domain specialists**, people who have expert knowledge of the problems under study. A domain specialist may be a problem owner, an end user of the required system, a sponsor, an outside specialist, a manager, etc. The result of analysis is represented in a cause-effect graph, which is a directed graph in which nodes represent problems and arrows point from cause to effect.

Case study.   Figure 5.4 contains a cause-effect graph for the library case. During analysis, a number of underlying problems are discovered. One cause of overspending the budget is that documents are multiply acquired by different departments and that different departments have subscriptions to the same journals. This is called the problem of multiple acquisitions. It can be in turn traced to the fact that acquisitions of different departments are not coordinated. The problems of multiple acquisitions and lack of coordination are added to the problem list.

The problem of the high reservation/borrowing ratio is caused by the bad availability of books, which is in turn caused by the two problems of losing/stealing books and of not returning books. One of the causes of lost/stolen books is improper supervision on the return of documents, which makes it possible for library members to steal a book that someone else returned but is not yet registered as taken in by the library. Another cause of lost/stolen documents is that all books and journals are stored in rooms open to the library members, so that they can browse through them but can also easily steal them. This problem is added to the problem list.

The librarian insists that an important cause of lost/stolen documents as well as for the fact that documents are kept too long is bad member mentality. It is quite possible to see this as a fact of nature, like the problems of shrinking budgets and fluctuating dollar rates, but the librarian believes that an education campaign can change this mentality, so the developer adds it to the problem list and cause-effect graph.

Finally, it is discovered during analysis that one cause of the overlong borrowing periods is that library personnel has no time to go through the list of borrowed books each week to find out which books have been borrowed longer than their allotted borrowing period. Manual procedures also increase the cost of levying fines. The cause-effect graph and problem list are updated accordingly. The matrix of problems against problem owners is updated into the one shown in figure 5.5.

In addition to doing a cause-effect analysis, a **quantitative study** should be made of the problems. The reason for this is simple: in order to decide upon investing in a solution process, the severity of the problems must be assessed first. For example, how many documents are stolen each year? For how long do borrowers exceed allowed borrowing periods? What is the ratio between reservations and borrowings?

Quantifying the problems has three advantages. First, only a quantitative characterization of these problems can give an indication of the potential benefit to be derived from solving the problems. Second, only if a problems is quantified is it possible to know in the future whether and to what extent it is solved. Third, if quantification shows that a problem has only a slight impact on the business, the sponsor may make only a small budget

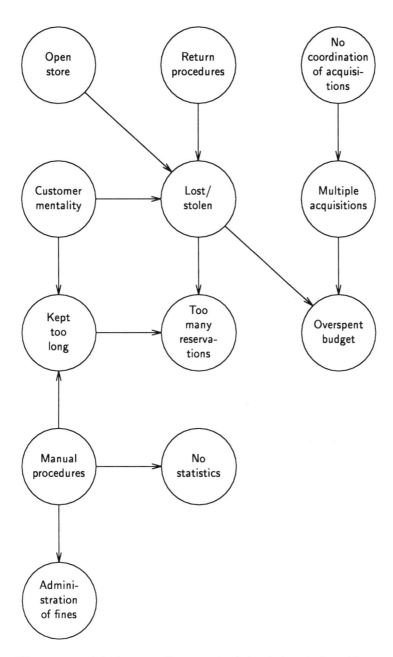

Figure 5.4: Initial cause-effect graph of circulation desk problems.

	Faculties	Library members	Librarian	Treasurer	Circulation desk clerks
P1. Too many documents are lost or stolen		X	X	X	
P2. Documents are kept too long by members		X	X		
P3. There are too many reservations in proportion to borrowings		X			
P4. There are no reliable use statistics			X	X	
P5. Overspent budget	X		X	X	
P6. Multiple acquisitions			X	X	
P7. No coordination of acquisitions			X	X	
P8. Sloppy return procedures		X			X
P9. Bad member mentality		X			X
P10. Open store			X		
P11. Manual procedures				X	X
P12. Cost of levying fines			X	X	

Figure 5.5: Revised matrix of problems and problem owners. Underlying problems are printed in boldface.

P1. Too many documents are stolen.	A total of 4500 titles are known to have been stolen. On the average, 200 titles are stolen each year, with an increase of 10% per year.
P2. Documents are kept too long by members.	On the average, a document is returned three weeks after it ought to be returned.
P3. There are too many reservations in proportion to borrowings.	The average ratio is 30 reservations for every 100 borrowings, with an observed maximum of 50 per 100.
P4. There are no reliable use statistics.	All figures in this table are estimates.
P5. The budget is over-spent.	The current annual budget of Dfl 900 000 is overspent with Dfl 200 000.
P6. Multiple acquisitions.	20% of the 3000 journal subscriptions are duplicates.
P7. No coordination of acquisitions.	
P8. Sloppy return procedures.	
P9. Bad member mentality.	
P10. Open store.	
P11. Manual procedures.	
P12. Cost of levying fines.	Total amount of fines levied each year is Dfl 2000, the cost of which is Dfl 1000.

Figure 5.6: A quantification of some identified problems. For the unquantified problems, it will be harder to know in the future whether and to what extent they are solved than it is for the quantified problems.

available for solving it, or the problem owners may drop it from the problem list completely.

Case study. A possible quantification of the problems identified in the library is shown in figure 5.6. Not all problems could be quantified. It can be seen that the cost of levying fines is a negligible problem compared with the other problems, so the sponsor gives us the order to put this low on the list of problems to be solved. We will ignore this problem in the rest of the case study.

5.2.4 Make activity model of current business

ISAC now prescribes making an **activity model** of the current situation in the business. A current activity model represents the activities as they are currently performed in the business and the flows of material information between those activities. The purpose of making a current activity model is to be able to discuss possible changes to the business in the next step. The activity model will be the platform for generating and discussing alternative solutions. Activity models are made only after the problem analysis, for this will help the analyst to draw boundaries around the systems under development. In particular, it will help the analyst to distinguish relevant from irrelevant systems when activity models are made.

The ISAC technique for representing activity models is the *A-schema*. We will not use this, because ISAC tends to be identified with the use of these schemas, and using them would lead attention away from the real core of ISAC, the identification of problems and problem owners and the modeling of business activities. Instead, we use a simple diagram notation already used in chapter 2. Figure 5.7 gives an example. The following conventions are used.

- Subsystems are either *activities* or *stores*. Stores are passive entities in which an unlimited supply of data items or material items can be kept. Activities and stores may be decomposed into subsystems. An activity can have activities and stores as subsystems, but stores can only have stores as subsystems. The decomposition of a subsystem is shown in a separate diagram, so that each diagram contains a nesting only one level deep. For example, figure 5.7 shows three of the activities of the library as subsystems. A decomposition of the circulation activity is shown in figure 5.8. The name of an activity or store should make clear whether the subsystem is an activity or store.

- Transactions between subsystems are represented by arrows, whose direction indicates the direction of the *flow* of data or material items in the transaction. Interactions may be bidirectional. The names of the flows indicate the kind of data or material item passing through the flow. To distinguish transactions from accidental line intersections, a black dot is drawn on the intersection that represents the interaction. The *borrow_request* flow in figure 5.8 is an example of this. To keep the top-level diagram simple, only the major flows are shown in this diagram.

For the moment, this suffices to determine the meaning of the diagrams. As an aside, we remark that the subsystem diagrams used here could equally well be replaced by the data flow diagrams of chapter 9, by the activity charts of Statemate [153, 139], or by other suitable notation systems. In this chapter, we will call the subsystem diagrams drawn according to the above conventions **activity diagrams**.

Case study. Figure 5.7 shows an activity model of the library. The diagram shows three groups of activities performed in the library. There are no stores in this diagram. The two external systems, *PUBLISHER* and *MEMBER*, represent systems that generate input for the library or that receive output from the library. Because *PUBLISHER* and *MEMBER* are types that can have many instances, arbitrary instances P and M of these types are declared. The library interacts with many publishers and many members, but only one typical member of each class of systems is shown. The model as shown does not show all details, but it does give an impression of the major activities performed in the library, and their interfaces.

Looking at our problem list (figure 5.6), we see that we have problems in the acquisition and circulation activities. The problem in the acquisition activity is that duplicate acquisitions are performed. To solve this problem, we should zoom in on this activity and see how it is actually performed. The resulting model of the acquisition activity can then serve as a basis for discussing possible alternative ways of performing the activity.

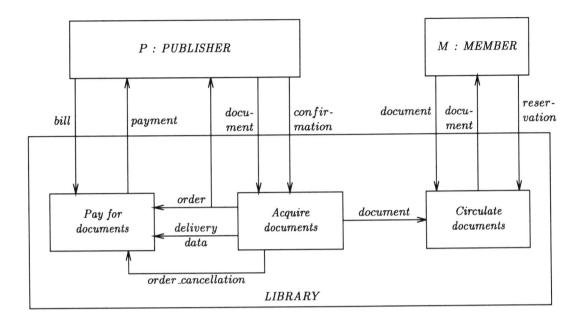

Figure 5.7: An activity diagram showing the activities in the library at a high level.

We will zoom in on the other problem area, the circulation activity. Figure 5.8 shows an activity model of this activity. It shows three subactivities, borrowing, returning, and reservation, and three stores, a reservation shelf, a file with document data and the store room where the documents are kept. This may not be the best possible decomposition of the system; in the exercises, another decomposition is discussed. In the current decomposition, all activities communicate with each other via the store with document data. When a borrow request arrives, the borrowing activity consists of checking the document data to see whether the document is available and is not reserved. If the document is reserved, the borrower must be the reserver, otherwise the request is refused. If the document is borrowed by the reserver, the reservation record is deleted and the document is taken from the reservation shelf. If it is borrowed by someone else and the document is not reserved, it is taken from the store room. In both cases, the document data are updated accordingly. When a document is returned, the returning activity puts it in the right place and updates the appropriate records. If the document is reserved, it is put on the reservation shelf and the reserver is notified of the arrival of the document. If the reserver does not borrow the document within ten days, the reservation record is deleted. If a returned document is not reserved, it is returned to the store room. In both cases, the document data is updated accordingly.

This small example illustrates that the pattern of interactions in a relatively simple activity can be quite complex. This is not surprising, for most of the activities in an organization consist of keeping each other informed (or, unkindly, uninformed) about what happened, what should happen, and what can be expected to happen. Most of the problems in an organization are problems with internal or external communication, and all of the problems that can be addressed by an information system are basically communication problems.

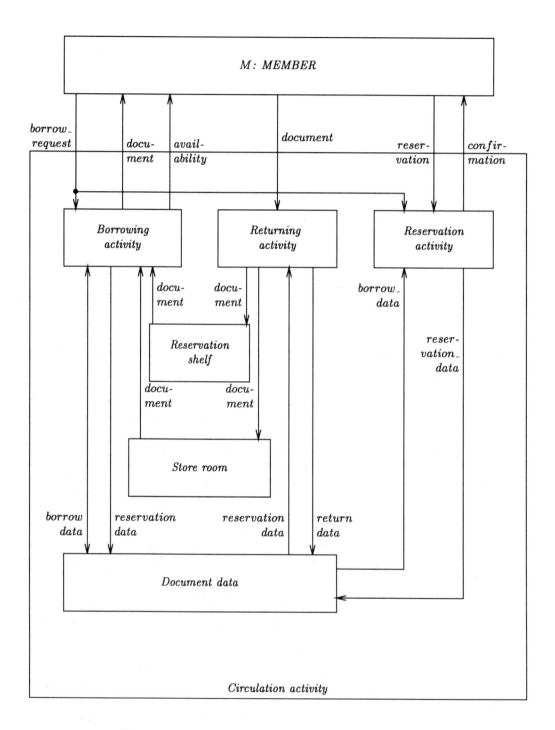

Figure 5.8: An activity diagram of the circulation activity.

5.2.5 Analyze goals

We now understand the problems, know who the problem owners are, and have a model of current business activities. Before we investigate possible changes to the current situation, we should list the goals of the development process. A **goal** is simply a desired situation. We must specify goals at this stage in order to know how to evaluate solution proposals. The specification of goals allows us to understand why the problems identified earlier are problems at all, and what sponsors and problem owners want to achieve by the development process.

A goal specification should be *declarative*; it specifies the desired result, not a way to reach this result. For example, instead of specifying the goal that an information system should provide payment information within one day, we should specify the goal that this information should be available within one day. This opens up the possibility that this information could be made available by other means than the company information system.

Even if all goal specifications are declarative, we can order goals in a tree such that the descendants of each node represent subgoals of the node. The root of this tree is the business mission. Since any goal in this tree is a means to a higher goal, the injunction to specify goals, not means, is strictly speaking vacuous. This is fully analogous to the confusion about what are requirements and implementations. Only the root of the tree is not a means to a higher goal (in the tree). However, only a subset of nodes in the tree represent goals that allow us to evaluate change proposals. These goals can be found by interviewing problem owners and asking them which situation they would like to achieve. We should specify goals that lie in this subset but are otherwise as high up in the tree as possible, but not higher.

Drawing up a list of goals may require a lot of negotiation, because different problem owners may have contradictory goals. To resolve contradictory goals, one moves to a higher level goal in the tree upon which all problem owners can agree. Ultimately, the mission of the business is reached, and it is to be hoped that there is at least agreement about that.

Case study. A discussion with the different problem owners reveals the following list of goals:

- Library members and faculties:
    - All books and journals in the relevant research area should be borrowable.
    - Documents should be optimally available.
    - The library should have several copies of books used for courses given by the faculty, to be used by students.
    - Students should be able to use educational material in study rooms of the library.
- Librarian and treasurer.
    - Documents should be optimally available.
    - The expenses of the library should remain within budget.
    - Accurate and up-to-date statistics on library use should be available.
- Circulation desk.
    - The number of reservations done because some member does not return a borrowed document in time should be minimized.

  — The work done in connection with members who are too late with returning the documents should be minimized.

  — The work done in connection with lost documents should be minimized.

We try to harmonize this list by moving to higher level goals about which agreement can be reached. After negotiation, we get the following goals. The first goal is worked out by already specifying two means by which this goal can be reached.

  G1 Documents should be maximally available.

     G1.1 Books should be returned in time.

     G1.2 The number of losses should be minimized.

  G2 Keep library expenses within budget.

  G3 Optimize the service of the circulation desk.

  G4 Keep statistics accurate and up-to-date.

These goals are general enough to be related to the mission of the library, yet specific enough to be related to the goals of the different problem owners. It is instructive to trace these goals to the initial list of goals above, and check which of those initial goals have not made it to the final list. The relation between this final goal list and our initial goal list is that if we ask "Why?" of any of the goals in the initial list that does not appear in the final list, we should be able to answer with one of the goals in the final list. The final goal list is related in the same way to the library mission: The mission answers the "Why?" question for any of our final goals.

5.2.6   Define change needs

One of the functions of a list of goals is to be able to give the reason why the problems are problems at all. Conversely, for each goal we can identify the reasons why it is not achieved by listing the problems that impede achievement of the goal. If we do this, we find that we can cluster problems into groups of similar problems that are related to the same or similar goals. One way to do this is to make a matrix of problems against goals and try to find clusters of related problems. There is no algorithm to do the clustering; the understanding of the situation gained by analyzing it from different angles should suffice to make the clusters. Each cluster defines a *change need* that will act as a goal of the development process.

Case study. Comparing the problem list with the goal list, we get the following clusters, each of which is a change need. For each change need, we list the problems it is intended to solve and the goals that the change should help to achieve.

  • *Return procedures should be improved* so that document availability and the service to the customer are maximized.
    Problems: P2, P3, P8, P11.
    Goals: G1, G3.

  • *Acquisitions should be coordinated* so that multiple acquisitions are reduced.
    Problems: P5, P6, P7.
    Goals: G2.

  • *Statistics should be improved.*
    Problem: P4.
    Goal: G4.

- *The possibility of theft should be reduced.*
  Problem: P10.
  Goal: G1.

In accordance with the directives of the sponsor, solving problem P12 is not part of our change needs.

5.2.7 Generate change alternatives

We are now armed with sufficient ammunition to generate change alternatives. This is best done in a brainstorming session, in which any idea at all is written down without evaluation or critique. Initially, the alternatives are only sketched in the barest outline. Elaboration and evaluation will be done in the next steps.

Case study. Here are some alternatives for the library case:

A1 Reduce theft by removing all documents from the reach of members.

A2 Reduce theft by marking all books with an indelible and invisible magnetic marker and place ports with sensors at library entries.

A3 Improve supervision on document return procedures by reducing the number of entries/exits to the library department to one, and by organizing a strict schedule under which there will always be one library functionary at the entry/exit desk.

A4 Facilitate the production of use statistics by implementing an automated information system.

A5 Facilitate automatic reporting on members who extend their borrowing period beyond allowable limits by implementing an automated information system.

The alternatives are not all mutually exclusive, but some, such as the first two, are. Some of them involve changes to the information system of the library, including automation; others take measures not involving automation or even the information system.

5.2.8 Make activity model of desired situations

We now make *packages* of one or more change alternatives that are worth investigating. To investigate a package, we make an activity model of it. This makes the package a possible topic of rational discussion and allows us to compare it with the current situation.

Case study. Here are a number of packages that can be constructed from the available alternatives.

1. Change nothing at all (the null package). This package should always be included, simply because we want to compare the possible changes with the current situation.

2. A1: Put all documents in a separate store room.

3. A2 & A3: Use magnetic markers and reduce the number of entries.

4. A4 & A5: Implement an automated information system.

Elaborating the automation package, we find that we have to add at least two activities to the communication diagram of figure 5.8: producing a list of overdue documents and their borrowers, and sending reminders to members. Both activities should be performed daily. This has become feasible by automation. Activities for other functions, related to the production of statistics, could be added as well. The extended communication diagram is not shown here.

The package in which a separate store room is introduced for documents, inaccessible for library members, introduces a new system, the Store Room, with a number of interactions when documents are put into the Store or fetched from it. Making a model of this situation is left as an exercise for the reader.

If you try to model the magnetic marker package (A2+A3), you find that it has exactly the same communication diagram as the current situation. This is because only the implementation technology changes, not the pattern of communications. Communication diagrams will not represent every change made to the situation. (The same holds for the A-schemas used in ISAC.)

5.2.9   Evaluate alternatives

For each of the packages that are modeled, we now estimate what their problem solving power is. Very few solutions are such that they do not introduce problems; in fact, every solution is the seed of a new batch of problems. We therefore also investigate which problems are introduced by each package, and for whom. This is done by making, for each package, a matrix of problems against problem owners, and indicating in this matrix which problems are solved and which are introduced.

Case study. Figure 5.9 contains the matrix for the automation package (A4 & A5) together with A1 or with A2 & A3 (it is immaterial for the matrix which is chosen). An "O" in an entry means that the problem is solved for the problem owner.

Two extra problems are introduced, P13 and P14. Problem P13 is that the library members would experience this new situation as a rigid borrowing discipline. There is no guarantee that this would change member mentality, so this problem is not indicated as being reduced by this alternative. Problem P14 is introduced by solving problems P6 and P7. The faculties and library members have a problem with not being allowed multiple acquisitions, for now they have to go by foot, bicycle or car to another department to find the books or journals they want! Evaluation of this situation may lead to extra measures, such as a facility for internal document transfers.

Solving problems is a good thing and introducing problems is a bad thing. The question is, how good and how bad is it? We must evaluate the expected impact of a package against the goals of development, identified earlier. Different alternatives should *not* be compared with each other, because this could lead to a war over pet proposals.

Case study. The automation package (A4 & A5) together with the magnetic marker and single entry options (A2 & A3) score best with respect to the development goals. In particular, they do not introduce the problem introduced by A1, that users of the library cannot browse through the books anymore.

5.2.10   Choose an alternative

The sponsor is presented with a report about the evaluation of alternatives and then chooses one of them. The developer may suggest a choice, but it is important that the sponsor authorizes this choice because it significantly affects the use of resources in the rest of the development process.

Case study. Altogether, it is decided that the following changes will be implemented in the library:

- Terminate double journal subscriptions.

	Faculties	Library members	Librarian	Treasurer	Circulation desk clerks
P1. Too many documents are lost or stolen		O	O	O	
P2. Documents are kept too long by members		O	O		
P3. There are too many reservations in proportion to borrowings		O			
P4. There are no reliable use statistics			O	O	
P5. Overspent budget	X		X	X	
P6. Multiple acquisitions	X		O	O	
P7. No coordination of acquisitions	X		O	O	
P8. Sloppy return procedures		X			X
P9. Bad member mentality		X			X
P10. Open store			X		
P11. Manual procedures				X	O
P12. Cost of levying fines			X	X	
P13. Rigid borrowing discipline		X			
P14. No multiple acquisitions.	X	X			

Figure 5.9: Matrix of problems and problem owners for the automation package (A4 & A5) together with one of the other packages (A1 or A2 & A3). An "O" means that a problem is solved for a problem owner. An "X" means that a problem exists for a problem owner.

- Books already in the possession of some library department should not be bought by another department, unless there is very good reason to do so.

- Journals cannot be borrowed anymore.

- Photocopiers will be installed in all library departments.

- An automated IS will be implemented that registers all borrowings. Daily, it will produce a list of members who have not yet returned a borrowed book.

- Reservations will also be registered by the system.

- Each year, a list of lost or stolen books will be produced and distributed among members of staff at all faculties.

Note that this decision is reached after extensive discussion and negotiation with all problem owners, including faculties and (representatives from) library members.

As illustrated by this example, it is not necessary that the chosen alternative should contain the development of an information system. Indeed, at least one package in the case study, using a separate store room for the documents, does not involve any information system development. This situation is asymmetric: for alternatives that do involve information system development, organization developments are always necessary, but for alternatives that involve organization development, information system development may not be necessary at all. Any development always involves organization development and some developments additionally involve information system development.

5.3   Activity Study

If an information system is not part of the chosen solution, then ISAC is exited at this point. For those development projects where an information system *is* part of the chosen solution, an Activity Study should be performed. The purpose of an Activity Study is to decompose the chosen activity model into information subsystems, specify required subsystem properties, and specify interfaces between the subsystems.

5.3.1   Decomposition into information subsystems

The chosen activity model is elaborated until information systems can be identified.

Case study. In the example, no elaboration is necessary, for information subsystems can already be identified in the activity model produced by Change Analysis. Two candidates are the information system for the circulation desk and the information system for document acquisition. The activity models show precisely what the required interface between these systems and their users is, and Change Analysis as a whole shows why providing this interface to users of the information system is useful.

For each desired information subsystem, it is then determined whether it can or should be automated. This is done by classifying each information subsystem under one of the following headings:

1. *Impossible to formalize.* Examples of information subsystems that cannot be formalized are informal activities in which information is exchanged with clients informally.

2. *Formalizable.*

Attribute	Measure	Current	High ambition	Low ambition
Response time	Seconds in real time	Not applicable	2 sec. avg. per day 5 sec. max.	5 sec. avg. per day 20 sec. max.
Volume of trans- actions	Total number per day for library	30 avg. per day 60 max.	200 avg. per day 300 max.	50 avg. per day 100 max.
Latency of data	Real time be- tween event oc- currence and da- tabase transac- tion	1 day avg. per year 1 day max.	1 second avg. per day 1 hour max.	1 sec. avg. per day 1 day max.

Figure 5.10: Table of ambition levels for some system attributes.

(a) *Not suitable for automation.* Photos made by X-ray scanners can be printed and stored in manual archives or they can be digitized and stored in computer memory. Due to privacy reasons, however, it may be decided that this activity is not suitable for automization.

(b) *Suitable for automation.* The library administration is an example of this.

Case study. The Circulation and Acquisition information systems are both going to be automated. Note that we already chose an automation alternative in Change Analysis, so this analysis seems su- perfluous. One can also turn this around and say that this part of activity analysis has already been performed simultaneously with Change Analysis.

Having identified the information subsystems that will be automated, the activity model of the desired situation is elaborated to the point where each future information system is represented by one activity in the model. The resulting model then represents the orga- nizational context of all desired information systems, and represents the interfaces of each system to its organizational context.

5.3.2   Analysis of information subsystems

For each system to be automated, desired properties are specified, called **ambition levels**. Examples of ambition levels are limits on response time, timeliness of output, volume and frequency of input, and requirements on the quality of input and output data. These are often specified nonbehaviorally, or behavioral specifications of proxies are given.

Case study. ISAC uses a cumbersome specification of desirable system attributes and ambition levels, which is too elaborate to use for illustration here. A simplified presentation of a list of ambition levels is given in figure 5.10.

Each ambition level is then tested for its feasibility. ISAC recommends the following ways for feasibility testing:

Social system	**Change Analysis**: Analyze business problems and indicate a solution direction.
Computer-based systems	**Activity Study**: Work out the solution and identify computer-based information systems in it; specify required properties of these systems.
Software systems	**Information analysis**: Specify external behavior of automated information system(s).
Software subsystems	**Implementation**: Construct automated information system(s).

Figure 5.11: ISAC's coverage of aggregation levels.

- Find out if projects with similar objectives have realized information systems with similar ambition levels.

- Simulate the ambition levels by means of computational models.

- Build a prototype that satisfies a number of the properties of an ambition level and do a field test with it, i.e. let users actually work with it.

In addition to these tests a *cost/benefit analysis* of each ambition level is performed. On the basis of these tests and analyses, the ambition levels are evaluated and a choice is made for one ambition level.

5.3.3   Coordination of information subsystems

Activity Study ends with a precise definition of the interfaces of the information systems, and the assignment of priorities to them. It can be argued that the precise specification of interfaces is already part of the next task, called information analysis in ISAC, and which is concerned with giving a precise external behavior specification of each information system. The specification of priorities of information systems is an important task in planning the specification and implementation of the information systems.

5.4   Methodological Analysis

5.4.1   The place of ISAC in the development framework

ISAC can be mapped to the aggregation hierarchy of systems as shown in figure 5.11. The figure also contains the motivation for allocating the stages of ISAC to these levels.

Figure 5.12 shows that Change Analysis follows the requirements engineering cycle step by step. It also shows that half of the energy in Change Analysis is devoted to trying to understand the problem. This agrees with the advice of experienced consultants: don't rush to solutions.

Having indicated a business solution in the form of a high-level activity model of the desired situation, ISAC continues, in the Activity Study, to elaborate this into a more

Requirements engineering cycle	Change Analysis
Analyze needs	• List problems • List problem owners • Analyze problems (matrix, causes) • Make current activity model • Analyze goals • Define change needs
Synthesize alternative solutions	• Generate change alternatives
Simulate solutions	• Make activity model of each change proposal • Make problem/problem owner matrix of each change proposal
Evaluate solutions	• Evaluate against change goals
Choose a solution	• Choose

Figure 5.12: Change Analysis as an iteration through the requirements engineering cycle at the business level.

detailed model of activities and to identify those activities that (1) are information systems that (2) must be automated. For each information system to be automated, required properties are specified. Figure 5.13 shows that the specification of the required properties follows the requirements engineering cycle with almost as exact a match as Change Analysis has with the requirements engineering cycle.

After the required system properties have been specified, the behavior of each subsystem is specified in information analysis. Since, according to figure 5.11, information analysis is one level lower in the aggregation hierarchy, one may wonder where the decomposition takes place that is needed to move to the next lower level. This decomposition takes place by focusing, in information analysis, on the external behavior of software systems. A computer-based information system has two kinds of subsystems, software systems and people, also called (end-)users of the information system. The specification of procedures to be followed by the users is not listed explicitly as a separate task in ISAC. In practice, this means that the specification of user procedures is taken to be a derivative task of the specification of external software behavior. There is something to say for turning this around, and continuing after Activity Study with the specification of user procedures. After the user manuals have been written, one can then turn to the specification and implementation of software to support these procedures. Howes [147, 148] discusses the advantages and limitations of this way of working.

Logical development task	Activity study
Decompose system	• Decompose chosen activity model into information subsystems. — Elaborate chosen activity model. — Identify information subsystems. — Analyze suitability for automation. — Elaborate activity models until each information system is one activity.
Specify subsystem requirements	
Analyze	• Analyze information subsystems. — Analyze contribution of each information subsystem to change objectives.
Synthesize	— Generate ambition levels for each information subsystem.
Simulate Evaluate	— Test the feasibility of ambition levels. — Perform cost/benefit analysis of ambition levels.
Choose	— Choose ambition level.
	• Coordinate information subsystems — Determine interfaces between information subsystems. — Assign priority to information subsystems.

Figure 5.13: Activity Study as organization decomposition and information subsystem specification.

5.4.2   Activity modeling

Notations.   The diagram technique used in this chapter to represent activity models has a close resemblance to known techniques such as A-schemas in ISAC, data flow diagrams in structured analysis (chapter 9) and activity charts in STATEMATE [153, 139]. It shares with these other graphical notations the separation of subsystems into passive and active ones. However, in these other notations, stores cannot be decomposed into substores. I do not see why this should be prohibited. Databases can be decomposed into tables, and these can be further partitioned into fragments as needed. Anything goes, as long as it allows us to specify the required business activities with the required clarity.

Activities and stores.   The decomposition of activities into subactivities and passive stores is a principle that pervades structured behavior modeling. It is responsible for the unnecessarily complex communication pattern in figure 5.8. Some flows in the activity diagram represent access of an activity to a store to retrieve data that it has itself put there. If we had encapsulated the stores in the activities to begin with, then we would have a diagram that shows less interaction and should therefore be easier to understand. Exercise 2 gives an example of this.

Primary and secondary flows.   A-schemas use a convention to distinguish the flow of material from the flow of data. Material flows are represented by bold lines, data flows by thin lines. The intention behind this notation is to distinguish the primary flow of goods from the secondary flow of data. However, the distinction between material and data flows does not coincide with the distinction between the primary process and secondary, supporting business processes. For example, the primary process of organizations like banks and insurance companies consists of data flows. The obvious thing to do is to invent a convention by which primary flows are highlighted in bold, regardless of whether they transport data or matter. For example, one can highlight the flow of documents in figure 5.8 by drawing the flow of documents in bold.

Advantages and disadvantages of activity modeling.   Making an activity model of the current situation has advantages as well as dangers.

- The advantage is that it allows discussion of alternatives in terms of a shared model of the current situation. Without a shared model of the current situation, discussion of alternative futures may lead to misunderstanding, because what one person thinks is a change may be viewed by another person as the current situation.

There are three potential disadvantages of current activity modeling:

- There is a danger that the developer will work out the model in so much detail that too much time will be lost in modeling a situation that should be changed. The guideline here is to elaborate the model of current activities only to the level of detail needed to understand the current problems and to represent possible solutions. That is, each activity in the model should be needed to understand some problem.

- The activity model, detailed or not, may not be understandable by all problem owners, so that it cannot serve as a means of communicating about alternative future situations.

- Not all changes proposed by a change alternative may be visible as changes in an activity model. For example, the magnetic marker alternative in the library case has the same interaction structure as the current situation.

The developer will have to weigh these advantages and disadvantages against each other in order to decide whether to make a current activity model, which representation technique to use, and when to stop adding detail to the model.

5.4.3 Participation

The orientation of Change Analysis and Activity Study on business problems and business activities makes a high degree of user-participation in these tasks possible and even necessary. In general, there are three forms of user participation in a development process [188, 235].

1. **Consultative participation** consists of regular consultations with key users. Information Engineering is an example of a method that uses consultative participation.

2. **Representative participation** consists of the participation of representatives of user groups in the development process. ISAC is an example of a method that uses representative participation.

3. **Consensus participation** consists of consultations with all users about all development decisions, so that a consensus exists among all users about these decisions. ETHICS (appendix C) is an example of a method that uses consensus participation.

The demand on the time and energy of users increases from consultative to consensus participation, and the role of the developer changes from that of an active participant making proposals for change to that of a facilitator of the change process.

In ISAC, representatives of users perform Change Analysis, and the developer plays the role of facilitator at this stage. This requires communicative and social skills of the facilitator, and it assumes that all problem owners are willing to resolve their differences by discussion and negotiation. This may not always be the case. Simply making a matrix of problem owners against problems is a political act that may cause a war; doing the same for every possible future situation and then actually choosing among the matrices has an explicitness rarely shown in politics. As remarked earlier, ISAC talks about *interest groups* rather than problem owners. An interest group is a group that has an interest in the development process, but this interest may be positive or negative. One group may be interested in obstructing development, where the other may be interested in speeding it up. To deal with these situations, ISAC must be supplemented with methods and techniques to facilitate organizational change.

5.5 Exercises

1. Describe the meaning of figure 5.8 in words. Which description of the model (the diagram or the verbal description) is easier for you to grasp? Can you identify people with the opposite preference, i.e. who grasp easily what you find difficult to grasp?

2. Make an activity model of the circulation system (figure 5.8) using the following guidelines:

   - Data about documents are locally available within the borrowing activity and reservation data are maintained locally in the reservation activity.

   - The flows between activities are labeled by the name of the *action* which causes a material or data item to be sent along the flow. The direction of the arrow still indicates the direction of flow.

   Compare the resulting model with that of figure 5.8. Identify at least one point in which the model of figure 5.8 is worse than the one you built, and one point in which it is better than the one you built.

3. Make an activity diagram of alternative 4 of the case study (the automation alternative).

4. The activity model of a desired situation and the current situation may be the same, even though these situations differ. Give an example of this.

5.6 Bibliographical Remarks

The ISAC method. A concise description and motivation of ISAC is given in two companion papers by Lundeberg, Goldkuhl and Nilsson, published in 1979 [202, 203] and in a 1982 paper by Lundeberg [200]; a textbook on ISAC by Lundeberg, Goldkuhl and Nilsson was published in 1981 [204]. A summary of the case study used in this textbook is presented by Lundeberg [201]. The account in this chapter is primarily based on the textbook [204] and on course material [297]. Figure 5.1 is based on an introduction to ISAC given by Bots *et al.* [48, page 174]

Combinations of ISAC with other methods. ISAC emphasizes problem analysis and activity modeling but neglects data modeling. Hanani and Shoval [136] combine ISAC with NIAM, a method for data modeling. The information analysis stage of ISAC produces, for each information system, a specification of input information sets to be accepted by the system and output information sets to be produced by the system. Hanani and Shoval recommend modeling the structure of the data in these sets by means of NIAM.

Wrycza [372] proposes a combination of ISAC with Entity-Relationship modeling by a linguistic analysis of the activity model produced by Activity Study. The activities and information sets in the activity model are described in natural language, and the sentences in these descriptions are then analyzed to yield an ER model of the data that must be manipulated by the future information systems (see chapter 8 for the method of natural language analysis).

Participative development. Land and Hirschheim [188] give an introduction to the different forms of participation and list the reasons why participation is desirable and useful as a development practice. Mumford [236] gives a survey of participation practices in history and links it to different forms of democracy. Mumford's ETHICS method [235, 237] (appendix C) is one of the few methods that practices consultative participation. Carmel,

Whitaker and George [59] compare participative development with Joint Application Design (JAD), a collection of methods and techniques to develop information systems in a series of intensive user-developer sessions.

6

Information Strategy Planning

6.1 Introduction

Information Engineering (IE) was developed in the 1970s by Clive Finkelstein and James Martin [217]. Most of the ideas were in place in the early 1980s; several books about it were published in the late 1980s [103, 214, 215, 216]. There are two basic ideas behind the method.

- Information Engineering tries to deliver the information systems that a business really needs. To achieve this goal, Information Engineering starts with an analysis of the business strategy and its consequences for the use that the business should make of information technology. Thus, Information Engineering has a strong top-down, managerial view of the business and its needs.

- The information technology of a business must be based upon a model of the data relevant to the business. This model plays a central role in the information strategy of the business. Required system functions change as the desires of people change, but the data model changes only as fast as the meaning and relevance of data changes. The assumption of Information Engineering is that human desires change faster than the meaning and relevance of data. A data model is therefore more stable than a function model.

The global structure of Information Engineering is shown in figure 6.1. The figure shows two tracks of analysis and development, an *activity track* on the left, in which business activities are analyzed, and a *data track* on the right, in which the data needed by the business activities are analyzed.

During **Information Strategy Planning** (ISP), the current business situation, the business strategy and the needs of management are analyzed and an information strategy plan is determined. Two important components of this plan are an identification of relevant activities in the business, called *business functions*, and an identification of topics of interest to the business, called *subject areas*. The relation between the two is that in order to perform the business functions, data about the subject areas will have to be maintained. A third important component of the information strategy plan is the identification of the *business*

109

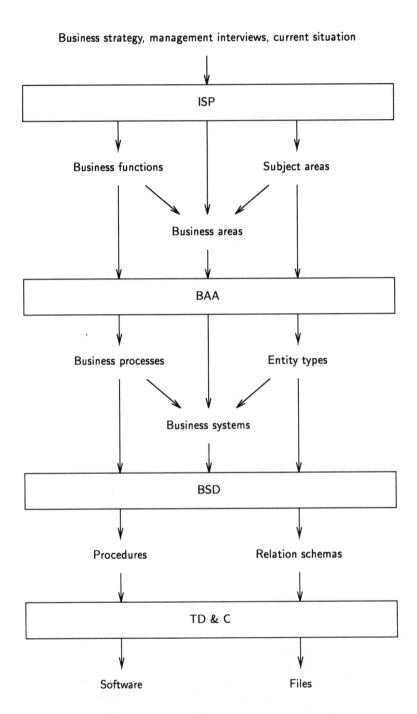

Figure 6.1: The global structure of Information Engineering.

areas of the business. Each business area is a coherent collection of business functions and subject areas.

During **Business Area Analysis** (BAA), the business functions within one business area are decomposed into *business processes* and the subject areas into *entity types*. These are correlated in order to identify *business systems*. Each business system is an information system that maintains a coherent collection of data and supports a coherent collection of processes that manipulate this data.

During **Business System Design** (BSD), a logical design for each business system is made. Physical design and implementation are performed during **Technical Design and Construction** (TD & C).

There are several strategies to perform this process. The most elaborate is to perform all tasks by hand in a classical system development process. Alternative strategies include the development of small systems by end-users on a PC and buying packages off the shelf. In all cases, Information Strategy Planning is performed, followed by a decision about the optimal strategy to perform the rest of the development process. Information Engineering can be viewed as a toolbox from which to select the tools to perform the rest of development. James Martin emphasizes the use of CASE tools to ensure coherence and mutual consistency of the architectures and specifications delivered during development.

Figure 6.2 shows the tasks of Information Engineering in more detail. The structure of ISP is analyzed and explained in section 6.2. In sections 6.3 to 6.5 we then discuss two of the tasks within ISP, viz. the analysis of a business strategy (section 6.3) and the specification of an information architecture (sections 6.4 and 6.5). You should refer to figure 6.2 to place these tasks in their context. Section 6.6 contains a methodological analysis in which we place ISP within our development framework and compare Information Engineering with ISAC.

6.2   The Structure of ISP

An **information strategy plan** for a business consists of an analysis of the business strategy, the definition of a number of architectures and an indication of a number of alternative strategies to implement these architectures. The following architectures are defined.

1. A high level **information architecture**, which represents the information that is relevant to the business and represents the use that the business makes of this information.

2. The desired **information system architecture** of the business. This is a list of the information systems to be designed and the interfaces between them.

3. The **technical architecture** is a definition of the software, hardware and communication facilities that will support the information systems of the business.

4. The **organizational infrastructure** defines the stucture of the organization of information supply for the business, the use of standards and procedures, allocation of responsibility, authority to perform tasks, location of expertise, etc.

---

1. Information strategy planning (ISP)

- Preliminary analysis

    — Analyze business strategy.
    — Determine preliminary information architecture.

- Evaluate current situation.

    — Evaluate current technical architecture of information supply.
    — Evaluate current organizational infrastructure of information supply.
    — Evaluate current and planned information systems.

- Determine information needs and priorities.
- Determine architectures.

    — Determine desired information architecture.
    — Determine desired system architecture.
    — Determine desired technical infrastructure.
    — Determine desired organizational infrastructure.

- Determine information strategy plan.

2. Business area analysis (BAA)

- Specify desired information architecture.
    — Specify Entity-Relationship model of business area.
    — Specify process model of business area.
    — Analyze interaction between entities and processes.
    — Identify business information systems.
- Model current information systems.
- Verify information architecture by comparing with current systems model.

For each business information system do:

3. Business system design (BSD)

- Specify system design.

    — Transform ER model into database schemas,
    — Specify data flow model of system,
    — Define data access paths and procedure/entity matrix.

- Specify user procedures.

    — Specify dialogue flow,
    — Specify screen layouts,
    — Specify clerical user steps.

4. Technical design and construction (TD & C)
5. Conversion
6. Production

Figure 6.2: The tasks of Information Engineering.

ISP starts with a preliminary definition of an information architecture on the basis of an analysis of the business strategy. It proceeds with an evaluation of the current state of the technical architecture and the organizational infrastructure as well as of current and planned information systems. Management is interviewed to determine information needs and priorities. The results of these evaluations and interviews are then used to define the four architectures. Figure 6.3 shows connections between the tasks and deliverables of ISP and shows how the four architectures are used in Information Engineering.

In addition to the four architectures, an information strategy plan contains a definition of a number of alternative strategies to implement these architectures. A strategy may recommend the application of client-server technology, a network of PCs, the use of commercial off-the-shelf software, etc. Different strategies may recommend different ambition levels for the implementation of the four architectures and should provide a cost-benefit analysis as well as a risk analysis of the alternatives. Finally, the information strategy plan should define follow-up projects, identify needed resources and indicate dependencies between projects. The information strategy plan is presented to the sponsor of the ISP project and must lead to a decision about the strategy to be followed and follow-up projects to be performed.

6.3 Analysis of Business Strategy

The first task to be performed in ISP is the analysis of the business strategy. Sources for the analysis of the business strategy are interviews with top management and documents relating to the business strategy (see figure 6.3). These documents may include, among others, business plans, information technology plans, annual reports, and executive memos and reports [215, page 78]. An analysis of a business strategy consists of at least the following tasks:

- an analysis of the business mission,

- an analysis of the long-term goals of the business,

- an analysis of the problems that make it difficult to achieve those goals, and

- an analysis of the critical success factors (CSFs) perceived by management.

Figure 6.3 shows that this preliminary analysis of the business strategy can be performed in parallel to the evaluation of the current situation. It leads to a preliminary information architecture, which is refined after a second round of management interviews is held. Whereas in the first interviewing round top management is interviewed, in the second round middle management is interviewed as well, and the results from the preliminary analysis and the evaluation of the current situation are used to determine information needs and priorities.

6.3.1 Analyze business mission

The business **mission** is the general purpose and nature of the business. As explained in section 2.5, the business mission is to the business what the product idea is to an industrial product. A business mission gives answers to the questions

- What business are we in?

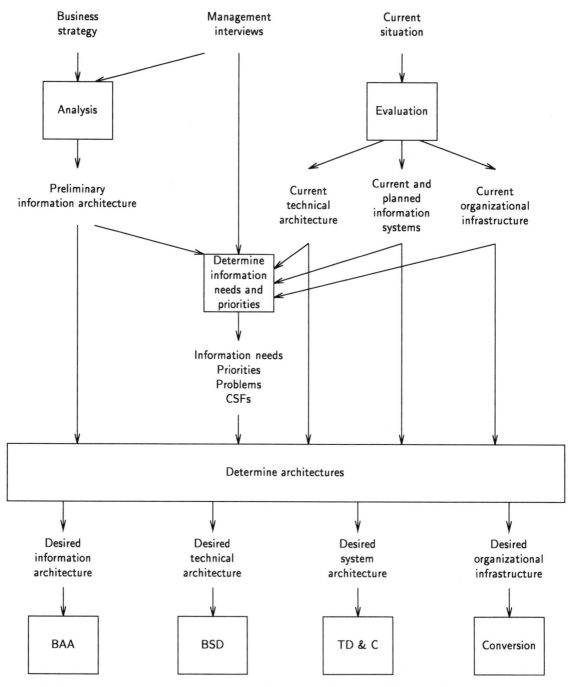

Figure 6.3: The structure of ISP and the role of the four architectures in Information Engineering.

- The mission of a hospital is the care and treatment of the ill.

- The mission of transport company is the efficient movement of goods from sender to receiver.

- The mission of a particular software consultancy may be the solution of business problems by means of information technology.

Figure 6.4: Some examples of business missions.

- The goal of a transport company may be to increase its market share. A particular objective to realize this goal may be to increase market share from 30% to 35% within the next 36 months.

- The goal of a software company may be to improve customer relations. An objective related to this goal may be to have all employees follow a particular human relations training during the next 12 months.

- The goal of a hardware manufacturer may be to decrease downtime of its products. An objective related to this goal is to decrease the number of service calls for its printing equipment to less than one per month on the average within the next 24 months.

Figure 6.5: Examples of business goals and objectives.

- What will our business be?

- What should our business be?

The mission statement gives the reason of existence of the business and describes what the underlying idea is of the product or service delivered by the business to its environment. Some examples of business missions are given in figure 6.4. The mission statement of a business may imply success or failure of the business in a changing environment. For example, in the early 1960s a Dutch manufacturer of home heating equipment formulated its mission as the manufacture of coal stoves. When the Netherlands switched to natural gas heating systems in the late 1960s, this manufacturer went broke [349, page 163]. Had the mission been formulated as the manufacture of heating equipment, this might not have happened.

6.3.2 Analyze business goals and objectives

A **goal** is a medium to long term result to be achieved by the business. The business mission is the highest-level goal of the business. Typically, goals are formulated as desirable states to be reached at an unspecified time in the future. Goals can be made measurable by means of **objectives**, which are measurable states to be achieved within a specific time frame. Some examples of goals and objectives are given in figure 6.5.

- Achievement of the goal of an increased market share may be inhibited by an inadequate information system about competitors.

- The goal of decreased product downtime may be inhibited by an unreliable component delivered by a third party.

- The goal of improving customer relations may be inhibited by an inadequate information system about employee performance.

- The goal of having a smaller inventory may be inhibited by the fact that orders tend to be for smaller batches and increase in frequency.

Figure 6.6: Business problems and the goals whose achievement they inhibit.

6.3.3 Analyze business problems

A business **problem** is a phenomenon that makes the achievement of objectives and goals, and hence of the business mission, more difficult than it has to be. The relation between problems and the goals whose achievement they inhibit can be represented by means of a **problem/goal matrix**. Construction of such a matrix for the library case study is straightforward and is left as an exercise for the reader. Figure 6.6 gives some examples of business problems and the goals whose achievement they inhibit.

6.3.4 Analyze critical success factors

A **critical success factor** (CSF) is an area in which, according to management, the business must perform well. Thus, a CSF is an area of concern to management. If the business performs well in this area then (according to management) it is likely that it achieves its objectives and if the business performs badly in this area then (according to management) it is likely to fail to reach its objectives. The identification of CSFs is partly a matter of cognitive style of management and different managers may identify different areas as CSFs. CSF thus bridge the impersonal world of business objectives with the subjective world of management information. CSFs are identified by management based on experience with the business. One manager of a supermarket listed the following CSFs for a supermarket [285]:

- Product mix

- Inventory

- Sales promotion

- Pricing.

Each CSF should be decomposed into factors for which measurement units and observation procedures are given. CSFs and their decompositions are thus extremely important to the information system developer, for they indicate what the system must provide information about.

Case study. The mission of the library is

> to acquire and make available documents containing information that is of use for scientific research and education.

An important current library goal is to improve the level of service to library users. Subgoals of this goal are

- to increase the availability of documents,
- to provide on-line access to its catalogue and
- to provide on-line access to all university library catalogues in the Netherlands.

Problems that inhibit the achievement of these goals are

- a decreasing budget,
- inefficient budget spending by multiple document and journal acquisitions,
- a large rate of document loss and
- habitual late returns of documents.

Given these goals, the chief librarian identifies the following areas of concern as critical success factors for the library:

- The coverage of the scientific fields by the documents possessed by the library.
- The availability of documents to the library members.
- Optimal use of the available budget.

To measure the performance of the library on these CSFs, the librarian will need such data as the number of borrowing requests placed, through the library's own circulation desks, to other libraries, and the ratio between the journals in a particular field present in the library to the total number of journals in that field. To measure availability, the librarian will need data like the ratio of reservations to borrowings, the number of missing documents, etc.

6.4 Determination of Information Architecture

An information architecture has four components:

- an entity model of the data relevant for the business,

- a list of relevant business functions, organized hierarchically in a function decomposition tree,

- a definition of dependencies between functions, and

- a function/entity matrix that correlates functions with the entity model.

We show how to define three of these four architecture components in this section. The specification of dependencies between functions is not treated here, because this would take too much space and would obscure the message of this chapter.

6.4.1   The function decomposition tree: structure and meaning

A **business function** is a group of activities that together support one aspect of furthering the mission of the business. A **business process** is an activity that transforms an input into an output and is performed in order to achieve a business function. Where a function is usually an ongoing activity such as *acquire orders* or *dispatch products*, a process is an activity performed in a particular time interval, and that can be repeated at different time intervals. Business processes and functions can be organized into a **function decomposition tree**, whose root is the business mission. Descending from the root, we encounter first the business functions, and then the business processes. Each higher-level function is refined into a collection of functions at the next lower level in the tree. A function decomposition tree of a system does not make any statement about the decomposition of the system into subsystem. To avoid misunderstanding, a more accurate name for the tree would be **function refinement tree**, but because the term "function *decomposition* tree" is widely used, we will continue using it. The business mission is thus the root of at least two trees: one in which it is decomposed into goals and subgoals (section 6.3) and one in which it is decomposed into activities (functions and processes).

The function decomposition tree indicates the relationship between *what* is done in the business and *why* this is done. The tree thus answers the following questions:

- What is the mission of the business? In other words, why does it exist?

- Which activities must be performed in order to achieve this mission?

- Why is a certain activity performed?

During ISP, the business mission is decomposed to the level of functions. During business area analysis, the tree is further decomposed so that it includes all business processes.

Figure 6.7 shows a function decomposition tree of a student administration. The root of the tree is labeled with the mission of the administration. Described more fully, this mission is

> To keep an administration of the educational achievements of students with respect to the examinations of the faculty.

This mission provides the rationale of all activities below the root in the function decomposition tree. If an administration activity cannot be allocated to a node in the tree, then there is no reason to perform it — or more accurately, the mission of the administration does not provide a reason to perform it.

The purpose of a function decomposition tree is to understand what happens in a business and why. There are many things that are *not* represented in a function decomposition tree [23]:

- A function decomposition tree does not show *mechanism*. It does not show *how* activities are performed, merely *that* they are performed. For example, activities in the tree may be performed manually, mechanically, electronically or mentally.

- A function decomposition tree is independent from the *organization structure*. The tree does not show a breakdown of the organization into departments. One department may perform activities at many different nodes, and different parts of the activity at one node may be performed by many different departments.

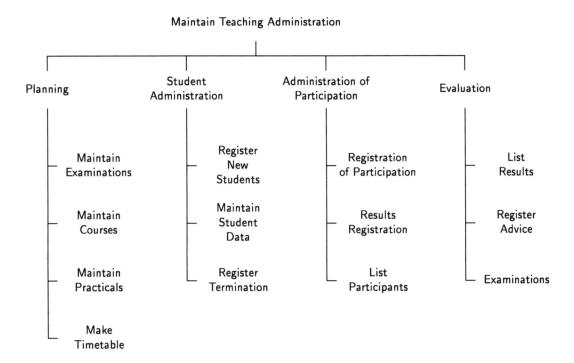

Figure 6.7: A function decomposition of a student administration.

- A function decomposition tree does not show *sequences* of activities. The ordering of nodes from left to right or top to bottom has no meaning and is merely intended to provide a convenient layout.

- A function decomposition is independent from the *jobs* people do. Nodes are not job descriptions. What any one person does may be scattered all over the tree, and conversely different parts of a task at one node may be performed by many different people.

The independence of the function decomposition tree from mechanism, organization structure, procedures and job roles makes it more stable than it would otherwise be, for it will not be affected by changes in these things. The function decomposition tree is an **essential model** of the business, i.e. given the business mission, the business should perform the activities in the tree. Changes in implementation mechanisms, job roles, organization structures and procedures must all keep the function decomposition tree invariant. Only changes in the business mission (or its interpretation by management) should change the tree. It is for this reason that it is important to draw a function decomposition tree before a change is initiated. The tree serves to represent what must remain constant in the change process.

Given an overall system function and a set of business activities, there are often several different trees that relate the activities to the overall function and it depends upon the interaction between the domain specialists and developers what the result will be. There is not a single tree that is the "best" model of the business activities. The function of the tree is to serve as a common framework for discussing the information architecture, and to fulfill this function the tree should be geared to the needs of those who use it. The utility of the tree lies in the fact that it is an extremely simple notation, that requires very little explanation to be understood by all stakeholders, and yet conveys a very important message about the business, viz. what the business does and why.

Case study.   Figure 6.8 shows a function decomposition tree of the library.

6.4.2   The function decomposition tree: construction heuristics

The process of building a function decomposition tree is highly iterative. One may start top-down (if one knows the system function) or bottom-up (if one knows which activities the system performs), but along the way one is likely to have to backtrack to revise a part of the tree already drawn. A very useful technique to build the first versions of the tree, recommended by Barker and Longman [23], is to use small sticky notelets and write one activity on each notelet. The notelets easily stick to a glass wall or to a table surface and can be moved around quickly as the ideas about the best organization of the tree change. When the tree is stable, and only then, a graphical editor could be used to draw the tree and give it a nice layout.

A useful heuristic for building the tree is to divide the activities in the business into the **primary activity**, in which material, energy or information is used to produce a product or service, and the **management activity**, in which the primary activity is managed. The primary process can be further divided into activities typical for the different stages of the life cycle of the product or service: acquisition of raw material, energy or information,

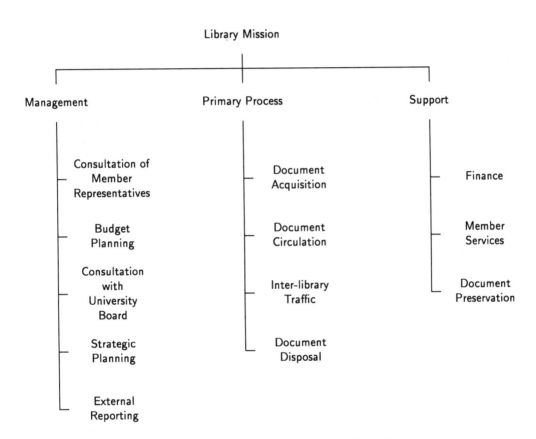

Figure 6.8: A function decomposition of the library.

followed by production, distribution, support and disposal of the product or service. Figure 6.9 gives some examples of each of these activities. Typical management activities are: planning of the business organizing it, acquisition of resources to do the business, directing the work done, and controlling the performance of the work done. Figure 6.10 gives some examples of each of these activities. We return to management activities in chapter 15, where we discuss the management of the development process.

For each of the identified activities, one can distinguish further activities by describing different aspects. For example, one can describe subactivities related to the financial aspect, the information aspect, the legal aspect, the human aspect, the technological aspect, etc. Acquisition of material from suppliers requires maintaining a database of information about potential and actual suppliers (information aspect), placing orders and making payments (financial aspect), signing contracts (legal aspect), defining interesting job roles (human aspect), etc.

6.4.3   The entity model: structure and meaning

Each business is interested in a certain part of the world with which it interacts. This is the **Universe of Discourse** (UoD) of the business. The UoD of a business may contain suppliers, customers, raw materials, finished products, payments, obligations and rights of the business and of its suppliers and customers, etc. As a preparation for making an entity model of the UoD, the UoD can be partitioned into subject areas, where a **subject area** is a topic of interest for the enterprise. Example subject areas for a travel agency are

- Travelers

- Destinations

- Airlines

- Tour operators

- Insurances

Subject areas are named by nouns. Count nouns must be plural (e.g. "Destinations"), mass nouns are in the singular (e.g. "Cash").

Referring to figure 6.3, after the information needs and priorities of the business have been determined, the list of subject areas is refined to an ER model of the UoD. An **Entity-Relationship model** (ER) of a UoD, or *entity model* for short, is a representation of the types of entities and their relationships in the UoD of the business. The phrase "in the UoD of the business" in the previous sentence is synonymous with "of interest to the business". Without restriction to things of interest for the business, there would be infinitely many entity types and relationships.

Figure 6.11 shows a fragment of an ER model of three subject areas of a travel agency. An ER model groups entities in the UoD into **types**. An entity type is represented in an ER diagram by a rectangle, labeled by the name of the type. In figure 6.11, *AIRPORT* is an entity type. Individual airports are **instances** of this type. A relationship links existing entities of two types; a relationship may relate entities of the same type. The instances of a relationship are called **links**. For example, a *RESERVATION* instance is a link between a particular *TRAVELER* and a particular *FLIGHT*. Each relationship may be subject

- **Acquisition**
  - Purchase material, information, energy, buildings, machinery, furniture, vehicles, etc.
  - Test procured material or information
  - Store procured material or information
- **Production**
  - Research new product or service opportunities
  - Develop and design new products or services
  - Schedule production
  - Produce product or service
  - Control quality of product or service
- **Distribution**
  - Store product
  - Pack the product or service
  - Advertise the product or service
  - Match product or service to customer needs
  - Sell the product or service
  - Manage fleet
- **Support**
  - Handle customer complaints
  - Product maintenance
  - Improve the product or service
  - Correct product faults
- **Disposal**
  - Retirement
  - Scrap
  - Recycling
  - Renewal

Figure 6.9: Examples of activities in different stages of the life cycle of products and services.

- **Planning**
    - Analyze environment (competitors, markets, products)
    - Identify trends
    - Set goals and objectives
    - Formulate business strategy
    - Determine critical success factors
- **Organizing**
    - Identify and group tasks
    - Define organization structures
    - Create organizational positions
    - Establish qualifications for each position
    - Define responsibilities and authority
- **Acquisition**
    - Raise funds
    - Purchase equipment
    - Recruit staff
    - Train staff
    - Compensate
    - Terminate assignments
- **Directing**
    - Delegate authority
    - Motivate personnel
    - Coordinate activities
    - Facilitate communications
    - Resolve conflicts
    - Manage changes
    - Supervise
- **Controlling**
    - Establish reporting systems
    - Develop standards of performance
    - Measure results
    - Reward and discipline

Figure 6.10: Examples of management activities in a business.

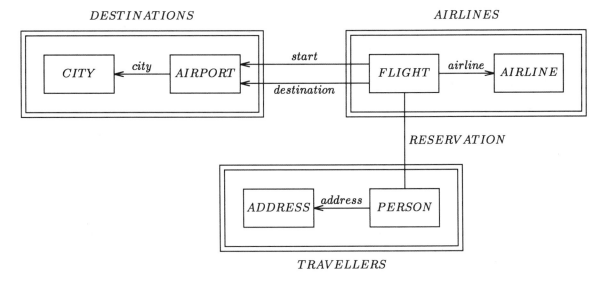

Figure 6.11: An ER diagram of three subject areas of a travel agency.

to **cardinality constraints**, which restrict the number of entities that can be linked at any point in time. In this chapter, we only discuss two cardinality constraints. In a **many-many** relationship R between E_1 and E_2, any number of existing instances of E_1 can be linked to any number of existing instances of E_2. A many-many relationship is represented by an undirected line. In a **many-one** relationship from E_1 to E_2, each existing instance of E_1 is linked to exactly one existing instance of E_2. A many-one relationship from E_1 to E_2 is represented by an arrow from E_1 to E_2. For example, in figure 6.11, each $FLIGHT$ has exactly one *destination* and one *start*.

There are many different notational conventions for ER models, some of which will be reviewed in chapter 7. In this book, we use the following conventions.

- The name of an entity type is always a singular noun written in uppercase letters.

- A many-many relationship is represented by an undirected line. If the meaning of the relationship can be expressed by a noun, then this noun can be used as a label of the line, written in uppercase letters. The name of a relationship R between E_1 and E_2 must be such that the sentence

   An R relates an E_1 and an E_2

   is a grammatical sentence (i.e. a syntactically well-formed and semantically meaningful sentence). For example, "a $RESERVATION$ relates a $PASSENGER$ and a $FLIGHT$" is a grammatical sentence.

- Sometimes, the meaning of a many-many relationship can be expressed by indicating the role that a participating entity type plays in the relationship. In these cases, the role name can be written in lowercase letters at the corresponding end point of the relationship line. If instances of E_1 play role r in a relationship with E_2, then the grammatical sentence that we can build from this is

Figure 6.12: If a relationship is not named, the role of at least one of the linked entities must be named.

"Each existing E_1 is the r of zero or more existing E_2s".

Figure 6.12 gives an example. It says that each existing *CONTAINER* is the *transported_item* in a relationshop with zero or more existing *ROUTE_SEGMENT*s. A many-many relationship line must be adorned with at least one role name or with a relationship name.

- The name of a many-one relationship from E_1 to E_2 represents the role played by E_2 in the relationship. It is a noun written in lowercase letters. If relationship a points from E_1 to E_2, then the grammatical sentence that we can build from this is

    "Each existing E_2 is the a of zero or more existing E_1s".

    For example, in figure 6.11, each existing *AIRPORT* is the *destination* of zero or more existing *FLIGHT*s and it is the *start* of zero or more existing *FLIGHT*s.

Subject areas are not normally represented in an ER notation, because they clutter up the diagram. However, if they are shown, as in figure 6.11, they are shown as double-barred rectangles and their name is shown in uppercase letters. In chapter 7, we also give a detailed analysis of the concepts of entity and relationship, and give a more detailed classification of cardinality constraints.

Case study. Example subject areas of the library include

- documents,
- library members,
- document orders,
- publishers,
- payments, etc.

Figure 6.13 shows a fragment of an ER model of the UoD of the library, containing entity types from each of these subject areas.

6.4.4   The entity model: construction and validation heuristics

Detailed heuristics for finding relevant subject areas, entity types and relationships are given in chapter 8. Here, we give two guidelines that can be used to find subject areas and an ER model using the results of business analysis. The first guideline is to run through the activities in the function decomposition tree and ask what topics are relevant for these activities. Figure 6.14 gives a rather arbitrary list of subject areas related to primary activities and management activities (figures 6.9 and 6.10). The second guideline to construct the ER model is to analyze the list of CSFs identified by management. Any relevant ER model must represent the data needed to derive the CSF values.

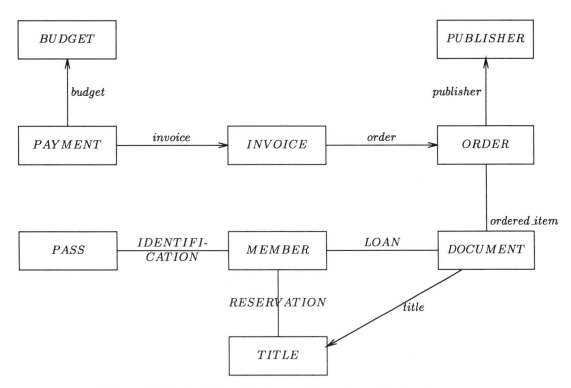

Figure 6.13: An ER model of some data relevant for the library.

Figure 6.14: Some example subject areas of a business.

	Document acquisition	Document circulation	Document disposal	Inter-library traffic	Finance	Member services	Document preservation	Budget planning
PASS		R				CD		
MEMBER		R				CUD		
TITLE	C	U	D					
DOCUMENT	C	U	D	U			U	
PAYMENT					CD			
INVOICE					CD			
ORDER	C				UD			
PUBLISHER	C							
BUDGET					R			CRU

C = Create access
R = Read access
U = Update access
D = Delete access

Figure 6.15: Function/entity matrix for the library.

Case study. The librarian listed the following CSFs:

- The coverage of the scientific fields by the documents possessed by the library.
- The availability of documents to the library members.
- Optimal use of the available budget.

The ER diagram in figure 6.13 can serve as a basis to accommodate the data needed to assess these factors. For example, these data can be specified as attributes of entity types in the model.

A useful heuristic to validate the ER model is to correlate the subject areas and entity types with the activities of the business. This tells us what is the relevance of the subject areas and entity types for the activities and what is the use that each activity makes of data belonging to the entity types. The correlation can be represented by means of a matrix in which all activities are listed along one dimension and all subject areas or entity types along the other. An entry in the cell indicates whether the activity creates, uses, updates or deletes data belonging to the subject area or entity type. The matrix of activities versus subject areas should be separated from the matrix of activities versus entity types. This gives is two types of matrices, the **function/subject area** matrix and the **function/entity matrix**.

Case study. Figure 6.15 shows a function/entity matrix for the library. Only the budgeting activity of the management function is shown in the table. The other activities do not manipulate instances of the entity types shown. For each function, we indicated the kind of access it has to instances of an entity type, Creation of an instance, Reading the state of an instance, Updating the state of an instance, or Deletion of an instance.

A function/entity matrix can be used for two completeness checks:

- A row without a C represents an entity type for which there is no activity that creates instances of the type. This may indicate that some activity is missing from the model.

- A column without any entries represents an activity that does not use or produce any data. This may indicate that some entity types are missing from the model.

6.5 Identification of Business Areas

A third use of the function/entity matrix is the identification of relevant business areas. A **business area** is a coherent collection of activities and data. Cohesion within one business area should be high, coupling between business areas should be low. Business areas do not necessarily coincide with departments or other kinds of business units. Different departments may use data from the same business area and one department may use data from different business areas. Business areas are represented in a function/entity matrix by interchanging the order of rows and columns, until for each business area the cells belonging to that area fall into one square. Because the data and activities in one business area must have a high coherence, a business area that creates data will ideally also update and delete these data. The best decomposition into business areas thus encloses all C's, U's and D's into business areas; any other arrangement would increase the coupling between business areas. An R outside a business area shows that an activity allocated to one business area reads data created and maintained in another business area. These R's thus represent data flows between business areas.

Case study. Figure 6.16 shows a possible arrangement of the function/entity matrix that encloses the C's, U's and D's as much as possible inside business areas. The business areas identified here are called, from left to right, Documents, Expenditures and Members (figure 6.17). There are a U and a D outside a business area (finance updates and deletes orders). Moving these into the Expenditures area would cause the creation of orders to be moved out of the Documents area. This is a choice that should be discussed with domain specialists. Figure 6.17 shows the data flows between the business areas of the library.

Rearranging a function/entity matrix so that business areas become visible is called **diagonalization** in Information Engineering, because the business areas appear on a diagonal of the matrix. There are CASE tools that perform diagonalization by moving the C's close to a diagonal. The identification of business areas is however something that requires domain knowledge which, so far, has eluded formalization. This knowledge is not captured by an algorithm that manipulates rows (or columns) so that C's are moved close to a diagonal.

	Document acquisition	Document disposal	Document circulation	Inter-library traffic	Document preservation	Finance	Budget planning	Member services
TITLE	C	D	U					
DOCUMENT	C	D	U	U	U			
ORDER	C					UD		
PUBLISHER	C							
BUDGET						R	CRU	
PAYMENT						CD		
INVOICE						CD		
PASS			R					CD
MEMBER			R					CUD

Figure 6.16: Partitioning of the function/entity matrix into business areas. The three identified areas are Documents, Expenditures and Members. Each of these areas is a coherent set of entity types and functions.

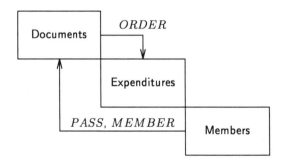

Figure 6.17: Data flows between business areas of the library.

Social system	**Information Strategy Planning**: Determine desired information architecture, system architecture, technical architecture, organizational infrastructure.
Computer-based systems	**Business Area Analysis**: Model business areas, identify business systems and specify their external behavior.
Software systems	**Business System Design**: Specify architecture of automated information system(s).
Software subsystems	**Technical Design & Construction**: Specify physical designs and implement business systems.

Figure 6.18: Information Engineering's coverage of aggregation levels.

6.6 Methodological Analysis

6.6.1 The place of Information Engineering in the development framework

The system hierarchy. Figure 6.18 shows the coverage of aggregation levels by Information Engineering. ISP analyzes the business strategy and produces a strategy plan for the information aspect system of the business. The core of the strategy consists of the four architectures, which must be used in any implementation of the information strategy. Within this core, the information architecture plays a central role. It has a peculiar structure, which links the activities in the organization with the structure of the UoD:

- Business activity is decomposed into subactivities needed to achieve the mission of the business.

- The UoD is decomposed into types of entities about which the business wants to maintain information.

These are decompositions of two distinct systems (the business and its UoD). The function/entity matrix links the two decompositions and identifies business areas as coherent sets of activities and entity types. The system hierarchy of figure 6.18 places the business at the top level and decomposes this repeatedly into subsystems that are interesting from the software engineer's point of view. The decomposition of the UoD into entity types does not belong to a particular level in this hierarchy. The UoD can be partitioned into its own aggregation levels, separate from the hierarchy used for computer-based systems.

The allocation of business area analysis to the level of computer-based systems is justified by the observation that some activities in a business area will be supported or performed by a computer-based system. In business area analysis, business areas models are elaborated until one or more business systems can be identified. Before the business systems are identified, however, the function decomposition tree and entity models have been elaborated to a level of detail that is sufficient to serve as model of observable behavior of the business systems. The observable behavior of these systems is thus modeled *before* the business area is decomposed into business systems.

Engineering. The engineering cycle plays a minor role in Information Engineering — which is curious, given the name of the method. The essence of engineering is the exploration of alternative actions by simulating the actions and evaluating their results before they are implemented. Simulation may take the form of exploration of alternatives by means of discussion, computation of likely effects, construction of mock-ups, throw-away prototyping, asking specialists what the likely effects are, etc. Any exploration of alternatives is however absent from ISP. Function decomposition and entity modeling are treated as analytical activities whose results follow more or less deterministically from their inputs (the business strategy, management interviews and an analysis of the current situation). There is no visible search for alternatives in Information Engineering in these tasks.

Two activities in ISP do however indicate an engineering orientation. The first is that the desired business situation is specified (by means of the four architectures) before it is implemented. It is a precondition of the engineering cycle that the desired situation is specified before it is realized. The second indication of an engineering orientation is that ISP ends with the generation of a list of alternative strategies to be followed in the rest of the development process. Each strategy suggests an ambition level for the implementation of the four architectures. The strategies must be evaluated using techniques such as cost-benefit analysis, risk analysis, and an analysis of threats and opportunities in the environment of the business. All of this introduces an element of engineering into Information Engineering. However, it is clear that the engineering cycle does not play as central a role as it does in, for example, ISAC Change Analysis.

6.6.2   Function decomposition

Function decomposition in product development. Function decomposition is a well-known technique in industrial product design. The root of a product function decomposition tree is labeled by the underlying product idea. This represents the reason why the product should exist. The other nodes represent activities performed by the product and by which it achieves its underlying idea. It is useful to stop decomposing the product function when we reach the level of observable product transactions. This is analogous to the decomposition of the business mission down to the level of business processes, which usually include internal and external business transactions.

Since we can build a function decomposition tree of a business as well as of each information system in the business, it is important to be aware of the system of which one is building a function decomposition tree: the business, a business unit (department) or a business information system. These trees may look like each other, but they represent the function of quite different systems and will therefore have different transactions at their leaves.

Function refinement and system decomposition. A function decomposition tree decomposes a product idea or business mission into activities. At the higher levels of the tree, these activities are called product functions or business functions. The term "function" is then used in its meaning of "useful activity" (see section 2.5). In chapter 3, we observed that a decomposition of functions into subfunctions is orthogonal to a decomposition of a system into subsystems. This is represented graphically by the magic square in figure 3.10 (page 55). The same observation can be made at the business level. A function decomposition tree of a business decomposes functions (useful activities) into subfunctions, which

Figure 6.19: Naming a many-many relationship by a verb creates the problem of in which direction the verb should be read.

are again activities. All of these activities may or may not exist at the same level of aggregation. Remember that each level of an aggregation hierarchy is characterized by its own concept of observability and often has its own natural level of transaction atomicity (see subsection 2.4.2). For example, we can choose to decompose the mission of a business into observable interactions between the business and its environment. In the terminology of chapter 4, this decomposition is a refinement of behavior. Internal interactions like "send copy of shipping advice to the accounting department" are absent from such a function decomposition tree. Alternatively, we can choose to decompose (refine) the mission only into internal interactions between subsystems of the business; or we can choose to decompose (refine) the mission into external as well as internal interactions. These are all good choices for some purposes and they are bad choices for others. The point is that decomposition (refinement) of an activity into subactivities is orthogonal to decomposition of a system into subsystem.

6.6.3   Entity models

Conventions.   The conventions for representing cardinality constraints vary wildly with different authors. Chapter 7 reviews most conventions used for ER models. Here, we should note that the naming of relationships is problematic in those conventions that require a relationship to be named by a verb. For example, in figure 6.19, we intuitively read *PASSENGER RESERVES FLIGHT*, but this is a consequence of the accidental fact that *PASSENGER* is drawn to the left of *FLIGHT*. In a complicated diagram, layout may be improved by drawing *FLIGHT* to the left of *PASSENGER* or above or below it, and this should not affect our reading of the relationship. The sentence *PASSENGER RESERVES FLIGHT* suggests more about the relationship than is represented by the diagram because, unlike the diagram, the sentence constrains the order of the entity types: *FLIGHT RESERVES PASSENGER* does not have a meaning and *PASSENGER RESERVES FLIGHT* has a meaning. This problem disappears by labeling the relationship with a noun, for the two sentences

- a *RESERVATION* relates a *PASSENGER* and a *FLIGHT*

- a *RESERVATION* relates a *FLIGHT* and a *PASSENGER*

have the same meaning.

Advantages and disadvantages of entity modeling.   The use of entity models in the early stages of development has similar advantages and disadvantages as the use of activity models (see section 5.4). The advantage is that the entity model provides a shared conceptual model of the data needed by the business. A disadvantage is that the analyst may spend too much time on too many details of entity modeling — although, to the

extent that the entity model is more stable than a model of business activities, this time
is not wasted. A second disadvantage of entity modeling is that the model may not be
understandable by management, which means that it cannot fullfil its role as a means of
communication with management.

6.6.4   Information Engineering and ISAC

Norm-driven and problem-driven.   A major difference between ISAC and Information
Engineering is that ISAC takes experienced problems as the starting point, while Information Engineering takes a business strategy as the starting point. Jointly, they cover the
possible starting points for client-oriented development: deterioration of performance with
respect to norms that themselves may be unchanged, and a change of norms with respect
to a situation that itself may not have changed. Of course, these two starting points are
not mutually exclusive. Correspondingly, in ISAC Change Analysis one finds tasks in which
the business goals are analyzed, and in ISP one finds tasks in which business problems are
analyzed.

Given their differences and agreements, it is easy to identify possibilities of combination.
Putting both methods in one bag of tools, one can pick and choose among the following
methods and techniques according to the needs of the situation:

- Analysis of problems and interest groups (ISAC)

- Analysis of problem causes (ISAC)

- Function decomposition (ISP)

- Activity modeling of the current or desired situation (ISAC)

- Entity modeling of the UoD (ISP)

- Linking activities to entity types (ISP)

This list is not complete but does indicate the possibilities for combination.

Function decomposition and activity modeling.   Function decomposition trees and
ISAC activity models are closely related and can be built in a mutually consistent way.
Activity models are organized in a hierarchical way which, when function decomposition is
used, should correspond to the function decomposition tree. Figure 6.20 shows a part of a
function decomposition tree that shows the hierarchical decomposition relation of the two
activity models of the library shown in chapter 5 (figures 5.7 and 5.8).

Participation.   Just like ISAC, Information Engineering stresses the importance of user
participation. However, since the intended system users in Information Engineering include
top management, and managers tend to have little time for representative participation,
management participation in Information Engineering tends to be of the consultative kind.

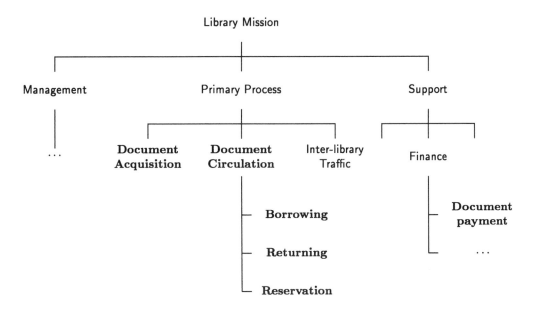

Figure 6.20: A function decomposition tree. The activities in the ISAC activity models are printed in boldface.

6.7   Exercises

1. Make a problem/goal matrix of the library, using the analysis of subsection 5.2.6.

2. Compare the functions in the function decomposition tree of the library of figure 6.8 with the example activities in figures 6.9 and 6.10 and explain any differences.

3. For every activity in the product life cycle of figure 6.9, try to find an example in the student administration (appendix B). Make a function decomposition tree of the administration based on this analysis, and compare the result with figure 6.7.

4. Use the business activities of figures 6.9 to draw a function decomposition tree of the primary process of a travel agency three levels deep. Check the tree by going to a local travel agency and asking what they do.

5. Adapt the ER diagram of figure 6.11 so that it represents the following situation: Each flight can consist of several segments and is scheduled on a regular basis several days of the week. A flight with segments that lead the traveler from start to final destination and back again is called a return flight. A return flight in which the time interval between departure and return date includes a Saturday night has a different price from a flight which does not satisfy this condition.

6. Use figure 6.14 to list the relevant subject areas for a travel agency. Indicate these areas on the ER diagram of exercise 5.

7. Using the results of exercises 4 and 5, make a function/entity matrix of a travel agency and identify business areas.

8. Consider the following three models made in ISP: a function decomposition tree, an entity model and a function/entity matrix.

   (a) Is making a function decomposition tree a descriptive activity (for which the empirical cycle is the appropriate method) or is it a prescriptive activity (for which the engineering cycle is the appropriate method)?

   (b) Is making an entity model of the UoD a descriptive or a prescriptive activity?

   (c) Given a function decomposition tree and an entity model, is there one unique function/entity matrix that combines the two?

6.8   Bibliographical Remarks

A large number of methods and techniques went into Information Engineering, among which are Business Systems Planning (BSP), a strategic planning method developed by IBM, Entity-Relationship modeling, and a number of other diagraming techniques. Information Engineering was developed in the 1970s by Clive Finkelstein and James Martin. A joint book about Information Engineering was published in 1981 [217]. A year later, a widely cited work by James Martin on methods for strategic data planning appeared [212], which should be viewed as part of Information Engineering. In 1989, James Martin published a revision of the Martin/Finkelstein volumes [214, 215, 216]. Meanwhile, Finkelstein had started his own company and published a book about his own version of the method also in 1989 [103]. This differs considerably from the earlier Martin/Finkelstein version. In addition to Finkelstein's and Martin's brands of IE, there is a third version marketed by the Arthur Young Information Technology Group [72]. This is close to the original Martin/Finkelstein version.

In this chapter, James Martin's version of Information Engineering is described, based upon Martin's 1989 description of it [215], course material by James Martin Associates [166], and on a very clear exposition of Information Strategy Planning given by Simons and Verheijen [319].

In addition, use is made of a book on function analysis written by Barker and Longman [23]. This book is part of a trilogy that describes a method similar to Information Engineering, called Case*Method [21, 22, 23]. This method goes back to a comprehensive method for data and activity analysis presented by Rosemary Rock-Evans [280, 281, 282, 283].

The list of activities in the product life cycle (figure 6.9) and the list of management activities (figure 6.10) are based on similar lists given by Barker and Longman [23], Martin [212], and the list of management activities given by Thayer [342].

7

The Entity-Relationship
Approach I: Models

7.1   Introduction

Entity-relationship (ER) modeling is a method for building conceptual models of a
UoD. It was introduced by Peter Chen in 1976 as a reaction to the *relational data modeling*
approach [65] proposed by Ted Codd in 1970 [69]. Relational data modeling was itself a
reaction to still earlier approaches to the specification of database systems, in which the specification of conceptual data structures was mixed with the specification of implementation
structures. In those earlier approaches, a model that represented entity types and relationships in the UoD was not distinguished from a model of access paths and pointer structures
in a computer-based system. The relational approach proposed by Codd eliminates this
problem by abstracting from implementation structures. However, it also abstracts from
many of the structures present in the UoD: all that is represented in a relational data model
is that certain data items can be grouped together in tuples. As a consequence, relational
data models are useful high level models of the data stored by a computer-based system,
but they are not well-suited to modeling structures present in the UoD of the system. Chen
proposed the ER approach as a means to represent the structure of the UoD without at the
same time saying anything about implementation structures in a computer-based system.

There are many versions of the ER approach that disagree about the graphical conventions used and about the extensions added to the initial version of the approach presented
by Chen. This chapter ends with a survey of some major graphical conventions and their
relationship to the convention used in this book. The conventions and concepts defined
in this chapter stay close to Chen's original proposal but avoid a number of ambiguities
present in that notation. In sections 7.2 to 7.4, we lay the groundwork by defining entities, attributes, types, existence and identity. In section 7.5 we define relationships and
in section 7.6 cardinality constraints. In section 7.7, a very brief introduction to the *is_a*
relationship is given. Section 7.8 contains a methodological analysis of the ER approach.

7.2   Entities, Values and Attributes

7.2.1   ER entities

To distinguish the entity concept in ER modeling from the concept of entity in other model-ing approaches, as in JSD, I will often speak of *ER entities* instead of just entities. We define an **ER entity** as any actual or possible part of reality that, if it exists, can be observed. Note that this is identical to the concept of a system given in chapter 2. Consequently, all examples of systems are examples of entities:

- Physical objects like cars, sticks and stones are ER entities.

- Intangible objects like operating systems, editors and compilers are ER entities.

- Social constructs like organizations, employees, obligations and bank accounts are ER entities.

- Ephemeral objects like events, actions and transactions are ER entities.

- Unobservable things like truth values, numbers and characters are *not* ER entities, but physical symbol occurrences used to represent these abstract things *are* ER entities.

7.2.2   Attributes

Entities are observable, and they therefore have observable properties. For example, a particular person can be observed to have a weight of 90 kg. In this observation, *weight* is called an attribute and 90 kg is called an attribute value. More generally, we define attributes and their values as follows:

- An **attribute** is a type of non-disturbing observation that can be made of an ER entity.

- An **attribute value** is a particular instance of an attribute. That is, it is a particular non-disturbing observation that has been made of an ER entity.

Observing the value of an attribute should not change the attribute value nor the value of any other entity attribute. Hence, we require attributes to be types of *non-disturbing* observations. In database terms, an attribute value is the answer to a query, and queries should not change the state of the queried system.

Attribute values represent part of the state of an ER entity. Suppose that a physical object has attributes *weight*, *color* and *shape*, then we can represent part of the state of the object by a tuple of attribute/value pairs as follows:

$$\langle color : green, weight : 10\ kg, shape : cube\rangle.$$

7.2.3   Values

Abstract, unobservable things such as numbers are called **values** in this book. The set of all possible values is disjoint from the set of all possible ER entities, for the first consists of unobservable things and the second of observable things. Values are used to represent observations in a system of measures. For example, we say that the weight of an ER entity is 10 kg or that someone is called *John*. The symbol occurrences "10" and "*John*" are themselves observable parts of the world and they are therefore ER entities. Often, *ad hoc* values are invented to represent certain system observations. We may invent for example the set of values {*green, red, blue*} to stand for observations of the three colors green, red and blue.

7.2.4 Null values

The use of **null** values must be avoided as far as possible, because their meaning is unclear and their logic is unknown. Null values are used, among others, to represent the following things:

- To indicate that an event *has not yet taken place* (e.g. *termination_date* has value **null** when termination has not yet occurred).

- To indicate attribute values that are *unknown* (e.g. *birth_date* has value **null**).

- To indicate *nonexistence* of an entity (e.g. no car *owner* exists). (This would be more properly called a **null entity**.)

- To indicate *confidentiality* of attribute values (e.g. *telephone* has a null value when it is secret but is known to exist).

- To indicate *inapplicability* of attribute values (e.g. *maiden_name* of male employees).

If the same **null** value is used with all these meanings, then if an attribute value is **null**, we do not know what it means. Even if we were to disambiguate the **null** and use, say, *nonexistent* when we mean that an attribute value is unknown, then the logic of this value is unknown. How do we count **null** values with this meaning? If two attributes values are both **null**, are these attribute values equal? Similar questions can be asked of the other possible meanings of **null**. Because **null** values are highly ambiguous and ill-understood, they should be avoided as much as possible, and when they cannot be avoided, be treated with special care.

7.3 Types and Existence

7.3.1 Intension and extension

Values and ER entities with similar properties are classified into *types* according to the properties they have in common.

- A **property** of a thing is the contents of any true proposition about that thing.

- A **type** is a set of properties shared by a set of things.

- The **extension** of a type is the set of all *actual and possible* things that share the properties in the type.

- An element of the extension of a type is called an **instance**

- The **intension** of a type is the set of *all* properties shared by the extension of the type.

We illustrate these definitions with a number of examples. Examples of properties of a particular person are

- that this person has a height and a weight (i.e. the attributes *height* and *weight* are applicable);

- that this person has height 192 cm. (i.e. the attribute *height* has value 192 for this person);

- that the age of this person never decreases;

- that if this person borrows a book, he or she must return it.

Any set of properties, including a singleton set, defines a type. For example, the first property above defines the type of things that have a height and a weight. The first two properties jointly define the type of things that have a weight, and have a height of 192 cm. If the defined type consists of ER entities, we call the type an **ER entity type**.

Just like ER entities, values have properties. The properties of values are unobservable but can be investigated by symbol manipulation. Some properties of the number 2 are that it is the smallest prime number, that it is even, etc. The properties shared by all natural numbers are defined by Peano's axioms, and the properties shared by propositions are defined by any axiom system of propositional logic. If the defined type consists of values, we call the type a **value type**.

Suppose we define a type by properties $\{p_1, \ldots, p_n\}$. Then there are usually many properties, not in the type definition, that are shared by all instances of the type. Here are two examples:

- The type of thing with height 192 cm has the following infinite set of properties: It has a height less than n cm for any $n > 192$.

- The natural numbers have all properties derivable from Peano's axioms.

Related to this, there are often different, equivalent definitions of the same type. For example, there are different equivalent sets of axioms that define the type of natural numbers. Whatever set of defining properties is used, the set of *all* properties of the extension is called the intension of the type. For example, the intension of the type of natural numbers is the set of all properties shared by all natural numbers.

7.3.2   Representation

An **ER model** consists of a collection of diagrams and accompanying documentation. Figure 7.1 gives an example of a graphical representation of entity types, attributes and value types. Each entity type is represented graphically as a rectangle labeled with the type name, each value type is represented by an ellipse labeled with the type name, and each attribute applicable to the entity type is represented by an arrow from the entity type to a value type, labeled with the attribute name. Type names are nouns written in uppercase letters, attribute names are nouns written in lowercase letters that indicate which role the attribute value is playing with respect to the entity type.

A graphical entity type declaration has an equivalent textual representation of the form

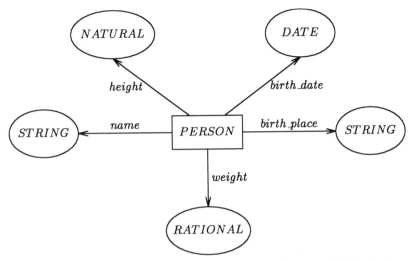

$PERSON(name : STRING, height : NATURAL, birth\_date : DATE, birth\_place :$
$STRING, weight : RATIONAL)$.

Figure 7.1: Graphical representation of entity types, attributes and value types, and its equivalent textual representation.

$$E(a_1 : T_1, \ldots, a_n : T_n).$$

The graphical or textual declaration can be supplemented with a specification of other properties shared by all instances. For example, the $PERSON$ type could have the additional defining property that

- all $PERSON$ instances have a weight less than 150 kg.

It is useful to interpret an attribute as a mathematical function from the extension of the entity type to the set of possible attribute values. A **mathematical function** is a relation between two sets, called **domain** and **codomain**, such that each element of the domain is linked to at most one element of the codomain. The concept of mathematical function is entirely different from the concept of system function introduced in chapter 2. For example, let $ext(PERSON)$ be the extension of $PERSON$ (i.e. the set of all current and possible persons) and $ext(NATURAL)$ the extension of $NATURAL$ (i.e. the set of all natural numbers). Then we can view $height$ as a mathematical function

$$height : ext(PERSON) \rightarrow ext(NAT).$$

The extension of $PERSON$ is called the **domain** of $height$ and the extension of $NATURAL$ the **codomain** of $height$. By abuse of language, the types $PERSON$ and $NATURAL$ will themselves also be called domain and codomain of $height$, respectively. Note that in relational databases, the codomain of an attribute is called the *domain* of the attribute!

7.3.3   Existence

The extension of the type of persons is the set of all *possible* person entities and the extension of the type of natural numbers is the set of all natural numbers. At any moment, a subset of the set of all possible persons exists. In subsection 2.2.1, the concept of existence of a system was equated with the possibility to interact with other existing systems. Since ER entities and systems are the same thing, we also say that an ER entity **exists** if it is capable of interacting with other ER existing entities. It follows that values do not exist, at least not according to the existence concept defined here. Values are unobservable, so they don't interact with anything. Of course, *symbol occurrences* that represent values can exist, i.e. they can be created and destroyed. However, events in the life of a symbol occurrence are not events in the life of the represented values.

The set of instances of a type that exists in a state of the UoD is called the **existence set** of the type in that state of the UoD. Each attribute is only defined for the existence set of its domain. Let us write σ for an arbitrary state of the UoD and $ext_\sigma(PERSON)$ for the existence set of $PERSON$ in state σ. Then $ext_\sigma(PERSON) \subset ext(PERSON)$, for the set of existing persons is a subset of the set of all possible persons. The *height* attribute is only defined for the existence set of $PERSON$, so that we have

$$height : ext_\sigma(PERSON) \rightarrow ext(NATURAL).$$

7.4   Entity Identification

7.4.1   The importance of identification

It is extremely important for value types to be able to test on equality. For example, it is by means of equations like $a + b = b + a$ that we define the meaning of addition for integers, and it is by means of reductions like $2 + 3 = 5$ that we can compute the value of integer expressions.

Equality is also important for entity types. For each entity type we must define an **identification criterion** that tells us when to count two observations of an entity as observations of the *same* entity, and when to count them as observations of different entities. Consider the entity type $MEMBER$ in an ER model of the UoD of a library. If we make two observations of library members at different times, we can ask if these are observations of the same member. If, by independent criteria, we know that the same person was observed both times, did we then observe the same member? This depends upon the library regulations. One person may quit being a member and after a while register anew as a member. In these two incarnations as a library member, the person will receive a library pass with *different* identifiers. We will have to look at library regulations to find out whether they are considered to be one or two member instances.

On the other hand, suppose we do not know whether we have observed the same person or not. In this case, the answer seems easy: ask for the library pass. If we observe the same pass both times, we observed the same member. However, library members occasionally lose their pass and then receive a new one, with another identifier than the previous one. This means that *difference* of pass identifiers does not imply that we have observed different persons. Apparently, a careless definition of identification criteria can lead to wrong conclusions.

7.4.2 Identifiers

If computer-based systems represent entities that exist in the UoD, then they must have a means of representing the *identity* of entities. In particular, they must be able to do two things:

- The system must be able to represent *different* entities that are in the same state. Otherwise, two entities that in one state of the world happen to have the same attribute values would be counted as one. Queries about how many entities there are would be given the wrong answer, and control signals sent out to the UoD could arrive at the wrong entity.

- The system must be able to represent the *same* entity in different states. Otherwise, a system would not be able to accumulate historical data about an entity. A query about the past state of an entity could then not be answered, and a control decision based upon the history of an entity could then not be made.

To represent the identity of an entity in the UoD, the computer-based system must use an **identification scheme** that assigns a globally unique **identifier** to each relevant entity in the UoD. Each identification scheme has a **scope** of actual and possible entities to which it assigns identifiers. An identifier is a *value* that is assigned by the identification scheme when the entity becomes relevant. The identification scheme must enforce the following **identifier requirements**:

1. **Singular reference**: An identifier never refers to more than one ER entity. This excludes *homonyms*. Even if two ER entities are in exactly the same state, and cannot be distinguished, they must still have different identifiers.

2. **Unique naming**. An entity never has more than one identifier as name. This excludes *synonyms*.

3. **Monotonic designation**: Once an identifier denotes an entity, then this identifier will always denote this entity. The set of identifier-entity pairs in which we pair identifiers with the ER entity which they name, therefore only grows.

The first two requirements demand that there be a 1-1 correspondence between identifiers and identified entities, and the monotonicity requirement demands that assignments of identifiers to entities never be deleted.

Examples of identification schemes are the employee numbering scheme in a company, the student numbering scheme in a university, the serial numbering scheme of industrial products, etc. There is no identification scheme that is watertight. All schemes allow violation of any of the three identifier requirements. Some people manage to have no social security number, others have two, some social security numbers may be given mistakenly or fraudulently to two different people, etc. To make the situation more complex, most entities are within the scope of different identification schemes, and therefore have several different legally valid identifiers.

Note that an identifier is a *value*. For example, an employee number is a natural number. One employee number may be represented by many different symbols (e.g. as a natural number in binary notation or as binary coded decimal), but these symbols all represent the same identifier. One such symbol may have many occurrences in different machines (or even in the same machine), and all these occurrences represent the same identifier.

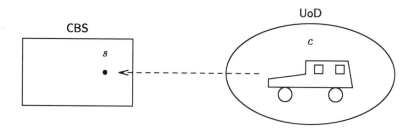

Figure 7.2: A car c in the universe of discourse (UoD) is represented in a computer-based system (CBS) by a surrogate s.

7.4.3 Surrogates

In order to be aware of what we are identifying, it is important to distinguish entities in the UoD from entities in a computer-based system. The representation of a UoD entity in a computer-based system is called a **surrogate** for the UoD entity (figure 7.2). Surrogates are observable parts of the world, for they can interact with other observable things. This means that the concept of existence is applicable to surrogates just as it is applicable to UoD entities. The existence of surrogates and the existence of the entities they represent do not have to coincide, however. For example, a CAR surrogate can be created in a database system before the car that it represents has been manufactured, and the surrogate may continue to exist after the car in the UoD is destroyed. On the other hand, when a surrogate for a library member is created, the member already existed in the UoD (as a person), and this person will continue to exist after the surrogate is destroyed.

Because a UoD entity is represented by a surrogate in a system and the surrogate has a different identity from the represented UoD entity, we need an identification scheme for surrogates in addition to an identification scheme for UoD entities. We call the identifiers of the surrogate identification scheme **internal identifiers** and the identifiers of the UoD identification scheme **external identifiers**. The scope of the internal identification scheme is the system itself, which may be distributed over several locations. The scope of an external identification scheme is external to the system and overlaps with the UoD. Internal identifiers are not observable for an external system observer but external identifiers are observable for observers of the UoD (otherwise they would not be useful).

External identifiers are declared in an entity declaration by an exclamation mark:

$$E(a : V_1, !b : V_2, \ldots).$$

An identifier always consists of a single attribute. An entity type may have several identifiers. The exclamation mark does not give us all information we need, because for each identifier, we must know what the identification scheme of the identifier is. This information must be provided in the documentation of the ER model.

7.4.4 Keys

A **key** of an entity type E is a set of attributes whose combination of values is unique within each possible existence set of E. For example, suppose that $PERSON$ has attributes *name*,

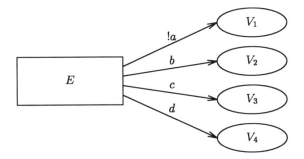

!a	b	c	d		!a	b	c	d		!a	b	c	d
1	b_1	c_1	d_1	*swap*	1	b_2	c_2	d_1	*reuse*	1	b_2	c_2	d_1
2	b_2	c_2	d_2	$\Longrightarrow$	2	b_1	c_1	d_2	$\Longrightarrow$	2	b_1	c_1	d_2
3	b_2	c_3	d_3		3	b_2	c_3	d_3		4	b_2	c_3	d_3

Figure 7.3: Key values may be changed and reused. The figure shows three existence sets and two state transitions, in the first of which key values are swapped and in the second of which a key is reused.

address, birth_date, birth_place, age, ssn (social security number). If in each state of the UoD, different existing persons have different values on the combination {*name, birth_date*} then {*name, birth_date*} is a key of *PERSON*. Keys are often underlined in an entity declaration, as in

$$PERSON(!ssn, \underline{name, birth\_date}, \ldots).$$

(For brevity, the codomains of the attributes are not shown.)

It is compatible with the definition of a key that in a state change of an entity, the attribute values of a key change and that after a key value has been used for an existing entity it may be reused for another entity that exists or is created. This distinguishes them from identifiers. Figure 7.3 illustrates this. Entity type E is declared as

$$E(!a, \underline{b}, c, d).$$

The three tables represent three existence sets for E. In the state transition from the first to the second, two entities swap their key values and in the transition from the second to the third, a key value of a deleted entity is reused for a new entity.

7.5 Relationships

7.5.1 Identity and existence

A **link** between ER entities is a tuple of ER entities with labeled components. Links are represented by writing down a labeled tuple of entity *identifiers*. An example link is

$$\langle borrowed\_document : d, borrower : m \rangle,$$

where d and m are identifiers of a document and a library member, respectively. Link components are not ordered, which means that

$$\langle borrower : m, borrowed\_document : d \rangle$$

is identical to the link listed above. The number of components in a link is called its **arity**. If the arity is two, the link is called **binary**, if it is three, it is called **ternary**. The positions in the link are identified by the name of the **role** that the entity plays in the link.

A **relationship** is a set of properties shared by a set of links — in other words, it is a **link type** and an individual link is an instance of a relationship. An essential part of the definition of a relationship is the specification of which components the instances of the relationship have. This part of the relationship can be specified as follows:

$$R \subseteq r_1 : E_1 \times \cdots \times r_n : E_n,$$

where $\times$ is a commutative Cartesian product. The following two declarations are therefore equivalent:

$$LOAN \subseteq borrowed\_document : DOCUMENT \times borrower : MEMBER \text{ and}$$
$$LOAN \subseteq borrower : MEMBER \times borrowed\_document : DOCUMENT.$$

A link is an observable part of the UoD and hence an ER entity. We will follow the usual way of speaking and talk of links and entities as if links are not a special kind of entity. However, note that just like any other kind of ER entity, links can have attributes. We can declare the attributes of links in the same way as we declare attributes of entity types:

$$R(a_1 : V_1, \ldots, a : m : V_m).$$

Thus, a relationship declaration consists of at least two parts: a specification of the relationship components and a specification of relationship attributes. A possible third part consists of all other properties of the relationship instances. For example, every $LOAN$ instance may have the property that the borrowed document is less than 100 years old.

Every link has the **dependent identity** property, which says that the identity of the link is the labeled tuple of identities of its components. Consequently, the identifier of a link is a labeled tuple of identifiers of component identifiers. This has the important consequence that a relationship cannot link the same entities twice at the same time but it can link them twice at different times. For example, there cannot exist two occurrences of

$$\langle borrowed\_document : 123, borrower : 567 \rangle$$

at the same time, because the equality of these identifiers means that the identified links are equal. This is reasonable, because one member cannot borrow the same document twice *simultaneously*. However, an occurrence of $\langle borrowed\_document : 123, borrower : 567 \rangle$ can exist for a while, disappear, and then reappear to exist for another while. Again, this is a reasonable model of reality. If this is not what the modeler wants, then the relationship should be replaced by an entity type with its own identifier.

Every existing link is also required to satisfy the **component existence assumption** that all its components exist. This is reasonable, for an observation of a link may require an observation of any of its components. So if the $LOAN$ existence set contains $\langle borrowed\_document : 123, borrower : 567 \rangle$ as an element, then the $DOCUMENT$ existence set contains 123 and the $MEMBER$ existence set contains 567 as element. The

Kind	Example	Explanation
Duration	*LOAN*	A library member lends a document for a certain period.
Event	*DELIVERY*	A transport company delivers parts from a company for a project.
Component link	*DECOMPO-SITION*	An engine is part of the decomposition of a car.
	MEMBER-SHIP	An employee is member of a department.
Obligations	*LOAN*	Within three weeks after the borrowing date, the member who borrowed the document should either return the document or extend the borrowing period. This is represented by for example the attribute *return_date* of *LOAN*.
	SUPPLY	A supplier has a contract to supply a business with a certain product at a certain price every week.
Permission	*READ_ACC-ESS*	A user has read access to a file.
Prohibition	*BLOCKING*	An account owner is not allowed to withdraw money from an account.
Instantia-tion	*copy*	A document is a copy of a title.
Representa-tion	*pass*	A member pass represents a member in transactions with the library.
Specializa-tion	*is_a*	A car is a special kind of vehicle.
Role playing	*played_by*	An employee role is played by a person.

Figure 7.4: Examples of frequently occurring kinds of relationships.

converse is not true in general: If a *MEMBER* and a *DOCUMENT* exist, then there does not necessarily exist a *LOAN* link between them. Figure 7.4 shows some frequently encountered relationships.

7.5.2 Representations

Binary relationships can be represented by a line connecting the related entity types, as shown in figure 7.5. The line must be labeled by the name of the relationship, which must be a noun written in uppercase letters, and/or by the role played by at least one of the components in lowercase letters. The advantages of this representation are that it is visually simple and that the labels can be read in a natural way. The disadvantages are that we cannot show relationship attributes, and that we cannot use it to represent relationships with arity larger than 2.

These disadvantages are not present in the diamond representation shown in figure 7.6.

$$LOAN \subseteq borrower : MEMBER \times borrowed\_document : DOCUMENT$$

Figure 7.5: A binary relationship represented by a line, and its corresponding textual declaration.

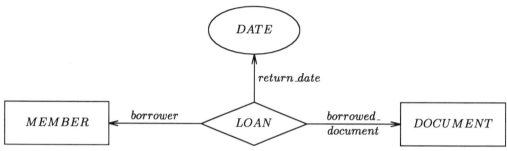

$$LOAN \subseteq borrower : MEMBER \times borrowed\_document : DOCUMENT$$
$$LOAN(return\_date : DATE)$$

Figure 7.6: Diamond representation of relationships. In any state of the UoD, the arrows represent projection functions on the existence set of the relationship.

In the diamond representation, we must label the arrows with the corresponding role names. If there is no danger of ambiguity, the arrows may be unlabeled. The diamond representation represents the role names, can represent attributes and can be used for relationships of any arity. Its disadvantage is that it is visually restless. The arrows from the relationship diamond to the component types are projection functions that retrieve a component from a cartesian product. For example, *borrower* is a function

$$borrower : ext_\sigma(LOAN) \rightarrow ext_\sigma(MEMBER)$$

and we have borrower

$$\langle borrowed\_document : d, borrower : m \rangle = m.$$

Figure 7.7 shows an ER diagram in which two of the role names are shown; without these role names, it would be impossible to find out from the diagram what the role of two companies in a *DELIVERY* link is. An instance of *DELIVERY* has the form

$$\langle supplier : s, transport\_company : c, PROJECT : p, PART : q \rangle$$

7.6   Cardinality Constraints

7.6.1   Representations

A **cardinality constraint** is a constraint on the cardinality of existence sets in an ER model. An example of a cardinality constraint on the existence set of an entity type is:

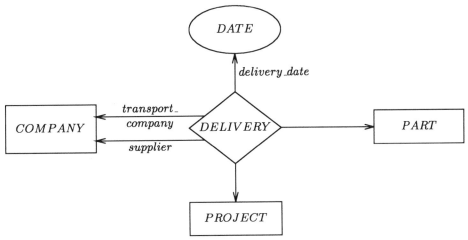

$DELIVERY \subseteq supplier : COMPANY \times transport\_company : COMPANY \times$
$PROJECT \times PART$
$DELIVERY(delivery\_date : DATE)$

Figure 7.7: A relationship with arity 4.

- The number of documents with a publication date before 1900 is less than 10 000.

Most cardinality constraints state that the number of entities with a certain property is restricted in a certain way. In most examples, this property is that the entity must be linked in a certain way to something else. Most cardinality constraints are therefore constraints on the existence set of relationships. Two examples follow:

- A document is borrowed by at most one member at the same time.

- One member can borrow at most 20 documents at the same time.

Figure 7.8 shows the representation of cardinalities in the line and the diamond representation of relationships. Reading from left to right in the line representation, we read that an existing member can borrow 0, 1, ..., or 20 existing documents. Reading from right to left, we get that an existing document is borrowed by 0 or 1 existing members. In the diamond representation, the cardinalities are placed at the roots of the arrows, so that the same cardinality constraints are represented. For example, going from $MEMBER$ to $LOAN$, we read that each existing member is the borrower component of 0, 1, ..., or 20 existing $LOAN$ links; continuing from $LOAN$ to $DOCUMENT$, we read that each existing $LOAN$ has exactly one existing $DOCUMENT$ component. As a consequence, each existing member can borrow 0, 1, ..., or 20 existing documents.

The specification of cardinality constraints obviously depends upon our definition of identity criteria, because these constraints tell us how many different instances can have a certain property. Less obviously, cardinality constraints also depend upon our definition of existence. In the model of figure 7.8, currently existing members can borrow up to 20 currently existing documents, and currently existing documents can be borrowed by at

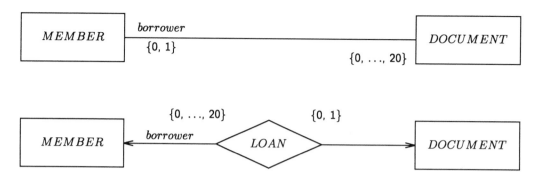

Figure 7.8: Relationship cardinalities. In the diamond representation, the cardinalities are placed at the roots of the arrows.

Cardinality set	is represented as
$\{0, 1\}$	0, 1
$\{1\}$	1
$\{1, 2, \ldots\}$	≥ 1
$\{0, 1, 2, 3, \ldots\}$	(Omitted from diagram.)
$\{0, \ldots, n\}$	$\leq n$
$\{n, n+1, \ldots\}$	$\geq n$

Figure 7.9: Frequently occurring cardinality constraints.

most one currently existing member. This is true in the UoD, but if we turn to a computer-based system, the situation may be different. For example, in a historical database system, all *LOAN* instances are stored even after the loan in the UoD has ceased to exist. In that database system, one *DOCUMENT* surrogate may be related to any number of *MEMBER* surrogates through different *LOAN* links. The model of figure 7.8 would not be a valid representation of this situation.

7.6.2   Special cardinalities

Cardinality constraints can always be represented in a diagram by sets of natural numbers. A number of common cardinality sets are represented in a simpler way without the curly brackets, as shown in figure 7.9. For example, in figure 7.10, each existing order has at least one existing order line and each existing order line belongs to exactly one existing order. An existing order line is for exactly one existing product, but an existing product can occur in any number of existing order lines, including 0. This cardinality information also gives us some information about existence constraints: an order cannot exist without at least one existing order line, and an existing order line cannot exist without a corresponding existing order. An order line cannot exist without a corresponding existing product, but a product can very well exist without being ordered for. The relationship between *ORDER* and *ORDER_LINE* is often called a **master-detail** relationship. All global information such as customer address and order number is attached to *ORDER* (the master), and all detail information is attached to *ORDER_LINE* instances.

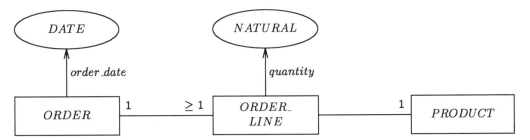

Figure 7.10: A master-detail relationship between $ORDER$ and $ORDER\_LINE$.

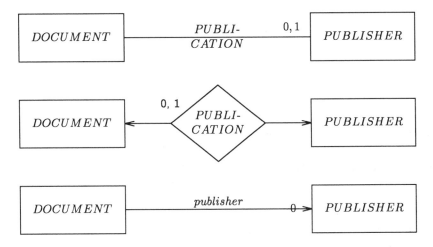

Figure 7.11: Representations of partial many-one relationship, also called partial functions.

For some of the special cardinalities shown in the table above, we can use an *arrow* representation as an alternative to the line and diamond representations. In the following paragraphs, we give a number of examples.

Many-one relationships

Figure 7.11 shows three representations of a **partial many-one** relationship, also called a **partial function**. A partial many-one relationship from $DOCUMENT$ to $PUBLISHER$ relates each existing document to at most one existing publisher. The function is partial because there are documents that have no publisher. In general, in each state σ of the world, a partial many-one relationship from E_1 to E_2 is a partial function

$$ext_{\sigma}(E_1) \rightarrow ext\_\sigma(E_2).$$

The partiality is represented in the arrow representation by writing a 0 through the head of the arrow in the diagram. It is customary to drop the adjective "partial", but we will not follow this custom.

Figure 7.12 shows three representations of a **total many-one** relationship, also called a **total function**. A total many-one relationship from $DOCUMENT$ to $TITLE$ relates each existing document to exactly one existing $TITLE$. The function is total because each

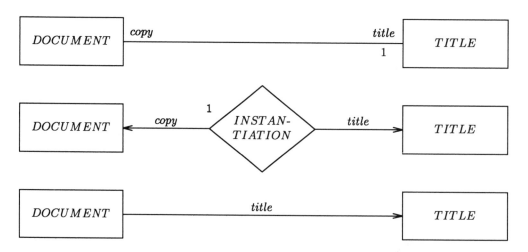

Figure 7.12: Representations of a total many-one relationship type (also called total function).

existing document has a title. In general, in any state σ of the world, a total many-one relationship from E_1 to E_2 is a total function $ext_\sigma(E_1) \rightarrow ext\_\sigma(E_2)$. A master-detail relationship is always a total many-one function from detail to master.

Independently from the distinction between partial and total many-one relationships, we can distinguish injective and surjective many-one relationships. Figure 7.13 shows three representations of an **injective many-one** relationship, also called an **injective function**. The diagram says that each existing manager manages at most one existing department. This means that different existing departments are managed by different existing managers. This is the distinguishing feature of injective many-one relationship types: if E_1 has an injective many-one relationship to E_2, then different existing instances of E_1 cannot be related to the same instance of E_2.

Finally, figure 7.14 shows three representations of a **surjective many-one** relationship (which happens to be total), also called a **surjective function**. The diagram says that each existing university has at least one existing faculty. This means that the function assigning universities to faculties goes *onto* the existence set of $UNIVERSITY$: there is no university that does not participate in the $DECOMPOSITION$ link with at least one faculty. In general, if E_1 has a surjective many-one relationship R to E_2, then instance of E_2 cannot exist without participating in R.

One-one relationships

In addition to many-one relationships, we are interested in one-one and in many-many relationships. A relationship is called **partial one-one** if it has cardinality 0, 1 at one or both sides. If both sides have cardinality 1, then we call it a **total one-one** or a **bijective function**. Figure 7.15 shows three representations of a total one-one relationship.

Many-many relationships

Any binary relationship that is not many-one or one-one is called **many-many**. Figure 7.16 shows two representations of a many-many relationship. Note that by the component exis-

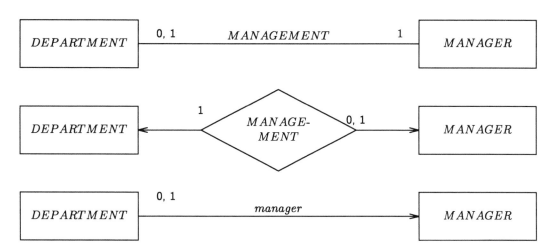

Figure 7.13: An injective many-one relationship, also called an injective function (which happens to be total).

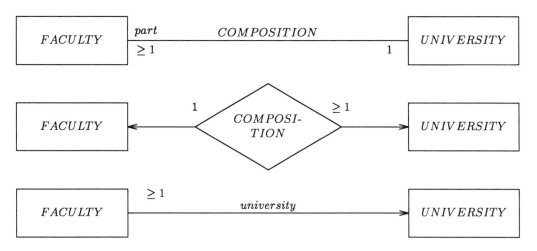

Figure 7.14: A surjective many-one relationship, also called a surjective function (which happens to be total).

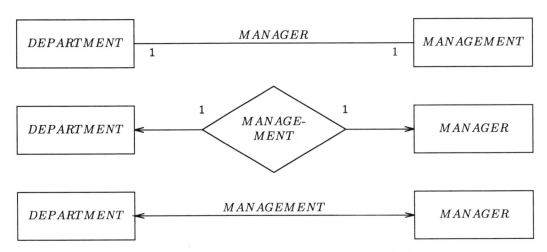

Figure 7.15: A total one-one relationship (also called a bijective function).

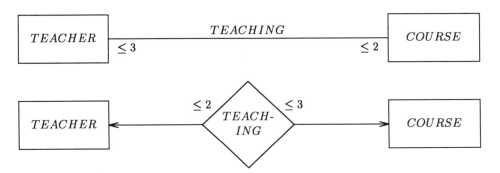

Figure 7.16: Two representations of a many-many relationship.

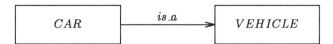

Figure 7.17: Representation of specialization and generalization. Each CAR instance is identical to a $VEHICLE$ instance. Note that the cardinality $\{0, 1\}$ of is_a has been omitted.

tence assumption, the projection functions of any relationship are total (for every existing link, they will yield an existing component).

7.7 The is_a Relationship

There is one function that deserves special mention: the is_a relationship. An is_a relationship from E_1 to E_2 is the inclusion function from the extension of E_1 to the extension of E_2. In other words, we have E_1 is_a E_2 if and only if

$$ext(E_1) \subseteq ext(E_2).$$

We call E_1 a **specialization** of E_2 and E_2 a **generalization** of E_1. In figure 7.17, each possible instance of CAR is identical to an instance of $VEHICLE$. This means that if we look at a CAR, what we see is (also) a $VEHICLE$. Note that for convenience, we drop the cardinality $\{0, 1\}$ from the diagram.

Note that all *possible* instances of a specialization are identical to an instance of the generalization. If all existing students in the current state of the world happen to be male persons, we cannot conclude that $STUDENT$ is_a $MALE$. To draw such a conclusion, it must be true that all *possible* students are males.

The is_a from a specialization to a generalization is a special relationship, because its instances are identity links of the form $\langle x, x \rangle$ for an entity x. To check whether E_1 is a specialization of E_2 we must ask whether an instance of E_1 is also an instance of E_2.

7.8 Methodological Analysis

7.8.1 The place of ER models in the behavior specification framework

In figure 4.3, we showed a simple framework for behavior specifications, that distinguished specifications of a system from UoD specifications and, independently from that, a static and a dynamic dimension of the specified systems. ER models can be used to specify the state space of the UoD as well as of the system under development (SuD). The state of the SuD or the UoD is represented by

1. the set of entities that exist in that state and

2. the state of each existing entity.

System dynamics is not modeled in the ER approach. For example, it is not represented which updates are possible, what is the effect of the updates on the system state, and what constraints there are, if any, on updates.

7.8.2   Cardinality constraints

There are many cardinality constraints that are not expressible as cardinality constraints on the existence set of relationships but are nevertheless relevant:

- Constraints on the maximum and average number of existing instances of an entity or relationship.

- If R is a relationship from E_1 to E_2, then we can give the average number of instances of E_2 linked by R to an existing instance of E_1.

- Constraints on the frequency with which entities or links are created, deleted or updated.

These constraints are often regarded as constraints on the implementation of the SuD, but this is not necessarily the case. All of the above constraints have a meaningful interpretation in the UoD of the system.

7.8.3   Constraints on the UoD and constraints on the system

ER models can represent the state space of the SuD or the UoD of the SuD. We saw that there is an important difference in the meaning of the statement "an instance of E exists" when interpreted as a statement about the UoD and when interpreted as a statement about the SuD. A UoD instance of E can exist even if no system instance of E (i.e. a surrogate) exists and vice versa.

The difference is even more dramatic when we look at the meaning of cardinality constraints. Take the statement

- A member has at most one *LOAN* link to the same document at the same time.

Interpreted as a statement about the UoD, this is an analytical truth that follows from the meaning of the words used in it. Assuming that the statement is interpreted in the normal way, it is impossible that it is falsified by a state of the UoD. On the other hand, interpreted as a statement about a system that represents a UoD, it is a constraint on the valid states of that system. It is quite possible that the system contains several *LOAN* links between the same member and the same document surrogate at the same time. Take as a second example the statement

- A member has at most 10 000 *LOAN* links to documents at the same time.

(This statement is implied by the constraint that a member has at most 20 *LOAN* links to documents at the same time. If a member cannot borrow more than 20 documents, he or she cannot borrow more than 10 000 documents.) As a statement about the UoD, this statement is always true. However, its truth does not follow from the meaning of the words used in it, but from observations of the UoD. We have never observed a falsification of this statement in the UoD and we can safely assume that we never will observe a falsification in the UoD. On the other hand, interpreted as a statement about the SuD, it is a constraint on the valid states of that system. It is quite possible that the system contains more than 10 000 *LOAN* links between a member surrogate and document surrogates at the same time.

Let us call statements that are true in all states of a system **regularities** of the system. The above two statements are examples of regularities about the UoD but thethere are also regularities that apply to the SuD. For example all laws of mechanics and electronics are regularities in the behavior of the system.

Regularities must be constrasted with **norms**, which are statements that we would *like* to be true of a system, but that may be violated. The very same statement may be a regularity when interpreted in the UoD but a norm when interpreted in the SuD. For example, the two example statements used above are regularities in the UoD but they are norms for the SuD. The name "cardinality constraint" for those two statements is therefore not accurate. A more accurate term would be **cardinality statement**. Depending upon our interpretation, a cardinality statement could be a **cardinality regularity** in the UoD or a **cardinality constraint** on the UoD or on the SuD. However, unless explicitly stated otherwise, we will follow accepted usage and use the term "cardinality constraint" for cardinality regularities as well.

An interesting methodological consequence of this analysis is that a good justification of interpreting a sentence as a norm for a computer-based system is that the sentence expresses a regularity in the UoD of that system. Because the system represents its UoD, we know that if the system falsifies the sentence, it cannot be in a state that represents a UoD state. Of course, there are many other good justifications for interpreting a sentence as a norm for the system. For example all product objectives are norms for the system because they help in realizing business goals.

The UoD is also subject to norms. Take the following example statement:

- A borrowed document must be returned within three weeks of the borrowing date.

This is a norm for the UoD that can easily be falsified by the UoD. Such a falsification must be represented by the system, and therefore cannot be treated as a norm for the system. Indeed, an important function of the system is precisely to represent these violations and signal them to library personnel. There are also UoD norms that *are* translated into system norms. Take the following example:

- A member has at most 20 *LOAN* links to documents at the same time.

This is a norm for the UoD that can easily be falsified. If this norm is not effectively enforced by the library, the system may validly represent 21 *LOAN* links between a member and documents at the same time. However, an important means to enforce this norm is to let the system refuse to register a borrowing if this would result in a violation of this constraint. Thus, this UoD norm is translated into a system norm. These two examples show that UoD norms may or may not be translated into system norms. Thus, it is *not* a good justification of interpreting a sentence as a norm for a computer-based system that the sentence expresses a norm for the UoD of that system.

7.9 Summary

The set of all possible things is partitioned into *ER entities*, which are observable parts of the UoD, and *values*, which are unobservable. The concept of an ER entity is thus the same as that of a system defined in chapter 2. ER entities have *attributes*, which are types of non-disturbing observations, and attributes have *values*, which represent possible observations of the ER entity. ER entities and values are instances of *types*. A type is the set of properties shared by its instances. ER entities may be related through *links*. The type of a link is called a *relationship*.

An ER model may represent the state space of a computer-based system or of its UoD. Instances of a type may exist in the UoD or in the system; in the second case, they are called *surrogates* for UoD instances.

An *identifier* of an entity type is an attribute that has different values for different instances, always has the same value for the same instance, and that is never changed. Links have no independent identity nor an independent existence. The identity of a link is the tuple of identities of its components. A link can only exist if its component ER entities exist. Relationships may represent part-of relations, events, durations, permissions, obligations, etc.

UoD instances (entities or links) are identified by an *external identifier*, which is visible for the user and assigned by some external authority. Surrogates are identified by an *internal identifier*, which is invisible to the user and assigned by the system itself. A combination of attributes whose values are unique on existing ER entities of a type in each state of the world is called a *key* of that type. Key values may change from time to time, and key values may also be reused.

Cardinality constraints of relationship R limit the set of existing ER entities related with each other through instances of R. By means of cardinalities we can distinguish many-one, one-one and many-many relationships. For the first two kinds of relationships, we can distinguish partial, total, injective and surjective variants.

A special kind of relationship is the *is_a* function. It is the inclusion function from the extension of a *specialization* to the extension of a *generalization*. To test if a relationship is an *is_a* relationship, we must test whether each instance of the specialization is identical to an instance of the generalization.

ER models can be used to represent the state space of a computer-based system or of its UoD. The existence of a UoD entity need not coincide in time with the existence of its surrogate in the system. Cardinality constraints should be more accurately called cardinality statements. A statement that expresses a *regularity* about the UoD can be used as a *constraint* on the system. A sentence that expresses a constraint on the UoD may or may not be interpreted as a constraint on the system. This depends upon the desired functions of the system.

7.10   Exercises

1. Discuss possible identification criteria for $DOCUMENT$, $TITLE$ and $JOURNAL$.

2. Add cardinality constraints to the diagram of figure 6.11 interpreted first as a model of the UoD, and next as a model of the system. In both cases, motivate your choice of constraints.

3. Draw ER diagrams of the example relationships in figure 7.4. Include cardinality constraints for the case that the relationship is interpreted in the UoD, and for the case that the relationship is interpreted in the system. In both cases, motivate your choice of constraints.

4. Consider figure 7.7. One of the following two constraints cannot be expressed as a cardinality constraint in the diagram. Which one? Explain your answer.

(a) A supplier cannot deliver parts to more than two projects.

(b) A supplier cannot deliver the same part to more than two projects.

5. We can use the *is_a* relationship to eliminate *null* values of the type *not applicable*. Explain how this can be done.

6. A diagram containing a partial function from E_1 to E_2 can always be replaced by an equivalent diagram containing only total functions. Explain how this can be done.

7. Suppose that we allow relations to be components of other relations. Use this construct to change the model in figure 7.7 so that, without using *null* values, we can represent the situation in which a transport company has not yet been selected for the delivery, but the supplier, part and project are selected, as well as the situation in which the transport company has been selected.

8. Change the model in figure 7.6 so that historical information about loans can be maintained. What should be the cardinality constraints in this new model?

9. What is the difference between the referential integrity constraint in relational database theory and the component existence constraint defined in this chapter?

10. There is a connection between many–many relationships and the fourth normal form of relational database theory. Explain this connection.

11. Some of the following sentences can be interpreted as sentences about the UoD or sentences about a database system. In the first case, they can be interpreted as constraints or as regularities, in the second case, they must be interpreted as constraints. For each sentence, answer the following questions:

(a) Can it be interpreted as a regularity in the UoD?

(b) If so, what are the consequences of interpreting it as a constraint on the system?

(c) Can the sentence be interpreted as a constraint on the UoD?

(d) If so, what are the consequences of interpreting it as a constraint on the system?

Answer these questions for the following sentences.

- Less then 100 students follow course CS101 every year.
- Course CS100 is a prerequisite for course CS101.
- Students always follow CS100 before they follow CS101.

7.11   Bibliographical Remarks

Models of UoD semantics. The ER approach is not the only modeling method that proposed a level of modeling above that of the relational model. In addition to the ER approach, Nijssen developed NIAM [243, 244] (Nijssen's Information Analysis Method), also known as the **binary relationship method**. NIAM has evolved into what is now often called a **fact-based approach** or a **role modeling approach**. Another influential approach stemming from the mid-70s is the study of aggregation and generalization structures in UoD models by Smith and Smith [320, 321], who used techniques from artificial intelligence to add more semantics to data models.

Introductions to ER modeling. The ER approach originates with Chen's 1976 paper [65]. The *International Conference on the Entity-Relationship Approach to Systems Analysis and Design* has been held since 1980 [64]. Navathe and Elmasri [94] give a good introduction in two chapters. A good book-length introduction is given by Batini, Ceri and Navathe [25]. This includes integration with data flow models and transformation of ER models into relational, network and hierarchical models. Teory [338] has a less wide scope and concentrates on a method of implementing an ER model into a relational database system. Rosemary Rock-Evans [280, 281] gives a very elaborate and practical introduction to ER modeling and its place in the system development life cycle.

Different definitions of "ER entity." There is no universally accepted definition of "entity" in the ER approach. The ambiguity can in most cases be resolved if we ask whether "entity" is used to refer to a type or to an individual, and whether it is used to refer to something in the system or in the UoD. This gives four possible meanings of "entity," all of which occur in the literature.

1. *Individual in the UoD.* Chen [65, page 10] defines an entity as "a 'thing' which can be distinctly identified." Elmasri and Navathe [94, page 40] define an entity as "a 'thing' in the real world with independent existence."

2. *An individual in the system.* Elmasri and Navathe [94, page 42] talk about entities as if they exist in the database system: "A database will usually contain groups of entities that are similar."

3. *A type in the UoD.* Batini, Ceri and Navathe [25, page 31] say that "entities represent classes of real-world objects." Instances of this type are called "entity occurrences".

4. *A type in the system.* Storey and Goldstein [328, page 307] define an entity as "a 'thing' of interest in a database, for example *STUDENT*." An entity occurrence is now a record in the database system.

A fifth meaning is also sometimes used, illustrated by the following quotation from Chen [65]: "Let *e* denote an entity which exists in our minds ⋯" I use the following terms for these different concepts.

Entity concept	Term used in this book
1. An individual in the represented UoD.	ER entity, system.
2. An individual in the database system.	Symbol, data item, ER entity, surrogate, system.
3. A type in the represented UoD.	ER entity type, system type.
4. A type in the database system.	Data type, ER entity type, surrogate type, system type.
5. An individual mental concept.	—

Entities, identity and surrogates The concept of identity is discussed in the context of object-oriented programming by Khoshafian and Copeland [178]. Some of these ideas go back to a paper by Hall, Owlett and Todd [134], who introduced the concept of the surrogate.

Figure 7.18: Mandatory participation in a link.

Surrogates are also used by Codd in RM/T [70]. A clear discussion of the concept of identity in object-oriented databases and models is given by Kent [176, 177]. The concept of identity as presented in this chapter comes from Wieringa and De Jonge [365]. An interesting paper which also argues for the need to distinguish objects from values is MacLennan [207].

Mandatory (total) and optional (partial) participation. It is customary to distinguish mandatory from optional participation of an entity in a link. For example, in figure 7.18, *EMPLOYEE* participates **mandatorily** in *EMPLOYMENT* and *DEPARTMENT* participates **optionally** in *EMPLOYMENT*. This is because an employee cannot exist without participating in at least one existing *EMPLOYMENT* instance. In the terminology of this chapter, the projection function from *EMPLOYMENT* to *EMPLOYEE* is *surjective*. An alternative terminology often used is that *EMPLOYEE* participates **totally** in *EMPLOYMENT* and *DEPARTMENT* participates **partially** in *EMPLOYMENT*. I refrain from using this terminology because it does not add anything to what we can already express and because it may confuse things by using "total" in the meaning of "surjective".

Differences in graphical representation techniques. There is a lot of difference in graphical representation techniques within the ER approach. Figure 7.19 shows some alternative ways to depict many-one cardinality of a binary relationship. Using diamonds for relationships, a commonly used convention is the one at the bottom of figure 7.20. Another convention used is to limit cardinality sets to *closed intervals*, which are then represented by their lower and upper bounds (figure 7.21). Most confusing are the alternative conventions for contingent participation in a relationship, shown in figure 7.22. The bottom two conventions represent, equivalently, that each E_1 *may* be related to *one* or more E_2. They put the *may* at the E_1 side, which distributes the representation of the cardinality constraint over two places.

The technique used in this book is motivated by the fact that in using it, all arrows in a diagram represent functions and all cardinalities are denoted and interpreted in a single, uniform way. This allows borrowing the terminology from mathematics about partial, total, injective, surjective and bijective functions, which have clear definitions and known properties. It also facilitates implementation because functions from entity types to entity types can always be represented by pointer-like constructs like location-independent surrogate references. Functions from entity types to value types are always represented by attribute values. Using arrows instead of undirected lines also indicates in which direction we have to read the names along the arrows. Finally, the representation technique used here puts the cardinalities at the place where they most naturally belong. This is seen when you try to represent cardinalities for a relationship with arity greater than 2, using the techniques of figure 7.20. Only the top representation, which is the one used in this book, scales up

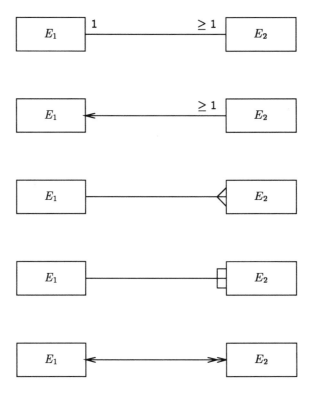

Figure 7.19: Alternative representations of a many-one relationship. The two representations at the top follow the convention of this book.

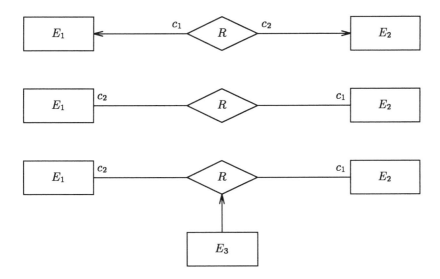

Figure 7.20: Three representations of binary relationship cardinalities using the diamond representation. Some authors use the diagram at the bottom for the case where R has attributes. These attributes are not attached to R but to E_3, which is called an "associative entity". We use the representation at the top.

naturally to relationships of higher arity.

Cardinality constraints and regularities.   The distinction between constraints and regularities was introduced by Wieringa, Meyer and Weigand [366] and is further elaborated by Wieringa [362]. Liddle, Embley and Woodfield [192] give an exhaustive classification of cardinality statements.   Thalheim [340] gives a formalization and defines some intricate types of constraints not present in the classification given by Liddle *et al.*

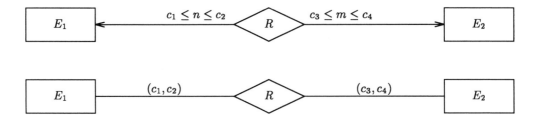

Figure 7.21: Interval representation of cardinality constraints (bottom) and its arrow equivalent (top). The representation at the top follows the convention of this book.

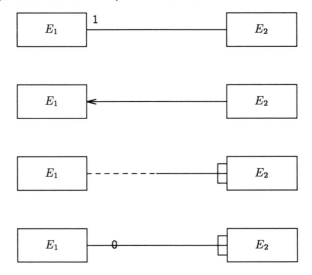

Figure 7.22: Different representations for optional participation of E_1 in a relationship. Each convention intends to express the fact that each existing E_1 is related to zero or more existing E_2's. The two representations at the top follow the conventions of this book.

8

The Entity-Relationship
Approach II: Methods

8.1 Introduction

There is no single method for ER modeling, but there are many heuristics proposed by
many different researchers. In this chapter, we gather a number of these heuristics and
group them into two classes: heuristics for finding an ER model (section 8.2) and heuristics
for evaluating an ER model (section 8.3). In section 8.4, we show how an ER model of a
database system can be transformed into a relational database schema. ER models can be
made of a computer-based system or of its UoD. Because the first can only be found by
way of the second, we restrict ourselves to finding an ER model of the UoD of a system.
Section 8.5 contains a methodological analysis of the heuristics discussed in this chapter.

8.2 Methods to Find an ER Model

There are four methods to find an ER model of a UoD (figure 8.1).

- In **entity analysis of transactions**, required system transactions are analyzed on
  which data they manipulate.

- In **natural language analysis**, one analyzes natural language sentences on words
  that indicate entity types and relationships.

- In **form analysis**, forms used within a business are analyzed to discover the structure
  of the data entered on these forms.

- In **record analysis**, record declarations in a database schema are analyzed to discover
  their structure.

In addition, if one has built a number of ER models of different parts of the same UoD,
using one or more of the above methods, then one can merge these different ER models into
a more complex model of that UoD. This is called **view integration**. In this chapter, we

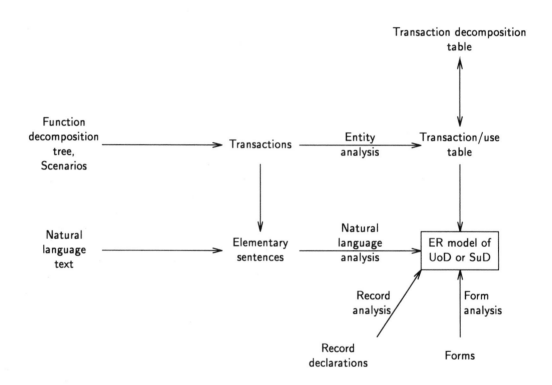

Figure 8.1: A road map of methods to find an ER model.

- **Elementary sentences.** Transform sentences into elementary sentences (sentences that contain one main verb).

- **Common nouns.** A common noun in an elementary sentence usually represents an ER entity type.

- **Transitive verbs.** A transitive verb in an elementary sentence usually indicates an action in which a link is created.

- **Adjectives.** An adjective in an elementary sentence usually represents an attribute of an ER entity type.

- **Adverbs.** An adverb in an elementary sentence usually represents an attribute of a relationship.

Figure 8.2: Heuristics for natural language analysis.

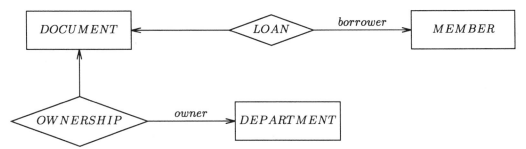

Figure 8.3: An ER diagram made using the noun and verb heuristics.

discuss the first of the two methods above. Pointers to the literature on the other methods are given in section 8.8.

8.2.1 Natural language analysis

Natural language analysis is a method to produce an ER model from a text written in natural language. There is no fixed sequence of steps to natural language analysis, but there are common heuristics, shown in figure 8.2 [66].

As an example of the elementary sentence heuristic, consider the statement

(1) A document is owned by a department and may be borrowed by a library member.

This can be transformed into the following two elementary sentences:

- A document is owned by a department.

- A document may be borrowed by a library member.

Using the common noun and transitive verb heuristics of figure 8.2, this gives us the ER diagram in figure 8.3. Note that the verb *borrow* corresponds to the relationship *LOAN* because a borrow action creates a *LOAN* instance. As an example of the adjective and adverb heuristics, the sentence

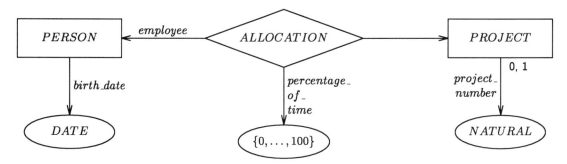

Figure 8.4: An ER diagram made using the adjective and adverb heuristics.

(2) A 40-year old person works on a project with project number 2175 for 20% of his time

leads to the ER diagram in figure 8.4. We used some background knowledge that we share with whoever produced sentence (2): we know that persons have a birth date and that the age of a person is the number of years that the birth year is past. Similarly, some shared background knowledge about percentages and people's ages was used to define the codomains of *age* and *percentage_of_time*. This shared background knowledge is part of an implicit conceptual model of the UoD shared with the people who produced sentence (2).

Using our background knowledge, we also assumed that all existing projects are identified by their project number. This is represented in the diagram by the cardinality constraint $\{0, 1\}$ of the *project_number* attribute. We have not attached a cardinality constraint to an attribute before, but the meaning of this is clear: each natural number is a project number of at most one existing *PROJECT* instance. We must verify with the domain specialists whether this is true, and whether project numbers of past projects can be reused.

An advantage of natural language analysis is that it is simple. A disadvantage is that it may lead to many irrelevant ER entity types and relationships. For example, sentence (3) may very well occur in a statement of information needs or in some other document describing the UoD:

(3) The database system shall register members of the library.

Applying natural language analysis, we find the following elementary sentences:

- The database system registers members.

- The library has members.

This gives the diagram shown in figure 8.5. Obviously, this represents irrelevant structures for almost any database system that is to be used by the library. The library has no database system that contains data about which members it registered in which database system, or about which library a person is a member of. Only if we wanted to make, say, a national database system that registers data about all libraries in the country, the database systems they use, and the library members registered in those database systems, would this diagram be relevant.

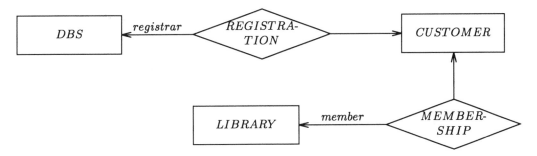

Figure 8.5: An ER diagram containing irrelevant types.

8.2.2   Natural language analysis of transactions

We can reduce the number of irrelevant entity and relationships found if we concentrate on a small number of highly relevant sentences. One set of highly relevant sentences is the set of **queries** of which we know beforehand that the required database system will have to answer them. This brand of natural language analysis is also called **query analysis**. For example, a database system for the library circulation desk must at least be able to answer the following queries:

- Which members have reserved this document?

- When is this document due for return?

- How many copies of this title are in the library?

This leads to such potentially relevant entity types as *MEMBER, DOCUMENT, COPY, TITLE* and *LIBRARY*. Further investigation should reveal that *DOCUMENT* and *COPY* are the same, and that for the reason mentioned above, *LIBRARY* is irrelevant.

Query analysis can be generalized into a natural language analysis of all transactions. To do that, we must first find all required system transactions, including all database updates and queries. One way to find this out is to go through a number of **scenarios** that the system must be able to engage in. Another way is to start with the product idea and decompose it into required product transactions. We will list all possible starting points to find required system transactions in chapter 13.

Once we have a list of transactions, we can describe each transaction by means of an **elementary sentence**, which is a sentence consisting of a subject, verb and, possibly, an object. For example, two transactions that a student administration must be able to perform may be

- Enroll a student in a course.

- Register a student for a test.

Natural language analysis gives three relevant entity types, *STUDENT, COURSE* and *TEST*, and two relationships, *ENROLLMENT* and *TEST_REGISTRATION*.

8.2.3   Entity analysis of transactions

A second way to analyze transactions, which gives more information, is **entity analysis of transactions**. In this method, we write down for each transaction which entities or links are created, read, updated or deleted. We write this down in a table called a **transaction/use** table and use this as a source for entity types and relationships to put in an ER diagram. We illustrate this method by applying it to the student administration.

Figure 8.6 shows part of a function decomposition tree of a student administration. We focus on the middle branch, because the leaves of this branch are transactions that the administration must be able to perform. Figure 8.7 shows a transaction/use table that lists the entities or links created, read, updated or deleted *in the administration* by the transaction. Because of its format, the table can be easily constructed line by line. Note that the we focus upon *data* created, read, updated or deleted in the system itself. This is because we are analyzing transactions of the system, and these transactions have access to the data in the system, not to their entities and links in the UoD. For example, the system does not "read" the course in the UoD (whatever that may mean) but a course surrogate in the system. Nevertheless, this data represents entities or links in the UoD, and we therefore end up with a model of the UoD.

Building a transaction/use table is an iterative process in which we may have to back-track several times. It is likely to be performed in parallel with drawing an ER diagram of the contents of the table so far, because the diagram allows us to keep track of the contents of the table more easily.

The transaction/use table is equivalent to the **transaction decomposition table** shown in figure 8.8. The transaction decomposition table is called a *process/entity* matrix in Information Engineering, because transactions are called processes there; it is a more detailed version of the function/entity matrix made in ISP (chapter 6). The reason for calling it a transaction decomposition table is that each transaction is decomposed into actions performed on entities or links. The transaction decomposition table plays a central role in the integration of methods in chapter 13.

Figure 8.9 shows the ER diagram obtained from the transaction/use table. Inclusion of the attributes of the entity types and relationships would clutter up the diagram, so these have been added as textual declarations. Note the *null* value in two of the attribute result types. The reason they appear here is that *TEST_REG* and *PRACTICAL_REG* stand for *registration events*, whereas the *result* attributes are attributes of two other events that occur later, viz. doing the test and finishing the practical work. The ER method does not help in distinguishing these events. We return to this in chapter 13, where we discuss the integration of the ER method with Jackson System Development.

Building an ER diagram from a transaction/use table is not automatic. It requires analysis of the meaning of the names of the entity types and relationships. For example, by choosing to represent some types as relationships, decisions about (structured) identity have been made. As before, the modeler is not likely to get it right the first time.

8.2.4   Case study: the library

In this section, natural language analysis and entity analysis of transactions are used to find an ER model of the UoD of the circulation department of the library described in appendix B. We start with an entity analysis of transactions.

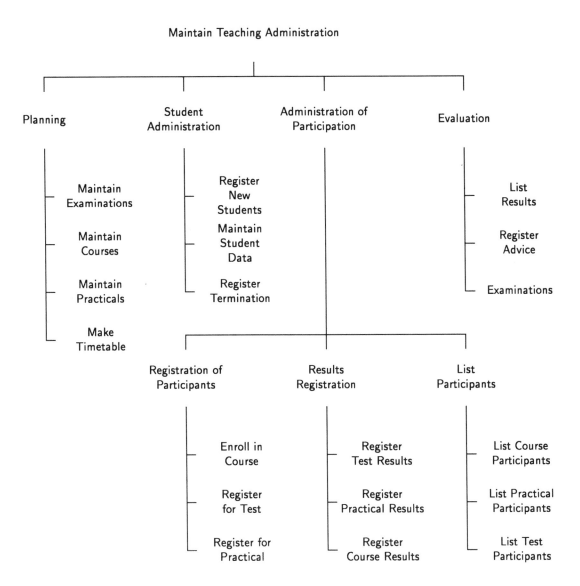

Figure 8.6: Fragment of a function decomposition tree of a student administration.

	Create	Read	Update	Delete
Enroll in course	*ENROLL-MENT*	*COURSE, STUDENT*		
Register for test	*TEST_REG*	*TEST, STUDENT*		
Register for practical	*PRACTICAL_REG*	*PRACTICAL, STUDENT*		
Register test result			*TEST_REG*	
Register course result			*ENROLL-MENT*	
Register practical result			*PRACTICAL_REG*	
List course participation		*ENROLL-MENT, STUDENT, COURSE*		
List test participation		*TEST_REG, STUDENT, TEST*		
List practical participation		*PRACTICAL_REG, STUDENT, PRACTICAL*		

Figure 8.7: A transaction/use table for the Administration of Participants. *TEST_REG* and *PRACTICAL_REG* stand for test registration and practical registration, respectively.

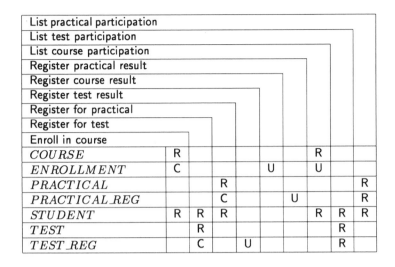

	Enroll in course	Register for test	Register for practical	Register test result	Register course result	Register practical result	List course participation	List test participation	List practical participation
COURSE	R						R		
ENROLLMENT	C				U		U		
PRACTICAL			R						R
PRACTICAL_REG			C			U			R
STUDENT	R	R	R				R	R	R
TEST		R						R	
TEST_REG		C		U				R	

Figure 8.8: A transaction decomposition table.

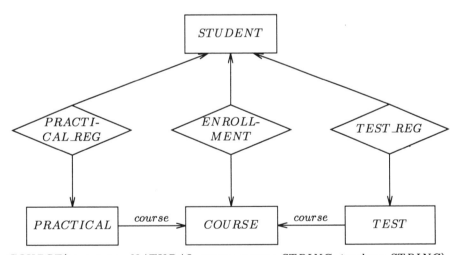

$COURSE(\underline{course\_nr} : NATURAL, course\_name : STRING, teacher : STRING)$
$ENROLLMENT(date : DATE)$
$PRACTICAL(starting\_date : DATE, duration : NATURAL)$
$PRACTICAL\_REG(result : NATURAL \cup \{null\})$
$STUDENT(\underline{student\_nr} : NATURAL, student\_address : STRING, parent\_address :$
$STRING, name : STRING)$
$TEST(date : DATE, room : STRING)$
$TEST\_REG(result : NATURAL \cup \{null\})$

Figure 8.9: ER diagram and attribute declarations.

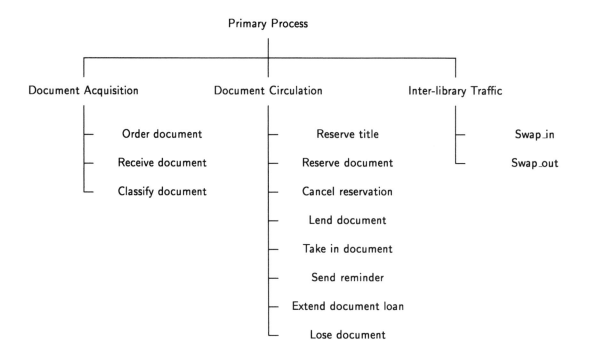

Figure 8.10: Decomposition of the primary process of the library to the level of transactions.

Entity analysis of transactions

In chapter 6, we gave a function decomposition of the library (figure 6.8). Figure 8.10 decomposes the primary process of the library to the level of transactions. Figure 8.11 contains the transaction/use table for the circulation desk database system. The relationships *T_RES* and *D_RES* represent title reservations and document reservations, respectively. The title reservation transaction needs data about members and documents to check if a member is allowed to place a reservation and whether no document of that title is available for borrowing. It creates a title reservation record if both checks are positive. Borrowing a document may cause deletion of a reservation link. Extending a document loan can only be done if there are no reservations for the title of that document, and if the member is allowed to extend the loan (so these records must be read). If these conditions are satisfied, the *LOAN* relationship is updated by setting a new return date. When a document is lost by a member, a *LOST* record is created that relates the lost document and the member, and a *FINE* is created that records the fine to be paid for this loss. The other entries of the table are self-explanatory.

Figure 8.12 shows an ER diagram for the types shown in the transaction/use table. It contains attributes and cardinality constraints. The presence of the entity type *DEPART-MENT* is the result of a natural language analysis of queries, explained below.

Natural language analysis of transactions

The following elementary sentences describe the circulation desk transactions of figure 8.10.

	Create	Read	Update	Delete
Reserve title	T_RES	TITLE, MEMBER, DOCUMENT		
Reserve document	D_RES	MEMBER, DOCUMENT	DOCUMENT	
Cancel reservation				T_RES, D_RES
Lend document	LOAN	T_RES, D_RES, MEMBER		T_RES, D_RES
Take in document				LOAN
Send reminder		LOAN, MEMBER	LOAN	
Extend document loan		T_RES, D_RES, LOAN, MEMBER	LOAN	
Lose document	LOSS, FINE	LOAN	DOCUMENT	LOAN

Figure 8.11: A transaction/use table for the circulation desk database system.

- A member reserves a title.

- A member reserves a document.

- A member extends the loan of a borrowed document.

- A member returns a document.

- A member loses a document.

- A reservation is canceled.

- A member is sent a reminder that a borrowing period has extended beyond the date that returning is due.

Most nouns and verbs in these sentences represent relevant entity- and relationships. However, even in these sentences, we find irrelevant nouns, that do not correspond to entity types, such as "reminder" and "period". Natural language analysis can at best be a heuristic that guides the modeler to some of the relevant entity types and relationships.

Not all relevant queries of the circulation desk database system have been included in the function decomposition tree. The following list gives some examples:

- Which documents are borrowed by a member?

- Which borrowings are overdue?

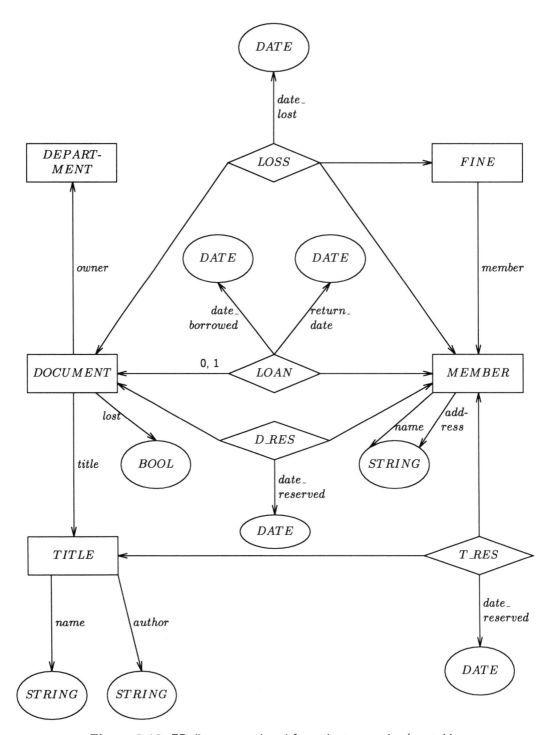

Figure 8.12: ER diagram produced from the transaction/use table.

- ER entities are observable, values are not.
- ER entities have a state, values do not.
- ER entities have an identity independent from their state, values *are* their identity.
- ER entities can interact with other ER entities, values cannot interact with anything.
- ER entities have a history and values do not.

Figure 8.13: Entity/value checks.

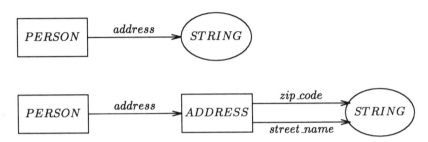

Figure 8.14: Modeling an address as an attribute value type or as an entity type.

- Who is the owner of this document?

Analysis of the last query shows that there must be an owner for each document. Further analysis then leads to the discovery of the entity type *DEPARTMENT*, related as *owner* to the documents it owns. This entity type was already included in figure 8.12.

8.3   Methods to Evaluate an ER Model

Like all models, ER models are found in many iterations and we must check their quality repeatedly before we can be sure that we have a valid model. In this section, we discuss the checks that can be applied to ER models.

8.3.1   Entity/value checks

A frequent dilemma in ER modeling is whether to model something as an ER entity or as a value. For example, should we model *ADDRESS* as a value type or as an entity type? Figure 8.13 gives some checks that we can use to determine whether we modeled something correctly as an entity or as a value type. These checks all follow from the definition of ER entities as observable parts of the world and from the definition of values as abstract, unobservable things.

To give an example of the application of the entity/value checks, how do we decide whether to model an address as an ER entity or as a value (figure 8.14)?

- As an ER entity, an address has a state, consisting of such information as its zip code, street name, etc.

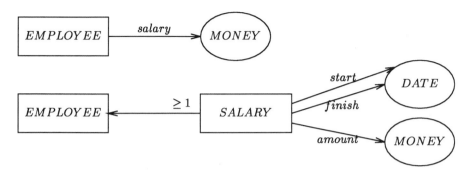

Figure 8.15: Two ways to represent the salary of an employee. In the second representation, salary is an entity type, because it has a history. We can represent the salary the employee had in different periods of time.

- As a value, an address does not have a state. It could be modeled as a value of type *STRING*, containing a zip code, street name etc. as substrings.

The difference between the two representations is that as an ER entity, one address *could* have had other values for its attributes *zip_code*, *street_name*, etc. If a government were to assign new zip codes to addresses, then this can be modeled without modeling at the same time that everybody is changing address. It is merely the states of addresses that would change, not the addresses themselves. This would not be possible if address were modeled as a value. Changing the zip code of an address is then strictly not possible: we can only replace one *STRING* representing an address by another that differs from the first one only in its zip code.

Another way to say the same thing is that ER entities have an identity. Saying that something has a state that *could* have been different, is tantamount to saying that there is something that remains identical to itself under changes of state. That is, ER entities have an identity that remains invariant under state change.

Taking yet another view on the same difference, ER entities can initiate or suffer events (which may change the state of the entity), but values cannot. This means that ER entities can *interact* with other ER entities. An address modeled as an ER entity will be able to participate in an interaction like *observe_zip_code* with an observer who reads the zip code, and it can engage in interactions like *change_zip_code* and *change_street_name*, in which the zip code or street name is changed. Since interaction is regarded in this book as the same thing as observation, we can also say that ER entities can be observed and values cannot — which is their definition to begin with.

But when ER entities have a state, they potentially have a *history*. An address modeled as an ER entity can suffer the event *change_zip_code* but an address modeled as a *STRING* cannot. If we model an address as an ER entity, then we can model its history as the trace of events which occurred in its life. This difference is illustrated in figure 8.15, using a *salary* attribute as example. In one representation, *salary* is an attribute that can have different values at different times. The history of these values is not represented. In the second representation, salary is an entity type, because it has a history. We can represent the salary the employee had in different periods of time. Note, incidentally, that *MONEY* is a value type in both representations.

- The identity of a link is a labeled tuple of the identities of its components. An ER entity is not composed of another identity.

Figure 8.16: Entity/link check.

Relationship	Components
LOAN	Member, document
WRITE_PERMISSION	User, file
PART_OF	Car, engine
MEMBERSHIP	Student, student society
ER entity type	"Components"
DEPARTMENT	Department members
CAR	Engine, wheels, ...
SCHOOL	Faculties

Figure 8.17: Some entity types and relationships.

8.3.2 Entity/link checks

Another dilemma in making an ER model is the decision whether to model something as an ER entity or as a link. Figure 8.16 gives the only difference between ER entities and links. The dependent identity check is an immediate consequence of the definition of links in chapter 7. It is stated in terms of identities instead of identifiers, because the decision concerns the entities themselves, not their names. Of course, modeling something as an ER entity or a link has a consequence for the structure of their identifiers. As an example of the application of the entity/link check, take the types in figure 8.17. All of the instances of the types in the table can be viewed as having *components* in some sense of the word. The difference is that instances of the first four types are identified by means of their components, whereas instances of the last three types are identified independently from the identity of their components. A document loan is identified by identifying the document and the member who borrows it, a write permission is identified by identifying the file and the user who has the permission, etc. We cannot replace the document identifier in a *LOAN* link by another document identifier without destroying the link and replacing it with another one. By contrast, a car does not become another car when parts are replaced, a school keeps its identity when faculties are added or deleted, and a department does not become another department when members leave it.

Historical relationships

A link is identified by its components. This means that every time the same components enter into a relationship, the *same* link exists. The upper diagram in figure 8.18 shows the *LOAN* relationship between a member and a document. If the same member borrows the same document at different times, then the existence set of *LOAN* contains, at different times, the same instance of *LOAN*. It is impossible that the existence set of *LOAN*

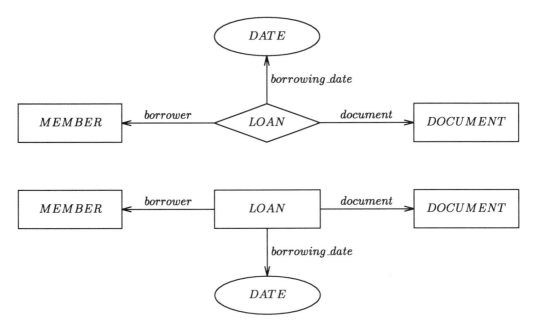

Figure 8.18: Different occurrences of a link (e.g. at different times) cannot be distinguished. In the entity representation, the occurrences are different entities.

contains both "copies" of this instance at the same time, for it is a *set*. That is, the set $\{\langle borrower : m, document : d \rangle, \langle borrower : m, document : d \rangle\}$ is equal to the set $\{\langle borrower : m, document : d \rangle\}$, even if both links existed at different times (and therefore have a different *borrowing_date* attribute). We cannot therefore represent the history of the link in an ER diagram.

One way to be able to represent the history of an instance is to model it as an entity type, as shown in the lower diagram. In this case, a *LOAN* instance has an identity that is independent from its state and different from all other *LOAN* instance identities. The elements of an existence set of *LOAN* are identifiers l_1, l_2, ..., some of which may have the same *borrower* and *document* attribute values. Those with the same *borrower* and *document* attribute values are historical occurrences of the same link. This representation has, however, the disadvantage that we can now have two different instances of *LOAN* (with different identifiers) with the same *borrowing_date*. This situation is correctly excluded by the relationship representation. In addition, we cannot count the number of existing loans by counting the members of the existence set of *LOAN*, because some members of this existence set may represent loan links that existed in the past. The identity information of different occurrences of one borrowing link is therefore not properly represented.

Another possible way to represent a historical link is to represent *LOAN* as a ternary relationship between *MEMBER*, *DOCUMENT* and *DATE*. The *borrowing_date* of the *LOAN* instance is now a component rather than an attribute. This means that the identifier of *LOAN* instances has the form

$$\langle borrower : m, document : d, borrowing\_date : c \rangle.$$

Possible attributes (which are not part of the identifier) would be the return date and the

Figure 8.19: Example of a "weak" entity type. We will not use weak entity types in this book.

- If T_1 is a specialization of T_2 then each instance of T_1 is identical to an instance of T_2.

Figure 8.20: The specialization check.

number of reminders sent. This solution adds a historical dimension to relationships. It combines the advantages of the two representations in figure 8.18. We can generalize this by also adding a historical dimension to entities, so that we can represent different historical versions of the same (identical) entity.

However, there is no agreed convention to represent historical relationship types in the ER approach. Addition of a historical dimension to the Entity-Relationship approach is a substantial extension to classical Entity-Relationship modeling that would greatly improve its modeling power. We will not treat this extension, as how this can best be done is still a research issue.

Weak entities

In many texts on the Entity-Relationship approach the concept of a **weak entity** is used. Roughly speaking, this is an entity that must be identified by a key of another entity concatenated with some of its own attributes. The archetypical example is shown in figure 8.19. Each employee has key *emp#* and each employee has zero or more children, who are identified, per employee, by an attribute *dependent#*. If we want to identify a child in the existence set of *CHILD*, we must therefore concatenate the value of *emp#* with the value of *dependent#*.

Each weak entity type always has a "parent type" that must supply part of its identifying information. The relationship from parent type to weak entity type is always a master-detail relationship. In the days of sequential storage media (magnetic tapes), weak entities were implemented as repeating groups within their parent record; this explains the use of a "local key", that is only unique within the parent record. In a hierarchical data model, weak entities are descendants of their parent entity.

Obviously, the concept of a weak entity has a meaning in the implementation of a software system but not in a model of the UoD. Children have their own identity that can be represented in a UoD model by their own identifier, that does not contain an identifier of any other ER entity. In this book, we will therefore not use weak entity types.

8.3.3 Specialization check

There is only one check to find out whether an *is_a* relationship is correct, and that is to test the identity statement shown in figure 8.20. By performing this deceptively simple test, we are forced to make explicit what we mean by an *is_a* arrow. For example, is a *STUDENT* a *PERSON*? The answer seems to be yes, until we realize the consequence of this answer: each *STUDENT* instance is identical to a *PERSON* instance. Suppose we want to be able to represent that one person is a student at two different times in his or her life. According to the national student registration authority in the Netherlands, such a person is two students. Since $1 \neq 2$, this administration cannot represent students as being identical to persons. As another example, consider the library *MEMBER* example analyzed in section 7.4. It is clear from that analysis that *MEMBER* instances are *not* identical to *PERSON* instances, and therefore that we have *not MEMBER is_a PERSON*.

8.3.4 Elementary sentence check

One way to validate that an ER model is a correct representation of a UoD is to discuss it with a domain specialist. However, many domain specialists do not understand the ramifications of an ER diagram, and it is therefore useful to translate the model into elementary sentences and discuss these sentences with the domain specialist. This is called an **elementary sentence check**. Translation of an ER model into elementary sentences amounts to traveling a road in figure 8.1 in the backwards direction.

Example elementary sentences that correspond to our library model (figure 8.12) are:

- At each moment, each *DOCUMENT* has an *owner*.

- At each moment, the *owner* of each *DOCUMENT* is a *DEPARTMENT*.

- At each moment, each *DOCUMENT* is borrowed by at most one *MEMBER*.

- At each moment, each *MEMBER* has a *LOAN* relationship with zero or more *DOCUMENT*s.

The phrase "at each moment" emphasizes that an ER diagram represents what is common to all states in the state space of the UoD. Any ER diagram can be translated this way into a set of sentences in natural language. Upon reading it, a domain specialist may improve the model by adding extra information, such as that the owner of a document never changes, or the specialist may correct mistakes, for example by remarking that in the first part of their lives, documents have no owner at all.

8.3.5 Population check

A second means to facilitate the understanding of the domain specialist is the **population check**. This is done by drawing a **population diagram** of the ER model, which is just a representation of a possible state of the system represented by the diagram. Figure 8.21 shows a population diagram of the *LOAN* relationship. Below each ER entity type and relationship, a small existence set of that type is drawn in the form of a table. The diagram shows clearly that *MEMBER* and *DOCUMENT* instances can exist without being related by an existing *LOAN* instance. Each population diagram should exhibit the cardinality properties of the relationship; if some cardinalities are not possible in the UoD, then the domain specialist can discover these omitted cardinality properties by means of a population diagram that violates them.

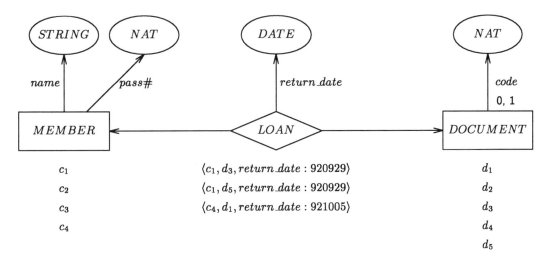

Figure 8.21: A population diagram.

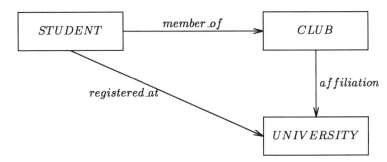

Figure 8.22: If the equation $registered\_at(s) = affiliation(member\_of(s))$ is always true, then $registered\_at$ is a redundant relationship.

8.3.6   Derivable relationship check

In the **derivable relationship check**, we check whether there are relationships that can be derived from other relationships. A simple case of this where all involved relationships are functional is illustrated in figure 8.22. If *in every possible state of the modeled part of the world*, for every existing student s we have

$$registered\_at(s) = affiliation(member\_of(s)),$$

then the $registered\_at$ relationship is redundant.

It is a choice of the modeler whether or not to remove a derivable relationship from the model. One reason why we should remove it is that this would make the model more understandable. A second reason why we should remove it is that the specification of state changes is more complex if we include a derived relationship. If either of the relationships $registered\_at$ or $member\_of$ changes, then $affiliation$ should be specified to change as well. This may lead to an *update anomaly* if one of these relationships is updated but $affiliation$ remains unchanged.

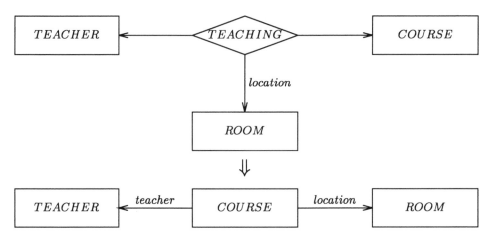

Figure 8.23: Applying the minimal arity check. The *TEACHING* relationship can be decomposed without loss of information into two relationships with smaller arity, *teacher* and *location*.

These are not decisive arguments for dropping derivable relationships from an ER diagram. In special cases, a diagram may become more understandable if we include a derivable relationship. The domain specialists, users or sponsor or even the law may prescribe inclusion of a redundant relationship in an ER model.

8.3.7 Minimal arity checks

Connected to derivable relationship checks is the **minimal arity check**. In the minimal arity check, we check whether for any relationship R in a diagram there are relationships, possibly not yet all in the diagram, with smaller arity, such that R can be derived from these new relationships. Consider the diagram in figure 8.23. Suppose each course in a faculty has one teacher and is given in one room. Then the representation of the relationship between *COURSE*, *TEACHER* and *ROOM* can be decomposed without loss of information into the two many–one relationships in the lower half of figure 8.23. The decomposition is lossless because the two relationships *teacher* and *location* are many–one. When they are joined at their first argument, we recover the *TEACHING* relationship.

Again, a reason to prefer relationships with minimal arity is that it makes the model more understandable and avoids update anomalies. Replacement of a $\langle t, c \rangle$ tuple in the *teacher* relationship in the lower part of figure 8.23 would correspond to a set of updates to the *TEACHING* relationship in the upper part. If not all of these updates would be performed an update anomaly would arise.

A well-known mistake that can be made in reducing the arity of relationship types is called the **connection trap**. The *SALE* relationship in figure 8.24 relates shops to the products and clients involved in a sale. There is no lossless decomposition of the *SALE* relationship into relationships with smaller arity.

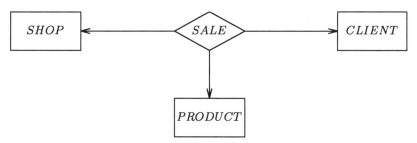

Figure 8.24: The connection trap. The *SALE* relationship cannot be decomposed into relationships with smaller arity without loss of information.

8.3.8   Creation/deletion check

The creation/deletion check can be used to check the completeness of our ER model. We use the transaction decomposition table shown in figure 8.8 to check whether for every entity type or relationship in it, there are transactions that create or delete it. If there is no C or no D in a row of the table, we must either explain this absence or repair this omission to the model. For example, in the *COURSE* row of table 8.8, there is no C or D transaction because course administration has not been modeled. We should add these transactions in a more complete ER model of the UoD.

It is not always necessary that every entity or relationship be created or deleted. For example, in a model of an elevator system, relevant entity types are *BUTTON*, *FLOOR*, etc. The existence sets of these entity types are fixed during the useful life of the system. Even if they are not fixed, e.g. because the building is renovated and new floors are added, then the creation of new *FLOOR* instances is not done in a transaction with a user of the elevator system.

8.3.9   Cross-checking

One way to check the mutual consistency of different parts of the model is to perform cross-checking. **Cross-checking** consists in traveling in different directions through the map of induction methods shown in figure 8.1, and checking if we get mutually consistent results. For example, we can perform natural language analysis starting from a piece of text and, independently, do an entity analysis of transactions starting from a function decomposition tree. The resulting models are likely not to be identical, and we can improve the quality of both by merging them in the way described in the section on view integration below. The result should be consistent with the natural language analysis as well as with the transaction analysis.

Similarly, we can independently perform an entity analysis of transactions starting from a natural language analysis of transactions, and check whether the results are the same. For example, in a natural language analysis of transactions of the student administration system, we should have found the following elementary sentence for the transaction List Course Participants:

- List students who are enrolled in a course.

This elementary sentence is consistent with the description of the transaction in figure 8.7.

1. Draw a double arrow pointing to the entity type(s) where the path starts (or can start).

2. Write a C, R, U or D in each entity an relationship that is accessed along the way, corresponding to the type of access performed.

3. Indicate how one travels through the diagram by drawing arrows along the arrows drawn on the diagram, annotated with access conditions.

4. Check for each entity and relationship whether the attributes read or updated when traveling the path are present.

Figure 8.25: Drawing a navigation path for a transaction.

Yet another useful way to cross-check is to travel the map *against* the direction of the arrows. Starting from an ER diagram, we can describe its contents in elementary sentences and check whether these describe the transactions in the function decomposition tree. Alternatively, starting from an ER diagram, we can ask for each entity and relationship what happens to it. When is an instance created, read, updated or deleted? This gives us a list of relevant transactions, that should be identical to the list of transactions in the function decomposition tree we started with.

8.3.10   View integration

An ER model of the UoD of a business is likely to be too large to be built and understood as a whole. It is good practice to build ER models of different aspects of the UoD separately, and integrating these models afterwards. Each of these models is called a **view** of the UoD. Integrating different views acts as a quality check on the merged models, because different views may make up for each other's omissions.

8.3.11   Navigation check

A **navigation check** is a special kind of cross-check, in which we verify whether all transactions can be performed by a system that would implement the ER model. This is done for each relevant transaction by drawing a **navigation path** through the ER diagram, that represents the path that a system would follow through the data in order to execute the transaction. The navigation path is drawn by the procedure shown in figure 8.25.

For example, suppose we want to check whether the diagram in figure 8.12 is sufficient to answer the query

> Give the names and addresses of all members who are due to return one or more documents.

The navigation path through the diagram is shown in figure 8.26. Apparently, a system that implements the diagram can answer the query, since the name and address of members are represented on the diagram. As an example of a correction that can be made this way, suppose that the query would have required the system to sort the members on their family name. Then the diagram would have had to be changed by replacing *name* : $MEMBER \rightarrow$

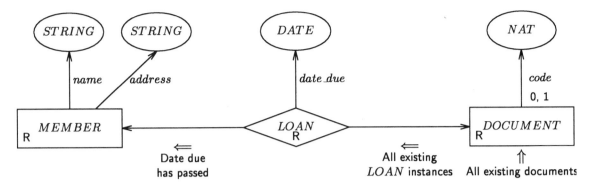

Figure 8.26: Navigation path through an ER diagram for the query "Give the names and addresses of all members who are due to return one or more documents".

1. Transform all many–many relationships into their diamond representation.

2. Write down the declarations of the attributes of all entity types and relationships.

3. Indicate an external identifier attribute for each entity type.

4. Add compound identifiers to each relationship declaration.

5. Indicate the primary key of each declaration.

6. Add many–one relationships as referential keys.

Figure 8.27: Method for transforming an ER model into a relational schema. The resulting schema must still be optimized for performance.

STRING by *family_name* : *MEMBER* → *STRING* and *initials* : *MEMBER* → *STRING*.

A navigation path can be drawn for every transaction. For example, the transaction Extend Document Loan has a navigation path that starts from *MEMBER*, travels to *LOAN*, and then performs an Update access to a *LOAN* instance.

8.4 Transformation to a Database System Schema

An ER model can be transformed into a relational database schema in a simple manner. Figure 8.27 contains a procedure for transforming an ER model into an relational database schema. We explain it by means of a small example.

The upper diagram in figure 8.28 is a part of an ER model of the library UoD. The first step in the transformation to a relational schema is to replace every many–many relationship into its diamond representation. The resulting diagram is called a **functional ER model**, because all lines are arrows and hence represent mathematical functions. The second step is to write down the declarations of the attributes of all entity types and relationships. These declarations have the format defined for the declaration of attributes in figure 7.1. In the example, we assume that all entity types have external identifiers defined by the

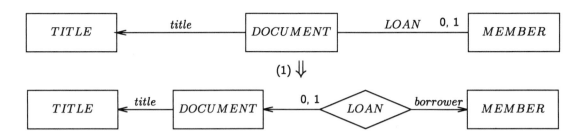

$(1) \Downarrow$

$(2) \Downarrow$

TITLE(*title_id* : *NATURAL*, *name* : *STRING*, *author* : *STRING*)
DOCUMENT(*doc_id* : *NATURAL*, *location_code* : *STRING*)
LOAN(*date_borrowed* : *DATE*, *return_date* : *DATE*)
MEMBER(*member_id* : *NATURAL*, *name* : *STRING*, *address* : *STRING*).

$(3) \Downarrow$

TITLE(!*title_id* : *NATURAL*, *name* : *STRING*, *author* : *STRING*)
DOCUMENT(!*doc_id* : *NATURAL*, *location_code* : *STRING*)
LOAN(*date_borrowed* : *DATE*, *return_date* : *DATE*)
MEMBER(!*member_id* : *NATURAL*, *name* : *STRING*, *address* : *STRING*).

$(4) \Downarrow$

TITLE(!*title_id* : *NATURAL*, *name* : *STRING*, *author* : *STRING*)
DOCUMENT(!*doc_id* : *NATURAL*, *location_code* : *STRING*)
LOAN(!⟨*document* : *NATURAL*, *member* : *NATURAL*⟩, *date_borrowed* : *DATE*,
return_date : *DATE*)
MEMBER(!*member_id* : *NATURAL*, *name* : *STRING*, *address* : *STRING*).

$(5) \Downarrow$

TITLE(<u>!*title_id* : *NATURAL*</u>, *name* : *STRING*, *author* : *STRING*)
DOCUMENT(<u>!*doc_id* : *NATURAL*</u>, *location_code* : *STRING*)
LOAN(<u>!⟨*document* : *NATURAL*, *member* : *NATURAL*⟩</u>, *date_borrowed* : *DATE*,
return_date : *DATE*)
MEMBER(<u>!*member_id* : *NATURAL*</u>, *name* : *STRING*, *address* : *STRING*).

$(6) \Downarrow$

TITLE(<u>!*title_id* : *NATURAL*</u>, *name* : *STRING*, *author* : *STRING*)
DOCUMENT(<u>!*doc_id* : *NATURAL*</u>, *title* : *NATURAL*, *location_code* : *STRING*)
LOAN(<u>!⟨*document* : *NATURAL*, *member* : *NATURAL*⟩</u>, *date_borrowed* : *DATE*,
return_date : *DATE*)
MEMBER(<u>!*member_id* : *NATURAL*</u>, *name* : *STRING*, *address* : *STRING*).

Figure 8.28: Transforming an ER model into a relational database schema.

library and visible to library employees; these identifiers are indicated in the third step by exclamation marks. Addition of identifier attributes requires some care. As indicated by the discussion in section 7.4, we may have to consult library regulations to find out how entities are identified. If there are entity types without external identifiers, we must consult the sponsor and customer to decide how to add these identifiers. If identification is not important for some entity types, we should add internal identifiers, which are generated by the system and which are invisible to the user of the system.

Having provided a mechanism to identify entities, we can in the fourth step add compound relationship identifiers. The components of the relationship identifier are the identifiers of the component entity types. Note that *document* is really a function $LOAN \rightarrow DOCUMENT$, but that in the attribute declarations, we replace $DOCUMENT$ with $NATURAL$. We can do this because in the function composition

$$LOAN \xrightarrow{document} DOCUMENT \xrightarrow{doc\_id} NATURAL$$

the function *doc_id* is one-one. By replacing $DOCUMENT$ with $NATURAL$, we prepare ourselves for the translation into types available in DBMS schema languages.

In step five, we add the relational concept of a key. A key is a combination of attribute values whose value is unique in each existence set. The simplest thing to do is to define each external identifier to be a key. If an entity type does not have an external identifier, then we must consult domain specialists to determine which combinations of attribute values is unique in each existence set. A relationship may now get a compound key in which one component is a compound key of an entity type.

Finally, in step six we add many–one relationships as referential keys to entity types. The resulting declarations have the form of relation schemas. Translation of these schemas into a database schema definition language such as SQL requires one more decision, viz. the translation of the value types into the data types available in the schema definition language. There are algorithms to support the transformation of an ER diagram into a relational database schema, which perform optimizations in special cases.

8.5 Methodological Analysis

8.5.1 The place of the ER method in the development framework

System hierarchy. The ER modeling notation has been developed to represent the UoD of database systems. However, it can be used to represent the UoD of any data manipulation system, including the UoD of organizations, of computer-based systems and of software systems. This has already been indicated in figure 3.15.

We remarked in section 6.6 that the decomposition of the business into computer-based systems and of these into software systems is independent from a decomposition of the UoD into subsystems. For any particular UoD, we can define an aggregation hierarchy; but since we make no assumptions about the kind of UoD we are modeling, we do not assume any particular hierarchy in the UoD. As a consequence, we cannot allocate ER modeling to any level in the aggregation hierarchy of our development framework, for this hierarchy decomposes a business into computer-based systems, these into software systems etc.

Moreover, because the UoD of a business may also be the UoD of a software system, an ER model of the UoD of a business can be used as an ER model of the UoD of a software system. We saw this already in chapter 6: Moving from ISP to business area analysis, we may add cardinality constraints, but the subject areas and entity types relevant in a business area are also subject areas and entity types relevant for the entire business.

The transformation of an ER model into a relational database schema brings us into the realm of software subsystems. In the system hierarchy, this is a decomposition. In the example of figure 8.28, the relation schemas correspond one–one with entity types and relationships, so there does not seem to be much of a decomposition in this move. However, there is a decomposition of focus: in the ER model, the atoms of the model are entity types and their relationships; in the relational schemas, the atoms of the model are attributes. Furthermore, optimization of the schemas may lead to splitting of relation schemas on the basis of access patterns.

8.5.2   Modeling and engineering

As spelled out in section 7.8, an ER model can represent the state space of a computer-based system (or a business or a software system) as well as of the UoD of that system. The meaning of statements made by the model may be quite different in these two interpretations. A cardinality statement that expresses a regularity about the UoD is a norm when interpreted as a statement about the system, and a cardinality statement that expresses a norm for the UoD may or may not be interpreted as a norm for the system. This has an obvious methodological consequence for model validation. If there is a mismatch between an ER model and the UoD, then the model is wrong; but if there is a mismatch between the model and the system, then the system is wrong.

This is a consequence of the fact that when modeling the UoD, we should follow the empirical cycle of discovery, but when specifying a system, we should follow the engineering cycle. As explained in chapter 3, in both cycles we follow a rational problem solving process in which we generate alternative solutions, estimate likely effects, evaluate these and then make a choice. In the empirical cycle of modeling a UoD, we estimate effects of a model by deducing observable consequences, and evaluate these by performing experiments. The population check and the elementary sentence checks are (very simple) ways to deduce consequences of an ER model and test these. Most other evaluation heuristics of ER models are quality checks in which we verify the use we made of the modeling constructs.

Once we have an ER model of the UoD, we can turn around and view it as a model of the state space of a computer-based system. Entities and links in the system are then surrogates for entities and links in the UoD, and cardinality regularities in the UoD model now become cardinality constraints on the system. Viewed as a model of the system, we can now add a specification of how many instances of a certain type we want the system to be able to handle, even if this constraint does not correspond to a regularity in the UoD. We may also decide to enforce some constraints on the UoD by implementing them as constraints on the system. The UoD constraint that a member must not borrow more than 20 documents simultaneously may be translated into a system constraint, but the UoD constraint that a member must return a document within three weeks will not be translated into a system constraint. As a consequence of these decisions, a system that represents one member to have borrowed 21 documents simultaneously is wrong (it violates a system constraint), but a system that represents one member to have borrowed a document for four weeks may be right (when it represents a UoD entity that violates a UoD constraint).

Estimation of the likely effects of the ER model involves thinking through likely usage scenarios in order to check whether the constraints imposed on the system allow effective and efficient handling of these scenarios. The navigation check is an evaluation of the capability of the SuD to perform some of its functions, viz. to answer certain queries.

Thus, during ER modeling we start with empirical modeling of the UoD and end with engineering a system. In the process, our interpretation of statements changes from regularities to constraints, and our interpretation of model evaluations changes from a descriptive mode in UoD modeling to an prescriptive mode in system engineering.

8.5.3   Natural language analysis in NIAM

Natural language analysis plays an important role in NIAM, a method for modeling the world as fact types and value types [244]. Fact types are similar to relationships, except that fact types can relate entity as well as value types. An attribute is modeled in NIAM as a binary fact type that relates an entity type and a value type. NIAM has also been called the **binary relationship method**, because in its earlier versions, it only accepted binary fact types. In more recent versions, NIAM also accepts n-ary fact types.

Fact types in NIAM correspond directly to elementary sentences. Fact types can be found using Nijssen's **telephone heuristic**: Imagine that you are phoning someone who has a grasp of elementary English and has no knowledge of the UoD you are trying to model, and that you try to describe the current state of the UoD to that person. The sentences that you then use describe a model of that state. The sentences describe particulars, such as

"The member with member number 123 has borrowed document with key ABC"

This statement about an individual state of affairs can easily be transformed into a hypothesis about all possible states of the UoD, such as

- There is a class of possible objects called *MEMBER*.

- *MEMBER* instances are identified by their member number.

- There is a class of possible objects called *DOCUMENT*.

- *DOCUMENT* instances are identified by a key.

- *MEMBER* instances can borrow *DOCUMENT* instances.

These elementary sentences can be translated directly into NIAM fact types, but they can also be translated into ER entity types, relationships and constraints on these.

The difference between NIAM natural language analysis and ER natural language analysis is that NIAM starts at the instance level and ER modeling starts at the type level. The example elementary sentence above describes a particular fact in which particular entities and links are described. The example elementary sentences in subsection 8.2.1 describe types of facts and do not refer to particulars. This difference is not essential and we can use either type of sentence in an ER or NIAM natural language analysis.

8.6   Summary

Two methods for discovering ER models from a set of observation data were treated: natural language analysis and entity analysis of transactions. *Natural language analysis* starts from elementary sentences describing the UoD and translates these sentences into ER diagrams. This may yield many irrelevant entity types and relationships. To focus on relevant entity types and relationships, we can start with the required system transactions, including the queries that the system must be able to answer, and describe these in elementary sentences. Because the required transactions manipulate data that has a meaning in the UoD, these sentences are elementary descriptions of the UoD. *Natural language analysis of transactions* results in an ER model of the UoD. *Query analysis* is a special case of this.

A different method is *entity analysis of transactions*, in which we, for each required transaction, ask what data are created, read, updated or deleted. These data have a meaning in the UoD, and if we make an ER model of them, we have a model of the UoD.

Several groups of methods were discussed to evaluate ER models. Entities have an identity and a state, values have no state (*entity/value check*). Entities have a simple identity, links have a compound identity (*entity/link check*). Each specialization instance is identical to a generalization instance (*is_a* check). Absent creation or deletion transactions for an entity type or relationship may indicate an incomplete model (*creation/deletion check*). Another way to check the completeness of the model is by means of *cross-checking* and *view integration*. The model is simplified if we take care that all relationships are minimal (*minimal arity check*) and if we remove derivable relationships (*derivable relationship check*). By means of the *elementary sentence check* and *population check*, we can validate the truth value of the model with domain specialists. This is a simple way to do empirical tests of the model. The *navigation check* can tell us whether the system will be able to perform the required functions.

Transformation of an ER model into a relational database schema brings us to the level of software subsystems. This represents a decomposition of entity types and relationships into attributes. Performance considerations can cause us to factor out groups of attributes into separate relation schemas.

ER models can be used to model the UoD of a business, of a computer-based system or of a software system. All these systems may have the same UoD, because the UoD is not part of the aggregation hierarchy of computer-based systems. Each UoD has its own aggregation hierarchy, about which we make no assumptions in this book. ER models can be used to represent the state space of the UoD or of a system under development. As a UoD model, it has a descriptive orientation and the empirical cycle of discovery must be followed. As a system specification, it has a prescriptive orientation and the engineering cycle of product development must be followed.

8.7   Exercises

1. One of the following constraints can be expressed as a cardinality constraint in figure 8.24, the other cannot. Add the representable one to the diagram.

   - Each client buys at least one part at a shop.
   - Each client buys at most two parts in one shop.

2. Discuss the consequences of modeling *AUTHOR* and *PUBLISHER* as a value type and modeling them as an entity type. What would you choose in a model of the circulation desk UoD?

3. Discuss the consequences of modeling *DELIVERY* in figure 7.7 as a relationship and as an entity type.

4. Which of the following relationships are *is_a* relationships?

   - This is a car.

   - A Ford is a car.

   - Ford is a type of car.

   - A teacher is a member of staff.

5. Change the ER model in figure 8.9 in such a way that the *result* attributes of *PRACTICAL* and *TEST_REG* do not need to have a *null* value in their codomain.

6. Add a type/instance distinction to *PRACTICAL*, *TEST* and *COURSE*. For example, there is a course "Conceptual Modeling" (a type) that is given every autumn (an instance).

7. In exercise 7 of chapter 7, you were asked to draw a relationship type that has another relationship as a component. What does this mean for the transformation of an ER model into a relational schema?

8.8 Bibliographical Remarks

ER methods. ER modeling methods are presented by Teory, Yang and Fry [339], and by Batini, Ceri and Navathe [25]. Another source used for this chapter is Storey [327]. A detailed and practical introduction to ER modeling is given by Rock-Evans [280, 281]. An abbreviated version is given in a later work [284].

Natural language analysis. Natural language analysis was proposed in 1983 by Chen [66]. It is used in several proposals for modeling, such as a method proposed by Abbott [1] to write ADA programs and a method proposed by Saeki, Horai and Enomoto [299] to perform software development. Natural language analysis at the instance level plays a central role in NIAM [244].

Transactions analysis. The method of entity analysis of transactions presented in this chapter is based upon a proposal by Flavin [105]. A thorough description of transaction analysis is given by Rock-Evans [280, 281, 282, 283]. An accessible summary of these methods is given in a later work [284].

Evaluation methods.   Some of the evaluation methods have been taken from existing literature on ER methods, such as Batini *et al.* [25], Teory *et al.* [339], and Storey [327]. The definition of ER concepts in chapter 7 is used in the entity/value and entity/link checks. The creation/deletion checks are taken from Information Engineering. The use of navigation paths to perform the query check is well-known in ER modeling and is described by, for example, Batini *et al.* [25]. The population check is taken from NIAM [244]. The minimal arity check is based on a step known in NIAM as the *arity check*. View integration techniques and methods are described in Batini and Lenzerini [26] and Navathe, Elmasri and Larson [242]. A survey of view integration methods is given by Batini, Lenzerini and Navathe [27].

Transformation to database system schema.   Many papers and books that propose ER methods have something to say about transformation of an ER diagram into a relational database system schema. Useful introductions and surveys are given by Batini *et al.* [25], Storey [327], Teory [338], and Teory, Yang and Fry [339].

9

Structured Analysis I: Models

9.1 Introduction

Structured analysis is a method to specify the observable behavior of a software system in a way that reflects the essential tasks to be performed by the software system. In a rational development process, structured analysis would be followed by structured design to develop a modular architecture of software systems, and by structured programming. The historical sequence in which these methods were proposed is the reverse of this: structured programming was proposed around 1970 and structured design and analysis were proposed in the late 1970s. The move from structured programming to structured analysis parallels the move from relational databases to entity-relationship modeling, because both movements turn away from implementation structures towards problem structures.

In this chapter, we treat the notation system used by structured analysis, the data flow notation. The notation is general enough to be used for systems that manipulate material and energy as well but in this chapter, we restrict ourselves to the representation of data manipulation. Extension of the notation to deal with material and energy manipulation is left as an exercise for the reader.

Sections 9.2 and 9.3 survey the structure of data flow models: a data flow model represents a system that receives data flows from the environment, transforms the received data, stores them and sends data flows as response to the environment (section 9.2). The environment with which the system communicates is represented by external entities and by time (section 9.3). Section 9.4 looks at data stores and the way in which we can use an ER diagram to represent the structure of data stores. Section 9.5 looks at data flows and section 9.6 discusses the specification and decomposition of data transformations. In section 9.7, data flow models are analyzed from a methodological point of view.

9.2 Components of a Data Flow Model

Data flow models can be used to represent any kind of data manipulation system, ranging from (the data manipulation aspect of) businesses to computer-based systems and software systems. Just like an ISAC activity model, a data flow model represents a data manipulation system by specifying the data manipulation activities performed by the system and the data

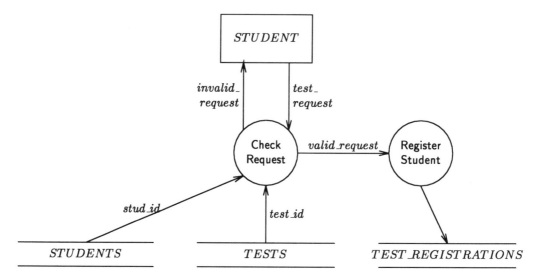

Figure 9.1: A DF diagram of a student test registration.

stores used by these activities. The main notation used for data flow models is the **data flow diagram** (DF diagram). A DF diagram consists of four kinds of components (see figure 9.1):

- A **data transformation** is an activity that manipulates data. Data transformations are also called **processes** or **functions** by some authors. A data transformation is represented by a circle on a DF diagram. If the data transformation is not decomposed into subprocesses, it is named by a verb and noun that together describe the activity. If the data transformation is decomposed into subprocesses, it is named by a noun. In this book, the first letters of the words in the name of a data transformation are written in upper case letters.

- A **data store** represents part of the observable memory that the system has of past activities. This memory is *observable* in the sense that it may lead to observably different behavior in the future. A data store is represented by a pair of parallel lines on a DF diagram. It is named by a plural noun whose singular form describes the individual data items in the store. In this book, this name is capitalized and written in mathematics font.

- An **external entity** is a part of the environment of the modeled system, with which the system interacts. An external entity is represented by a rectangle on a DF diagram. It is named by a singular noun that stands for a typical instance of that entity. In this book, this name is written in capitalized mathematics font.

- Data transformations, stores and external entities are connected by arrows called **data flows** that represent directed communication channels. Data items can travel through data flows in the direction of the arrow. A data flow is named by a singular noun, possibly with adjectives, that describe the data items that pass through it. A data flow into or out of a data store may be nameless, in which case it is assumed to carry the entire contents of one record in the store. If a data flow passes through a data transformation, the data flow name of the output flow must show what the difference between input and output flows is. In this book, data flow names are written in small letters in mathematics font.

The DF diagram in figure 9.1 says that there is a *STUDENT* external entity that can generate *test_request* data and can receive *invalid_request* messages. There are three data stores called *STUDENTS*, *TESTS* and *TEST_REGISTRATIONS* and the check of a registration request reads from the stores *STUDENTS* and *TESTS* to perform its task. It outputs a data flow called "*invalid_request*" back to a *STUDENT* entity and a data flow called "*valid_request*", which is sent to the data transformation called "Register Student". This data transformation has write access to the *TEST_REGISTRATIONS* data store. Note that nothing in the DF diagram says that the system is computer-based or that it is manual. In general, a DF diagram does not say anything about the implementation of a system.

In addition to a DF diagram, a DF model consists of the following supporting documentation:

- Just like activity models, complex DF models are hierarchical, such that a data transformation may be decomposed into a lower-level DF diagram. The hierarchy must be documented by a **transformation decomposition tree**. Each node in the tree corresponds to a data transformation that is expanded on the next lower level into a DF diagram.

- Each data transformation that is not decomposed into a lower-level DF diagram must be specified by other means. These specifications are called **minispecs**.

- The structure of the data contained in the data stores must be represented by an **ER diagram**.

- All names used anywhere in the model must be defined in a **data dictionary**.

9.3 Interaction Between the System and its Environment

A system interacts with its environment by reacting to events produced by its environment. The environment of a system consists of external entities and time. We discuss each of these in the next two subsections.

9.3.1 External entities

An **external entity** of a system S is a system in the environment of S with which S can interact. External entities are also called **terminators** or **sources/sinks** by some authors. An external entity is represented by a rectangle in a DF diagram. This rectangle may represent a type or an instance. For example, the *STUDENT* entity in figure 9.1 is really a type, whose instances may interact with the student administration. Suppose we had added the national student registration authority as an external entity that provides the administration with data about students, such as student administration numbers. The rectangle for the national student registration authority would then represent an instance rather than a type.

When the environment does something to which the system must respond, an **event** is said to occur. Events must be discrete in time. The continuous change of temperature in a room is not an event, reaching a specified temperature to which the system must respond (e.g. by shutting off a heater) is an event. The **response** of a system to an event is the observable activity of the system caused by the event. More in particular, the system response consists of any observable output produced by the system as well as any change in the data stores that may lead to observably different behavior in the future. When the response has been produced, the system settles into a state in which it is ready to receive another event. To illustrate this, some examples of events and their responses follow.

- A room whose temperature is controlled by a thermostat reaches the desired temperature. The thermostat responds by switching off the heater (observable output). As noted above, temperature data arrive continuously, but the event that the desired temperature has been reached is discrete.

- A user sets the desired room temperature in a thermostat. The thermostat responds by remembering the desired temperature (state change). If the actual room temperature is lower than the desired temperature, it additionally responds by switching on the heater (observable output).

- A student requests to participate in a test. If the preconditions for registration are satisfied, the student administration responds by remembering the registration (memory change). Otherwise, it responds by rejecting the request (observable output)

Events and responses are *not* represented in a DF diagram. Rather, the data flows entering and leaving the system as a result of the event are represented.

Because data stores are passive and cannot perform any interaction with an external entity, external entities never send data directly to data stores but only to data transformations. In addition, interactions between external entities are not represented in DF diagrams. This is not because those interactions are impossible — they often occur — but because they are not of interest.

The name of an external entity must indicate the *role* that the entity is playing for the system, not the physical implementation. For example, the student administration has an external entity *SUPERVISOR* for students who supervise during tests, and an external entity *STUDENT* for students who do the tests. The same person may play both roles at different times in his or her life but because the roles are different, they are viewed as different external entities.

The name of each external entity must be entered in the data dictionary along with any other relevant information. For example, in a data dictionary for a thermostat we may write assumptions about the **interface technology** of the *SENSOR* external entity. This may include the speed with which data arrives, the time between successive packets, etc. One important aspect of interaction with external entities that can be documented in the data dictionary is the **delay** between the time at which an external event occurs in an external entity, and the time at which the system learns of this occurrence. In an elevator control system this delay may be less than a microsecond, in a database system this delay may be several hours. A second important aspect that can be documented in the data dictionary is

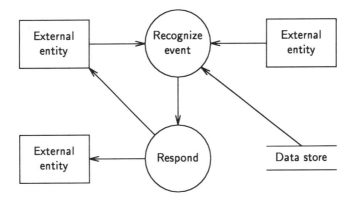

Figure 9.2: Due to an imperfect environment, the system often needs an event recognition mechanism to find out whether an external event has occurred.

the **response time** required of the system. This is the time interval from the moment at which the system learns that an event has occurred to the moment at which the response to this occurrence has been produced.

9.3.2 Time and temporal events

The environment of a system consists of external entities and time. An event is called **temporal** if it consists of the passage of a moment in time to which the system must respond. Examples of temporal events and their responses are:

- At midnight every day it is time to produce a report on late borrowers. The system responds to this temporal event by producing an overdue report.

- Three weeks after borrowing a document it is time to either return the document or request an extension of the borrowing period. The system responds to this temporal event by producing a report that a document loan is overdue.

We noticed before that events are not shown in a DF diagram, but that the data flows generated by the event are. Therefore, like all events, temporal events are not visible in the diagram. The only input that can be generated by a temporal event is the time of day and it is customary to omit this input data flow from a DF diagram. This means that temporal events are completely invisible in the DF diagram. To find out if a DF diagram defines responses to temporal events, look for output data flows that are produced without using any input data flows.

9.3.3 Event recognition

The occurrence of an external event must be distinguished from the *recognition* by the system that the event has taken place. Often, the system needs an **event recognizer**, which is a data transformation that accepts some data flows from the environment and monitors this for the occurrence of an event. When the event occurs, relevant data are then sent to a data transformation that produces the response (figure 9.2). This structure can often be found in data-intensive as well as control-intensive systems:

- In figure 9.1, the student administration must do some internal processing to verify that a request to participate in a test is a valid request. After this event recognition, the response to the event is generated by a different transformation.

- A thermostat that controls the temperature in a room receives a continuous signal which represents this temperature, and compares this with the desired temperature. This comparison is a data transformation performed by the control system, needed to recognize the event that the room has reached the desired temperature. The event is external, for it takes place in the room. The recognition that the event has taken place is a process performed by the thermostat itself.

- Temporal events always need event recognizers, because there is no external entity that notifies the system of the occurrence of the temporal event. The event recognizer is a data transformation that produces a temporal event without any apparent input.

9.3.4   Perfect technology

The need for event recognizers is a consequence of the assumption, made by data flow modeling, that the system is implemented by means of **perfect technology** and interacts with an environment that is implemented by means of imperfect technology. This corresponds with the idea that the environment of a system can be defined as that part of the world over which the developer has no control, and the system as that part of the world over which he or she has control. The developer ideally has complete freedom to choose the implementation of the system but has to accept all implementation decisions that have been made for the environment. In order to prepare for this decision, a DF model represents the system as if it were implemented using perfect technology, which is a model that is not subject to any implementation constraints. Data transformations execute infinitely fast, data stores have unlimited capacity and data flows have infinite transmission speed. This model represents the **essential behavior** to be implemented by the system. It is therefore also called an **essential model**.

The environment, by contrast, must be accepted as it is. The environment may send events to the system at the wrong moment, provide the system with incorrect data values, etc. The system must therefore perform event recognition in order to filter out incorrect input events. Event recognizers therefore act as an interface that shields perfect technology from an imperfect environment. The amount of work to be done by event recognizers is determined by the nature of the imperfection of the environment.

Conversely, the response of a system is needed by the environment because the environment is imperfect. If the environment were perfect, then the system would not have been needed at all. The complexity of the response of the system is determined by the extent of the imperfection of the environment. Take for example a system that controls a barrier to a parking garage. If the barrier happens to be implemented using intelligent technology, the control system can open the barrier by sending it the command *raise*. If the barrier uses less intelligent implementation technology, the control may have to send the command *start_opening*, monitor an input data flow *angle* on the correct angle, and send a command *stop_opening*. The nature of the imperfection of external entities therefore determines the complexity of the system response.

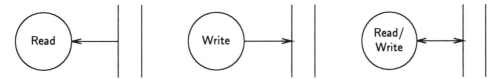

Figure 9.3: The three kinds of data store access.

9.4 Data Stores and the ER Diagram

9.4.1 Data stores

Data stores contain the observable state of the system. Any part of the system state that does not make a difference to any possible future system behavior is part of *internal* system state. Data stores only contain the observable system state. In a computer-based system, data stores may be implemented as variables or files that are read from or written to by data transformations. In a manual system, data stores may be implemented as card files, dossiers or even human memory. A data store can only have an interface (through data flows) with data transformations; it cannot be connected directly to other data stores or to external entities. There are three kinds of data flows between a data store and a data transformation: read, write and read/write shown in figure 9.3.

- In a *read* access, a data item stored in the data store is read by a data transformation.

- In a *write* access, a data item in the data store is created, deleted or updated by a data transformation. A write access must be implemented by first reading the record to be updated from the store; this is not represented.

- In a *read/write* access, a read takes place to show part or all of the data store contents to another data transformation, and to update the contents of the store. This is shown by a bidirectional arrow.

In order to decide which kind of data store access a data transformation needs, we should describe the meaning of the transformation by means of a precondition and a postcondition. The **precondition** describes the assumptions made by the transformation about its inputs, the **postcondition** describes the state brought about by the transformation. The heuristics for deciding what kind of access to data stores the transformation needs, are as follows:

- If the preconditions refer to a data store, then the transformation needs read access to that store.

- If the postcondition refers to a data store, then the transformation needs write access to that store.

For example, suppose that we update a document record every time it is borrowed (figure 9.4). The precondition of the Borrow transformation is that the borrowed document exists and the member is allowed to borrow the document. This refers to the contents of the *DOCUMENTS* and *MEMBERS* data stores, so the transformation needs read access to those stores. The postcondition (in case of successful execution) is that a loan is created and that the document borrow count has been increased. This refers to the *LOAN* and *DOCUMENT* data stores and therefore a write access to those stores is needed.

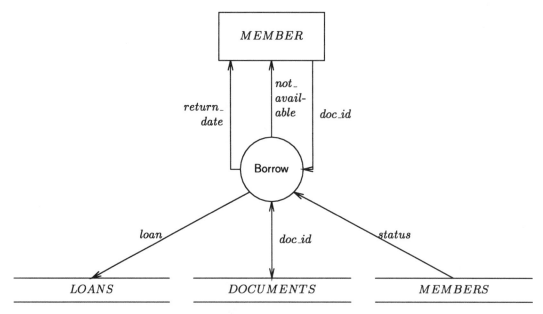

Figure 9.4: A read/write access.

Data stores are documented in the data dictionary by means of the conventions shown in figure 9.5. Using these conventions, we can specify for example the structure of the *STUDENTS* data store as shown in figure 9.6. The data dictionary can contain other information about data stores, such as the maximum and minimum expected size, expected growth rate, etc.

9.4.2   The ER diagram

Figure 9.7 shows part of a DF diagram for the test registration administration. The numeric labels of the data transformations are arbitrary numbers to identify the data transformations, and the letter P indicates that a data transformation is primitive (explained later). The diagram is part of a model of the following behavior of the student administration (see apppendix B for a case description).

We can document the structure of the data stores by means of an ER diagram in which each data store corresponds to an entity type or to a relationship. Figure 9.8 shows an ER diagram of the student administration that has already been discussed in chapter 8. The basic rule of correspondence between the ER diagram and the DF diagram is:

- Each entity type and each many-many relationship corresponds to a data store, whose name is the plural of the name of the type.

The ER diagram represents the state space of the UoD of the system as well as the state space of the system. Viewed as a model of the system state space, entities and links are *surrogates* for UoD entities and links. Existing surrogates are stored in data stores.

It is not obligatory to maintain a one-one correspondence between entity types and relationships in the ER diagram and data stores in the DF diagram. The only requirement

Data type specification	Meaning
T = an elementary data type	Depending upon the conventions in force for the project, elementary data types like $NATURAL$ and $STRING$ and enumeration types such as $\{red, white, blue\}$ can be used. In addition to the range of the datatype, the meaning of its instances in terms of the UoD is described.
$T = T_1 + \cdots + T_n$	An instance of T is a concatenation of instances of T_1 through T_n.
$T = !T_1 + \cdots + T_n$	Each instance of T is identified by an instance of T_1.
$T = [T_1 \vert \cdots \vert T_n]$	An instance of T is an instance of exactly one out of T_1, ..., T_n. That is, T is a supertype of all T_i.
$T = (T_1)$	An instance of T is an instance of T_1 or $null$.
$T = n_1\{T_1\}n_2$	An instance of T is a set of minimally n_1 and maximally n_2 instances of T_1. For example, an instance of $3\{STUDENT\}10$ is a set of minimally 3 and maximally 10 $STUDENT$ instances. If n_1 is omitted, the minimum is 0, and if n_2 is omitted, the maximum is infinity.

Figure 9.5: The conventions for describing the structure of data in the data dictionary.

$STUDENTS =$	$\{STUDENT\}$
$STUDENT =$	$!stud\_id + name + address + (parent\_address)$
$stud\_id =$	$NATURAL$
	Meaning: Unique identifier of students, assigned by the national student registration authority.
$name =$	$STRING$
	Meaning: Family name of the student.
$address =$	$STRING$
	Meaning: address to which correspondence should be sent.
$parent\_address =$	$STRING$
	Meaning: address to which mail should be sent in holidays.

Figure 9.6: Examples data dictionary specification of the $STUDENTS$ data store.

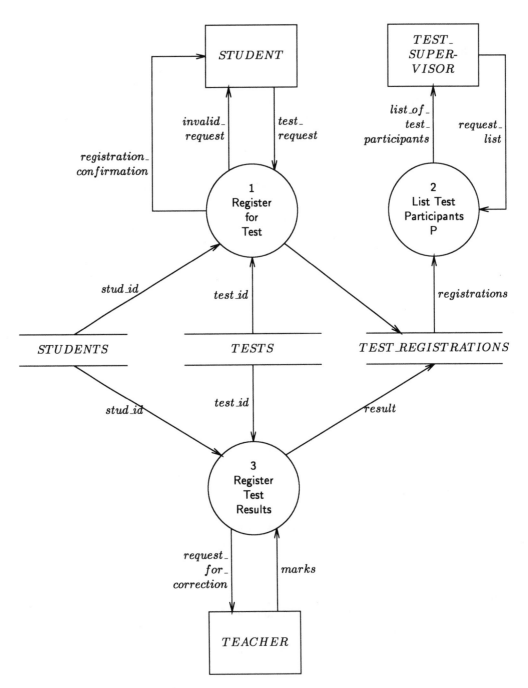

Figure 9.7: A DF diagram of part of the test administration.

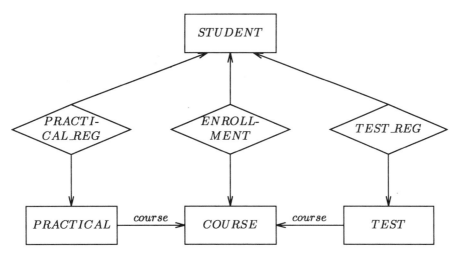

Figure 9.8: ER diagram of the student administration.

is that for each attribute of an entity type or relationship, there should be a data store in which it is stored, and for each field of a data store there should be an entity type or relationship whose attribute it represents. There are two extremes:

- It is possible to put only one data store in the DF diagram. Each record in this store corresponds to one existing entity or relationship, but different records in this stores can be instances of different types. This choice would lead to a badly structured data store and a badly structured DF diagram, but it is logically possible to do this.

- It is possible to store each entity and relationship attribute in a different data store. This would also lead to a badly structured DF diagram.

One should use criteria such as minimality of interfaces between activities and data stores to find out what the optimal partitioning into data stores is.

There is some redundancy between the documentation in the data dictionary and the ER diagram. For example, attributes are declared both in the data dictionary and in the ER diagram. Worse, both declarations follow a different convention. Compare, for example, the definition of the *name* attribute in figure 9.6 with the definition of *name* in the ER approach. In the ER model, *name* is a function

$$ext_\sigma(STUDENT) \rightarrow ext(STRING).$$

This means that we can distinguish the domain and codomain of *name*. In the data flow model, the distinction between attributes, their domains and their codomains is not made.

It is possible that external entities are part of the UoD of the system. For example, *STUDENT* is an external entity because it can generate events to which the system must respond. At the same time it is an entity type in the ER diagram, because it is part of the world about which the system stores data. Because in the example we let ER entity and relationship types correspond to data stores, we find a data store *STUDENTS* as well as an external entity *STUDENT* in the DF diagram.

$list\_of\_test\_participants = \{registration\}$
$registration = !stud\_id + student\_name + course\_nr + course\_name +$
$\qquad\qquad date\_of\_test$
$test\_request = !stud\_id + course\_nr + date\_of\_test$
$valid\_request = registration$

Figure 9.9: Example data flow specifications in the data dictionary.

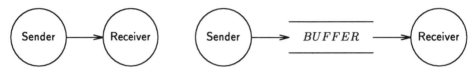

Figure 9.10: Synchronous and asynchronous communication between data transformations.

9.5   Data Flows

Data flows can be used to connect a data transformation with an external entity, with another data transformation, or with a data store. Data flows carry *discrete* packets of data, whose structure is specified in the data dictionary. Examples of data dictionary entries for data flows are given figure 9.9. The data dictionary can contain other information about data flows, such as the rate with which data flows through it.

A data flow that connects two data transformations represents a *synchronous* communication between the data transformations over a reliable channel. This means that the transport of data through the flow takes no time — remember that we assume perfect technology. Put differently, the sender and receiver simultaneously participate in the communication. If two data transformations must communicate *asynchronously* (i.e. the sender can continue its work even if the receiver has not yet received the data) they must do so via a data store, as shown in figure 9.10.

Data flows may be merged and split as shown in figure 9.11. Data flows merely represent the possibility of data transport and do not imply anything about the control structure of this transport. For example, in figure 9.1, we know that the Check Request needs all its three input flows to be able to produce any output, and produces either an *invalid_request* output or a *valid_request* output. This is *not* represented by the DF diagram but will be specified in the minispec for the data transformation, explained below. Figure 9.12 represents a data transformation that needs its input data disjunctively but produces its outputs conjunctively, which is the reverse of the situation in figure 9.1.

It is also possible that two disjunctive outputs are sent to the same destination. For example, figure 9.13 shows a *monthly_reorder* data flow, which carries data regularly once a month, and an *emergency_reorder* flow, which carries data at irregular times. The two flows are different, for when an *emergency_reorder* communication occurs, it need not occur synchronously with a *monthly_reorder* communication.

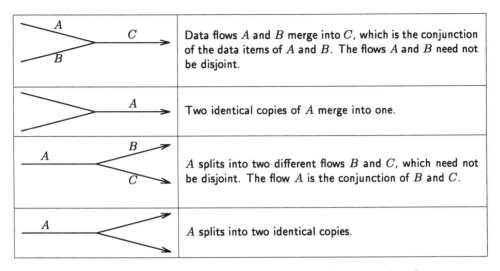

Figure 9.11: Conventions for splitting and merging data flows.

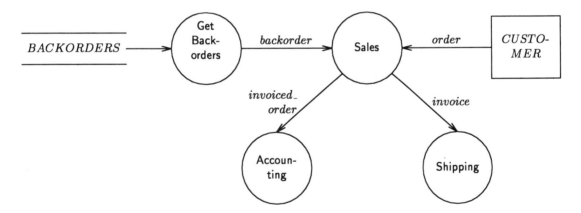

Figure 9.12: The Sales data transformation has disjunctive inputs and conjunctive outputs.

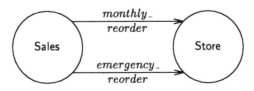

Figure 9.13: Two different data flows between two data transformations.

9.6 Data Transformations

A **data transformation** is an activity that manipulates data. There are two kinds of data transformations, combinational and reactive. A **combinational data transformation** does not have a memory of its inputs once it has produced an output. If a combinational data transformation receives inputs $I_1, \ldots, I_m$ and it produces outputs $O_1, \ldots, O_n$, then the outputs are a mathematical function of its inputs:

$$\langle O_1, \ldots, O_n \rangle = f(\langle I_1, \ldots, I_m \rangle).$$

A **reactive data transformation** has a memory of its past inputs that influences its response to current inputs. If the current state of a reactive data transformation is σ and its next state is σ', then the outputs and next state are mathematical functions of its inputs and current state:

$$\langle O_1, \ldots, O_n \rangle = f(\sigma, \langle I_1, \ldots, I_m \rangle) \text{ and}$$
$$\sigma' = g(\sigma, \langle I_1, \ldots, I_m \rangle).$$

A reactive data transformation must be specified in a DF model by decomposing it into a DF diagram that contains at least one data store. Note that the entire system modeled by a DF model is a reactive data transformation (assuming there is at least one data store in the DF model).

A combinational data transformation can be specified in two ways, by a DF diagram that does not contain a data store and by a minispec. Thus, combinational and reactive transformations both can be specified by decomposing them into a DF diagram but only combinational transformations can be specified by means of minispecs. We discuss decomposition and minispecs in the next two subsections.

9.6.1 Specification by DF diagram

If a data transformation is specified by a DF diagram, we say that the data transformation is **decomposed** into a DF diagram. Data transformation decomposition gives us a hierarchical structure of DF diagrams, that can be represented by a **transformation decomposition tree**. The root of the tree is a data transformation that represents the entire system, and the leaves of the tree are data transformations specified by means of minispecs. The data transformations at the leaves of the tree are also called **primitive data transformations** or **functional primitives**. Note that all primitive transformations are combinational.

A DF diagram that represents the entire system by one data transformation is called the **context diagram** or a **level 0 diagram** of the system. The data transformation in the context diagram is called the **system transformation**. Figure 9.14 shows a context diagram for part of the student administration. The system transformation in figure 9.14 is decomposed into the level 1 diagram shown in figure 9.7. Data transformations 1 and 3 of the level 1 diagram are specified in figures 9.15 and 9.16. The entire transformation decomposition tree is shown in figure 9.17.

The context diagram of a system is called the level 0 diagram of the system, and the decomposition of the system transformation is called the level 1 diagram. A diagram that decomposes a data transformation at level n is itself at level $n+1$. The data transformations in a level $n + 1$ diagram are identified by labels of the form $p.k$, where p is the identifier

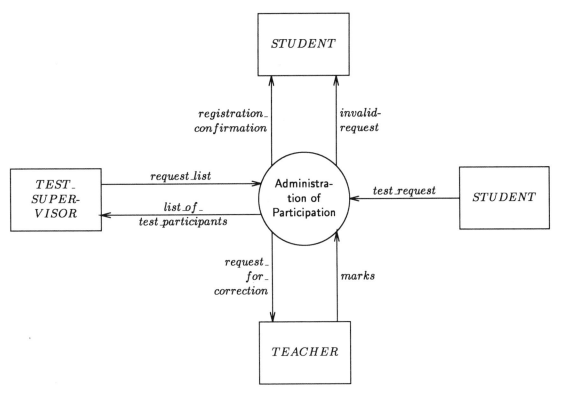

Figure 9.14: Context diagram of part of the student administration.

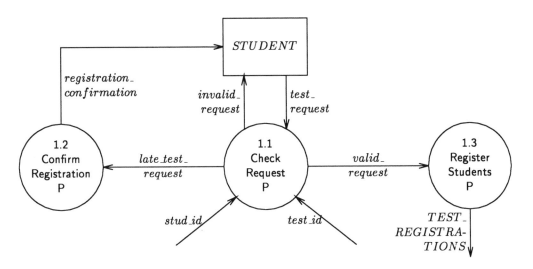

Figure 9.15: Diagram 1 (register for test).

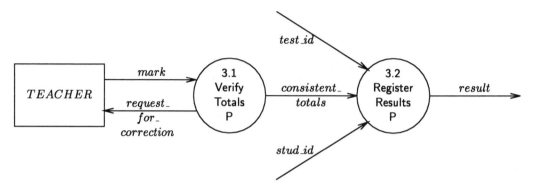

Figure 9.16: Diagram 3 (maintaining test results).

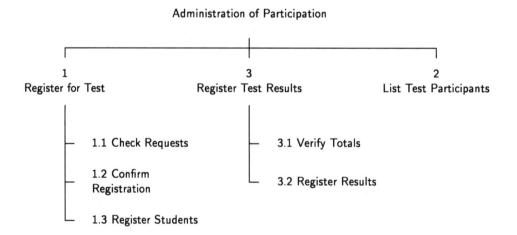

Figure 9.17: Transformation decomposition tree of the administration.

of the parent data transformation and k is an arbitrary number that is unique within the diagram. Primitive data transformations are additionally labeled by a P.

When we decompose a data transformation, we may also decompose the data flows entering and leaving the transformation subject to the principle of **data balancing**, which says that the sum of data items entering (leaving) a data transformation must be equal to the sum of data items entering (leaving) its decomposition. For example, *STUDENTS* and *TESTS* enter diagram 2 and *REGISTRATIONS* leaves diagram 2; this equals the input and output data flow of data transformation 2 in the level 1 diagram. Note that only the *sum* of input (output) data items of diagram n and data transformation n is required to be equal. This allows us to split or merge data flows when we go from a data transformation to its decomposition, as long as we preserve the total set of data items passing through the flow. The decomposition of a flow into finer-grained flows at a lower level must be documented in the data dictionary.

When we decompose a data transformation into a DF diagram, we must take care that the source (destination) of the flows entering (leaving) the decomposition can be traced. One way to do this is to take care that the flows entering (leaving) the data transformation have unique names and to use these names also for the input (output) flows of the decomposition. If a data transformation reads from a data store through a nameless flow, then we use the name of the data store as the flow name in the decomposition (see the flow *TEST_REGISTRATIONS* in figure 9.15).

We allow the repetition of external entities at different levels of the hierarchy, but data stores must be shown in one DF diagram only. If we were to repeat one data store in different diagrams, then the interfaces with the store would be distributed over different diagrams, which would reduce the modularity of the model.

9.6.2 Minispecs

A combinational transformation can be specified by decomposing it into a DF diagram without data stores or by writing a minispec. A minispec defines the relationship between inputs and outputs of a data transformation. Minispecs can also specify requirements on code size and execution speed of the implementation. Each minispec should not be larger than a page. Minispecs can be written in any language that is agreed upon and understood by all relevant people and that is unambiguous. Some frequently used specification techniques in minispecs are *structured English, pseudocode, decision trees, decision tables*, and *pre- and postconditions*. Formal specification languages such as VDM or Z are also possible. In this section I give examples of pre- and postcondition minispecs and pseudocode minispecs. In the next chapter, some examples of structured English, decision trees and decision tables are given.

The pre- and postcondition style of writing minispecs is a declarative way of specifying what a process does by means of rules of the form

PRE: precondition on input data flows
POST: postcondition on output data flows.

The precondition may be vacuously true, in which case it is given by the Boolean TRUE. Note that the postcondition is a *condition* on the output data, not an action that produces the data. This gives the designer the freedom to choose among different actions that would implement the minispec. Figure 9.18 gives a declarative specification of the Check Request

---

Check Request
PRE: $TEST.COURSE.course\_nr = test\_request.course\_nr$
        and $STUDENT.student\_nr = test\_request.student\_nr$
POST: $valid\_request = test\_request + \langle TEST.COURSE.course\_name \rangle.$

PRE: no $COURSE$ with $COURSE.course\_nr = test\_request.course\_nr$ in $COURSES$
        or no $STUDENT$ with $STUDENT.student\_nr = test\_request.student\_nr$ in $STUDENTS$
POST: $invalid\_request = ``error''.$

Figure 9.18: Minispec for Check Request. Note that the preconditions must jointly cover all possible input data.

Check Request
READ *stud_id, course_nr, date_of_test* FROM *test_request*.
DO in no particular order:
        SEARCH $STUDENTS$ FOR *student_id*.
        SEARCH $COURSES$ FOR *course_nr, date_of_test*.
END_DO.
IF not found THEN WRITE "Invalid request" TO *invalid_request*
ELSE READ *course_name* FROM $COURSES$.
        WRITE *stud_id, course_nr, course_name, date_of_test* TO *valid_request*.
END_IF.

Figure 9.19: Imperative specification of Check Request, using pseudocode.

---

process of figure 9.15. Note that two pre- and postcondition pairs are needed. These preconditions must be mutually exclusive and they must jointly cover all possible input data. For comparison, figure 9.19 gives an example of an imperative specification of Check request, using pseudocode. Structured Analysis does not prescribe a particular language for pseudocode. Any language which is understandable for analysts and implementors and domain specialists is acceptable. Figure 9.20 lists a number of constructs that can be used in pseudocode specifications.

Figure 9.21 gives a declarative specification of the Register Student process. It takes a *valid_request* tuple and takes the current state of the *TEST_REGISTRATIONS* data store, and adds the tuple to the data store. Even though the process performs an action on a data store, the postcondition is still specified declaratively as a condition on the contents of the data store. For comparison, figure 9.22 gives an imperative specification. The danger of imperative specifications is that they lure the analyst in writing detailed programs at a stage of development where this is not appropriate. This makes imperative specifications longer than necessary, and they are harder to read and harder to change than declarative specifications. On the other hand, if the effect of a process is to perform

---

- READ (data items FROM [input data flow | data store])
- WRITE (data items TO [output data flow | data store])
- CREATE data item IN data store
- DELETE data item FROM data store
- SEARCH data store FOR condition
- DO in no particular order: sentences END_DO
- IF test THEN sentences (ELSE sentence) END_IF
- CASE term IN labeled sentences END_CASE
- WHILE test DO sentences END_WHILE
- FOR_EACH term IN list DO sentences END_FOR

Figure 9.20: Examples of sentences that can be used in writing pseudocode specifications.

Register Student
PRE: *valid_request* is present
and contents of $TEST\_REGISTRATIONS = X$
POST: $TEST\_REGISTRATIONS = X \cup \{valid\_request\}$.

Figure 9.21: Declarative specification of the Register Student process. This is an update, but we still specify its postcondition as a *condition* and not as an action.

Register Student
READ *valid_request*.
WRITE TO $TEST\_REGISTRATIONS$.

Figure 9.22: Imperative specification of Register Student, using pseudocode.

an action, such as to update a data store, an imperative specification is usually shorter, simpler and more understandable than the corresponding declarative specification (compare figures 9.21 and 9.22).

9.7   Methodological Analysis

9.7.1   The place of DF models in the specification framework

DF models can be used to specify the behavior of any current or desired data manipulation system. They ignore the most important aspect of data manipulation systems, viz. that they have a UoD: In DF modeling the *system* is specified, not its UoD. Referring to the framework for behavior specifications in figure 4.3 (page 75), DF models represent both dimensions of system behavior, static and dynamic. Figure 9.23 details the aspects of state space and state transition specification represented by ER and DF specifications. Briefly, the system state space is represented in a DF model by data stores and the state transitions of the system are represented by data transformations. Some static constraints can be specified in the data dictionary as comments on data store definitions and some dynamic constraints on transactions can be specified as part of the documentation of external entities. It is clear from figure 9.23 that the ER model duplicates information already represented by the data stores. In addition there is information present on either side not represented by the other:

- ER models show of which entity types and relationships the existence sets are stored in the data stores. ER models also show cardinality constraints.

- DF models show what use is made of the data in the data stores. They also show where the data come from and where they go to.

The state transitions of the system are represented by the data transformations. In particular, data transformations and their specifications represent the response of the system to events. An event triggers one or more data transformations, which trigger other transformations, so that eventually an observable response is produced. All data transformations therefore represent observable activity of the system. A DF diagram provides the same information as a list of required observable system functions (in the sense of useful interactions) and adds to this the following information:

- Which external entities produce or consume data during an interaction.

- Which information about past interactions is accessible to each function.

This is represented by showing how each data transformation reads information from the data stores, and how it updates the data stores. In the simplest kind of DF diagram, each data transformation represents a single system function, contains no data stores itself, and accesses only system data stores; different transformations do not send data flows to each other. This is shown schematically in figure 9.24. Let us call this a **functional DF diagram**. In a functional diagram, there is a one-one relationship between data transformations and required system functions and the transformations have no direct interfaces with each other. The transformations are all combinational, because they have no memory.

	System behavior specification	
	ER model	DF model
State space		
Entities	Y	Data store records
Entity types	Y	Data stores
Entity attributes	Y	Data store fields
Relationships	Y	Structured data stores
is_a Relationships	Y	N
Relationship types	Y	Data stores
Relationship attributes	Y	Data store fields
Constraints		
Cardinality	Y	Data dictionary
Storage constraints	As annotation	Data dictionary
State transitions		
System transactions	N	Data transformations
Transaction effects	N	Minispecs
Transaction preconditions	N	Minispecs
Other constraints		
Interface technology	N	Data dictionary
Response time	N	Data dictionary
Delay	N	Data dictionary

Figure 9.23: Representation of the static and dynamic dimension of system behavior by ER models and by DF models.

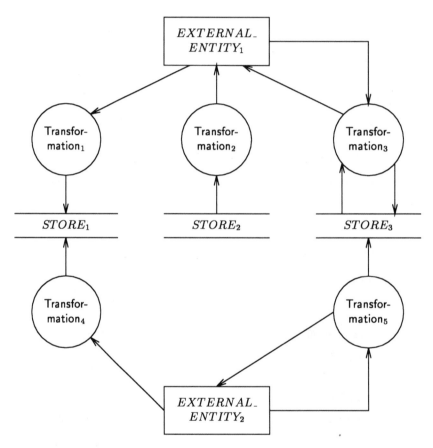

Figure 9.24: The structure of a functional DF diagram.

We can therefore assume that each transformation is specified by a minispec; if a transformation were to be decomposed into a DF diagram, then this diagram contains no data stores and we can write a minispec that specifies the same effect. Furthermore, we can always specify a function completely by specifying two things in its minispec:

- The **precondition** of the function. This is a condition on the triggering event of the function and on the contents of the data stores that, if false, prevents the function occurring. If the precondition is false, the transformation responds to the event by sending a message to the environment that the function cannot be executed.

- The *effect* of the function. If the precondition is satisfied, the transformation responds by updating data stores and/or sending output to the environment as required by the function. The effect may be specified by means of a postcondition specification, or by an imperative specification, etc. The effect is always observable. (Any update to a data store is observable because data store contents are by definition observable.)

Any DF diagram can always be brought into functional form, because this form represents the structure of a programmable computer. At the very least, we can represent a data manipulation system as a single data store and a single data transformation, representing the memory and processor of a computer, respectively. This represents the system as a single, complicated function with a single, complicated memory. In practice, we can usually do better than that and distinguish several orthogonal system functions. In any case, a DF model represents a system as a collection of functions, each of which has a precondition and an effect.

9.7.2 Transactions

Figure 9.23 defines the dynamic aspect of the system as consisting of *transactions* (useful interactions with the environment that are atomic) rather than functions (useful interactions with the environment that are not necessarily atomic). DF models do not represent system transactions but system functions — indeed, data transformations are often called *functions* by some authors. There is nothing in the concept of data transformation that forces us to use it to represent transactions. Nevertheless, even if transformations do not always represent transactions, an entire DF model represents system behavior as consisting of transactions. We explain this in the next paragraphs.

A transaction is represented in a DF model as consisting of an *event* generated by the environment and a *response* generated by the system. The atomicity property of transactions is satisfied because a DF model assumes a system implemented by means of *perfect technology*, which means that data transformations perform their task at infinite speed, data stores have unlimited capacity, and data access is instantaneous. This means that the response to an event occurs synchronously to the event! We call this the **synchronicity assumption** of DF modeling. It simplifies the representation of the system considerably. In practice, it means that the processes that will implement a transaction must be sufficiently fast as compared with the speed with which the environment produces events, so that the processing speed can be neglected. The synchronicity assumption leads to important constraints on the implementation of control systems, where the environment may produce events at a very high rate and these events must not be lost by the system.

An **essential DF diagram** is a is a functional DF diagram in which each transformation represents a single system transaction. An **essential DF model** is a model in which the

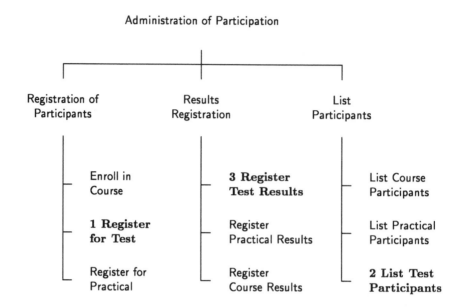

Figure 9.25: Function decomposition tree of the administration of participation.

DF diagram is essential. Once we have a list of required system transactions, we can try to represent required system behavior by means of an essential model. If all data transformations in figure 9.24 are transactions and different transformations are different transactions, then this is an essential DF model. If the system can perform more than five transactions, the essential model is likely to look like a bundle of spaghetti and it is useful to introduce a hierarchy in the model. In other words, even if we do not decompose transactions into lower-level data transformations, there will be higher-level transformations that are decomposed into transactions.

9.7.3   Transformation decomposition

For each product, we can draw a function decomposition tree whose root is labeled by the product idea and whose leaves are labeled by the product transactions. In theory, the *function* decomposition tree of a data manipulation system may differ from the *transformation* decomposition tree of the same system. For example, figure 9.25 gives a function decomposition tree of the student administration that differs from the transformation decomposition tree of figure 9.17. The nodes of the two trees that represent the same transactions have been numbered and are printed in boldface.

The two trees have been let to differ only to keep the DF model of the administration small and illustrative; in general, it is a bad idea to let the two trees differ this way. Figure 9.26 shows the relationship between the two trees that should be maintained. The figure shows the outline of a transformation decomposition tree that contains a function decomposition tree as a subtree with the same root. From the top down, the correspondence to be maintained is as follows:

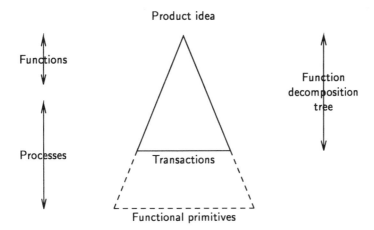

Figure 9.26: The transformation decomposition tree should contain the function decomposition tree as a subtree with the same root.

- The root of the function decomposition tree represents the *product idea*. This must coincide with the root of the transformation decomposition tree, which represents the system transformation in the context diagram. Consequently, we should label the system transformation by the product idea.

- The product idea is decomposed into required system functions, defined as useful system behavior. Thus, any product function is a product activity that contributes to the product idea, and all product activities must contribute to the product idea. This agrees with the definition of business function in Information Engineering as a group of activities that together support one aspect of furthering the mission of the business (page 118). Note, however, that we are now decomposing a product idea and not a business mission.

- A **process** is an activity with an input and an output, whose performance takes a finite interval of time (possibly of zero length). Processes are performed in order to perform a function. This agrees with the definition of business process in Information Engineering (page 118).

- The leaves of the function decomposition tree are the product transactions, which are processes that take no time. In an essential DF model, each transaction is represented by one data transformation, and each data transformation represents one transaction. If transactions are too complicated to be specified by a minispec, we may decompose their transformations further. This leads to functional primitives below the level of transactions.

By requiring the function decomposition tree to coincide with the upper part of the transformation decomposition tree, we achieve that the DF model represents no product mechanisms, no product structure, and no temporal sequences of activities. These required properties of the function decomposition tree were detailed in subsection 6.4.1 (page 118). In particular, the transformation decomposition tree makes no statement about the required system architecture. This parallels the independence of the function decomposition tree of a business from the decomposition of the business into subsystems, noted in the methodological discussion of ISP (page 132). Transformation decomposition stays at one level of aggregation in the development framework, system decomposition moves one level down.

All that is represented by the DF model of a system is that in order to perform a certain activity (data transformation), certain other activities must be performed (indicated by the decomposition of the data transformation). Conversely, the only reason for the presence of a data transformation lies in the fact that a higher-level transformation must be performed. The function decomposition tree thus represents a truly essential model of required system behavior.

Note that the activity of the system below the level of transactions is represented in more detail by the transaction decomposition table. For example, figure 8.8 (page 173) shows which data are created, read, updated or deleted as part of the transactions of the student administration. The part of the tree below the level of transactions shows how these sub-transaction processes produce and consume data.

9.8   Summary

A complete data flow model consists of the following components:

- A set of data flow diagrams.

- The corresponding process decomposition tree.

- Minispecs for the primitive processes.

- An ER diagram that represents the structure of the data stores.

- A data dictionary that contains the definitions of all names used in the model.

DF models partition the observable behavior of a system into activities called *data transformations*, which may change the system state as contained in the *data stores*, and whose behavior may depend upon the contents of the data store. The system communicates with its environment by data flows. The entire system is specified by the *system transformation* in the *context diagram*. This is decomposed into a DF diagram, whose transformation may be further decomposed into DF diagrams. The resulting hierarchical structure is represented by the transformation decomposition tree. The leaves of the tree are transformations that must be specified by *minispecs*.

The behavior of a system is represented by decomposing each transaction into an *external event* and a *response* to that event. External events can be generated by *external entities* or by the passage of time, in which case they are called *temporal events*. An event and its response together form a system transaction. Because of the atomicity property of transaction, a response is considered to occur simultaneously with its event.

The ER diagram of an ER model duplicates some information present in a DF diagram, but adds the information what the entity types and relationships are whose existence sets are stored in the data stores. For each entity type and for each relationship, the existence set should be stored in one or more system data stores; conversely, each data store should contain at least part of the existence set of at least one entity type or relationship. The DF diagram shows what kind of access the data transformations have to the data stores.

In a *functional DF model*, all data transformations correspond one-one with the required system functions, and the activities do not interface with each other. If the activities correspond one-one with required system transactions, we call it an *essential DF model*. The transformation decomposition tree should be made to contain the function decomposition tree of the system so that both trees share their root. The leaves of the function decomposition tree are data transformations that represent required system transactions; the transformation decomposition tree can further decompose these transformations into DF diagrams that accomplish the tasks listed in the transaction decomposition table.

9.9   Exercises

1. In figure 9.8, *TEST_REGISTRATION* really represents three events in the UoD: registering for a test, doing the test, and receiving a mark. An attribute of the registration event is *date_registered*, an attribute of doing the test is *date_of_test* and an attribute of receiving a mark is *result*. Change the ER diagram to represent these three events. Then adapt the DF diagram of the test registration so that each data store in the changed DF diagram corresponds to exactly one entity- or relationship type in the changed DF diagram.

2. (a) Draw an essential DF diagram of the student administration that represents the transactions of the functions Registration of Participants and Results Registration, shown in figure 9.25.

   (b) Abstract from this model a higher-level functional DF diagram that contains the two transformations corresponding to the functions Registration of Participants and Results Registration.

3. The DF diagram notation can also be used to represent material manipulations. Assume that we use thick lines to represent flows, transformations and stores of material.

   (a) Discuss the difference in behavior between flows, transformations and stores of data on the one hand and flows, transformations and stores of material on the other.

   (b) Suppose that we use dashed lines to represent energy flows, transformations and stores. Discuss the difference with data flows, transformations and stores.

4. Build data and/or material flow diagrams of the following processes. If there are temporal events, identify these. Try to build functional models.

   (a) To fill in my income tax form, I collect the yearly salary statement of my employer, leaf through a book with the latest tax-deduction tricks, gather the bills of deductible expenses of one year, fill in the form, use the income tax tables to compute the income tax return I am entitled to, copy the filled out form and send it to the income tax department.

   (b) A thermostat reads a sensor that indicates the current room temperature, accepts data from an input device that tells it what the desired room temperature is, and can send a signal to a heater to switch on and off. List the transactions of this control system and make a functional DF diagram.

(c) To wash clothes, they are separated into machine-washable clothes, hand-washable clothes, and clothes that must be cleaned chemically. The machine-washable clothes are separated into white and colored clothes to be washed separately. Hand-washable clothes are put aside to be done later and clothes to be cleaned chemically are put on another pile. After washing, the clothes are separated into those that can be put in the tumble dryer and those that must be hung to dry. After drying, the clothes are folded and put in cupboards.

9.10   Bibliographical Remarks

The importance of data flow modeling for business problem analysis was already realized in the early 1960s. Two early references which recognized this need are Gatto [110] and Miller [230]. The DF modeling notation received wide attention after papers by Ross and Brackett [293] and Ross [291] were published in 1976 and 1977. This notation distinguishes input flows into data input and control, and additional uses an flow to represent the mechanism by which the transformation is carried out. It became known as the Structured Analysis and Design Technique (SADT). Marca and Gowan published a book about this in 1988 [210].

The DF notation discussed in this chapter is a simplification of the SADT notation and was introduced in the late 1970s by DeMarco [84], V. Weinberg [358], Gane and Sarson [108], and Yourdon and Constantine [378]. DeMarco introduced the concept of leveling.

The use of ER models in combination with DF modeling is promoted in the early 1980s by Flavin [105]. The DF-ER modeling notation reached its final form in the late 1980s in a book by Yourdon [376]. Kowal [185] and Goldsmith [118] give good surveys of the combined DF-ER modeling approach.

The concept of essential model is due to McMenamin and Palmer [225]. Reactive systems are defined by Manna and Pnueli [209] and by Harel and Pnueli [140]; they are called planned response systems by McMenamin and Palmer. The synchronicity assumption is due to Berry and Cosserat [31] and is called the *synchrony hypothesis* by them.

10

Structured Analysis II: Methods

10.1   Introduction

Structured analysis (SA) was developed in a period in which manual administrations were automated for the first time. The computerized administrations had roughly the same functionality as the manual ones, but they could perform these functions faster. Consequently, the dominant method for finding a DF model of a SuD is to first model the current administration, abstract an essential model from this, and reimplement this as a computerized administration (figure 10.1). This is the method of *essential system modeling* discussed in subsection 10.2.1.

When DF models were used to specify requirements for control systems, it was found that there is no current manual system to be modeled first; instead, there are interface agreements with other engineering groups in which the transactions with other systems are laid down. A second method to find DF models therefore emerged, called *event partitioning*, in which the DF model is built starting from a list of event-response pairs that represent the required transactions with the environment. A refinement of this method, called *process analysis of transactions*, starts from the transaction decomposition table and builds the DF model from there. These methods are discussed in subsections 10.2.2 and 10.2.3. Section 10.3 lists the evaluation methods used in structured analysis. In section 10.4, we take a brief look at system decomposition and in section 10.5 we analyze structured analysis from a methodological point of view.

10.2   Methods to Find a DF Model

10.2.1   Essential system modeling

Figure 10.2 shows the structure of system development by essential system modeling. The current (manual or computer-based) system is modeled, including all its physical details. In the physical model, all model components are named after the physical entities that

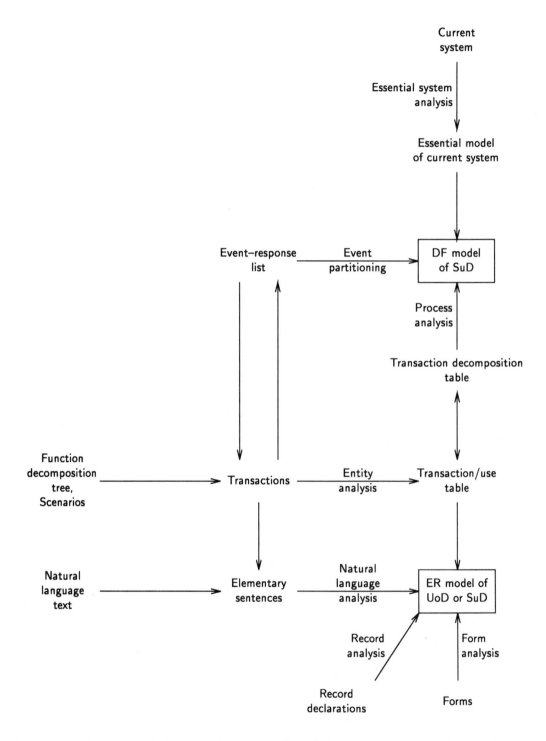

Figure 10.1: Road map for finding a DF model of the SuD and an ER model of the UoD or SuD.

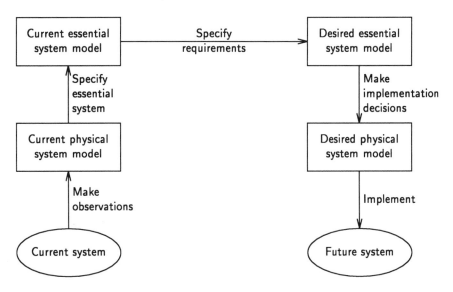

Figure 10.2: System development by essential system modeling.

- Assign logical names to the model elements.
- Flatten the DF diagram hierarchy.
- Remove unnecessary communication infrastructure.
- Remove unnecessary administrative activity.
- Partition into activity fragments.
- Integrate essential activity fragments by joining data flows and data stores.

Figure 10.3: Essential system modeling heuristics.

implement the component. Data transformations represent activities or processors (human or machine) that perform the activities.

The components of a physical DF model receive the names that are actually in use in the current system and which may indicate the current implementation technology. Thus, a transformation may be called "Monday morning's work", "Bob's speciality" or "Alice". Data stores may be called "In-box" or "Green cabinet" and data flows may have names such as "pink form" or "customer's copy". The resulting DF diagram is called the **current physical model**. Since it describes the current system exactly as it is and uses names borrowed from those currently doing the work, it should be easy to build and verify this model. If the current system is manual, the current physical model represents the flow of paper documents through the organization.

The current system model describes the system as it is currently implemented, and therefore contains activities, flows and stores that are due to current, imperfect implementation technology. We now eliminate all traces of current technology by extracting an essential model from the current physical model. Figure 10.3 lists the heuristics of essential system modeling. These should be followed in the order listed.

- **Remove nonlogical naming**. Any indication of persons, departments, locations, material, machines etc. is eliminated by choosing names that only describe the data that are manipulated, transported or stored. As a result, all transformations, flows and stores have logical names.

- **Remove inessential partitioning into tasks**. The partitioning of the current system into data transformations may be the result of historical contingencies, power games and other imperfections of the real world. For example, the sales department may maintain a shadow financial admininistration because in the past the department manager did not trust the financial department. By flattening the DF diagram hierarchy, current boundaries between task groupings dissolve.

- **Remove unnecessary communications infrastructure.** There may be a communications infrastructure in place that deals purely with imperfect implementation technology. For example, one department, person or machine may process its inputs so slowly that inputs sent to it from other departments have to be batched. This is visible as a data store in the DF diagram that would be unnecessary with perfect implementation technology. Other communication tasks that are the result of imperfect implementation technology are formatting, translation, sorting, merging etc., that take place to make data produced by one subsystem ready for consumption by another subsystem. All these communication tasks must be removed from the current system model by assuming that the system is implemented using infinitely fast processors and infinitely large data stores.

- **Remove unnecessary administrative activities.** There may be administrative activities in the system that are due to imperfect implementation structures. For example, one activity performed by the system may correct errors in data received from another activity performed by the system. Since the system is now assumed to be perfect, this kind of error correction is unnecessary and must be removed. Other examples of such unnecessary activities are checking whether input received from some system activity conforms to certain standards, auditing the correct performance of these checks, measuring the performance of the system, monitoring and regulating resource use, maintaining transaction logs, writing backup files, etc.

- **Partition the model into activity fragments**. Those data transformations that are part of the response to an event are grouped together into an activity fragment. This is the method of event partitioning, discussed in the next subsection. The activity fragments may still contain some traces of current implementation technology, such as unnecessary sequencing of data transformations, unnecessarily complex access to data stores, and storing multiple copies of data in different places. These traces must be removed.

- **Integrate essential activity fragments**. The resulting activity fragments are glued together at the data stores and data flows, and the integrated DF diagram should be given a logical hierarchical structure.

Once we have an essential model of the current system, we transform it into an essential model of the required system. We then make implementation decisions on the basis of the available technology, specify a physical model of the desired system, and implement this.

---

1. Build the context diagram.

   (a) Understand the purpose of the system.

   (b) Identify the external entities.

   (c) Define the data flows entering and leaving the system.

   (d) Check the context diagram.

2. Build an event list.

   (a) List the events in the environment to which the system must respond.

   (b) For each event, list the response of the system to the event.

   (c) Classify each response as data-intensive or as control-intensive.

3. Build a behavioral model.

   (a) Build a DF fragment for each event-response pair.

      • Define one data transformation for each event-response pair. Usually the transformation is named after the response of the system to the event.

      • Connect each response transformation to external entities that must sense the response.

      • If the response depends upon the current state of the system, connect the response transformation with a read data flow to the data store that holds the relevant part of the state.

      • If the response involves a change of state of the system, connect the response transformation with a write data flow to the relevant data store.

   (b) Merge the diagrams.

   (c) Divide the DF diagram into levels.

   (d) Complete the data dictionary.

   (e) Add implementation constraints.

Figure 10.4: Event partitioning.

10.2.2   Event partitioning

During essential system modeling, we are asked to partition the current system model into activity fragments that each deal with one event. This technique became known as **event partitioning**. It can be used not only to model current systems, but also to model future systems, and it is applicable to data-intensive as well as control-intensive systems. Figure 10.4 shows the tasks of event partitioning as listed by Goldsmith [118]. The basic idea of event partitioning is to identify external entities, identify data flows between the SuD and the external entities, identify events that lead to input flows, and draw a DF fragment for each event that shows how the input flows lead to the output flows. To deal with temporal events, the procedure should be completed by additionally starting from each system response and reasoning back to the event that triggered the response. The procedure is likely to iterate over the tasks listed in figure 10.4 until a satisfactory model is found. In

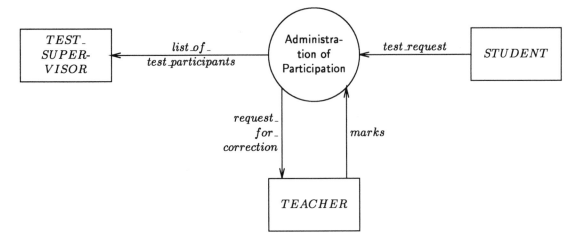

Figure 10.5: Initial context diagram of part of the student administration, that shows only the major data flows in each transaction.

Event	Response
Student requests participation in a test	Register for test
Time to produce result lists	Produce result lists
Administration requests list of test participants	Produce list of test participants
. . .	. . .

Figure 10.6: Part of an event list for the student administration.

the beginning, only normal events and responses should be considered. The occurrence of errors and exceptional conditions must be considered later.

To give an example, the initial context diagram for the student administration system could look like figure 10.5. Later iterations would improve this diagram. Part of the event list for the same administration is shown in figure 10.6. The procedure of figure 10.4 recommends classifying each event-response pair as data-intensive or control-intensive. This is a heuristic to determine whether, as a next step, we should build a DF model or a state transition diagram first. In this book we do not treat state transition diagrams, so we omit this part. (State transition diagrams and related notations are important for modeling control systems and are treated in *Requirements Engineering: Semantic, Real-Time and Object-Oriented Methods*.) Figure 10.7 shows the DF fragment built for the event-response pair "Student requests to perform a test – register for test". Note that it does not yet produce a response *invalid_request*, since we decided to deal with error conditions later.

10.2.3 Process analysis of transactions

Process analysis of transactions is a refinement of event partitioning that takes care that we produce mutually consistent ER and DF models (cf. the road map in figure 10.1). It is based upon the assumption that each event-response pair is a system transaction

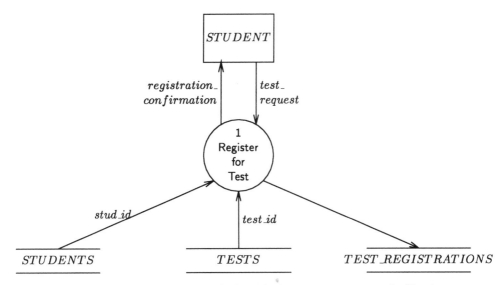

Figure 10.7: DF diagram fragment that deals with the event-response pair "Student requests to perform a test – Register for Test'.

and that each system transaction is an event-response pair. We start from the transaction decomposition table of the student administration shown in chapter 8 (figure 8.8, page 173). Figure 10.7 shows the DF fragment that deals with the transaction Register for Test. Note that the R and C entries in the Register for Test row indicate exactly which data store access must be represented in the DF diagram.

10.2.4   Case study: The Circulation Desk

Figure 10.9 gives the transaction decomposition table that corresponds to the transaction/use table given in chapter 8, figure 8.11 (page 175). For simplicity, the document reservation transaction and the *FINE* entity type have been omitted. In addition, not all situations in which a fine can be created are modeled.

We classified the circulation transactions into three groups and merged the DF fragments of each group as shown in the function decomposition tree of figure 10.10. Note that the root of this tree represents the product idea of a system for the administration of the circulation of documents. Since this is the task of the circulation department of the library, the decomposition tree of this function is a subtree of the function decomposition tree of the library, shown in figure 8.10. The DF diagrams of the three functions Reservation, Borrowing and Document loss are shown in figures 10.11, 10.12 and 10.13. Figure 10.14 gives the level 1 diagram and figure 10.15 shows the context diagram. Because the level 1 diagram merges some data flows of the Borrowing function, figure 10.14 shows a data dictionary entry that defines the connection between the higher and lower level data flows. Minispecs for the functional primitives of the DF model using various notations are given in figures 10.16 to 10.22. The DF diagrams and minispecs do not deal with errors or exceptional conditions.

The minispec for Lend Document uses a decision tree. This is a useful technique for

	Enroll in course	Register for test	Register for practical	Register test result	Register course result	Register practical result	List course participation	List test participation	List practical participation
COURSE	R						R		
ENROLLMENT	C				U		U		
PRACTICAL			R						R
PRACTICAL_REG			C			U			R
STUDENT	R	R	R				R	R	R
TEST		R						R	
TEST_REG		C		U				R	

Figure 10.8: Transaction decomposition table for the student administration.

	Required system transactions						
	Reserve title	Cancel title reservation	Lend document	Take in document	Send reminder	Extend document loan	Lose document
DOCUMENT	R						U
FINE							C
LOAN			C	D	RU	RU	RD
LOSS							C
MEMBER	R		R		R	R	
TITLE	R						
T_RESERVATION	C	D	RD			R	

Figure 10.9: Transaction decomposition table of some transactions of the circulation administration.

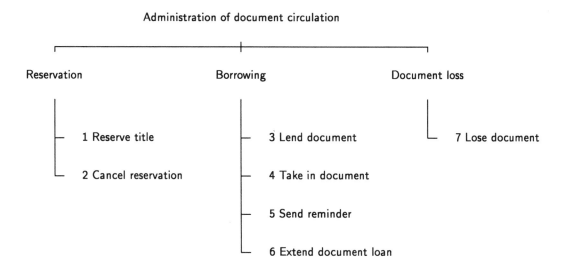

Figure 10.10: Function decomposition tree of the administration of document circulation.

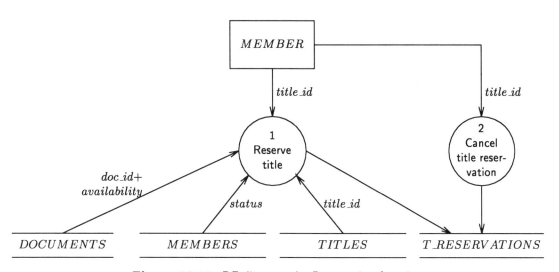

Figure 10.11: DF diagram the Reservation function.

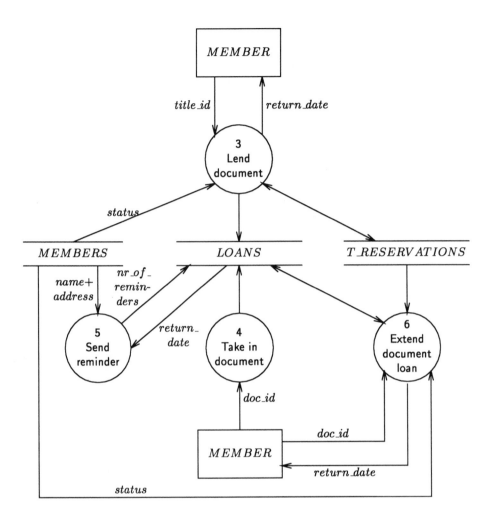

Figure 10.12: DF diagram of the Borrowing function.

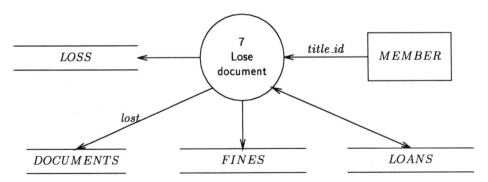

Figure 10.13: DF diagram of the Document loss function.

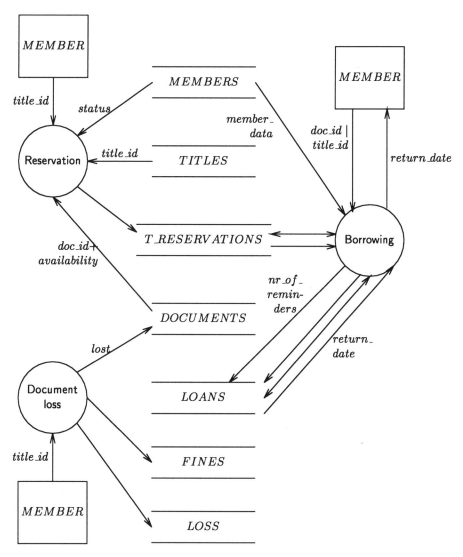

Data dictionary entry:
$member\_data = status \mid (name + address)$.

Figure 10.14: Level 1 DF diagram of the circulation administration plus two relevant data dictionary entries.

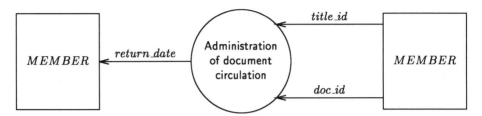

Figure 10.15: Context diagram of the circulation administration.

Reserve title

- Check whether title exists.
- Check whether all documents of this title are available.
- Check whether the member is allowed to reserve documents.
- If all checks are positive, create a title reservation record.
- Otherwise, refuse the reservation request.

Figure 10.16: Minispec of Reserve Title in natural language.

Cancel title reservation

- Remove title reservation by this member from $TITLE\_RESERVATIONS$.

Figure 10.17: Minispec of Cancel Title Reservation in natural language.

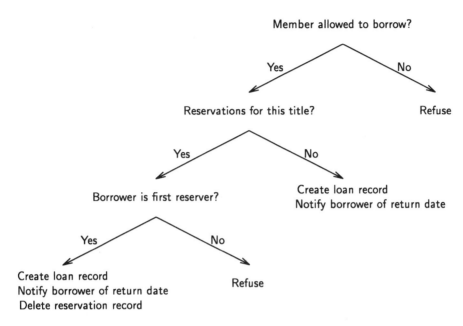

Figure 10.18: Minispec of Lend Document, using a decision tree.

Loan exists	Y	
Reservation exists	N	Other
Member has permission	Y	
	Update return date of loan	Refuse

Figure 10.19: Minispec of Extend Loan, using a decision table. The upper rows give an exhaustive listing of all possible conditions on the input data flows. The bottom row lists the actions done for each possible condition.

Take in document
• Delete the loan record of this member for this document.

Figure 10.20: Minispec of Take In Document in natural language.

Send reminder

- Read all overdue loans from *LOANS*.

- Produce for each loan a record containing the loan identification, the member name and address, and the return date for this loan.

- Update each overdue loan record by increasing the count of the number of reminders sent.

Figure 10.21: Minispec of Send Reminder in natural language.

Lose document

- Update document record with flag indicating that it is lost.

- Create fine record.

- Create loss record.

- Delete loan record.

Figure 10.22: Minispec of Lose Document in natural language.

specifying data transformations with a complex decision logic. A disadvantage of decision trees is that actions that must occur under several conditions may have to be repeated. The minispec for Extend Loan uses a decision table. This has been done for illustrative purposes, for the transformation is so simple that we do not need a decision table to specify it. Decision tables are useful if an exhaustive enumeration of all possible conditions is needed. A disadvantage of decision tables is that they tend to become voluminous, so that the overall picture becomes obscured.

10.3 Methods to Evaluate a DF Model

10.3.1 Walkthroughs and inspections

If a data flow model represents the current system, it can be validated by doing observations of this system and comparing them with the model. If the model represents a future system, no observations can be made and we must resort to other means, such as walkthroughs. A **walkthrough** is a peer review of a product specification. Walkthroughs are the traditional way of validating DF models in structured analysis. In its simplest form, a walkthrough is a meeting of developers and user representatives, in which someone very familiar with the model walks through the model. This may be the model builder but it may also be someone who studied the model in detail before the meeting. Any errors or mistakes in the model are noted, but not discussed. The model builder corrects them later on and, if necessary, the revised model is subjected to a second walkthrough. In order for the walkthrough not to become a walkover, the topic of the walkthrough must be focused on the model, not on the builder of the model. Participants in the walkthrough must not stand in a hierarchical relation with the model builder.

Inspections are a more formal variant of walkthroughs defined by Fagan [99, 100], in which the participants use a list of features to be checked in the specification. Inspections are part of a learning cycle, in which the model builder may be sent to courses to learn extra skills, and in which company practices are updated according to the results of inspection meetings.

10.3.2 Simulation and animation

A completely documented DF model can be executed by a suitable processor. The model builder can simulate the behavior of the specified system by simulating an event and following the data through the system until the response is produced. The same can also be done by a software interpreter. A simulation of a single system transaction consists of a sequence of alternating system states and system actions.

- Each system state is a snapshot of the simulation, consisting of the contents of all system data stores and the contents of all data flows.

- Each system action in the simulation is the firing of one primitive data transformation.

In the initial state of the simulation, all data flows are empty, except the input data flows that are filled by the event that triggers the transaction. The simulation then selects one data transformation for firing, which consumes its input flows and fills its output flows. In the final state of the simulation, all data flows are again empty, except the output data flows filled by the transaction response.

An **animation** is an animated presentation of a model simulation. An animated simulation could for example present the DF diagram to the user, and could represent the presence of data in a data flow or in a data store by a bullet. The firing of a data transformation could be presented by moving the bullets through the diagram (figure 10.23). If done at the appropriate speed, this results in an apparent movement of bullets through the diagram. The actual data values manipulated by the simulation could be gathered in a written simulation report.

If the model is not yet completely specified, then **token-based simulation** is still possible. In this kind of simulation, input data is represented by meaningless tokens. A data transformation that has tokens on all its input flows, fires by moving all these tokens to its output flows. Although rudimentary, token-based simulation does give an impression of system behavior. Token-based simulation can be animated in the same way as full-fledged value-based simulation.

10.3.3 Minimality principles

The **simplicity checks** of figure 10.24 can be used to enhance the understandability, and hence the communicability, of a data flow model. The 7 ± 2 check suggests the point at which, for reasons of comprehensibility, we should divide a DF diagram into levels. The other two principles are two formulations of the principle of loose coupling, formulated in table 2.1 (page 12). Simplicity considerations can cause us to split or merge data stores, because this would simplify data store access (e.g. reduce the number of arrows to or from a data store).

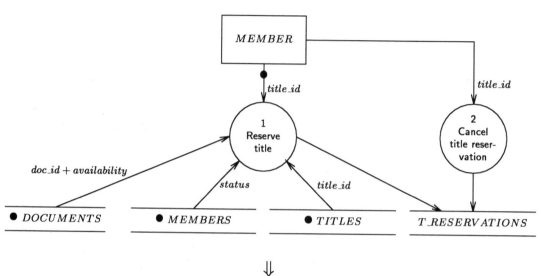

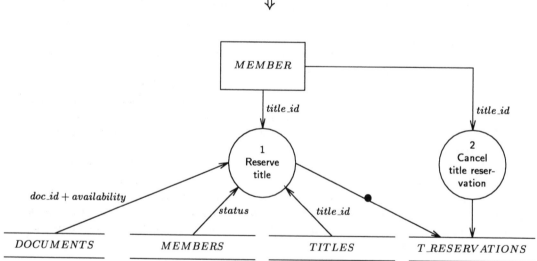

Figure 10.23: Animation of a DF diagram. A token placed on an input flow leads to the production of a token on the output flow. In the Ward/Mellor method of animation, data stores are not populated with tokens.

Minimality:

- **Seven plus or minus two.** The number of data transformation in a DF diagram should be 7 ± 2.

- **Minimal interfaces.** The number of interfaces between data transformations should be as small as possible.

- **Minimal access.** The number of accesses to a data store, and the number of data items transferred to and from a data store in each access, should be minimal.

Determinism:

- The data produced by a data transformation must be a function of the data that (ever) entered the transformation.

Balancing:

- **Vertical balancing.** The sum of data items entering (leaving) a compound data transformation equals the sum of data items entering (leaving) its defining DF diagram.

- **Horizontal balancing.** The DF diagram and ER diagram should be consistent with each other.

Figure 10.24: Quality checks for data flow models.

10.3.4 Determinism

The **determinism check** in figure 10.24 can be used to verify the completeness of the specification of data transformations. It is a check that the output of each data transformation is a function of its inputs. A data transformation should make no choice that is not determined by its input, so that to an observer the transformation behaves deterministically. For combinational data transformations, this means that the output of a transformation is a mathematical function of its input. For reactive transformations, this means that the output is a function of the input and its current state.

10.3.5 Vertical balancing

A leveled DF diagram is **vertically balanced** if each data transformation has exactly the same data interfaces as its decomposition. It is possible to split a data flow when we decompose a data transformation, but this must be done while conserving the data passing through the flows. Figure 10.14 contains an example.

10.3.6 Horizontal balancing and data usage

A DF diagram and an ER diagram are **horizontally balanced** if for each entity type and each relationship there is a set of one or more data stores that jointly contain the existence sets of these types, and for each data store there is at least one entity type or relationship that defines the contents of the data store. This means that all types of entities and relationships are actually used by some data transformation. In terms of the transaction decomposition table, each entity or relationship row should have an entry in it. This is a generalization of the creation/deletion check of ER modeling, where we check each row for creation and deletion events.

1. Allocate data transformations and data stores to available processors and devices.

2. Specify the human-computer interface.

3. For each processor, allocate behavior to

   (a) standard software already available on the processor or to

   (b) software tasks to be implemented manually.

4. Translate each DF diagram allocated to a task into a structure chart.

Figure 10.25: Decomposing a system into processors and tasks.

The dual of this check is the check of whether every transaction accesses at least one data store. This corresponds with a check of whether every column in the transaction decomposition table contains at least one entry. Columns without an entry indicate superfluous transactions, or transactions that have not been defined yet. We call this the **data usage check**.

10.4   System Decomposition

System decomposition consists of identifying subsystems that will jointly realize the behavior specified by the DF model. The subsystems may be processors, devices, people, index cards, etc. Devices may be sensors, terminals, actuators, etc. Allocation of the components of a DF diagram to different subsystems involves repartitioning the DF diagram hierarchy so that in the level 1 diagram, each data transformation represents one subsystem. The resulting model is called the **processor environment model**. Where the essential system model contains only the data transformations required to perform the system functions, the processor environment model contains additional transformations and stores needed to handle communication between different components. Essential data transformations and data stores may be split over several subsystems. For example, one data store may be duplicated over several file servers, a data transformation may be duplicated or split over several processors, etc. Allocation of essential data transformations and data stores to subsystems must be documented by means of **traceability tables** of the form shown in figure 10.26. A traceability table is a tabular representation of the existence set of a binary relationship. Each entry represents a binary link between a requirement at one level of aggregation and a subsystem at the next lower level of aggregation. The meaning of the link is that the subsystem helps implementing the requirement. Traceability tables are crucial when implementing changes to system requirements, for they allow developers to trace changes in requirements to changes in software modules.

Having allocated DF diagrams to subsystems, and having decided which subsystems are people and which are machines, we know which machines must implement the human-computer interface. Because users are only aware of the system through this interface, it is extremely important to get the user interface right. Specification of the user interface involves addition of transformations that deal with user dialogues, menu structures, screen forms, report formats, etc.

For each machine, certain software may already be available for many of the tasks

	Subsystem 1	Subsystem 2	· · · · · ·
Data transformation 1		X	
Data transformation 2		X	
Data transformation 3	X	X	
· · · · · ·			
Data store 1		X	
Data store 2	X	X	
Data store 3	X		
· · · · · ·			

Figure 10.26: Format of traceability tables. A traceability table links elements at one level of aggregation (vertical dimension) to subsystems at the next lower level of aggregation (horizontal dimension) to which they are allocated.

specified by the DF model of that machine. Libraries of reusable software components such as graphical routines, mathematical libraries, operating system libraries (e.g. routines for disk access), database management systems, etc. can be used to buy software to perform certain standard tasks. To exploit the availability of this software, the DF diagram for each machine is reorganized so that as many transformations as possible correspond to these ready-made software packages. These transformations then need not be implemented by handcraft but by means of reusable components. The resulting model is called **a software environment model**.

The data transformations for which no reusable software is available are now grouped into tasks, where a **task** is a sequential process. Tasks are allocated to one machine, which treats them as execution units that can be scheduled. Each task is a sequential process that does the work of one or more data transformations. Allocation of data transformations from the processor environment model to tasks in the software environment model must be documented by means of additional traceability tables.

Each task can now be designed by drawing a module diagram called a **structure chart**. This shows the organization of the code for the task into a hierarchical collection of modules, and show the flow of data and control between modules. Task design by means of structure charts is traditionally called **structured design**. Traditional structured development assumes that all tasks the SuD must be programmed manually and that the hardware consists of one processor; in this case, structured design follows structured analysis without intermediary decomposition or allocation steps.

10.5 Methodological Analysis

10.5.1 Essential system modeling

Essential system modeling is also called **reverse engineering**, which is a curious but correct term that indicates *system modeling*. The term reverse engineering connotes the idea of extracting requirements from a current system. These requirements may never have been written down, and they are needed if we are to replace a current system with another system, for we must know which essential requirements must be satisfied by the future system. Essential system modeling is a sensible thing to do when we want to **reengineer** a current system, i.e. to reimplement the current functionality with new technology. It is a reassuring activity from a modeling point of view, because there exists a system against which we can verify our model. In addition, if there is a current system, it is important for the developer of a future system to know what the current system is doing. Some of the functions of the current system may be so obviously needed in the opinion of the client, that the developer may never hear that they are needed.

The danger of the essential system modeling process proposed by McMenamin and Palmer is that one gets stuck in what they call the *current physical tarpit*. The modeler can lose too much time modeling too many details about the current physical system, that will be replaced anyway. Current physical system modeling may be useful, but the returns of this effort diminish quickly as the effort increases.

Current systems modeling is impossible if there is no current system to model. However, even if there is a current system, its functionality may be so inadequate that it is not worth the effort to model it. Approaches like ISAC and Information Engineering are oriented to developing systems with an enhanced functionality compared to the current system. In these approaches, system development is always part of business development, and the future information systems are therefore likely to have different functions than the current systems have. Thus, the effort spent on current system modeling must be determined by the balance between the need to get a true model of current functionality and the need to get a model of truly useful future functionality.

In an interesting empirical study of nine developers in three different companies by Bansler and Bødker [20], it was found that all interviewed developers did not make a current system model but immediately started by making a DF model of the required system. Bansler and Bødker also report a number of other interesting findings:

- The data flow models built in the investigated projects did not represent the essence of the required system, but described the required system in physical terms. In other words, during requirements engineering, implementation decisions were made.

- One of the implementation decisions made immediately was the determination of which part of the future system would be automated. This agrees with the ISAC, where this choice is made during activity study at the latest, which is before a precise model of the required systems is made. DF diagrams are used only to model the automated parts of the new situation; the manual part was modeled by other means.

- With one exception, the data flow models were not validated by users or domain specialists. In fact, they were never shown to users or domain specialists, because in the experience of the interviewed developers, users and domain specialists don't understand data flow models. The domain specialists felt comfortable with plain text but had a hard time reading (or even looking at) diagrams, so the developers validated the diagrams themselves. An interesting exception to this is the case where the domain specialists were engineers and technicians, used to constructing technical diagrams. These had a hard time reading text but felt comfortable with the diagrams.

- In one case only, the data flow model was updated to reflect changes to the system after it was implemented. In all other cases, changes to the implemented system were not reflected in the data flow model, so that the model was allowed to become obsolete during the system maintenance phase.

10.5.2   Event partitioning and data flow orientation

The method of event partitioning as presented in figure 10.4 starts with identifying the data flows between the SuD and its external entities, and identifies relevant events later. This is the natural thing to do if data flows are visible as paper forms that enter and leave an organization. It is then easy to first identify these forms, and next identify the events of receiving and sending a paper form. It is not the natural thing to do if the environment consists of other systems for which a list of input and output events is known. For control systems, it is more natural to think in terms of events and responses and worry about the data flows later. In addition, control system usually must respond to a large number of temporal events, for which no input data flows exist at all. The order of tasks in figure 10.4 should therefore be taken with a grain of salt; what is important is that for each transaction, a DF fragment is built. Each transaction consists of an event and a response, which at the requirements specification level are assumed to occur simultaneously; and each event and each response consists of zero or more data flows. It is just a matter of convenience whether we start with identifying relevant data flows, with identifying relevant events, or identifying relevant transactions. Note however that in order to build a functional DF model, we must at some point identify the relevant transactions. It is therefore always a good strategy to try finding the relevant transactions first, and turn to data flows or events only when it is hard to find the transactions immediately.

10.5.3   Specification of user procedures

Part of the system decomposition task is the determination of the boundary between people and machines. Because the specification techniques of DF models are oriented to automated systems, a consequence of postponing the choice of human-machine boundary until the design task is that the requirements specification represents human work in the same way as automated work. This totally ignores the important subject of work satisfaction. People do not tend to function very well if all they can do is perform tasks that are prescribed in minispecs down to the smallest details. One way to increase work satisfaction, and therefore human productivity, is to fix the human-machine boundary much earlier and specify human work by techniques from social psychology. As already remarked in the ISAC methodological discussion, there is something to say for specifying human work first and specifying machine work later. The study of Bansler and Bødker indicates that this agrees with what happens in practice anyway. One could turn to methods like ETHICS (appendix C) to borrow methods for the analysis of human work problems and for the specification of human work procedures.

10.6   Summary

A DF model of a future system can be found by means of *essential system modeling*, where we model the current physical system first, extract the essential model from this, and use this as the basis for the requirements on the future system. Part of the process of finding an essential system model is *event partitioning*, where we make a list of events to be handled by the current system, and for each event list the response produced by the system. The list of event-response pairs is used to define DF fragments of system activity. Event partitioning can just as well be used for future system modeling. An alternative to event partitioning is *process analysis of transactions*, which uses the transaction decomposition table to define DF fragments.

DF models can be evaluated by means of *walkthroughs* or *inspections*, in which developers and other relevant people evaluate a model on certain criteria. The model may be *simulated* and the simulations *animated* to enhance the understanding the behavior specified by the model. Simulations may be value-based or token-based. *Minimality checks* of a DF model check whether the number of transformations in a DF diagram is small enough to be comprehensible, whether the number of interfaces between data transformations is minimal, and whether the data fetched or stored in a data store should be minimal. In the *determinism check*, we verify that each transformation produces output that is a mathematical function of the input that ever was received by the transformation. The *vertical balancing* check consists of verifying that the data that flow into or out of a transformation equal the data that flow into or out of its decomposition. The *horizontal balancing* check verifies that the data stores in a DF diagram correspond to entity or relationship types in the ER diagram, and that the ER diagram is consistent with the data structure definitions in the data dictionary. This extends the creation/deletion check of ER modeling. The *data usage check* verifies whether every system transaction uses some data.

Essential system modeling has the advantage that there is an existing system against which we can verify the model, but it has the danger that we can spend too much effort in modeling a system that is no longer useful. Empirical research indicates that DF models are only used for the automated part of the required system, and that from the start they represent the physical structure of the system. They are not validated with the domain specialists, they are used for system implementation without going through an intermediate design stage, and after implementation they are not updated when the system is maintained.

Structured analysis tends to treat human work in the same way as mechanical work. The decision where to draw the human-machine interface is made only during design, and until that time all transformations are specified as if they had to be performed by machine. This is likely to result in user procedures that degrade the quality of work for the system user.

10.7   Exercises

1. Why is the Lend document transformation connected to the *T_RESERVATIONS* data store with a bidirectional arrow in figure 10.12?

2. Extend the library model with the following functions:

   (a) Specify two different Document Lending transactions, one in which the document is reserved (through a title reservation) and one in which it is not reserved.

   (b) After a document return, the administration checks whether there are outstanding reservations for this title, and if so, puts the document aside for one week and notifies the first reserver. If this reserver does not collect the document within one week, his or her reservation is canceled and the next reserver is notified. If there are no more reservers, the document is returned to the store.

3. Make a list of event-response pairs for the circulation administration and indicate for each pair, with which DF fragment it corresponds.

4. Analyze the method of classical structured development, listed in appendix C, according to the framework for development methods in figure 3.9. In particular, for each task in classical structured analysis, indicate whether the task is concerned with behavior specification at a particular aggregation level, or with system decomposition, and indicate any occurrence of the engineering cycle.

5. Appendix C describes the steps in modern structured development. Analyze this method according to the guidelines in exercise 4.

10.8 Bibliographical Remarks

Genealogy. The original 1977 paper by Ross and Schoman [294] is mandatory reading to get the major ideas behind structured analysis. The SADT flavor of structured analysis is elaborated in some later papers by [290, 292] and described in detail by Marca and Gowan [210].

In this chapter, we discussed a different flavor of structured analysis, dues to De-Marco [84], V. Weinberg [358], Gane and Sarson [108], and Yourdon and Constantine [378]. A milestone in the development of structured analysis is the definition of essential system modeling and of event partitioning by McMenamin and Palmer [225] in the mid-1980s. The method was further elaborated with real-time extensions, not treated in this chapter, by Ward and Mellor [352, 354, 355, 227] and by Hatley and Pirbhai [141].

The transition to structured design is described by Stevens, Myers and Constantine [325], Yourdon and Constantine [378] and by Page-Jones [251]. The definition of a system architecture for real-time systems is treated by Ward and Mellor [352, 354, 355, 227], Hatley and Pirbhai [141], and Goldsmith [118].

Rock-Evans [282, 283] gives a comprehensive survey of techniques and heuristics of DF modeling, called activity modeling by her. The presentation in this chapter is based primarily on DeMarco [84], which is still very readable, Goldsmith [118], and McMenamin and Palmer [225].

Seven plus or minus two. The 7 ± 2 check comes from psychological experiments performed by Miller [229] in 1956. It is cited by Ross in his initial paper on structured analysis [291] and repeated in probably every text in structured analysis after that, including this chapter.

Determinism and data conservation. DeMarco introduces the determinism check under the name **data conservation** check [84, page 109]. By data conservation is meant that the data transformation does not invent something out of nothing. The data that leave the transformation is the data that enter it, plus possibly some constant difference. This is a misleading way of stating it, for whatever a data transformation does, it does *not* conserve all the data that enter it. In fact, reactive data transformations implemented on a finite-state machine can have only a finite memory, so that most data that enter them are eventually destroyed.

11

Jackson System Development I: Models

11.1 Introduction

Just like Structured Development, Jackson System Development (JSD) was developed in the 1970s by lifting the structured approach from the level of programs to the level of software systems. Despite this common background, JSD differs considerably from structured analysis. To understand this difference, we must understand the background of JSD in Jackson Structured Programming.

11.1.1 Jackson Structured Programming

Where Structured Analysis has as its background the structured programming school of Hoare and Dijkstra, JSD has a different background, that of **Jackson Structured Programming** (JSP). JSP is a method for developing programs whose task is to transform a number of input files into a number of output files. Let us call this class of programs **administrative programs**. An example of such an administrative program is a database query. For example, a query to the student administration database takes as its input the data stores of the database and produces as output a printable file that contains a report about the contents of the data stores.

The three crucial ideas of JSP with respect to the construction of administrative programs are the following:

1. The structure of the input and output files of administrative programs can always be described as a structure built from elementary data items, where the structuring operators are concatenation, choice and iteration.

2. A program can be described as a structure built from elementary programming statements, where the structuring operators are concatenation (i.e. sequencing), choice and iteration.

3. The structure of the program is derivable from the structure of the input and output files.

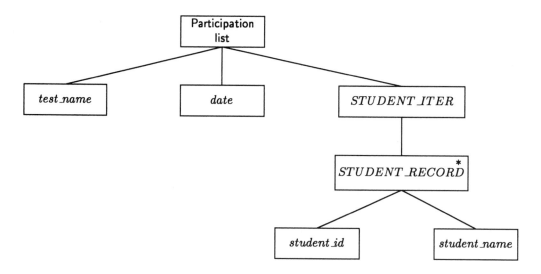

Figure 11.1: A file structure represented by a tree.

For example, suppose that we want to program the database function "List test participants". This is shown in figure 9.7 (page 204) as a data transformation that is triggered by a request and reads the data store *TEST_REGISTRATIONS*. The structure of the output file is represented in figure 11.1 by a tree whose root has the name of the file and whose leaves represent data items in the file. Left-to-right ordering of boxes represents sequence, and an asterisk represents iteration. There is also a construct to indicate choice, not used in the figure. The input file needed to produce this report is *TEST_REGISTRATIONS* (to get the list of student numbers of registered students). We assume that the output must be readable for people, and to achieve this, we also use as input files the data stores *COURSES* (to get the name of the test), *TESTS* (to get the test date), and *STUDENTS* (to get the name of each student). (This differs from the simple DF diagram of figure 9.7.) All of these files have a simple structure as an iteration of records that can be described by simple tree diagrams similar to the one shown in figure 11.1. What can we infer from the structure of these files about the structure of the program?

In this simple case, the structure of the program is isomorphic to the structure of the output file. It is shown in figure 11.2. The important thing about this example is that we use the same representation technique for the program as we use for the data structures. In the program structure diagram, however, the leaves of the tree represent atomic *actions*, left-to-right ordering represents sequential *execution*, and an asterisk represents iteration of *execution*. The choice, not shown here, represents alternative execution.

Like all structured programming approaches, it tells us to structure the program after the problem to be solved and not after the machine which happens to execute the program. However, JSP goes further than this, because it gives a systematic way that tells us, for the class of administrative programs, *how* to structure the program after the structure of the problem to be solved: the structure of the program is determined by the structure of the input and output files. It is this little extra that is the important difference between JSD and structured analysis.

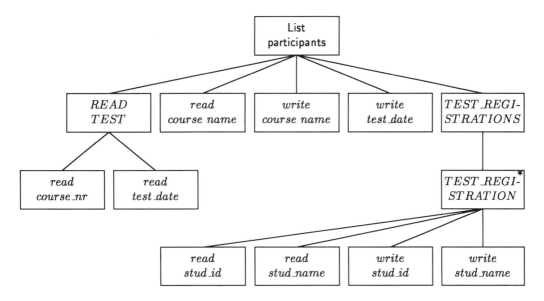

Figure 11.2: The structure of a program to produce the list of test participants. Each leaf represents an atomic action of the program. Left-to-right ordering of leaves represents sequential execution, the asterisk represents iteration. There is also a construct to represent choice, not used here.

11.1.2   From JSP to JSD

To lift this approach from structured programming to structured system development, we must generalize the idea of JSP in such a way that we do not refer to program structures and files, but refer to systems and their environment instead. This generalization is simple: the basic idea is to structure a software system after the environment with which it has to interact, just as JSP programs are modeled after the files with which they have to interact.

The environment of a computer-based system consists of its UoD and of other systems with which it has to interact, like such as its users. To make a model of the computer-based systems, we should therefore make a model of its UoD and of the systems with which it interacts. For example, to build a database system for the student administration, we should make a model of the UoD from which the system accepts input data. Each entity in the UoD will be represented by a tree diagram that represents its *life cycle* (figure 11.3). Each leaf of the tree is an action in the life of the entity, which will lead to an update of the database system. The tree diagram represents the structure of the input stream of action occurrences that the database system must register. Note that a model of the life cycles of *entities* in the UoD of the database system is also a model of the life cycle of *surrogates* in the database system, where these surrogates represent the UoD entities. After making a model of the UoD of the system, we therefore use it as the first version of a system model. This initial system model represents the life cycle of the surrogates stored in the system.

In addition to the UoD, the environment of a database system consists of the database users. The database state remembers part of the life of the surrogates, and if we assume that the system has unlimited memory, the tree structure representing the structure of the life

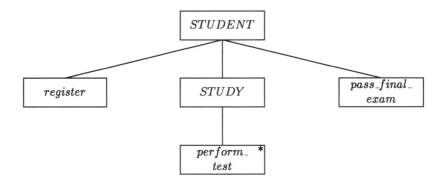

Figure 11.3: A simple student life cycle.

of a surrogate also represents the structure of a file containing the history of a surrogate. A database function that answers a query must match the structure of these history files with the structure of the output reports. It is shown later in this chapter that the specification of system functions is done along the same lines as programs are structured in JSP.

The same approach is applicable to any computer-based system. For example, the UoD of an elevator control system consists of elevator motors, cages, buttons, lights, etc. The life cycle of these entities will be represented by tree diagrams, whose leaves represent atomic actions that can occur in the life of the entities. After this UoD is modeled, the elevator control system can be structured along the same line as programs are structured in JSP.

To sum up, JSD uses the following structuring principles:

- To model a system, we must first make a model of its UoD.

- The UoD of the system is modeled as a set of entities that perform life cycles.

- This UoD model is then used as initial system model, and system functions are specified that match this model with the required output.

These three principles make JSD a precursor of object-oriented development. This connection is further explored in chapter 13.

11.2   The Structure of JSD Models

A JSD model of a computer-based system has the following structure:

- The **UoD model** represents the UoD of the system as a collection of communicating entities. For each entity, a life cycle is specified. Entities communicate with each other through shared actions. As illustrated in figure 11.4, each UoD entity e is represented by a surrogate s that exists in the system; the dashed arrow indicates the representation relation from each surrogate to the entity that it represents. Because of this representation relation, the UoD model is also a model of the system as a collection of communicating surrogates. The UoD model is also called the **initial system model**, because it is used as the first version of a model of required system functions.

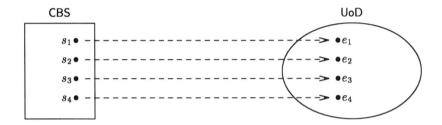

Figure 11.4: Each UoD entity is represented by a surrogate in the system. The dashed arrows indicate that each surrogate represents a UoD entity.

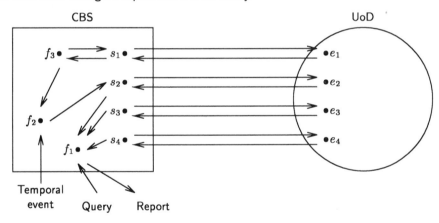

Figure 11.5: The structure of JSD model of a computer-based system. The arrows represent interactions.

JSD entity characteristics	JSD action characteristics
An entity is a possible or actual part of the UoD.	Each action takes place in the UoD and is not merely an action of the system itself.
Each entity participates in a time-ordered set of actions.	Each action is performed or suffered by an entity.
Each entity is atomic.	Each action is atomic in two ways: 1. it takes place at a particular point in time and 2. it is not decomposable into subactions.
Each entity has a unique identity.	Each action has a unique identity.

Figure 11.6: Characterizing features of JSD entities and JSD actions.

- The **system network** is a collection of surrogates and **function processes**. As illustrated in figure 11.5, each surrogate receives messages from its UoD entity and may also send messages to it. When a UoD entity performs an action, its surrogate receives the message to perform a corresponding update, and in control systems a surrogate may respond by sending a signal to its UoD counterpart. In addition, there are function processes f_1, f_2, etc. that interact with each other, with surrogates, and with the environment of the system. This environment may overlap with the UoD but it need not coincide with it. The environment provides the system with input events (which always come from the UoD), temporal events, queries, etc. For example, a function f_1 may receive a query about the state of the surrogates and respond by sending a report about a collection of surrogates to the environment. Another function f_2 may receive a temporal event and respond by sending a message to a surrogate. Function f_3 may collect historical data about surrogate s_1 and provide an aggregate summary to f_2 when asked for it.

The specification of UoD models is discussed in section 11.3 and the specification of system models in section 11.4. In section 11.5, JSD is analyzed from a methodological point of view.

11.3   The UoD Model

11.3.1   JSD entities and attributes

JSD models the UoD of a system as a set of entities. The characterizing features of **JSD entities** are listed in figure 11.6. First of all, a JSD entity must exist in the UoD and not in the SuD. A record in the student administration database is not a JSD entity, but the student itself is a JSD entity. A bank account is a JSD entity, but the record that represents it in a database system is not a JSD entity. JSD therefore strictly distinguishes entities in the UoD from their *surrogates* in the system. Second, JSD entities must be atomic, which means that the composition of a committee or of a queue of members who reserved a book is ignored. If we want to represent a committee or a queue as JSD entities, we must represent them as atomic entities. Third, they must have a unique identity that is independent from the state of the entity and that cannot be changed by any action. This means that if a committee is represented as a JSD entity, and the committee changes membership, then in JSD this would not lead to a change in identity of the committee. Finally, JSD entities must have something to do or something must be done to them, or both. A student registers for a test, receives a mark and writes a thesis, a bank account suffers deposit and withdrawal actions.

JSD entities are classified into **types** such that all entities of one type have a life cycle with the same structure. If T is the type of e, then e is called an **instance** of T. Each entity is an instance of exactly one type. The **extension** of each JSD entity type is the set of all possible and currently existing instances. In each possible state of the UoD, the **existence set** of a JSD entity type is the set of existing instances of the type.

JSD entities can have **attributes**, which are types of observable properties. For example, *name* is a type of observable property of a person, hence it is an attribute. An instance of this type is the name "John", which is called an **attribute value** of *name*. JSD requires each entity to have an **identifier attribute**, which is unique over all possible instances of a type and which never changes.

11.3.2   Life cycles

JSD actions

A **JSD action** is an event in which one or more JSD entities participate by suffering or performing the action. JSD actions have the characteristics listed in figure 11.6. First, a JSD action must occur in the life of an entity in the UoD. Producing a report about test results or updating a student record are no JSD actions. On the other hand, "Become student" and "lose student registration card" can be modeled as JSD actions. If we can describe an action without mentioning or presupposing the SuD, then the action is a JSD action.

Sometimes, UoD actions only have legal validity if they are registered by a database system. For example, a student and a university can enter into an agreement in which the university promises to conduct a test and the student promises to perform the test. This event is normally called "registering for a test", because the agreement is sealed by a registration action. In other words, making the agreement is an action in the UoD that occurs synchronously with a database update in which the occurrence of this agreement is registered. Making the agreement is an action in the UoD; registering it in a database system is system action. Because successful occurrence of the registration is a precondition for the successful occurrence of the agreement, people describe this agreement as "registering for a test". Because this is the common name for it, I will continue to use it as a name for a UoD action.

We now turn to the other criteria for JSD actions. A UoD action can only be a JSD action if it occurs in the life of a JSD entity. If we have omitted certain UoD entities from our model, then all actions in the life of those entities are not modeled as JSD actions, even though they occur in the UoD. If we do not model the chairs in the course rooms, then moving a chair to another room is not a JSD action.

JSD actions must be atomic in two ways:

- An action must occur at a specific point in time. This distinguishes actions from *states*, which persist over a period of time. For example, walking is not a JSD action but a state, because it persists over a period of time. To start walking and to stop walking are JSD actions, though. It does not make sense of JSD actions to ask when they began or how long they lasted, for they are considered to be instantaneous. Instead, one can ask *how frequently* an action occurs.

- An action must not be decomposable into subactions. This distinguishes actions from *processes*. For example, doing a test is not an atomic action, because it can be decomposed into at least two subactions, registration for the test and receiving a mark for the test. For the purpose of the student administration, we consider these last two actions as atomic. Note that this is a choice of abstraction level, since we choose to ignore the lower-level process in which test registration is implemented (i.e. request test registration, verify existence of test and student, update the test registration record, confirm to the student). JSD actions are transactions of JSD entities, in the sense that we defined transactions in chapter 2.

Finally, a JSD action must have a unique identity. As in the case of JSD entities, this means it can be given a unique proper name as identifier. For example, in a model of the circulation desk, there is only one action called *borrow*. Without unique action identification, we could not refer to actions by their name. Note however, that an action is associated with an entity *type*. If the *borrow* action is associated with the type $MEMBER$, then every $MEMBER$ instance m can perform an instance of *borrow* that we will denote with $borrow(m)$, where m is the identifier of a $MEMBER$ instance. Furthermore, one member can perform the same action instance $borrow(m)$ any number of times. We write $borrow(m)@t$ for the occurrence of $borrow(m)$ at time t. To avoid cumbersome expressions, we will say that an entity performs an action rather than that it performs an action instance.

There is a special JSD action called *null*, which represents non-action. The *null* action represents the fact that nothing occurs during a tick of the clock. We may explicitly model a *null* action to indicate that a JSD entity has a choice between doing something and doing nothing, and after either of these cases can continue with other actions. An example will be given later.

Process structure diagrams

Each entity has a **life cycle** whose structure can be represented by a **process structure diagram** (PSD)[1]. Figure 11.7 shows a simple PSD for an elevator system. A PSD is a tree in which the nodes are drawn as rectangles. The root node carries the label of the JSD entity type, which is also used as the name of the life cycle. The following conventions are used to represent the basic structures of sequence, choice and iteration.

- A *sequential execution* is represented by a sequence of boxes from left to right.

- An *iteration* is shown as a box with an asterisk in the upper right corner. An iteration must be the only child of a sequence.

---

[1] In JSD, life cycles are called **entity structures** and process structure diagrams are called **entity structure diagrams** instead.

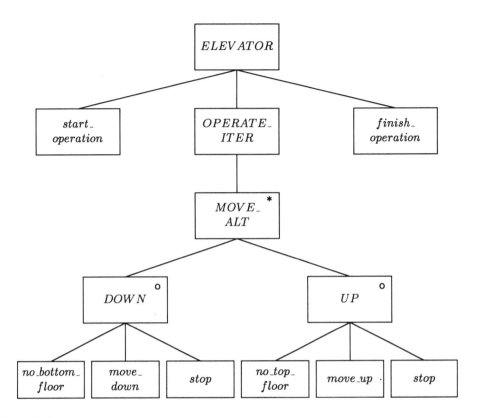

Attribute declaration:
$ELEVATOR(floor : NATURAL)$
Action definitions:

Action	Precondition	Effect
$start\_operation$		$floor := 1$
no_bottom_floor	$floor > 1$	
$move\_down$	Movement is only possible when all doors are closed.	$floor := floor - 1$
$stop$		
no_top_floor	$floor < max$	
$move\_up$	Movement is only possible when all doors are closed.	$floor := floor + 1$
$finish\_operation$		

Figure 11.7: PSD for the life cycle for an elevator. The PSD can be annotated with relevant information about *action preconditions* and *action effects*. The effect of actions on the state vector of the elevator is indicated by pseudocode attached to the actions. The events $floor > 1$ and $floor < max$ are outcomes of tests on the value of $floor$.

- A *choice* is shown as a set of children whose upper right corner is marked with a small circle. The choice boxes must all be children of one box, which may have an asterisk in it but may not itself be a choice box.

- *Parallelism* is represented implicitly. Each instance of an entity type executes an instance of the PSD for that type in parallel with all other entities. In addition, as explained later, we can define several PSDs for one entity, which are executed in parallel.

By labeling the root of the PSD with the name of an entity type, it is shown that the PSD represents the structure of the life cycle of all instances of the type. A PSD is *instantiated* in the life of a particular entity. Each entity executes an instance of the PSD defined for its type. The actions in the PSD are local actions of the entity, that can only change the local entity attributes.

A PSD may be annotated with information not representable in the PSD itself, such as a declaration of the attributes of the entity type, and a specification of the *action preconditions* and *action effects*. A **precondition** is a condition of the state of the world (not only the entity itself) that, if false, blocks the occurrence of the action. The **effect** of an action is specified by listing the changes of the local state of the entity that occur during the action. The local state of the entity is called the **state vector** of the entity in JSD and consists of the values of all attributes, including the value of a special attribute, called the **life cycle indicator** (*lci*). This indicates the position of the entity in its life cycle[2]. The effect of an action on the life cycle indicator is not specified in the annotation of the PSD, because it is already specified by the PSD itself.

At each moment, the entity is either waiting to perform or suffer its first action (i.e. it is waiting to be created) or it has a history that ends with the most recent action that occurred in its life. These states can be identified by adding leaves to the PSD as illustrated in figure 11.8. We omit this numbering from PSDs and assume that for each PSD there is an agreed labeling system, that defines the meaning of the values of *lci* in terms of the PSD. The state vector of the elevator in figure 11.7 has the form

$$\langle floor : m, load : n, lci : p \rangle.$$

For example, the occurrence of a *stop* action in figure 11.7 would increase *lci* by 1.

Premature termination

Often, an entity life cycle can be terminated by the occurrence of a certain action. This action can occur at any moment in the life of the entity, and when it occurs, it leads to a wind-up process, after which the life of the entity terminates. This is called **premature termination** in JSD. Premature termination is represented by indicating points in the life of an entity at which premature termination can occur, and specifying what happens during termination in a separate part of the PSD. Normal life is always represented by a branch that describes a process called *POSIT* (figure 11.9). At the start of the life of the entity, it is not known whether a normal or a prematurely terminated life is started, and the assumption is made (it is posited) that a normal life is followed. There is a second branch

---

[2]In JSD, *lci* is called a **text pointer**, because it points to a position in the program text associated with a life cycle.

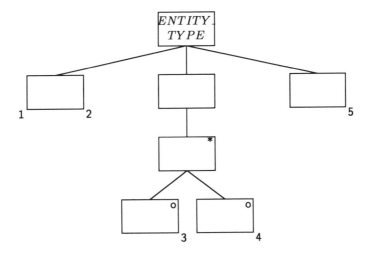

Figure 11.8: Identification of the positions in a life cycle.

leaving the root of the PSD, labeled *ADMIT*, that represents the process that starts when a premature termination ends the normal life of an entity. When the process jumps to the *ADMIT* branch, it admits that the assumption of normality is not true. The *POSIT* and *ADMIT* boxes are labeled by a question mark. The points in the normal process where premature terminations can occur are marked by adding *QUIT* boxes to the actions. Each *QUIT* box is labeled by an exclamation mark. A premature termination can occur after each action labeled by *QUIT*. It can then continue with any of the initial actions of the *ADMIT* branch. After processing the *ADMIT* actions, the entity has reached the end of its life cycle. Thus, in figure 11.9, the normal life of a holiday consists of a sequence of pleasant actions. After any action, an unexpected event can occur, causing the *fly_home* action to occur. The jump from the *QUIT* box to a next possible action in the admit branch is not an action in itself. Rather, figure 11.9 must be read as a shorthand for a larger diagram in which each of the four actions in the admit branch can occur after the *leave* action.

11.3.3 Parallelism and communication

Parallelism among and within JSD entities

Conceptually, a JSD model represents the UoD as an infinite set of JSD entities, some of which have started their life cycles and some of which have not. Of those who started their life cycles, some have reached a point at which no further action can be executed; these may be considered not to exist anymore. The entities that have started their life and not yet ended it, all executed their lives in parallel. In a state transition of the UoD, we may therefore see one or more entities performing or suffering an action in parallel. Thus, the UoD model contains parallelism across JSD entities.

JSD also allows parallel processes to be executed by a single JSD entity; these parallel processes are called **roles** of the entity. The life cycle of the entity then consists of the parallel composition of all its roles. For example, a person may perform several roles in

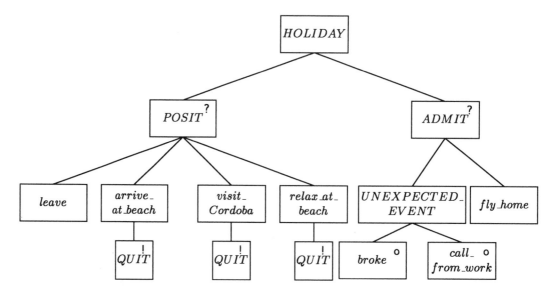

Figure 11.9: Premature termination.

parallel. He or she may be a student, a teaching assistant, a husband or wife, and a taxi driver all at the same time. Each of these roles can be represented by a PSD. To indicate that they are all executed by one entity in parallel, we label the root of each PSD by the identifier of the entity that plays these roles and declare this identifier in an annotation of the PSD. For example, figure 11.10 shows the student and teaching assistant roles of a person.

Remember that we may define preconditions of actions such that, when an action precondition is false, the action cannot occur. In the case of an entity playing multiple roles, we can define preconditions in terms of the life cycle indicator of the other roles that the entity is playing. For example, we may define as precondition of the *hire* action of *TA* that the *propaedeutical* action in its *STUDENT* role has been executed.

The model of parallelism used when one entity executed several processes in parallel is that of **interleaving**. This means that at each moment, *p* may execute *one* action. This may be an action local to one of its roles, or it may be a common action, shared by several of its roles. The trace of executed actions of one entity is totally ordered, and consists of an interleaving of the traces of each of its constituent roles. Contrast this with the parallelism of the UoD: different entities may perform or suffer different actions simultaneously. The trace of actions that occurred in the UoD therefore consists of a totally ordered sequence of **steps**, each of which is a set of actions that occurred in the life of different entities.

Common actions

Two or more parallel processes may communicate in JSD by executing a **common action instance.** sender and receiver participate in the communication simultaneously. The communicating processes may be the life cycles of different JSD entities or they may be two roles executed by a single entity. For example, figure 11.11 shows a customer and an order life cycle that share all their actions. The intention of the model is that there are

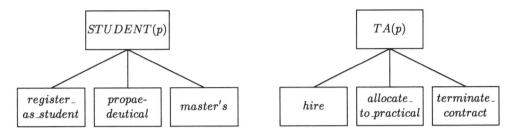

Remarks:

- p is of type $PERSON$.

- A precondition of $hire(p)$ is that $propaedeutical(p)$ has been executed in the $STUDENT$ role of p.

Figure 11.10: Two roles of a person. One person p performs these two roles in parallel.

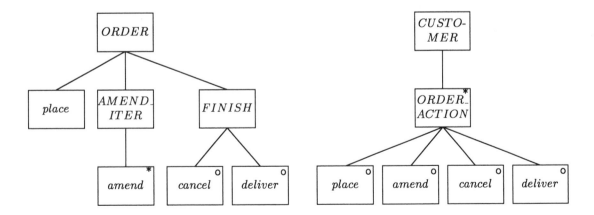

Figure 11.11: Common actions between two PSDs. Each common action enforces a synchronization between the PSDs.

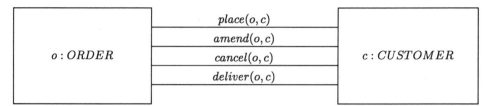

Figure 11.12: Explicit representation of common actions by a communication diagram. These diagrams are not part of the JSD method but help us to disambiguate communication by common actions.

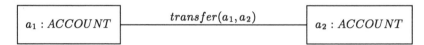

Figure 11.13: Communication between two different instances of one entity type.

many customers and orders, that a customer can place many orders. For each order of a customer, the customer must perform the order actions in the sequence prescribed by the *ORDER* life cycle, but across different orders, the customer can perform order actions in any sequence. Since identity of action names implies identity of named actions, the *place* action in both PSDs refers to one and the same action. However, this action has instances *place(c)* for customer identifiers c and *place(o)* for order identifiers o, and the intention is that a *place(c)* must occur synchronously with a *place(o)* and vice versa. This is not explicitly represented by the PSDs, so we add a **communication diagram** to represent communication by common actions. Figure 11.12 shows the communication structure intended by figure 11.11. Communication diagrams are not part of the JSD representation technique, but they help us to disambiguate communication by common actions. The communication diagram shows that there are shared action instances of the form *place(c, o)*, which represent communication between two entities o and c.

Common actions may be shared by more than two JSD entities. For example, if c can place an order at a particular branch office b, then we must introduce a JSD entity type *BRANCH_OFFICE* and provide the common action with three parameters *place(c, o, b)*, where b is of type *BRANCH_OFFICE*.

Without a communication diagram, the action *transfer* in which money is transferred from one bank account to another, cannot be represented. If the PSD for *ACCOUNT* contains the action *transfer*, then this does not indicate that this action is shared by two different bank accounts. The communication diagram in figure 11.14 does express this communication accurately.

Atomicity of common actions

Common actions are atomic like any other JSD action. For example, because *place(o, c)* is atomic, there is no state of the UoD in which an order is placed but the placed order does not yet exist. The atomicity of common actions means the following:

- The channel of communication is *error-free*: what is delivered is what is sent and nothing else.

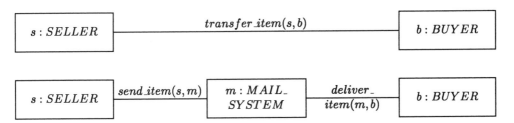

Figure 11.14: The atomicity of a common action can be resolved into an asynchronous communication if we choose a lower level of abstraction.

- The communication is *certain*: messages are not lost nor delivered at the wrong address.

- Communication is *synchronous*: The delay between sending and delivery is not modeled.

If we cannot make these assumptions about a communication, then this communication should not be modeled by a common action. Instead, we should then explicitly model the communication channel as a JSD entity and model communication of the sender and receiver with the channel as common actions. Errors, incorrect delivery and delay can then be modeled explicitly in the life cycle of the communication channel. For example, the upper part of figure 11.14 represents order delivery as a synchronous communication. This means that we ignore the possibility of garbling the contents of the communication, of delivering the item at the wrong address, and the time it takes to get the messages from sender to receiver. If we cannot or will not ignore one of these aspects, then we should model the communication channel as a JSD entity, as shown in the lower half of the figure. The life cycle for this communication channel can then be used to model unreliable asynchronous communication with the possibility of loss and errors.

11.4 The System Model

The UoD model represents the UoD as a collection of communicating entities. Let us call this model the **UoD network**. We represent this network by means of communication diagrams (not part of JSD) and PSDs. This network is now used as the initial version of the system model. The type instances are now *surrogates* for UoD entities and the actions are now *updates* of the state of surrogates, that correspond to UoD actions. The initial model is extended with function processes so that it becomes a **system network**. The system network is more complex than the UoD network, because it contains function processes in addition to surrogates. Moreover, as we shall see below, there are four different communication mechanisms in the system network.

11.4.1 Process communication in the system network

A communication between two nodes in the system network is called a *connection* in JSD. The simplest process connection in the system network is communication between surrogates through shared actions. There are three other kinds of process connections in the system network: data stream connection, state vector connection, and controlled data stream connection.

Data stream connections

A **data stream connection** between two nodes in the system network is a first-in first-out queue to which one node can add data and from which the other can remove data. Communication through a data stream is *asynchronous*, for the sender can continue after sending a message, even if the receiver has not yet received the message. Figure 11.15 shows a data stream connection D between account instances and instances of the function *ACCT_HISTORY*. The task of *ACCT_HISTORY* is to give a historical overview of updates to an account. The structure of the two communicating processes in figure 11.15 is shown in figure 11.16. The following features should be noted.

- When two processes communicate through a data stream D, the sender contains actions *add* ⟨*record*⟩ *to D* and the receiver contains actions *remove* ⟨*record*⟩ *from D*, where ⟨*record*⟩ is a brief indication of the data added to and removed from D. Such a specification should be precise enough for a programmer to write a program that implements the function.

- The structure of the *ACCT_HISTORY* process mirrors the structure of the report to be produced. The *ACCT_HISTORY* process is constructed according to the structured programming principles of JSP explained in section 11.1. *ACCT_HISTORY* is in this example a simple formatting function: upon request, it empties D and prints the data that it removes from D. More complex functions can also be specified, that manipulate the data before a report is produced. These more complex functions can be specified using the principles of JSP. Because we do not want to elaborate upon these principles, we only give examples of very simple function processes.

- *ACCT_HISTORY* is a **short-running function process**, which is a process that "exists" during one atomic system transaction only. In the system state *before* the transaction starts, the short-running function does not exist, and in the state *after* the transaction is finished, the short-running function does not exist either.

- Data stream connections have cardinalities. The default cardinality is 1 on both sides. The default cardinalities in figure 11.15 mean that one instance of *ACCT_HISTORY* reads a data stream filled by one existing *ACCOUNT* instance, and that one existing *ACCOUNT* instance sends data to a data stream read by many *ACCT_HISTORY* instances. As many *ACCT_HISTORY* instances are instantiated as queries are asked about account histories.

A **long-running function process** is a function process that exists for longer than a single transaction. Long-running function processes wait during most of their life for events to happen, and when these occur they produce a response in a single transaction. The *ACCT_HISTORY* function can be transformed into a long-running function process by embedding it into an iteration over the report production process. As a long-running function, an *ACCT_HISTORY* instance spends most of its life waiting for a query record to arrive. When such a record arrives, it produces a report in what is conceptually an atomic transaction, and waits for the next query to arrive. The connection cardinality would then

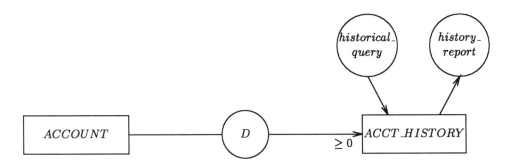

Figure 11.15: System network containing a data stream connection.

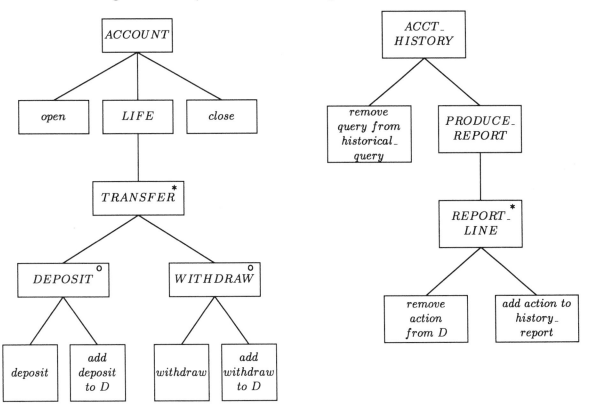

Figure 11.16: PSDs for *ACCOUNT* and *ACCT HISTORY*, *remove* and *add* actions embedded.

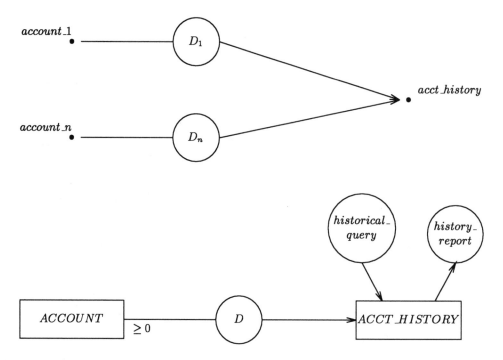

Figure 11.17: A single instance can read data streams originating from many instances in a fixed order, determined by the reader. This is a fixed merge.

be different: one existing instance of $ACCOUNT$ would send records to a data stream read by exactly one existing instance of $ACCT\_HISTORY$. There would still be many instances of $ACCT\_HISTORY$, one for each different $ACCOUNT$.

We can reduce the number of $ACCT\_HISTORY$ instances to 1 by allowing it to read data streams from different $ACCOUNT$ instances. The upper diagram in figure 11.17 represents the situation at the instance level, the lower diagram shows the system network diagram, which is at the type level. For each source-destination connection, there is a dedicated data stream.

If a process can receive data from several different data streams, we say that the data from these streams are **merged** by the process. The streams themselves remain distinct. In a **fixed merge**, the reader determines the order in which data is removed from the data streams. For example, in figure 11.17, $ACCT\_HISTORY$ reads data from the *historical_query* data stream and from all D data streams (one for each existing $ACCOUNT$ instance) in an order determined by itself.

In a **rough merge**, the reader cannot determine the order in which records are removed from its input data streams. Suppose the surrogate process $TEST$ has a life cycle in which one event consists of determining a date for the test, and the surrogate process $ROOM$ has a life cycle containing an action in which the purpose of the room is changed (administration, staff, courses, tests etc.). Suppose that we want to define a function process $ALLOCATE$, which allocates a $TEST$ instance to a $ROOM$ instance on a certain data and suppose that $ALLOCATE$ cannot control the speed with which records become available from the $TEST$ and $ROOM$ processes. For example, the messengers that inform the $ALLOCATE$ process

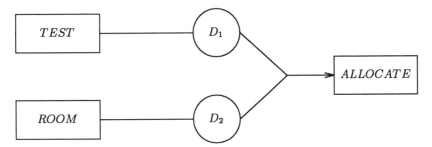

Figure 11.18: Rough merge of two data streams. The order in which messages from D_1 and D_2 are merged cannot be determined by the receiver, so the two input streams are joined outside the *ALLOCATE* box.

of state changes in the *TEST* and *ROOM* processes take arbitrary long times before they reach *ALLOCATE*. In that case, *ALLOCATE* may allocate a test to a room after the room has changed its purpose. *ALLOCATE* then receives the messages from *ROOM* and *TEST* in a rough merge, as shown in figure 11.18. To indicate that the receiver has no control over the order in which it receives messages from the two senders, the connections from senders to receiver are joined before they reach *ALLOCATE*.

State vector connection

Let N_1 and N_2 be two nodes in the system network, in which N_2 is a function process. A **state vector connection** from nodes N_1 to N_2 of the system network is a channel through which N_2 can read the state vector of N_1. The read action is synchronous and does not disturb the state of N_1. State vector connections are represented by a diamond which connects the observing and the observed process. For example, the upper half of figure 11.19 shows a state vector connection between a function process called *LATE* that reports on document loans that are late. The *LATE* process is an output function that reports on the current state of the system. *DOCUMENT*, *LOAN* and *MEMBER* are surrogate types. The *DATE* data stream receives the current date and time from an unspecified source, and the *LATE* function removes the contents of *DATE* to use it for its own processing. It fills a data stream *REPORT*, which can be emptied by an unspecified external entity.

The PSD of *LATE* is shown in in the lower half of figure 11.19. The process iterates of days, where each day it reads (and removes) a time record from the *DATE* data stream. How this record gets there is not specified. What is important is that in JSD, a process that is ready to read from a data stream will read and remove a record in this data stream as soon as it becomes available. Note that this is the equivalent of a temporal event in DF models. When triggered by a *DATE* record, the *LATE* process produces a report, which is an iteration of report lines. Each report line is produced by reading the state vector of a *LOAN*, checking whether it is late and if so, reading the appropriate states vectors of *DOCUMENT* and *MEMBER* instances to print the report line. There are four important things to note about this example.

- There is a special action *get_sv* that represents the action of observing the state vector through a state vector connection. For each *get_sv*, a search condition is specified that selects a subset of the existence set of a type. For example, *get_sv(SV₂) with*

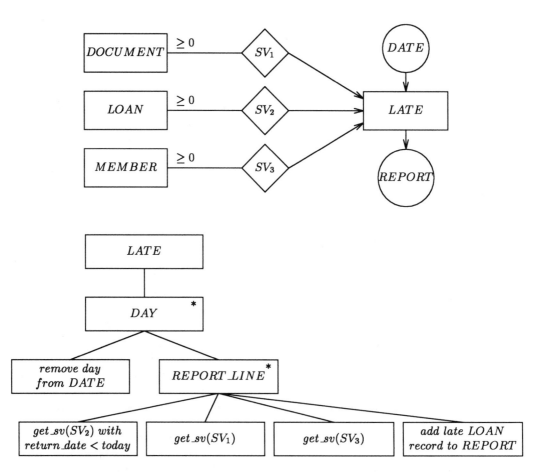

Figure 11.19: System network and PSD for the $LATE$ function process.

return_date < *today* selects the existing *LOAN* instances that are late. *get_sv* yields the entire state vector, i.e. all attributes of the observed process are visible to the observer. This data is available to the subsequent actions in the life of the observer.

- The structure of the *LATE* process mirrors the structure of the report to be produced. Again, the function process is constructed according to the structured programming principles of JSP explained in section 11.1. As pointed out before, we do not want to treat these principles here and our function processes are therefore trivial.

- *LATE* is a long-running function process, which waits most of its time on a temporal event (the arrival of a date) and then reponds in a single, atomic transaction.

- State vector connections have cardinalities, and the default cardinality is 1 on both sides. The cardinalities in figure 11.19 mean that one existing instance of *LATE* may read the state vector of many instances of *DOCUMENT*, *LOAN* and *MEMBER*, and that each existing instance of *DOCUMENT*, *LOAN* and *MEMBER* is read by exactly one existing instance of *LATE*.

The *LATE* function can be transformed into a short-running function process by removing the *DAY* iteration and by changing the cardinalities in the system network so that each existing instance of *DOCUMENT*, *LOAN* and *MEMBER* is read by arbitrarily many instances of *LATE*.

Controlled data stream connection

A **controlled data stream connection** is a connection over which one instance observes the state of the other and, depending on the observed state, performs an action on the observed process. The observation and action form one atomic transaction. Communication through a controlled data stream is therefore synchronous. The observation is done by means of a *get_sv* action and the action is performed by means of an *add ⟨record⟩ to data_stream* action. Thus, a controlled data stream connection combines the behavior of a state vector and a data stream connection. In figure 11.20, a *BLOCK* function process monitors the state of the existence set of *ACCOUNT* surrogates. It also receives all ticks of the clock, as sent to it by the *DATE* data stream. Each midnight, the *BLOCK* process becomes active and scans the existing accounts on the presence of the update condition *balance(a)* < −200. When the condition is satisfied by an account *a*, the action *block(a)* is sent to the account. Testing the condition on *a* and performing the action on *a* together is one atomic action that cannot be interrupted. If we were not to require this atomicity, then it would be possible that the condition that justifies the *block* action would be undone before the action is performed. Note that the *add block(a) to CD* action is not an addition to a queue, as it would be in the case of a data stream connection. The record written to *CD* is an action that is executed immediately by the receiver.

11.4.2   The specification of function processes

Input functions

An **input function** is a process that accepts messages from the environment of the SuD, filters out incorrect messages and sends the remaining ones to the appropriate processes

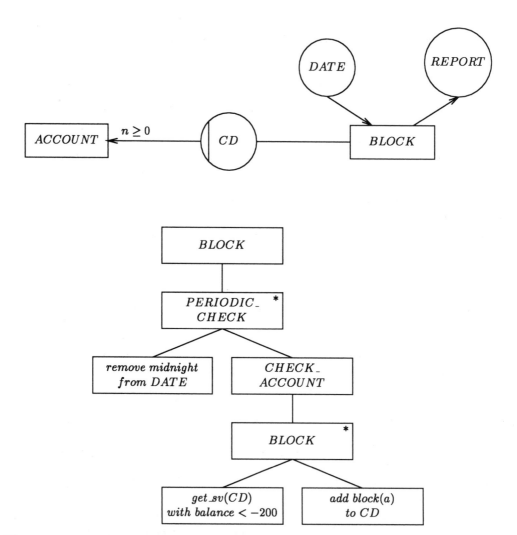

Figure 11.20: A controlled data stream connection from the *BLOCK* process to an *ACCOUNT* process, and a PSD for the *BLOCK* process.

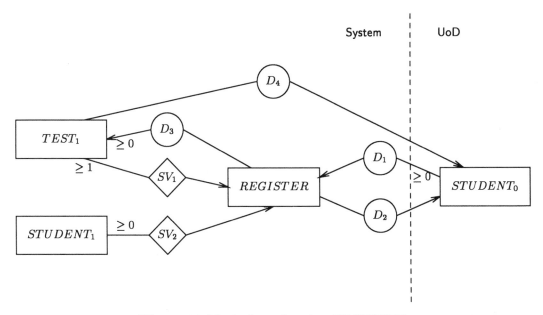

Figure 11.21: An input function *REGISTER*.

in the system. Figure 11.21 shows a system network containing an input function process. By way of illustration, the source of the input data is represented. $STUDENT_0$ is the *STUDENT* entity type interpreted in the UoD. $TEST_1$ and $STUDENT_1$ are the *TEST* and *STUDENT* entity types interpreted in the system. An existing instance of $STUDENT_0$ exists in the UoD and can send a registration request to data stream D_1, which is read by the *REGISTER* input function. We assume that this is a long-running function with exactly one instance. Without giving its PSD, we indicate what this function does: it checks whether the registration request is valid by checking whether surrogates of the test and student exist in the system and are in the required state for the registration action to occur. If there is something wrong, the registration request is refused and a message with this contents is sent to D_2. If the registration can be performed, this message is sent to the appropriate $TEST_1$ surrogate via data stream D_3 and a confirmation is sent along D_4.

The UoD entity types are normally not shown in a system network. The data streams D_1, D_2 and D_4 would be left dangling in the air and the surrogate types would not be indexed as they are in figure 11.21.

For each action of each entity type, there should be an input function process. These input functions are the update routines of databases and correspond to event recognizers in DF models. Input functions can be documented by additional requirements.

- For example, one can document the maximum delay permitted between the occurrence of an action in the UoD and the occurrence of the corresponding update of the system.

- One can specify the rate at which input messages arrive at the system.

- One can specify the error messages to be sent by the input function to the environment.

System

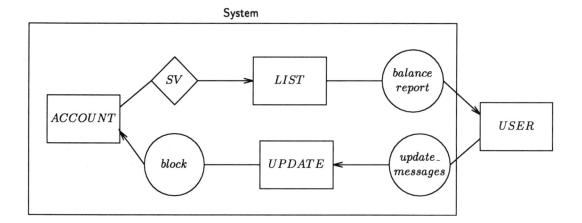

Figure 11.22: A feedback loop between the system and a user: system network and PSD.

- One can specify the layout of screens by which the input function parameters are communicated to the system, or the format of input records received from other systems.

Output functions

An **output function** is a process that selects, summarizes, and formats information about the system and sends it to the environment of the system. Very simple output functions can often be embedded in the PSD of a life cycle. These are called **embedded output functions**.

If an output function cannot be embedded in the life cycle of a surrogate without altering the structure of the life cycle, it must be added as a separate process to the system network. This process is defined by means of a PSD. Such an output function is called an **imposed** output function. There are two types of imposed output functions, short-running functions, such as *ACCT_HISTORY* in figure 11.15, and long-running functions, such as *LATE* in figure 11.19.

For each output function, one can specify additional requirements.

- One can specify the maximum response time for the output function, which is the time between the moment that the system learns that the function must be performed until the time that the response has been produced.

- One can specify the layout of reports to be produced by the function or the format of records sent to other systems.

Interacting functions

Often, the environment of a system asks a query about the system state and, based on the result of such a query, performs an update of the system state. For example, in figure 11.22, a user reads the state of a number of account surrogates and blocks those accounts with a certain negative balance. This is a feedback loop in which the environment controls the system based on the state of the system and a norm that this state must fulfill. Such a feedback loop is called an **interacting function**. We can specify this function in JSD by means of a controlled data stream connection as shown in figure 11.20. The *BLOCK* function process in figure 11.20 performs the task of the user in figure 11.22.

11.5 Methodological Analysis

11.5.1 The place of JSD models in the behavior specification framework

The behavior specification framework of chapter 4 (page 75) distinguishes UoD models from system models. We defer an analysis of UoD models to chapter 13 and restrict ourselves here to a comparison of system behavior specifications, shown in figure 11.23. When the system is ready to engage in a transaction with the environment, the state of a system is represented in JSD by

- the set of existing surrogates and their states,

- the set of existing long-running function processes and their states, and

- the contents of the data streams.

Between transactions, data streams may be empty. The system state may be changed by system transactions. JSD does not recognize relationships and models these in the same way as other surrogates for UoD entities. System dynamics is represented in JSD by means of system transactions of the following three kinds;

- updates to surrogates (input functions),

- responses to system inputs (output functions),

- conditional system updates (interacting functions).

11.5.2 Transactions

Transactions are represented as follows in JSD.

- In the UoD model, a transaction in which a surrogate is updated corresponds to an occurrence of an action instance $a(e)$, where a is an action and e a UoD entity. The action is a leaf in the PSD for the entity type of e. The entire PSD represents the entire life of entities; the leaves of the PSD correspond to system transactions, which represent actions in the life of UoD entities.

- In a model of the SuD, a transaction corresponds to a system function (input, output or interacting) specified by a PSD. The transaction effects and preconditions are specified as part of the PSD in the form of actions performed during the transaction and as annotations of PSDs that specify the meaning of actions.

	System models		
	ER model	DF model	JSD model
State space			
Entities	Y	Data store records	Surrogates, long-running function processes data stream records
Entity types	Y	Data stores	Surrogate types, long-running functions, data streams
Entity attributes	Y	Data store fields	Y
Relationships	Y	Structured data stores	Surrogate types
is_a Relationships	Y	N	N
Relationship types	Y	Data stores	Surrogate types
Relationship attributes	Y	Data store fields	Surrogate attributes
Constraints			
Cardinality	Y	Data dictionary	N
Storage constraints	As annotation	Data dictionary	As annotation
State transitions			
System transactions	N	Data transformations	Function processes
Transaction effects	N	Minispecs	PSDs and annotations
Transaction preconditions	N	Minispecs	PSDs and annotations
Process communications	N	Data flows	Process connections
Life cycles	N	In RT extensions	PSDs
Other constraints			
Interface technology	N	Data dictionary	N
Response time	N	Data dictionary	As annotations
Delay	N	Data dictionary	As annotations

Figure 11.23: Three kinds of models of system behavior.

	t_1	t_2	t_3	t_4	t_5	t_6	$\cdots$
E_1							
E_2							
$\cdots\cdots$							
D_1							
D_2							

Figure 11.24: Transaction decomposition in JSD. Each transaction is an atomic system function. The state of the system between transactions is stored in entities E_i and data streams D_i.

- More precisely, a transaction corresponding to a short-running function is specified by a PSD. The entire PSD represents one system transaction and is therefore atomic. The system is ready to accept new input when the PSD execution is ready. Intermediary states of the PSD are not observable to the environment.

- A transaction corresponding to one iteration through a long-running function is represented by a subtree of a PSD, which again must be treated as atomic.

The difference can be represented graphically by returning to the transaction decomposition table (figure 11.24). In JSD, the horizontal dimension of the table corresponds to the three kinds of system functions: input, output and interacting. Each transaction is an atomic system function. The vertical dimension represents all JSD entity types and the contents of the data streams between transactions. For an input function, each column represents the surrogates that must be updated; this represents a common action between UoD entities. For an output function, each column represents the data accesses performed to produce the output. For an interacting function, each column represents the surrogates whose state is read and the surrogates whose state is updated by the function.

11.5.3 Function specification

Using PSDs to represent entity life cycles as well as system functions is confusing, because the level of granularity is different in both cases. In addition, using PSD for a system function is one possible way to program this function, and this is a remnant of JSP. It is as if we would prescribe using PSDs for each minispec in DF models. This has the negative consequence that a requirements specification constrains the implementation of system functions unnecessarily. A model of required system functions should specify this function abstractly, without prescribing one particular implementation. One possible way to do this is to specify output functions declaratively in terms of pre- and postconditions to be realized by an implementation of this function. This would leave open whether the function would be implemented as a structured program, as in JSD, or as a relational calculus query expression that operates on sets of records, or by other means. One implementation decision already made in JSD is that output functions are programmed in JSD to operate in a record-at-a-time way. This precludes set-oriented query specification, which is the norm in relational database theory and practice.

	ER entity	External entity	JSD entity
Observable	Yes	Yes	Yes
In the UoD	Possibly	Possibly	Yes
In the system	Possibly	No	No
Suffers or performs events	Possibly	Yes	Yes

Figure 11.25: Differences between ER entities, external entities and JSD entities.

11.5.4 Entity concepts

Comparing the entity concept of JSD with those of ER modeling and structured analysis, we see that a JSD entity is an observable part of the UoD that has something significant to do, whereas ER entities may also live in the system and need not perform or suffer actions (figure 11.25). External entities exist outside the system and may or may not be part of the UoD.

ER models of the UoD represent the state space of the UoD and can be used to represent the state space of the system. JSD models of the UoD represent the behavior of the UoD and can be used as the initial version of a system model. External entities in data flow models are not used to represent the behavior of the UoD or of the system: they act as sources and sinks of data. The integration of ER models, DF models and JSD models will be discussed in detail in chapter 13.

11.5.5 Communication

There are a number of problems with the specification of communication in JSD. First of all, there are four different kinds of communication (common actions, data streams, state vectors and controlled data streams), three of which are represented in the system network. This is unnecessarily complex. The four kinds of communication can be reduced to two, synchronous communication and asynchronous communication using a queue as buffer. Communication by state vectors and by controlled data streams is synchronous, and communication by data stream is asynchronous, using a queue as buffer. Since a queue cannot be specified by a finite state machine (and hence not by a PSD), we cannot reduce this further in JSD. This brings the JSD network closer in form to a DF diagram, where there are also two kinds of communications: synchronous (through data flows) and asynchronous (via a data store). The data store buffer used for asynchronous communication does not have a particular structure such as a queue.

Assuming that we have reduced the number of kinds of communications to two, we still have a number of problems:

- Synchronous communication by common actions has the problem that the senders and receivers of the communication cannot be properly identified. In this book, this is solved by adding identifiers to the action instances, and defining communication diagrams to the model, which explicitly identify senders and receivers.

- The choice for a queue as buffer in asynchronous communication is understandable but not completely justified, for one can imagine situations in which the communication buffer must be a set, a bag, a stack, or even a priority queue, etc. For example, a scheduler of elevators may receive floor service requests in a set or in a priority queue that is periodically reorganized. The JSD notation could be made more flexible by leaving the organization of communication buffers open and specifying buffer properties in the model documentation. This turns the communication buffers effectively into data stores annotated with a specification of their behavior (queue, stack, set, bag, etc.)

- Synchronous communication by a controlled data stream has the problem that we may want to define an update condition that depends upon the global state of the system. For example, we may perform an update on *MEMBER*, triggered by the condition on *LOAN* that the member has 30 documents overdue. The notation would be more flexible if we allow global preconditions to be specified for synchronous communications.

11.6   Summary

JSD and JSP both structure a system after the environment in which it will function. In JSD this means that a *UoD model* is built and that required system functions are specified in terms of this UoD model. The UoD model represents the UoD as a set of communicating *JSD entities*. Each JSD entity must be discrete, exist in the UoD, have something to do and be uniquely identifiable. Each action must be discrete, exist in the UoD, occur in the life of a JSD entity and be uniquely identifiable. Each entity has a *life cycle* that is built by sequencing, iteration and selection from the actions. Life cycles are represented by PSDs. Entities communicate synchronously, through *common actions*. The presentation of the UoD model can be improved if we represent communication by *communication diagrams*, also called the *UoD network* in this chapter.

The system network consists of *surrogate processes*, that represent JSD entity processes, and of *function processes*, that implement the system functionality. Nodes in a system network are connected by a *data stream connection*, which is a queue acting as a buffer between a sender and a receiver, by a *state vector connection*, which is a window that one process may have on the state of another process, or by a *controlled data stream connection*, which is a synchronous conditional update.

Input functions accept messages from JSD entities and update the state of the corresponding surrogates. *Output functions* produce a report on the state of the system when they are requested to do so. *Interacting functions* update the state of a system process when a certain condition arises.

JSD models represent the state space of a system by means of the state of surrogates, long-running function processes, and data streams, and represent system transactions either by updates corresponding to actions in the UoD, or by function processes. The model would be simplified if functions were specified declaratively. The differences between an ER model and a JSD model of the UoD are small enough to be able to combine both models. The difference between the JSD system network and a DF model of the system is larger. The JSD network partitions a network representation of system activity into three kinds of nodes, surrogates, functions, and data streams, where a DF model has two different kinds of nodes, transformations and stores. The JSD network nodes are treated as types and the DF nodes as instances. Communication in the JSD network is complicated, where a

DF model has one simple representation for synchronous communication, in terms of which asynchronous communication is defined.

11.7   Exercises

1. Write a minispec in the pre- postcondition style for the input function *REGISTER* in figure 11.21. Then make a PSD for this input function.

2. (a) Turn *LATE* into a short-running function (figure 11.19).

   (b) Turn *ACCT_HISTORY* into a long-running function (figures 11.15 and 11.16).

3. Each test registration by a student starts its life by a *registration* action, in which a student and the university agree that the student will perform a test. It continues with the test itself, and finishes with marking the test. These actions are ordered for each student–test pair. Adapt the test registration model so that this ordering of actions per test registration is expressed.

4. The rough merge in figure 11.18 leaves open the possibility that the actions of *ROOM* and *ALLOCATE* are not properly synchronized, so that *ALLOCATE* continues allocating tests to a room even after the *ROOM* has changed its purpose. Change the model so that this possibility is eliminated.

11.8   Bibliographical Remarks

Jackson Structured Programming.   JSP was originally defined by Jackson [157] in 1975. The method is summarized by Jackson [162]. A brief and clear introduction to JSP is given by Sanden [300], who shows that it can be applied to a real-time system.

JSD.   The first version of JSD was published in 1983 [158]. A brief and readable introduction into JSD is given by Cameron [57]. Sanden [302] gives a brief introduction to JSD by means of a critical analysis of the elevator example given by Jackson [158]. Another short introduction is given by McNeille [226]. Sutcliffe [332] gives a good book-length introduction into JSD.

Pamela Zave and Daniel Jackson [380] compare PSDs with state transition diagrams and argue that PSDs are useful for the specification of grammars and step-by-step instructions, and state transition diagrams are useful for state-oriented descriptions. For example, premature termination is efficiently represented by state charts [137] and not by PSDs, but a sequential process such as a dialing session is more efficiently represented by PSDs. They show how the strengths of both notations can be combined.

In the preparation of this chapter, I used internal course material from Michael Jackson Limited [228]. Useful supporting material, explaining the rationale of the method and containing a few example applications of the method, can be found in a collection edited by Cameron [56].

Later developments. In an interesting paper [159], Jackson sketches the following methodological framework for describing computer-based systems: the *subject domain* is the real world about which the system will compute, the *target domain* is the real world that it will control, the *function* is a specification of the control that the system will exercise over the target, the *user domain* is the agency that determines when the system must start and stop computing, and the *machine* domain is the hardware part of the system. He shows how several complex problems can be decomposed in different descriptions that each use elements of this framework. A simple example is the decomposition of a parsing problem into lexical analysis, which produces lexemes as a target, and syntactic analysis, which has lexemes as its subject.

In a later work, Jackson [160] argues that the decomposition of a system model into a UoD model and a specification of system functions is not valid for all kinds of systems. Different kinds of systems need different frameworks. This is further worked out in joint work with Pamela Zave as a theory of multiparadigm system specification [161, 381].

12

Jackson System Development II: Methods

12.1 Introduction

There are several versions of the JSD method [158, 228, 332]. These differ in the grouping of tasks to be performed in JSD, but they all agree on the basic philosophy that a UoD model should be made before a system model is made. Figure 12.1 gives a slight adaptation of the 1986 version of the method. In the **modeling stage**, a UoD model is made. The JSD method for UoD modeling extends the methods already encountered for ER and DF modeling (figure 12.2). In the **network stage**, a system model is made, and in the **implementation stage**, the system model is implemented. We illustrate the modeling and network stages in section 12.2 by means of the circulation administration example. In section 12.3, we look at methods to evaluate the models built by JSD. Section 12.4 takes a brief look at system implementation in JSD and section 12.5 analyzes JSD from a methodological point of view.

12.2 Case Study: the Document Circulation System

The modeling stage starts with an identification of the relevant entities and actions in the UoD. As shown in figure 12.2, we can do this by analyzing the required system transactions. These transactions are input functions, output functions or interacting functions, and we can analyze them in the same way as we did when building an ER model. The difference is that we are now looking for actions that occur in the UoD, and for UoD entities that perform or suffer actions in the UoD.

The function decomposition tree in figure 8.10 lists all the input transactions of the circulation administration. These potentially represent UoD actions performed or suffered by UoD entities, so if we describe these transactions in elementary sentences, the chances are that the nouns in these sentences indicate JSD entity types and the verbs JSD actions:

- A *MEMBER* reserves a *TITLE*.

- A *MEMBER* reserves a *DOCUMENT*.

---

1. **Modeling stage**. Specify a conceptual model of the represented UoD.

   (a) List JSD entities and JSD actions.

   (b) Allocate JSD actions to JSD entities.

   (c) Specify JSD entity types and actions.

   (d) Specify life cycles of JSD entities.

   (e) Specify the effect of actions on the entities that participate in them.

   (f) Specify context errors.

2. **Network stage**. Specify a conceptual model of the system functions. Draw an initial system network diagram consisting of the JSD entities types only. For each input function, output function and interactive function:

   (a) Add the function to the system network diagram.

   (b) Specify the structure of the records which must pass over the data stream connections, state vector connections or control stream connections.

   (c) Elaborate the model where necessary.

   (d) Specify the process structure of the added function.

   (e) Specify timing requirements for the function.

3. **Implementation stage**. Transform system specification into an implemented system.

   (a) Design the database structure.

   (b) Design the program structures.

   (c) Code and test the system.

Figure 12.1: The JSD method.

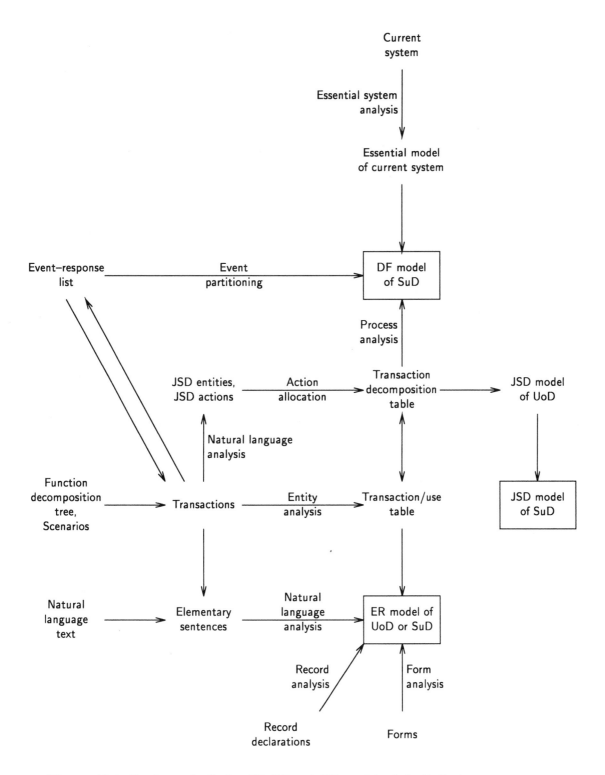

Figure 12.2: Road map for finding ER, DF and JSD models of the UoD, the current system, or the SuD.

- An action a cannot be allocated to entity type if we cannot say that an instance of the entity performed or suffered the action one or more times.
- Allocate an action to an entity in such a way that queries about whether, or how often, the action occurred in the life of an entity, can be answered.
- Allocate an action to an entity if it needs to change the local state of that entity.
- Allocate an action to an entity to enforce a sequencing of actions in the life of this entity. Allocate it to several entities to enforce sequencing by means of common actions.
- An action should be allocated to as few entities as possible.

Figure 12.3: Action allocation heuristics.

- A *MEMBER* borrows a *DOCUMENT*.

- A *MEMBER* returns a *DOCUMENT*.

- A *MEMBER* extends a document *LOAN*.

- A *MEMBER* loses a *DOCUMENT*.

- A *MEMBER* cancels a *RESERVATION*.

- A *MEMBER* is reminded of having to return a borrowed *DOCUMENT*.

The verbs in these sentences indicate potential JSD actions, the nouns indicate potential JSD entities. More potential JSD entity types can be found if we analyze the queries that the system must be able to answer. Example queries are:

- Which *DEPARTMENT* owns this *DOCUMENT*?

- When did we send a *REMINDER* to this *MEMBER*?

- Which *MEMBERs* reserved this *DOCUMENT*?

We next analyze the potential JSD entities and actions by checking whether they satisfy the JSD criteria for entities and actions. All of the potential entities above are atomic and identifyable, and they exist in the UoD. To check whether they can perform or suffer actions, we allocate actions to entities below. Looking at the potential actions first, we see that most verbs refer to actions in the UoD except one: owning a document is not an action.

12.2.1 Allocate actions to entity types

To see whether entities perform or suffer actions, the actions must now be allocated to entity types. (To simplify speech, I will also say that an action is allocated to an entity.) The heuristics for allocating actions to entities are listed in figure 12.3. A minimal condition for allocating an action to an entity is that we can ask how many times the action occurred in the life of the entity. For example, we cannot allocate the *borrow* action to a *DEPARTMENT*

	reserve_ title	*borrow*	*cancel*	*borrow res*	*extend*	*return*	*lose*	*remind*
DOCUMENT							U	
FINE							C	
LOAN		C		C	U	D	D	U
MEMBER								
RESERVATION	C		D	D				
TITLE								

Figure 12.4: Action allocation table for a model of the circulation UoD. This is a simplified form of the transaction decomposition table.

because we cannot ask how many times the department is borrowed. If an action occurs in the life of an entity, then this is relevant for the system if the system must answer queries about this action. For example, if the system must be able to answer the query whether this document is borrowed, then we should allocate *borrow* to *DOCUMENT*.

Actions must also be allocated to entities whose state they change. For example, if *borrow* would change the state of a *DOCUMENT*, we should allocate it to *DOCUMENT* as well as to *LOAN*. The definition of the effect of *borrow* in the *DOCUMENT* life cycle is local to the *DOCUMENT* entity in whose life *borrow* occurs, and is similar to the effect of *borrow* on the *LOAN* life cycle.

Enforcing sequencing by means of common actions can be done as follows. In figure 11.11, the life cycle of a *CUSTOMER* is an iteration over the actions *place*, *amend*, *cancel* and *deliver* in any order. There are constraints on the ordering of these actions, such as that an order cannot be delivered after it is canceled, but these are not expressible in the customer life cycle, for these constraints are valid per order, not per customer. In order to express them we must therefore introduce an *ORDER* entity type and define the life cycle of an *ORDER*. This life cycle is shown in figure 11.11. The common actions between *ORDER* and *CUSTOMER* enforce the proper ordering of actions in the life cycle of a *CUSTOMER*.

Applying these criteria to the lists of potential JSD actions and entity types, we get the **action allocation table** shown in figure 12.4. This is a simplified version of the transaction decomposition table, in which all R entries are omitted. The reason for omitting these entries is that reading the state of an entity is part of testing the preconditions of an action, but it does not mean that the action is allocated to the entity whose state it reads. An action must be allocated at least to the entities whose state it changes. Hence, we see all the C, U and D entries in an action allocation table. We also may see an occasional R entry if one of the other heuristics forces us to allocate an action to an entity whose state it reads.

The decisions made in building the action allocation table for the circulation UoD are explained below.

- To keep the model simple, we ignore *reserve_doc*. Addition of this action is not difficult and is left as an exercise.

- *reserve_title*. This creates a *RESERVATION*, so we should at least allocate this action to this entity type. Because a *reserve_title* is performed by a *MEMBER* and is directed at a $TITLE$, it seems natural to allocate *reserve_title* to these entity types as well. However, the event does not change the state of any entity of these types. Neither do we need to allocate *reserve_title* to $TITLE$ to remember the fact that *reserve_title* occurred in the life of a title. If we would define an attribute

$$title : RESERVATION \rightarrow TITLE\_IDENTIFIER,$$

then all this information could be retrieved by means of this attribute. The codomain of this attribute should be some unique identification of $TITLE$ instances, e.g. a key or an identifier attribute. We therefore allocate *reserve_title* to $RESERVATION$ only.

- *borrow*. This creates a $LOAN$ instance, so we must allocate it to $LOAN$. By a similar argument as above, we decide not to allocate it to $MEMBER$ and $DOCUMENT$ but define an attribute

$$document : LOAN \rightarrow DOCUMENT\_IDENTIFIER.$$

If we want to find out whether a document d is borrowed, we should look at the set of existing $LOAN$ instances and search for one whose *document* is d. If the $LOAN$ is done by a member who reserved the document (or the title of the document), then this reservation instance should be destroyed simultaneously with the creation of the $LOAN$ instance. This suggests that in some cases, *borrow* should also be allocated to $RESERVATION$ (as the last event in its life cycle). However, it is not possible to define a conditional participation in an action. Instead, we define a second transaction, *borrow_res*.

- *borrow_res*. This is a borrow action that terminates a reservation and starts a $LOAN$. We allocate *borrow_res* to $RESERVATION$ and $LOAN$.

- *cancel*. This terminates a $RESERVATION$, so we allocate it to this entity type. We don't allocate it to $MEMBER$, because we don't expect queries about how often a member canceled a reservation and *cancel* does not change the state of a $MEMBER$.

- *extend*. This changes the state of $LOAN$, so we allocate it to this entity type.

- *return*. This terminates the existence of a $LOAN$, so we allocate it to this entity type.

- *lose*. This terminates a $LOAN$, so we allocate it to this entity type. In addition, it changes the state of a document from present to lost. If we delete a $LOAN$ when the borrowed document is lost, then the information that the document is lost is not represented anywhere. We therefore add an attribute *lost* to $DOCUMENT$ and initialize it to *false*. The effect of *lose* is to set this attribute to *true*. We therefore also allocate *lose* to $DOCUMENT$.

  Yet another effect of $lose(m, d)$ is that m should pay a fine. We do this by introducing a $FINE$ entity type, with a history in which such events as *pay* and *waive* can take place. Instances of $FINE$ would be created by the circulation desk but be handled by the finance department. Thus, $FINE$ instances are a means of communication between these two departments. The *lose* action is also allocated to $FINE$ and should be the first event in the $FINE$ life cycle.

$DOCUMENT(\underline{doc\_id}, title\_id, location, ...)$

$FINE(\underline{pass\_nr}, total\_amount, amount\_paid, amount\_waived)$

$LOAN(\underline{pass\_nr}, \underline{doc\_id}, date\_borrowed, return\_date)$

$MEMBER(\underline{pass\_nr}, name, address, ...)$

$RESERVATION(\underline{pass\_nr}, \underline{title\_id}, date\_reserved)$

$TITLE(\underline{title\_id}, name, authors, publisher, year, isbn, ...)$

Figure 12.5: Entity types in the circulation desk UoD and their attributes.

- *remind.* A *MEMBER* is sent a reminder for returning a *DOCUMENT*, but this reminder is sent because a *LOAN* is extended too long. One member can be overdue for many *LOANS*, so we allocate *remind* to *LOAN*.

- The entity type *DEPARTMENT* has been omitted because there is no action for it in the UoD of the circulation desk.

- The entity type *REMINDER* has been omitted because it is suggested by a query that asks when the last reminder was sent for a document, and we can answer this query without introducing this entity type. For example, we can have the *LOAN* surrogate fill a data stream with *remind* messages, which is read by the query. Note that if we had kept *REMINDER* as an entity type, then the *remind* action would have been the creation action for this type.

The action allocation table shows that in our UoD model, *MEMBER* and *TITLE* are no JSD entities, because there are no actions in their lives. The reason for this is that we have a model of the world as viewed by the circulation desk. There are other views of the UoD, such as that of the member services department or the acquisition department, in which there are relevant actions that must be allocated to *MEMBER* or *TITLE*. For example, *MEMBER* actions like *become_member* and *change_address* will appear in a model of the UoD of the member services department, and *TITLE* actions like *order*, *arrive* and *classify* will appear in the UoD model of the acquisition department.

12.2.2 Specify JSD entity types and actions

Now that we have reasonable certainty about what the relevant JSD actions and entity types are, we specify them in more detail. The following items are specified:

- JSD entity type declarations, including their attributes. We do this in the same way as in ER modeling. Figure 12.5 contains the JSD entity specifications, with keys underlined.

- JSD actions are declared by listing their parameters and by giving an intuitive explanation of their meaning. Actions are specified in figure 12.6.

Action	Meaning
$reserve(m, t, c)$	A $MEMBER$ m reserves a $TITLE$ t at date c.
$borrow(m, d, c)$	$DOCUMENT$ d is borrowed by $MEMBER$ m at date c.
$return(m, d, c)$	$DOCUMENT$ d, which was borrowed by $MEMBER$ m, is returned by m to the circulation desk at date c.
$extend(m, d, c)$	The borrowing period of $DOCUMENT$ d, which is borrowed by $MEMBER$ m, is extended at date c.
$lose(m, d, c)$	$DOCUMENT$ d, which is borrowed by $MEMBER$ m, is lost by m at date c.
$cancel(m, t)$	A reservation by $MEMBER$ m for $TITLE$ t is canceled by m. It may be canceled by an explicit action of the m in which m says that the reservation is canceled, or it may be canceled by the omission of an action of the m, in which m fails to collect a document set aside for him or her due to a reservation.
$borrow\_$ $res(m, d, c)$	$MEMBER$ m borrows $DOCUMENT$ d at date c, whose $TITLE$ had a reservation placed on it by m. This $RESERVATION$ terminates by the $borrow\_res$ action.
$remind(m, c)$	At date c, $MEMBER$ m is reminded of not having fulfilled his or her obligation to return a document on time.

Figure 12.6: JSD actions in the circulation UoD and their informal descriptions.

12.2.3   Specify life cycle of JSD entities

The $LOAN$ life cycle is the central process in the circulation department. It is shown in figure 12.7. The leaves of the PSD have been labeled with the values of the life cycle indicator of a $LOAN$ instance. The *lose* action can occur after any action from the start and has been modeled as a premature termination of the $LOAN$. After the second reminder, there are two possible actions, both of which are final: a *return* or a *lose* action. This is a simplification, for after a reminder, the member can extend the loan as well.

The $RESERVATION$ life cycle is shown in figure 12.8. One of its final actions, *borrow_res*, is one possible first action of $LOAN$.

The $DOCUMENT$ and $FINE$ life cycles as seen by the circulation desk, contain only one action, *lose*, which terminates a $DOCUMENT$ life and starts a $FINE$ life. The rest of the life cycles of these entity types are part of the UoD models of the acquisition department and customer services department. This is not shown here.

12.2.4   Specify action effects

The preconditions and effects of the actions in the $LOAN$ and $RESERVATION$ life cycles are described in figures 12.9 and 12.10. The preconditions and effects of the only action in the life cycles of $DOCUMENT$ and $FINE$ visible in the part of the library UoD observable from the circulation desk, are described in figure 12.11. A default precondition of every action is that any parameter that refers to an entity, refers to an existing entity unless otherwise stated. A default effect of every action is that the life cycle indicator of the entity in which life the action occurs is updated according to the PSD of the entity.

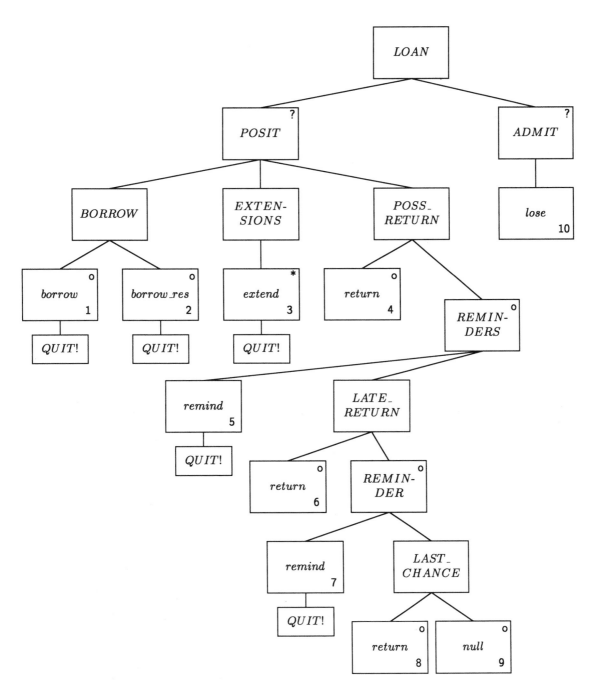

Figure 12.7: The *LOAN* life cycle. The numbers in the leaves are values for the life cycle indicator of *LOAN* instances.

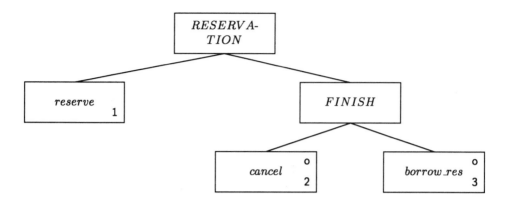

Figure 12.8: The *RESERVATION* life cycle. The leaves have been labeled with the possible values of the life cycle indicator.

LOAN		
Action	Preconditions	Effect
$borrow(m, d, c)$	• No *LOAN* instance $\langle m', d \rangle$ exists in the UoD for any m'. • There is no reservation for *title(d)*.	• A *LOAN* instance $\langle m, d \rangle$ exists in the UoD with *pass_nr* = *pass_nr(m)*, *doc_id* = *doc_id(d)*, *date_borrowed* = *c, return_date* = *c* plus three weeks.
$return(m, d, c)$	• The *LOAN* instance $\langle m, d \rangle$ exists in the UoD.	• The *LOAN* instance $\langle m, d \rangle$ does not exist in the UoD.
$extend(m, d, c)$	• The *LOAN* instance $\langle m, d \rangle$ exists in the UoD.	• *date_to_return($\langle m, d \rangle$)* = *c* plus three weeks.
$lose(m, d, c)$	• The *LOAN* instance $\langle m, d \rangle$ exists in the UoD.	• The *LOAN* instance $\langle m, d \rangle$ does not exist in the UoD.
$borrow\_res(m, d, c)$	• No *LOAN* instance $\langle m', d \rangle$ exists in the UoD for any m'. • There is a reservation for *title(d)* by *m*.	• A *LOAN* instance exists in the UoD with *pass_nr* = *pass_nr(m)*, *doc_id* = *doc_id(d)* and *date_borrowed* = *c, return_date* = *c* plus three weeks. • There is no reservation for *title(d)* by *m*.
$remind(m)$		—

Figure 12.9: Specification of the actions in the *LOAN* life cycle.

RESERVATION		
Action	Preconditions	Effect
$reserve(m, t, c)$	• No *RESERVATION* instance $\langle m, t \rangle$ exists in the UoD.	• A *RESERVATION* instance exists in the UoD with $pass\_nr = pass\_nr(m)$, $title\_id = title\_id(t)$, and $date\_reserved = c$.
$cancel(m, t)$	• The *RESERVATION* instance $\langle m, t \rangle$ exists in the UoD.	• The *RESERVATION* instance $\langle m, t \rangle$ does not exist in the UoD.
$borrow\_res(m, d, c)$	• The *RESERVATION* instance $\langle m, t \rangle$ exists in the UoD.	• The *RESERVATION* instance $\langle m, t \rangle$ does not exist in the UoD.

Figure 12.10: Specification of the actions in the *RESERVATION* life cycle.

FINE		
Action	Preconditions	Effect
$lose(m, d, c)$	• The *LOAN* instance $\langle m, d \rangle$ exists in the UoD.	• A *FINE* for losing d exists for m in the UoD.

DOCUMENT		
Action	Preconditions	Effect
$lose(m, d, c)$	• *DOCUMENT* instance d exists.	• $lost(d) = true$.

Figure 12.11: Specification of the *lose* action.

| RESERVATION | | Context error table | | |
LCI	Update	OK/ Error	Condition	Error message
0	$reserve(m,t,c)$	OK		
	$cancel(m,t)$	Error		Title is not reserved by member.
	$borrow\_res(m,d,c)$	Error		$title(d)$ is not reserved by member.
1	$reserve(m,t,c)$	Error		Title already reserved by member.
	$cancel(m,t)$	OK		
	$borrow\_res(m,d,c)$	OK		
2, 3	All			No reservation.

Figure 12.12: Context error table for *RESERVATION*.

12.2.5 Context errors

A **context error** is an attempt to inform the system that an JSD action occurred in the UoD that could not occur according to the PSDs of the UoD model. These errors can be systematically listed in a context error table, which can then be used in the specification of error-handling in input functions. Figure 12.12 gives a context error table for the *RESERVATION* process.

12.2.6 System functions

Examples of input, output and interacting functions have been given in chapter 11. In this section we give another example of an interacting function and in the exercises, there is another example of an output function. The interacting function to be specified is the following:

F1 Each day at 9:00 in the morning, suspend each member who has not responded for six weeks to a reminder.

A system network and a possible process structure for F1 are shown in figure 12.13. F1 requires elaboration of the UoD model and of the system specification. The UoD model must be extended with a *suspend* action in the *MEMBER* life cycle, and the system specification must be extended by adding the attribute *date_last_reminded* to the *LOAN* entity type,

$$LOAN(\underline{pass\_nr}, doc\_id, date\_to\_return, date\_last\_reminded).$$

Finally, the table of effect definitions must be updated with the effect of the actions on this attribute, as shown in figure 12.14.

12.3 Evaluation Methods for UoD Models

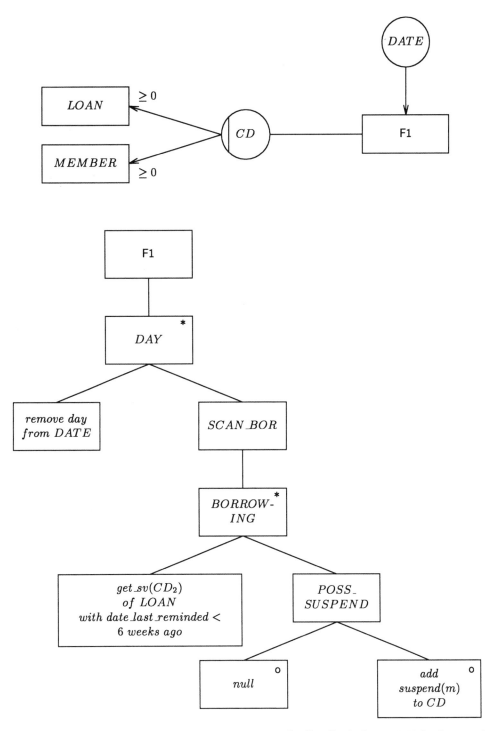

Figure 12.13: System network and process structure for F1: Each day at 9:00 in the morning, suspend each member who has not responded for six weeks to a reminder.

LOAN		
Action	Preconditions	Effects
$borrow(m, d, c)$	• No *LOAN* instance $\langle m', d \rangle$ exists in the UoD for any m'. • There is no reservation for $title(d)$.	• A *LOAN* instance $\langle m, d \rangle$ exists in the UoD with $pass\_nr = pass\_nr(m)$, $doc\_id = doc\_id(d)$, $date\_borrowed = c$, $return\_date = c$ plus three weeks, $date\_last\_reminded = none$.
$borrow\_res(m, d, c)$	• No *LOAN* instance $\langle m', d \rangle$ exists in the UoD for any m'. • There is a reservation for $title(d)$ by m.	• A *LOAN* instance exists in the UoD with $pass\_nr = pass\_nr(m)$, $doc\_id = doc\_id(d)$ and $date\_borrowed = c$, $return\_date = c$ plus three weeks, $date\_last\_reminded = none$ • There is no reservation for $title(d)$ by m.
$remind(m, c)$		• $date\_last\_reminded = c$

Figure 12.14: Effect definitions for the *date_last_reminded* attribute.

Entity checks:

- A JSD entity exists in the represented UoD, not merely in the DBS.

- A JSD entity must be able to perform or suffer actions.

- JSD entities must be atomic.

- A JSD entity must have a unique identity.

Action checks:

- Actions must occur in the represented UoD, not merely in the DBS.

- Actions are discrete in time.

- Actions cannot be decomposed in more elementary actions.

- Each action must have a unique identity.

Action allocation checks:

- An action cannot be allocated to an entity if we cannot ask how often the action occurred in the life of the entity.

- An action must be allocated to an entity if the system must remember occurrences of this action in the life of the entity.

- An action should be allocated to an entity if it needs to update the local state of the entity.

- Every entity should be created (deleted) sometime.

Common action checks:

- A message is delivered as sent.

- A message is never delivered at the incorrect address.

- There is no delay between sending and receiving.

Life cycle check:

- It should be impossible for a JSD entity to behave in another way than that described by its PSD.

Figure 12.15: Quality checks for JSD models.

Figure 12.15 summarizes a number of criteria by which to evaluate a model of the UoD. Most of them are simply a summary of the defining characteristics of the main concepts of UoD modeling. Only the life cycle certainty check is new. This check says that a life cycle gives a *necessary* process structure that covers all possible histories of a class of entities. It is an important quality check that prevents us from overlooking any exceptions, interrupts, premature terminations, etc., in the life of an entity. There are no evaluation criteria for the specification of system functions. If the function processes are specified following the JSP method, then they are guaranteed to be well-structured programs.

12.4   Implementation

The output of the network stage is a model of required system behavior that assumes an unbounded supply of processors, one for each surrogate process and function process, and a sufficient number of unbounded queues to act as data streams between processes. The implementation stage is concerned with mapping this abstract model to a model of a system with only one processor and limited memory. A simple way to transform a system network into a model of the implementation on a single-processor system is the following:

- Each surrogate process and each long-running function process becomes a module in the implementation. Short-running functions become modules that don't have an internal state that survives a call to the module.

- The state vectors of surrogates and long-running function processes are gathered together in files or global variables. There is one file or state variable for each surrogate type and for each long-running function process. This is called **state vector separation**.

- Each data stream is implemented as a file with a first-in first-out access discipline. Data stream access in the system modules is replaced by the appropriate file access statements.

- A scheduler reads all input to the system and calls any module in the system directly. When an update to a surrogate state is received, it calls the appropriate module on the appropriate state vector and advances the life cycle indicator of the surrogate accordingly.

This particular implementation strategy leads to a flat system, for each module is directly called by the scheduler. More refined implementation strategies are described in the literature on JSD, listed at the end of this chapter.

12.5   Methodological Analysis

12.5.1   Separation of UoD modeling from function specification

Jackson [158] motivates the JSD method by contrasting it with functional decomposition as practiced in structured analysis. He shows convincingly that a model of required system behavior that is based upon a model of UoD behavior is more maintainable than a model that decomposes a system into subsystems that correspond to required system functions.

The reason is simple: the UoD is more stable than the system requirements. The UoD is the part of the world about which the system computes. The UoD may consist of entities and processes that make up part of the business, or it may consist of entities whose behavior is to be controlled by the system. Either way, the entities and processes are more stable than the desires of system users. Requirements may change from requesting simple snapshot reports to requesting periodical historical summary reports or to complex interacting functions. All these functions are described in terms of the same UoD. If the system were structured in a hierarchical manner of a function decomposition tree, then any change in this tree could cause a major restructuring of the system. If the system is structured by separating the UoD model from the implementation of system functions, then a change in system function can remain localized to the affected function; the UoD model will remain constant during those changes.

An added benefit of building a separate UoD model is that this can serve as a common basis for understanding system behavior and for specifying system functions. The UoD model serves as a means of communication between customers, users, domain specialists and system developers.

12.5.2 JSD and Information Engineering

The above argument is built upon the same premise as Information Engineering, viz. that the UoD is more stable than human desires. The conclusion drawn from this premise is, however, different. Where Information Engineering concludes that the information strategy of a business must be based upon the foundation of a business data model (which is an ER model of the business UoD), JSD concludes that an information system must be structured by separating a UoD model from a model of system functions. The common denominator in these two different conclusions is that both methods agree that a UoD model must serve as a shared model in terms of which system requirements must be understood. The difference is that Information Engineering maintains a focus on functional decomposition of business needs, where JSD maintains a focus on system specification.

12.5.3 JSD and structured development

Note that JSD assumes that structured analysis leads to a system structure that is isomorphic to the function decomposition tree. We have seen in the methodological analyses of ISP (subsection 6.6.2) and data flow models (subsection 9.7.3) that function decomposition is orthogonal to system decomposition. Decomposing the product idea into functions down to the level of transactions yields a decomposition tree of the product idea that stays at one level of aggregation. This decomposition moves to the right along the horizontal dimension of the development framework of figure 3.9 (page 53). Decomposition of the product into parts leads us to the next lower level of aggregation. This is a movement downwards in the vertical dimension of the framework. It is only when we identify the two kinds of decomposition that we get into the maintainability trouble pointed out by Jackson. There is no assumption in structured development that system decomposition should be isomorphic to function decomposition — however, neither is there a guideline to keep these two decompositions distinct.

A related critique of JSD on function decomposition is that top-down decomposition of a problem only works well if we already know what the subproblems are. In the face of uncertainty about the solution, top-down decomposition of a problem is more likely to give us a wrong decomposition. Here, JSD assumes that a function decomposition tree is built top-down. There is no such assumption in structured development. The tree can be built top-down, bottom-up, middle out or in any other way, and in whatever way it is built we are likely to iterate many times before a stable tree is reached. The function decomposition tree is a representation of the product functions, not of the process by which we found those functions.

12.5.4   Modeling social processes

An important limitation of the JSD method is that life cycle modeling is only applicable in a limited manner to social systems. For example, the circulation desk model we developed in this chapter contains omissions in the dynamics of the represented UoD. Documents can be lost, but they can also be found, something we did not put in our model. Fines may be waived or refunded. Documents may get lost without being borrowed, and they may be damaged by their borrowers, or by other libraries, or by the binding department. Documents come in many forms: books, maps, journals, serial volumes, dossiers for which regular updates are published, manuals, and hand-written manuscripts; and many of these can appear on paper, microfiche or CD-ROM. All of these behave differently. If we include all of this in our UoD model, we get an extremely complex document life cycle and we can never be sure that we have really modeled all possibilities, or that new kinds of documents will not come into being. There is a trade-off between the complexity of the UoD model and the returns on this investment in terms of the utility of the model. If the UoD is mechanical, such as in an elevator system, it may be necessary as well as feasible to make a complete life cycle model of the UoD. But in the case of social systems, the number of exceptions, interrupts, premature terminations and backtrackings may be so high as to reduce the life cycle to the simple structure *create; do_anything*; delete*.

12.6   Summary

The JSD method consists of three stages, modeling the UoD, modeling the DBS and implementing the DBS. A UoD model can be found by an elementary sentence analysis of required system transactions or by analyzing a transaction system decomposition table that was already found by other means. The action allocation table is a simplified form of the transaction decomposition table and represents the communication structure within each system transaction. The evaluation methods for UoD models all follow from the definitions of the key JSD concepts such as JSD entity, JSD action, common action and life cycle.

The emphasis on the stability of the UoD model is shared with Information Engineering. Maintainability of the system is enhanced if it is structured after the UoD model rather than after the tree of required system functions. The UoD model can also serve as a common framework for communication about required system functions. A possible problem with JSD is that social processes do not have the required regularity to be modeled by anything other than an unstructured iteration over arbitrary actions between birth and death. Although JSD is contrasted with structured development, the critique that structured development requires a system to be structured top-down according to the function decomposition tree is unfounded.

12.7 Exercises

1. Reservations can be canceled because the reserver notifies the library of cancellation, or because ten days have passed since the reserver has been notified by the library of the availability of the reserved title. Change the system model by adding this function.

2. Add the entity type *D_RESERVATION* for document reservations to the UoD model of the library. Define a PSD for this entity type and make any other changes necessary to accommodate this process.

3. Assume that all fines of a *MEMBER* are collected in one *FINE* entity, so that the relationship between *MEMBER* and *FINE* would be one-one. Revise the model accordingly.

4. Define the system function F2: At the end of each week, make a list of borrowing actions that occurred in that week; add to this list a count of the loans of that week, plus a cumulative total of loans.

12.8 Bibliographical Remarks

Literature on the JSD method has already been given in the bibliographical section of the previous chapter. Case studies in the application of JSD can be found in Jackson's book [158], a collection of papers edited by Cameron [56], in Sutcliffe [332] and in Sanden [303].

Part III

Method Integration and Strategy Selection

13

A Framework for Requirements Engineering I: Models

13.1 Introduction

In this final part, we turn to the integration of the requirements specification methods of part II. In this chapter, we focus on integration of the modeling structures used in those methods and in the next, we concentrate on the integration of the methods to find and evaluate requirements specifications. We reviewed two kinds of methods in part II, methods for needs analysis at the organizational level (ISAC change analysis and Information Strategy Planning) and methods for behavior specification at the level of computer-based systems. In section 13.2, we show how the deliverables of ISAC change analysis and Information Strategy Planning can be integrated. In section 13.3, we turn to behavior specifications and compare the notations and techniques used in ER modeling, Structured Analysis and JSD by placing them in the framework for behavior specifications defined of chapter 4. In section 13.4 we then show how the notations of ER modeling and JSD can be integrated and in section 13.5, we show how to extend this with the DF modeling notation. In section 13.6, we step back and look at the different concepts of modularization used in the DF models and JSD models of a system.

13.2 The Specification of Product Objectives

In chapter 4, it was explained how the analysis of needs results in a specification of top level product objectives. If the product is a computer-based system, its environment is a social system and the the top level objectives must follow from an analysis of the needs in this social environment. ISAC Change Analysis and IE Information Strategy Planning are two methods to analyze the needs of the social environment. There are three characteristics shared by both methods:

- Both are methods to develop information systems.

- Both are methods for client-oriented development.

- Both methods represent the human activity in the environment of the SuD (by activity models and function decomposition trees).

The restriction of Change Analysis and ISP to information systems is not significant, because at this stage of development it is immaterial what kind of system will eventually be developed. The restriction to client-oriented development is more significant, because the methods and techniques recommended by Change Analysis and ISP can only be used for the analysis of individual clients and not for the analysis of a market. To analyze the needs of a market, one should turn to methods like Quality Function Deployment (QFD). In this method, product characteristics are analyzed from the viewpoint of users of the product, and these characteristics are translated into design characteristics of the product. The design characteristics then become the top level product objectives. Pointers to the literature on QFD are given in section 13.10.

Within the above shared orientation, there are three important differences between Change Analysis and ISP:

- In Change Analysis, needs follow from an analysis of *problems* experienced by an organization. In ISP, needs follow from an analysis of the *strategy* of the organization.

- In Change Analysis, the activity model represents interactions between activities. There is a hierarchical structure of the models, but this is not represented explicitly. Material or data manipulated by the activities is represented by stores. In ISP, the activity model is a tree that represents the contribution of each activity to the organization mission.

- ISP additionally represents the UoD of the business by an entity model. Interaction between data and activities is represented by a function/entity matrix. Entity modeling is absent from ISAC.

These differences are such that both methods supplement each other. Figure 13.1 shows an ER diagram of concepts from both methods and of some of the relationships between the concepts. Cardinalities are omitted; adding these is left as an exercise. Going from the top down, we see that interventions may solve some problems and introduce other problems, and that problems have owners and inhibit goals. The relationship *PG* is the matrix of problems against problem owners made in Change Analysis. Product objectives are objectives, which are subgoals, which are goals. The *is_a* fork below *GOAL* is intended to represent that all goals are either subgoals or missions. Not all subgoals are objectives, though, and not all objectives are product objectives. Goals form a hierarchy whose root is the business mission.

Persons are employed by organization units, may be members of groups that have problems, and may, as managers, want to monitor CSFs because they view these as indicators of goal achievement. Some organization units can be decomposed into other units. Activities are performed by organization units and form a function decomposition tree. In order to avoid crossing lines, *MISSION* appears twice in the diagram. The hierarchy of the function decomposition tree corresponds in ISAC to the hierarchy of activity models.

The interaction between activities is represented by the *INTERACTION* relationship and the interaction between activities and entities is represented by the *CRUD* relationship. The *CRUD* relationship is the function/entity matrix of ISP. The union of the *CRUD* and

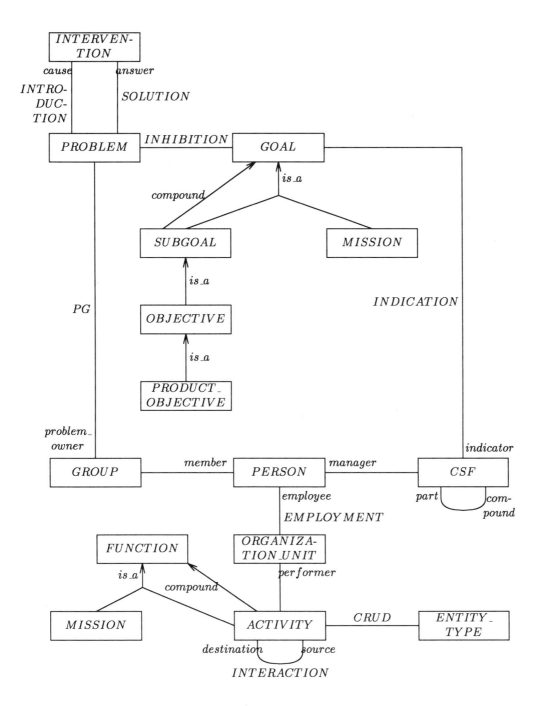

Figure 13.1: An integration of concepts from Change Analysis and ISP.

Deliverables		
	ISAC Change Analysis	ISP
Representation of product environment	• Matrix of business problems and problem owners • Graph of problems and causes • Activity model of desired business situation	• Decomposition of business mission into functions • Entity model of business UoD • Function/entity matrices • Critical Success Factors of the business
Representation of product objectives	• Change goals • Change needs • Ambition levels for product	• Matrix of business problems and business goals • Decomposition of business mission into goals and objectives • Ambition levels for product

Figure 13.2: Specification techniques for the representation of the product environment and of the product objectives.

INTERACTION relationships is represented in ISAC by the arrows appearing in activity models.

This model could be extended and refined in order to tailor it to a particular situation. For example, one could distinguish possible interventions from the intervention actually chosen and, for each possible intervention, represent the reasons for taking it and the reasons for not taking it. Objectives can be linked to activities that realize them, and they can be classified into constraints, essential objectives and preferences, and into technical and organizational objectives. Interventions may be regarded as lower-level objectives and they are linked to assumptions that, if they become false, would decrease the effectiveness of the intervention. Organization units can be linked to geographical locations, goals, and managers. Adding refinements like these, it is important to keep in mind what the use of such a data model is. The major use would be to serve as a data model for a database (often called **repository**) that records development decisions. The dangers of adding too many refinements to the data model are that one can end up in metaphysical discussions about the "true" meaning of terms like *objective* and *problem*, and that the model becomes so complex that it cannot be used effectively.

The point to be made here is that there is an amazing concurrence of ideas and techniques across Change Analysis and ISP. The diagram shows that there are two major concerns in needs analysis, the identification of objectives and the representation of the environment of the product. Adding these two concerns as subject areas to the diagram is left as an exercise for the reader. Figure 13.2 shows the techniques used by ISAC Change Analysis and by

ISP to represent the environment and the product objectives. From this list, it is easy to see that the techniques of both methods are complementary. This does not mean that all of these techniques *must* be used in any requirements engineering process. It means that, should the need arise, these techniques *can* be combined in a single requirements engineering process.

13.3   A Framework for Behavior Specifications

13.3.1   UoD models

In the methodological analyses of the preceding chapters, we have filled the skeleton framework for requirements specifications defined in chapter 4 with elements taken from ER models, DF models and JSD models. Figure 13.3 presents the resulting framework for UoD models. An explanation of the contents of the table follows.

First, the DF model column is filled almost completely with NA (Not Applicable). A DF model of a software system obviously does not represent the UoD of the system, but nevertheless some entities in the UoD of the system may appear as external entities in the DF model. For example, library customers are part of the UoD of the library circulation system and can be represented as external entities in a DF model system requirements. On the other hand, some entities (documents) are also part of the UoD but are not represented as external entity, and other entities (library employees) are external entities of the system but are not necessarily part of the UoD of the system. Moreover, external entities in a DF diagram may be types or instances; the distinction is not considered to be relevant for DF models. The external entities of a DF model are therefore not an adequate representation of the UoD of the system.

The other components of a DF model do not represent the UoD at all. The rest of the framework for UoD models therefore only contains a comparison of ER models and JSD models. An explanation of the entries of the table follows.

- The state of the UoD is characterized by the set of **entities** that exist in that UoD state, and by the state that each existing entity has. The entity state is represented by attribute values and, in JSD, additionally by the value of the life cycle indicator. In both approaches, entities are classified into *types*. A UoD entity in ER is any observable part of the UoD (i.e. a system in the general sense of section 2.2). A JSD entity is any observable part of the UoD that performs or suffers significant behavior. A JSD model of the UoD usually has less entity types than an ER model of the UoD.

- In the ER approach, there are special entity types called **relationships**. A relationship instance is a tuple of entities. There is in most ER approaches a special relationship, the *is_a* relationship, which represents subset inclusion. JSD does not distinguish relationships.

- The state space of the UoD is further constrained in an ER model by **cardinality constraints**. ER and JSD models of the UoD can additionally be annotated with constraints restricting the cardinality of existence sets of entity types or relationships. There is an ambiguity whether constraints in these models are *regularities*, propositions that are true in every state of the UoD, or *norms*, propositions that should be true in the UoD but may be violated by the UoD.

	UoD model		
	ER model	DF model	JSD model
State space			
Entities	Y	External entities	Y
Entity types	Y	Ambiguous	Y
Entity attributes	Y	NA	Y
Relationships	Y	NA	JSD entity types
Relationship types	Y	NA	Y
is_a relationships	Y	NA	N
Relationship attributes	Y	NA	JSD entity attributes
Constraints			
Cardinality	Y	NA	N
Existence set cardinality	As annotation	NA	As annotation
State transitions			
Entity transactions	N	NA	Actions
Transaction effects	N	NA	PSDs and annotations
Transaction preconditions	N	NA	PSDs and annotations
Entity communications	As relationships	NA	Common actions
Entity life cycles	N	NA	Y

Figure 13.3: Three kinds of models of UoD behavior.

- The ER notation does not allow the representation of behavior. In JSD, entity trans-actions (the smallest unit of interaction of an entity with its environment) are repre-sented by **actions**. For each action, preconditions and effects can be defined.

- UoD entities communicate in JSD by means of **common actions**. As will be ex-plained below, communications can end up in an ER model as relationships.

- Entity behavior is constrained in JSD by the definition of **life cycles**.

13.3.2 Models of system behavior

Figure 13.4 applies the framework to models of product behavior. It repeats the framework shown earlier in figure 11.23. Note that the framework can be applied to computer-based systems as well as to software systems. We collect here the remarks made in the method-ological analyses of the models produced by the ER approach, DF modeling and JSD.

- In each state of the system, a set of **entities** exist. These may be *ER entities*, *data store records* (DF), *data stream records* (JSD), *surrogates* that represent UoD entities (JSD), or *the state of long-running function processes* (JSD). Each existing entity, record, surrogate or long-running function process has a state, represented by *attribute values* (ER and JSD), *field values* (DF), or *local variables* of a function process (JSD). In JSD, an additional part of the state of a surrogate or a long-running function process is represented by a *life cycle indicator*.

- **Relationships** are represented as structured data stores in DF models and as surro-gates in JSD. Relationships may have attributes, and in ER models there are special relationships called *is_a* to represent the taxonomic structure of entity types.

- A number of **constraints** can be defined for the system state. ER models restrict the state space by means of *cardinality* constraints. *Storage constraints*, that limit the size of the existence sets, can be specified in DF models as annotations of data store definitions in the data dictionary, and as annotations of entity types in JSD models.

- ER models do not represent **system transactions**. In DF models, system trans-actions can be represented by *data transformations*, but this is not enforced by the notation. Preconditions and effects are specified as part of *minispecs* of data trans-formations. In JSD models, system transactions are represented as parts of *input functions*, *output functions* and *interactive functions*. These functions may be embed-ded, in which case they are actions whose preconditions and effects can be specified as annotations to a PSD for a surrogate process. Functions may also be short or long-running processes. A short-running process represents a single transaction, but a long-running process performs transactions on demand and continues to exist after the transaction has been executed. In either case, a transaction is represented by a PSD consisting of several actions, for which preconditions and effects can be specified as annotations to the PSD.

- DF models represent the system as a network of processes (i.e. data transformations) and data stores. **Communication** is through *data flows*. JSD models represent the system as a collection of (surrogate or function) processes that communicate through *data streams*, *state vectors* and *controlled data streams*.

	System model		
	ER model	DF model	JSD model
State space			
Entities	Y	Data store records	Surrogates, long-running function processes data stream records
Entity types	Y	Data stores	Surrogate types, long-running functions data streams
Entity attributes	Y	Data store fields	Y
Relationships	Y	Structured data stores	Surrogate types
is_a Relationships	Y	N	N
Relationship types	Y	Data stores	Surrogate types
Relationship attributes	Y	Data store fields	Surrogate attributes
Constraints			
Cardinality	Y	Data dictionary	N
Storage constraints	As annotation	Data dictionary	As annotation
State transitions			
System transactions	N	Data transformations	Function processes
Transaction effects	N	Minispecs	PSDs and annotations
Transaction preconditions	N	Minispecs	PSDs and annotations
Process communications	N	Data flows	Process connections
Life cycles	N	In RT extensions	PSDs
Other constraints			
Interface technology	N	Data dictionary	N
Response time	N	Data dictionary	As annotations
Delay	N	Data dictionary	As annotations

Figure 13.4: Three kinds of models of the SuD.

ER models	Same model, different interpretation
DF models	No UoD model
JSD models	UoD model is initial version of SuD model

Figure 13.5: The relation between the UoD model and the system model in the three behavior specification methods.

- System behavior can be constrained by means of **life cycle** diagrams for surrogate and function processes in JSD. There is no such possibility in the variant of DF modeling treated in this book, but in real-time extensions of DF models [122, 141, 354, 355, 227], the activity of data transformations can be controlled by state machines. These extensions are treated in *Requirements Engineering: Semantic, Real-Time and Object-Oriented Methods*.

- Other **constraints** on system behavior that can be expressed are constraints on the interface technology of external entities (DF), response time requirements (DF and JSD), and the permissible delay between the occurrence of a UoD action and its registration by the system (JSD).

13.3.3   Relationship between UoD models and SuD models

The three methods have different things to say about the way UoD models and SuD models must be combined (figure 13.5). It has been remarked in chapter 7 that ER models are insensitive with respect to the question of whether we model the UoD or the SuD. Looking at an ER model, we cannot discover which of the two it represents. To find that out, we must look at the documentation of the model. Of course, the *interpretation* of a UoD model is different from the interpretation of a system model. We have seen in chapter 7 that cardinality constraints that indicate regularities in the UoD are interpreted as norms for the SuD. DF models represent the SuD and not the UoD of this system, and JSD system models represent both. In JSD, the UoD model is used as initial version of the SuD model. We can retrieve the UoD model from a SuD model by removing the parts of the SuD model that represent system functions. These different views on what we are specifying will be taken in consideration when we try to build integrated models below.

13.4   Integrated JSD-ER Models of the UoD

In this section, we build an integrated JSD-ER model of the UoD of the student administration example. It is indifferent to whether this administration is automated or paper-based. Figures 13.6 to 13.8 give the PSDs of a JSD model of this UoD. In the following subsections, we extend this with an ER model of the same UoD, taking care to define the relations between these two views of the UoD, so that the two views jointly form an integrated model. Figure 13.9 shows the UoD network.

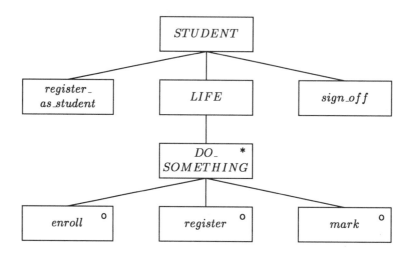

Figure 13.6: PSD for a simple *STUDENT* life cycle [364]. Reproduced by permission of Oxford University Press, 1994.

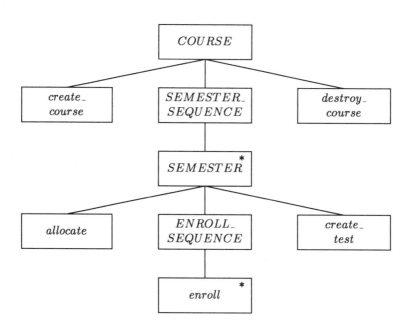

Figure 13.7: PSD for a simple *COURSE* life cycle [364]. Reproduced by permission of Oxford University Press, 1994.

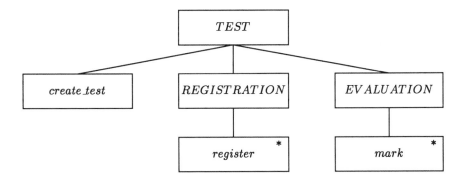

Figure 13.8: PSD for a simple $TEST$ life cycle [364]. Reproduced by permission of Oxford University Press, 1994.

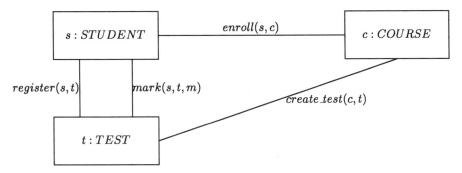

Figure 13.9: UoD network for the common actions between $STUDENT$, $COURSE$ and $TEST$ instances. For clarity, the action parameters are shown in the diagram [364]. Reproduced by permission of Oxford University Press, 1994.

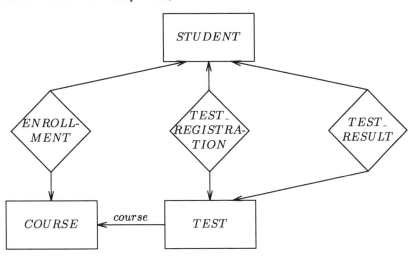

Figure 13.10: The ER version of the UoD network of figure 13.9. Each common action whose occurrence needs to be remembered has been turned into a relationship [364]. Reproduced by permission of Oxford University Press, 1994.

13.4.1   Entities

We saw in chapter 11 that a JSD entity is an ER entity with some extra requirements:

- It must exist in the UoD,

- it must have something significant to do,

- it must be atomic and

- it must have a unique identity.

Since we are currently looking at UoD models, we keep the first requirement. But since we want to extend JSD with the capability to model passive entities and their links, we drop the requirements that entities must have something to do; and because we additionally want to be able to model links, we also drop the requirement of atomicity. The requirement that an entity should have an identity is essential even in the ER approach, so we keep it. Spelling out the resulting definition of a JSD-ER entity, we get the following:

> A JSD-ER entity is an observable part of the UoD with a unique identity.

A glance at the definitions of ER entity given at the end of chapter 7 reveals that this is the way ER entities are defined in some ER methods.

13.4.2   Using relationships to remember common actions

There are two ways in which a relationship can appear in a JSD model of a UoD, as a common action or as a JSD entity type. Consider first the appearance of a relationship as a common action in the UoD model. Figure 13.10 gives an ER model in which all common actions in the UoD network of figure 13.9 appear as relationships.

- A link $\langle s, c \rangle$ in the existence set of *ENROLLMENT* corresponds to an occurrence of the *enroll*(s, c) action in the JSD model. Although it is not shown in the ER diagram of figure 13.10, a similar ER diagram of the student administration given in chapter 8 (page 173) reveals that *ENROLLMENT* has an attribute *date*, which represents the date of occurrence of the enrollment action. This attribute betrays the origin of *ENROLLMENT* as an action whose date of occurrence we want to remember.

- *TEST_REGISTRATION* corresponds to the common action *register* in the UoD network. It is instructive to now look carefully at the specification of the ER diagram of the student administration in chapter 8 (page 173), for it shows that in that diagram, this relationship has attribute *result*. This must have value *null* as long as the result is not available. As pointed out in chapter 7, *null* values must be avoided because their meaning and logic is ill-understood. The *null* value of this attribute means "will get a value, but has not received one yet". Figure 13.10 shows that we can avoid this null value by distinguishing the action in which a student registers from a test from the action in which he or she receives a mark for the test. By looking at the UoD from a dynamic perspective, we realize that we can split this relationship into two and so avoid the need for *null* values of the type "will get a value, but has not received one yet".

- A link $\langle s, t \rangle$ in the existence set of *TEST_RESULT* corresponds to the common action $mark(s, t, m)$ in the UoD model. The link has the attribute *result* with value m.

- The total many-one relationship *course* in the ER diagram corresponds to the *create_test* action in the JSD model. An occurrence of the *create_test(c, t)* action corresponds to a function application *course(t) = c. TEST* is an entity type with **dependent existence**, i.e. one whose instances are created by another entity in the model, i.c. *COURSE*. Because a course can create many tests, and each test is always created by exactly one course, the relationship from *TEST* to *COURSE* is a total function. This holds in general for the relationship between an entity type with dependent existence and the entity type upon whom its existence depends.

The guideline to be extracted from this is that if a relationship corresponds to a common action, then the components of the relationship are the identifiers of the objects that share the common action. The other action parameters end up as attributes of the relationship.

What is common in the above examples is that the common actions all need to be remembered by the system. The second guideline to be extracted from the example is therefore that common actions in a JSD model of the UoD must be represented as relationships in the ER model of the UoD if the system must remember their occurrence; otherwise, they need not be represented as a relationship in the ER model. For example, if an elevator and an elevator motor share the actions *start* and *stop*, this need not give rise to two relationships between the *ELEVATOR* and the *MOTOR* entity types, because there is no database that must remember which *start* or *stop* events occurred.

Note also that there may be other relationships in an ER model that do not correspond to common actions in a JSD model of that UoD. Relationships can stand for part-of relations, element-of relations, contractual obligations, permissions, authorizations, etc. These are not normally viewed as common actions.

Two advantages of defining relationships that correspond to common actions are that it allows us to specify which action occurrences must be remembered by the system, and conversely that it allows us to represent the meaning of some relationships more accurately. A third advantage is that it allows us to add cardinality information to the UoD model. For example, by translating the *create_test(c, t)* action into a total many-one relationship (the *course* arrow), we made explicit the information that *create_test(c, t)* can only be performed once per test but can be performed many times per course. This information is not represented explicitly in the JSD model. Similarly, the *TEST_RESULT* relationship adds cardinality information. In the JSD model, one student can receive several marks for one test. In the ER diagram, by contrast, each *TEST_RESULT* instance is a relationship between a student s and a test t, and for each pair $\langle s, t \rangle$ there is at most one such relationship in *TEST_RESULT*.

13.4.3 Reducing common actions by adding relationships

Relationships can also correspond to JSD entities in the JSD model. For example, in the ER model of the library given in chapter 8, *LOAN* is a relationship between *MEMBER* and *DOCUMENT*. In the JSD model of the same library given in chapter 12, we encounter *LOAN* as a JSD entity with its own life cycle. This can be explained as follows. The *LOAN* life cycle contains, among others, the actions *borrow*, *return*, *renew*, and *lose*. On the face

	t_1	t_2	t_3	t_4	t_5	t_6	$\cdots$
E_1							
E_2							
E_3							
E_4	C						
$\cdots$							

Figure 13.11: The transaction decomposition table of a system. The horizontal dimension represents all transactions of the system, the vertical dimension represents all types of which the system contains instances.

of it, these are all common actions shared by a member and a document. However, by modeling *LOAN* as a JSD entity type, we are able to allocate these actions and attributes to *LOAN* only and need not allocate them to *MEMBER* or *DOCUMENT*. The combined JSD-ER model more accurately represents what is happening, for in the ER model *LOAN* is a relationship between these two entity types. The JSD-ER model therefore represents the fact that all *LOAN* actions are *shared* by *MEMBER* and *DOCUMENT*, because they occur in the life of a link between a *MEMBER* and a *DOCUMENT*. Shared actions of *MEMBER* and *DOCUMENT* are allocated to *LOAN* only, just as shared attributes are allocated to *LOAN* only without loss of information.

The guideline to be extracted from this example is that we can reduce the number of entity types that share actions by introducing relationships to which the shared actions are allocated. Of course, the allocation of actions to entity types in the JSD model should still follow the heuristics for action allocation defined for JSD (figure 11.18). For example, if *borrow* increases an attribute of *DOCUMENT* that counts the number of times the document is borrowed, then *borrow* should be allocated to both *LOAN* and *DOCUMENT*.

13.4.4   The transaction decomposition table

ER models and JSD models of the UoD can be found by building a transaction decomposition table (figure 13.11). In a UoD model, the horizontal dimension represents all observable transactions of the UoD. If the SuD is a database system, then these are the actions in the UoD that must be registered by the database. If the SuD is a control system, then these are actions in the UoD that must be registered by the system as well as actions in the UoD that the system causes to occur. The vertical dimension represents all types of which the UoD contains instances. These are all the ER entity types and relationships. The entries of the table represent local actions in the life of instances, and the columns represent common actions.

Suppose that transaction t_i is a communication. If we want to remember the occurrences of this transaction, then we must add a relationship that corresponds this common action and add a "C" in the corresponding entry of the table. For example, each relationship E_4 in figure 13.11 remembers the occurrence of transaction t_1. If we then want to reduce the number of communications in the model then we can try to remove any other local events in the transaction according to the guidelines given above.

13.5 Integrated JSD-ER-DF Models of a System

It makes no sense to try to integrate a DF model of a computer-based system with a JSD-ER model of the UoD of that system, for the two models represent different systems. We therefore follow JSD and view the JSD-ER model of the UoD as an *initial system model*, which describes how the system models the UoD. In this section we extend this to an integrated JSD-ER-DF initial system model. Since the JSD network and the DF notation for system functions are so similar, further extension of an integrated initial model with a specification of required system functions should be done by using either the JSD notation or the DF notation for the representation of system functions.

13.5.1 A JSD-ER-DF initial system model

In chapter 9, we presented an integrated DF and ER modeling method in which, as a first approximation guideline, each entity type and each relation in the ER model corresponds to a data store in the DF model. This guideline can be overruled by considerations of modularity, which cause us to join or split data stores in order to minimize or otherwise modularize the access to data stores by data transformations. However, whatever is the result of splitting and merging data stores, it must satisfy the rule that the structure of all data in all data stores is described by the ER diagram, and that the ER diagram describes no other data than that in the data stores. This gives us one guideline to extend the JSD-ER model with a DF-ER model: the ER part of both models should be the same. This ER model gives us a single representation of the state space of the initial system.

Turning to behavior, the common denominator of the JSD part and the DF part of an integrated model lies in the fact that they both represent system transactions. In the initial JSD system model, the system is represented as consisting of a set of communicating processes, where each process is a surrogate for a UoD entity. A system transaction is then an update in the life of one surrogate corresponding to an action in the life of a UoD entity, or it is an update of a set of surrogates that corresponds to a common action in the life of a set of UoD entities. In either case, we abstract from the initiative of the transaction, which can lie with the UoD or with time (in the case of temporal transactions). In a JSD model we also abstract from the flow of data from the UoD to the system or back. The DF model, by contrast, represents a transaction as triggered by the arrival of one or more data flows at the system, or by the occurrence of a temporal event (which is not shown in a DF diagram). The DF model describes the transaction by specifying the data transformations that lead to a change of state of the system and/or to the production of output by the system, which it sends to one or more output data flows.

In order to represent transactions in a DF model, we have to show where their input data come from and where their output data goes to. This information is not represented by a JSD-ER model of the UoD nor in an initial JSD-ER system model. However, some external entities in a DF model may correspond to ER entity types.

Taking all these considerations together, we have the following guidelines for relating the initial JSD-ER and DF views of the system:

- The ER entity types and relationships jointly describe all and only the structure of the data stores. In the simplest case, there is one data store for each entity type and relationship, and for each data store there is one entity type or relationship. To express this, a data store should have the plural of the name of the entity type (e.g.

data store *STUDENTS* for the entity type *STUDENT*). Still in the simplest case, each data store contains the existence set of its corresponding entity type, and each record in the store is a surrogate for a UoD entity. In more complicated cases, data stores could have been split or merged.

- Each action in the JSD model corresponds to a DF fragment that accepts the input data of the action, updates data stores, and produces output. In the simplest case, an action occurring in the life of an entity of type E corresponds to exactly one data transformation, which updates the data store corresponding to E. A common action could update the data stores corresponding to all entity types that share the action. The data transformation may have to read other data stores in order to check preconditions for the action. In more complicated cases, a (possibly common) action could have been represented by a DF diagram fragment containing more than one data transformation. However, even in this case, this fragment can be represented by a single data transformation, decomposed into a lower level DF diagram.

- Some external entities in the DF model would correspond to some entity types in the JSD-ER model. These external entities should be given the same name as their corresponding entity type (as a side effect, this makes clear that they are *types* rather than instances). Other external entities will not appear in the JSD or ER parts of the model.

Figure 13.12 illustrates these guidelines by adding a DF diagram to our initial JSD-ER model. The *USER* is a person in the student administration department that uses the administrative system. Each data store corresponds to one entity type or to a relationship in the ER model of the system and each data transformation corresponds to a single action in the initial JSD model of the system. A transformation reads from those data stores that it needs for checking the action preconditions, and it writes to data stores that contain a surrogate whose state it must change. A full DF model would additionally contain a data dictionary describing all data residing or flowing through the system, and minispecs specifying the behavior of the primitive transformations (which all correspond to actions in our example). The DF model thus adds the following information to the JSD-ER model:

- It specifies the preconditions and effects of each action by means of data transformations and their minispecs.

- It describes the data flowing between the system and its environment in each transaction.

- It specifies with which external entities the system interfaces.

Conversely, the JSD part of the model adds life cycle information and provides a principle for partitioning the activity of the system into transformations that correspond to entity actions or entity communications.

13.5.2   A JSD-ER-DF model of system functions

The system network in JSD and the DF diagram of a DF model both represent the system as a network of communicating processes. The similarity between these two notations is sufficiently large to regard them as *alternative* ways to model system functions, rather than

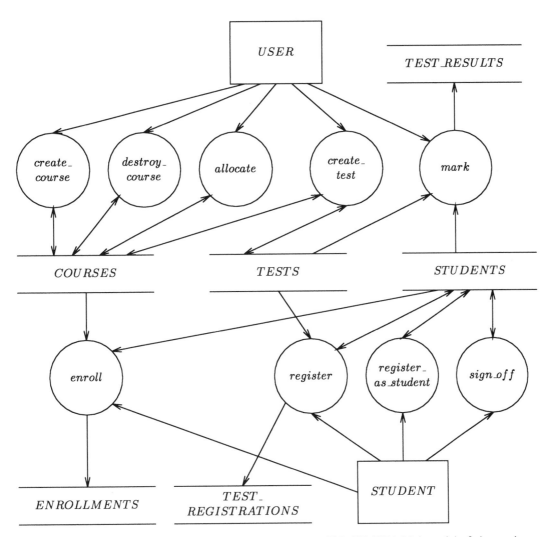

Figure 13.12: DF diagram belonging to an integrated JSD-ER-DF initial model of the student administration [364]. Reproduced by permission of Oxford University Press, 1994.

as supplementary ways. This means that in an integrated model, we should choose either one of these representations but not mix them.

Consider the JSD system network for the student administration given in figure 13.13 and the DF diagram of the same functions shown in figure 13.14. Both models represent two output functions, one to produce a list of individual student results upon request, and another one to produce, upon request, a list of participants in a test.

In the JSD network, *LIST_RESULTS* scans the existence set of *STUDENT* by means of a state vector connection. The initiative of this connection lies with the receiver of information (*LIST_RESULTS*). *LIST_RESULTS* is a long-running function process, and one instance of *LIST_RESULTS* can scan the state of many *STUDENT* instances. In the DF model, List results is a data transformation that receives a request, reads a data store, and produces output. In JSD terms, List results is a long-running function because, after it has produced output data, it is always ready to be activated by a new arrival of input data.

In the JSD network, *LIST_PARTICIPANTS* is a short-running function that, when instantiated, empties a data stream D and reads *STUDENT* instances in order to print the appropriate information. The data stream is filled because *TEST* instances write *register* actions to it every time a student registers for a test.

There are a number of differences between these representations. We review these here in the context of an integrated JSD-ER-DF model.

- The nodes in a DF diagram are data transformations or stores, the nodes in a JSD system network are surrogate types, function processes or data streams (figure 13.15). A data transformation in an integrated JSD-ER-DF model corresponds to an action in the life of a surrogate or to an atomic system function. A data store in an integrated model corresponds to the existence set of an entity type (e.g. *STUDENT*) or to a data stream (e.g. D corresponds to *TEST_REGISTRATIONS*). In the data store, the sequencing information inherent in the data stream (which is a queue) is not represented, unless a record field is added that holds the date and time at which the record was created.

- The nodes in a JSD network are *types* (whose instances are surrogates or function processes). *LIST_RESULTS* is a type with only one instance (the long-running function with the same name). The nodes in a data flow diagram are all *individuals*, viz. transformations or data stores. Because of this, the JSD network can show the cardinality of process connections, telling us how many instances of one node may be connected to how many instances of another node. A data flow model cannot show cardinalities other than the implicit one-one connection between individuals, represented by data flows.

- The function processes in a JSD network are all represented in the same way, viz. by means of PSDs. In a DF model, they can be represented by minispecs, using any specification language, or by lower level DF diagrams. In particular, a DF model allows declarative function specification by means of pre- and postconditions.

- There are three kinds of process connections in a JSD system network (state vector, data stream, controlled data stream) and there is only one kind of connection in a DF model (data flow). However, distinguishing different kinds of process connections

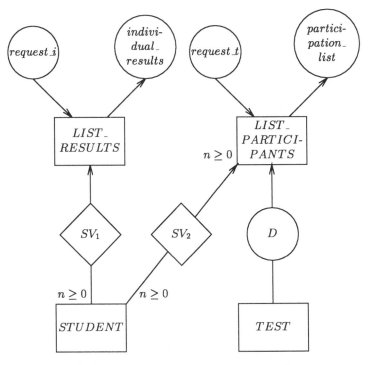

Figure 13.13: A simple system network showing two function processes.

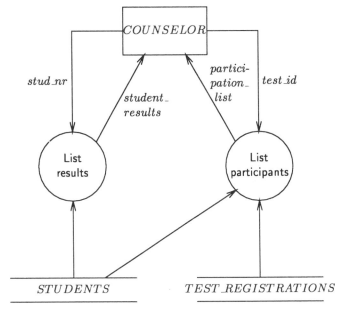

Figure 13.14: A DFD of the system functions of figure 13.13.

Essential DF diagram	JSD system network
Data transformation	• Action in life of surrogate • Function process
Data store	• Data stream (ignoring sequence) • State vector of surrogate process or of long-running function process

Figure 13.15: Comparison between DF diagrams and JSD system networks.

does not give the JSD network more modeling power. A state vector connection can be represented as a data flow, and a data stream that in any state of the system could hold more than one message can be represented in the DF model as a data store supplemented with a mechanism to take care of the first-in first-out behavior of the data stream. Controlled data streams consist of a state vector and a data stream connection that cooperate, and can therefore be translated as well. We look at this in exercise 4.

- A system network is not leveled, as a data flow model is. All processes in a system network are therefore "primitive".

Choosing one or the other notation for the specification of system functions does not give us different modeling capabilities. However, either notation has its advantages and disadvantages. The procedural way of defining system functions in JSD is cumbersome, but the notation does allow greater precision by allowing us to represent connection cardinalities. The DF notation gives very little guidelines as to modularizing the specification, but it does allow us to specify functions declaratively by means of pre- and postconditions.

Note that if we have chosen one notation, we can still use the other notation to specify some elements of the model in further detail. For example, if we choose to use the DF notation to represent system functions, then we can still use a PSD as a minispec of a primitive transformation. Conversely, if we choose to use the JSD notation for the system network, then we can still use DF models to specify the data interfaces of actions in a function process, as we did for actions in the surrogate processes earlier. Figure 13.16 summarizes the links we found among the different parts of an integrated model.

13.5.3 The transaction decomposition table

In a model of the SuD, the horizontal dimension of the transaction decomposition table lists all system transactions. This includes all registration transactions, control transactions, queries, etc. The vertical dimension lists all types that have instances in the system. In an ER-JSD model of the SuD this is a list of all surrogate types (entity types and relationships), all long-running function processes, and all data streams. Each column represents a synchronous communication:

- Common actions between surrogates,

DF-ER	• The ER entity types and relationships in an ER model of the UoD jointly describe all and only the structure of the data stores in a DF model of the system. In the simplest case, there is a one-one correspondence. • Some external entities in the DF model of the system correspond to some entity types in an ER model in the UoD.
ER-JSD	• If a relationship in an ER model of the UoD corresponds to a common action in a JSD model of the UoD, then the components of the relationship entity types that share the common action. The other action parameters are attributes of the relationship. • If the system must remember the occurrence of common actions in a JSD model of the UoD, then they must be represented as relationships in the ER model of the UoD; otherwise, they need not be represented as a relationship in the ER model. • The number of communications in a JSD model of the UoD can be reduced by introducing relationships into the ER model and corresponding JSD entity types in the JSD model, to which common actions are allocated.
JSD-DF	• In the initial SuD model, each action in the JSD model corresponds to a DF fragment that accepts the input data of the action, reads data stores to check preconditions, writes data stores to update the state of one or more surrogates, and produces output. • In a model of the system functions, either use a JSD network or use a DF model. Either notation can then be used to provide supplementary information for the other.

Figure 13.16: Links between the different views in an integrated model.

- state vector access by a function process,

- sending data to a data stream or receiving data from a data stream,

- communicating through a controlled data stream.

In a DF model of the SuD, the vertical dimension of the table is a list of all data stores and each column corresponds to a DF diagram fragment.

13.6   Modularization Principles

In this section, we look at different modularization principles used for behavior specifications in JSD and DF modeling.

13.6.1   Object-oriented and Von Neumann modularization

JSD and DF modeling both use modularization principles to partition the behavior specification into digestible chunks. This is not the same as decomposing the specified system into subsystems, i.e. descending in the aggregation hierarchy of systems. The decomposition of a behavior specification into specification modules stays at one level of the aggregation hierarchy. JSD and DF modeling use different modularization principles for partitioning the specification:

- DF models use the **Von Neumann modularization principle** that separates components that process data but do not remember data, from components that remember data but do not process data. This is a natural modularization principle in manual administrations, where people do the processing and paper provides the memory, and for computing systems that separate programs from files.

- JSD models use an **object-oriented modularization** principle, in which processing and memory are encapsulated into units that can perform their tasks in parallel. UoD entities, surrogate processes, and function processes all follow this principle.

The difference can be easily expressed in terms of the transformation decomposition table: in object-oriented modularization, each row of the transaction decomposition table is encapsulated in the life cycle of the surrogate type or long-running function. (Data streams have a simple life cycle that iterates over addition of items to a queue and removal of items from a queue.) In Von Neumann modularization, rows and columns are separated. In essential system models, each column corresponds to a single data transformation and each row corresponds to a data store.

One consequence of this difference is that a DF model does not contain any sequencing information. The DF model in figure 13.12 only shows which data transformations are triggered as a result of the arrival of some input, which data stores they access, and where they send their output. This is precisely the intention of a DF model, viz. to show which transformations and data stores must be realized by a system, and what their interfaces are if the system is to perform its function. All information about sequencing of data transformations has been eliminated. The JSD model, by contrast, allows the encapsulation of activity and memory into its models of UoD entities, and it is natural in this view to specify constraints on the sequencing of activity, i.e. to specify life cycles for UoD entities.

A related consequence is that the interfaces shown in a DF model are data flows, whereas the interfaces shown in a JSD model of the UoD are common actions. The separation of activity and memory in the Von Neumann modularization forces us to use data flows as interfaces. Since data stores have no activity, their interface will not consist of other actions operations that read and write data. By contrast, encapsulation of activity and memory into models of UoD entities allows the specification of interfaces by means of shared actions. Of course, in an integrated model, a DF diagram with accompanying minispecs may still be used to specify preconditions and effects of actions in a PSD. For example, the DF diagram can show what must be done when the precondition is not satisfied.

Separation of activity from storage adds interfaces to a diagram for another reason as well. Some data flows will show a read access of a transformation to a data store to retrieve information that it has itself put there earlier (cf. section 5.4). These interfaces will be removed in an object-oriented modularization. The remaining interfaces are essential communications between objects.

In chapter 12, we briefly described a simple way to implement JSD models of a system. In the implementation task, we descend in the aggregation hierarchy. One element of the JSD implementation method is the separation of state vectors of surrogate processes and long-running functions from the specification of the actions in these processes, and store these state vectors in files or global variables. This corresponds to a move from object-oriented modularization for a software behavior specification to a Von Neumann modularization for the software system implementation. In a specification of required external behavior of a data manipulation system, it is natural to imagine that each object has its own dedicated processor with its own unrestricted memory, whereas in an implementation of the system it is more natural if we view the system as a collection of processes that interface with a passive memory, that is shared by some processes. This means that in Von Neumann modularization, much care must be taken to avoid inadvertent access to the wrong state vectors. As remarked by Booch [44], in Von Neumann modularization any state vector in a store is globally accessible to any data transformation that accesses the store.

13.6.2   UoD-oriented modularization

There is a further difference between the modularizations followed by JSD and Structured Analysis, which is to do with the fact that JSD distinguishes a UoD model from a system model, whereas Structured Analysis recognizes only a system model. This means that there is a modularization principle available in JSD that is not available in Structured Analysis: partition the system into surrogates that correspond to UoD entities. Let us call this **UoD-oriented modularization**. Although the UoD can be a very chaotic place, it is still a useful place to look for help in defining natural boundaries between different components of our requirements specification. If we manage to find useful chunks in our requirements model that correspond to chunks in the UoD, then we have a requirements model that is more easily communicable to people who know a lot about the UoD, because the terminology with which we talk about the system requirements corresponds more closely to the terminology with which domain specialists talk about the UoD. As a consequence, validation of the model with engineers, working on systems in the UoD, or with users who have domain knowledge of the UoD, is facilitated.

In addition to leading to more understandable requirements models, UoD-oriented modularization leads to more maintainable requirements models because they are as stable as the UoD is. Usually, the UoD is more stable than the desires of the customers and users. A requirements model that is partioned into a UoD model and a system function model therefore consists of at least one part that is stable. The more variable part, the function model, can be defined in terms of this more stable one. And if the requirements model is more maintainable, the system is likely to be more maintainable too.

These advantages of structuring requirements models have already been pointed out at the end of chapter 11, as they belong to the motivations that Jackson gives for his approach to requirements specifications. Here, we add another argument, based on the specification of reactive systems. A *reactive system* was defined in section 9.6 as a system whose response to an input depends on the current input as well as on the past history of inputs, and a *combinational* system was defined as a system whose response to an input depends only upon the current input. The behavior of a combinational system system can be specified by a mathematical function, whereas the behavior of a reactive system must be specified by more complex means such as a state transition diagram or a PSD. DF diagrams are not a good way to specify the behavior of complex reactive systems, because all that is shown by the diagram is the data flow interfaces of each data transformation. In an essential DF model, these are the data interfaces of each transaction. The dependence of system behavior on past inputs is hidden in the minispecs and in the data store accesses.

The functional primitives in a DF diagram hierarchy are combinational systems, because they have no internal state that remembers previous inputs — all history is remembered by data stores. For the same reason, a transformation that remembers past inputs in a local data store such that the contents of this store determines the response to current inputs, is reactive. The JSD entities in a UoD model are also reactive systems, because they have a local state that remembers (part of) their history and that determines their possible future behavior.

In general, the behavior of a reactive system is harder to understand than that of combinational systems, because the effect of an input on the system depends upon the local state of the system. Consider the Borrow data transformation in figure 13.17, which has a local data store that determines part of its behavior, and is therefore a reactive system. Upon reception of a request for borrowing a document, the Check transformation looks at a condition on the data store $DOCUMENTS$, say the total number of documents currently borrowed. If this number is too high, the borrow request is refused, otherwise it is granted and the data store is updated accordingly. Note that this logic is not visible from the data flow diagram; it must be written down in minispecs. The response to a borrow request in this example depends in an obscure way on the local state of the data transformation, and this makes the effect of the transformation hard to understand. Contrast this with a functional transformation like Update Documents in the same diagram, which does the same thing every time it is activated.

Figure 13.18 specifies another reactive transformation, corresponding to a UoD object. The transformation contains a local data store that holds the state vectors of all existing student surrogates and of some local data transformations, each corresponding to one action in the life of a student surrogate. Because the transformation has a local data store, it is a reactive system, but because it corresponds to a UoD entity, its behavior is as easy to understand as that of the corresponding UoD entity. UoD-oriented modularization thus allows us to find reactive systems with a behavior that is more understandable than with another kind of modularization.

In terms of the modularity heuristics given in figure 2.1, UoD-oriented modularization

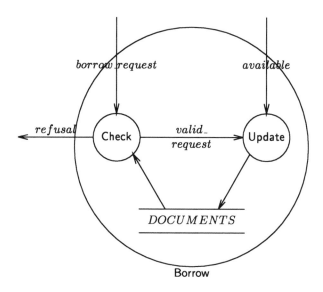

Figure 13.17: The reactive data transformation Borrow.

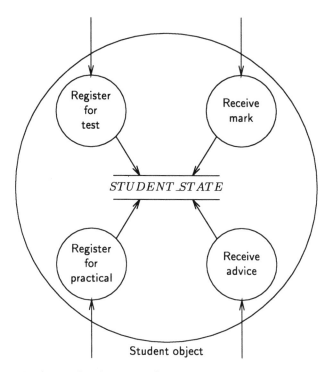

Figure 13.18: A reactive data transformation that represents a student object.

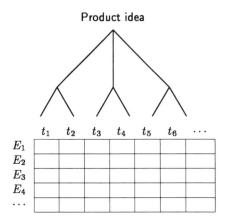

Figure 13.19: Linking the transaction decomposition table to the function decomposition tree of the product.

leads to modules in a requirements specification that have an underlying *system idea*. In terms of structured design guidelines, reactive systems that represent real world entities have the maximal degree of cohesion, viz. *functional cohesion* [251, 325]. According to these guidelines, JSD models thus have the best kind of modularity. Note that the cohesiveness of modules remains high when we go to the system network in JSD, for we then add processes that represent product functions. These processes have a clear intuitive semantics in terms of required system functions. In fact, the concept of functional cohesion is originally motivated by the high cohesion that system functions have.

13.7   Integrating System Models with Environment Models

The environment of a computer-based system is a social system which has been modeled in various ways in ISAC change analysis and in IE information strategy planning. A simple but powerful organization model used in information strategy planning is the function decomposition tree. Figure 13.19 shows that we can link the transaction decomposition table to a function decomposition tree that decomposes the product idea into atomic transactions required of the product. This connects the transaction decomposition table to the service that the system must provide to its environment.

In Structured Analysis, function decomposition is continued below the level of observable software system transactions down to the level of functional primitives. Figure 13.19 shows that at the point where we reach system transactions, we may, as an alternative, continue with object-oriented modularization.

In ISAC, we build a hierarchy of activity models with a diagram notation that has virtually the same semantics as DF models. Just like DF models, activity models are organized in a tree. They are used to model activities in an organization and not necessarily the activities of a computer-based system. Nevertheless, the transactions of a computer-based system are transactions with its social environment. If these transactions have any use for the social environment, then they will also appear as leaves in a function decomposition of this environment. In other words, they will appear in the leaves of the hierarchy of business activity models made in ISAC change analysis. Thus, some internal business transactions will appear in a function decomposition tree of a business information system, in a function decomposition tree of the business itself, and as atomic activities in an ISAC activity model of the business.

13.8 Summary

A method for modeling system behavior should provide concepts to describe the system *state space* and concepts to describe the *state transitions* of the system. This holds for methods to model the UoD as well as methods to model computer-based systems. Our framework for UoD models distinguishes *entity types*, *relationships*, *attributes* and *state space constraints* as concepts to look for in a state space description, and *transactions*, *communications* and *life cycles* as concepts to look for in state transition descriptions. Examples of state space constraints are *cardinality constraints* on links and constraints on *existence set cardinality*. Our framework for system models lists similar concepts, and adds behavior constraints such as *data rates*, *interface requirements*, *response time constraints* and *delay constraints*.

An ER model of the UoD is also an ER model of the system, DF models represent data manipulation systems but not the UoD of such systems, and JSD uses the UoD model as the initial version of a system model.

If we build an integrated ER-JSD model of a UoD, then we can use relationships to represent communications that must be remembered by the system. Relationships can additionally be used to reduce the number of communications in a model by allocating common actions to them. An integrated JSD-ER-DF initial system model extends a JSD-ER initial system model with DF models of transactions. DF diagram fragments can be used to specify preconditions and effects of transactions. In an integrated specification of system functions, we must choose either JSD's system network notation or the DF notation; the two cannot be mixed in the specification of system functions. However, if we choose the JSD notation, we can use DF diagram fragments to specify actions; and if we choose the DF notation, we can use PSDs as minispecs of primitive data transformations.

Analysis of the modularization principles used in DF modeling and in JSD reveals the following two differences:

- In JSD *object-oriented* modularization is used, and in DF modeling *Von Neumann* modularization is used.

- JSD uses a UoD-oriented heuristic for modularization.

Because DF models are intended to show data interfaces and no control, all sequencing information is lost in a DF model and all interfaces as data flows. In JSD, sequencing of actions is represented (by PSDs) and all interfaces are actions. The Von Neumann modularization of DF models appears in the JSD method when we move to implementation. The transaction decomposition table is partitioned horizontally by object-oriented modularization and vertically by Von Neumann modularization.

The UoD-oriented heuristic to identify specification modules generally leads to a more understandable and maintainable partitioning of the specification, because this partitioning corresponds to the UoD and the UoD is usually more stable than required system functions. This leads to a high form of cohesion of the specification modules, called functional cohesion in Structured Design.

The transaction decomposition table can be linked to a function decomposition tree of the product idea as well as to a function decomposition tree of the business mission. This links the transaction decomposition table, and hence an integrated system model, to higher level models of the social environment

13.9   Exercises

1. This exercise is about the model of deliverables of Change Analysis and ISP in figure 13.1.

   (a) Add cardinalities to the model.

   (b) Add the subject areas *PRODUCT_OBJECTIVES* and *PRODUCT_ENVI-RONMENT*.

2. In the JSD model of the UoD of the student administration of section 13.4, each student can receive multiple marks for a test. Prove this by constructing a trace of actions generated by the JSD model in which one student receives two marks for the same test in a row.

3. In subsection 13.4.3, we allocated *borrow* to *LOAN* only. Check that this conforms to the action allocation heuristics of figure 12.3.

4. (a) Build a DF model that simulates the behavior of a data stream.

   (b) Build a DF model that simulates the behavior of a controlled data stream.

   Discuss the accuracy of these simulations.

5. The solutions of the library case study given in this book are part of an integrated JSD-ER-DFD model of the circulation desk.

   (a) Show that the ER model of chapter 8 and the JSD model of chapter 12 can be combined so that they are part of one integrated ER–JSD model of the UoD of the circulation desk. Which additions would be needed to complete the model?

   (b) Show that the DF solution given in chapter 10 extends this model of the UoD of the circulation desk.

   (c) Specify the output function F1 of section 12.2.6 by a DF model.

13.10   Bibliographical Remarks

Data-function-behavior frameworks. Figure 13.20 compares two well-known frameworks for requirements modeling with the one used in this book. Olle *et al.* [246] distinguish the following three perspectives:

Olle *et al.* [246]	Harel [137], Wood & Wood [371]	This book
Process perspective	Functional view	Transactions, effects
Behavioral perspective	Behavioral view	Life cycles, preconditions
Data perspective	Data architecture view	State space
	System architecture view	

Figure 13.20: Two other frameworks for requirements models.

- The *process perspective* of a system focuses on the data processing performed by the system, i.e. on the processing to be performed when an event arrives at the system. This corresponds to the specification of transactions and their effects.

- The *behavioral perspective* focuses on the constraints applicable to event sequences. This corresponds to the specification of life cycles and transaction preconditions.

- The *data perspective* focuses on the structure and meaning of the data manipulated by the system. This corresponds with the structure of the state space of the system and the meaning of the system states in terms of the UoD.

The partitioning by Harel [137] and Wood and Wood [371] uses a slightly different terminology and adds a fourth view, that of the system architecture. This does not correspond to anything in figure 13.4 but to the decomposition of a system into subsystems. The data, process and behavior view also turn up in the Object Modeling Technique (OMT) [296] as the class model, the functional model and the dynamic model of a system, and in the Shlaer/Mellor method [309] as the information model, the process model and the state model of a system. This is explained in detail in *Requirements Engineering: Semantic, Real-Time and Object-Oriented Methods*.

The Zachman framework. In a famous paper, Zachman [379] gives a framework for information system architectures that classifies architectures according to the *perspective* by which it can be viewed and the *representation* of the system architecture from this perspective. He recognizes the following perspectives:

- The *scope* of the system. This is the top manager's view, representing the product idea, comparable to a rough architectural sketch of a house.

- The *business view* of the system is the view of the user of the system, comparable to the owner's view of a house.

- The *system model* is the designer's view of the system, comparable to the specifications produced by the architect for the designer.

- The *technology model* is the builder's perspective of the system.

- The *component model* is an explicit, context-free view of a component as would be given to a subcontractor.

These perspectives interleave the movement from vague to explicit specification (product idea to explicit behavior description) with the movement from high to low level of aggregation (compound system to component). These are the horizontal and vertical dimension of our framework for development methods, respectively (figure 3.9). Zachman recognizes three kinds of representations that can be used for each perspective, the *data description*, the *process description* and the *network description*. For example, the designer's data view could be represented by an ER diagram, his process view by a DF diagram, and his network view by a graph representing a network of processors. The data and process view correspond with the data and functional views in figure 13.20. The network view represents one particular decomposition of the system into subsystems that is interesting at the relevant level of abstraction. For example, the top level network view of a business could represent the geographic locations of the business, the network of the enterprise perspective could consist of a logistics network, etc. This view is thus already part of our framework for system development methods in figure 3.9. The data and process view are part of the framework for requirements specification models given in section 13.3.

In a later refinement of the framework, Sowa and Zachman [323] extend it with other views, viz. the *people* important to the business, the *events* significant to the business, and the important business *goals*. Relevant representation techniques for these views are organization charts, schedules, and business plans. The people view represents a move to the social system aspect, briefly discussed in section 3.6. The event view is part of the state transition view of section 13.3 and the goals view corresponds to the *objectives* view of figure 3.9.

Other frameworks.   There are many other frameworks for classifying requirements modeling and system development methods. A popular dimension in many frameworks is their coverage of different levels in the aggregation hierarchy. The assumption of these frameworks is that a top-down linear development strategy is used (see chapter 15), in which requirements for changes to a social system are determined first, after which these are decomposed to requirements on computer-based systems, and so on until the level of software subsystems is reached. Development methods can be classified according to their coverage of this sequence of top-down stages. Fitzgerald, Stokes and Wood [104] and Hackathorn and Karimi [130] use this as a classification principle. In other respects, these frameworks are not compatible with the one presented in this chapter. For example, the framework for information system development methods defined by Fitzgerald, Stokes and Wood [104] classifies methods according to the following dimensions:

- *Scope* of the method: this corresponds to its coverage of stages in the linear top-down development strategy.

- *Philosophy* of the method: this is the leading idea that informs the method (i.e. solution of user problems in ISAC, data structuring in ER, data flow modeling in Structured Analysis, etc.). We could call this the *product idea* of the method.

- *Assumptions* of the method: these are the assumptions that the method makes about its environment of use. Examples of such assumptions are that information needs can be modeled adequately, and that solutions to sub-problems lead to a solution of a compound problem.

- *Skills*: each method requires certain skills of its users, such as data processing skills, mathematical skills in case a formal specification language is used, etc.

- *Tool support*: for each method tool support may be provided.

Van Swede and Van Vliet [335] give a framework for information system methods and techniques that distinguishes *perspectives* from *aspects*.

- The *business perspective* models the way the business is done,

- the *information perspective* represents the information needs of the business,

- the *function perspective* represents the external behavior of the system, and the *implementation perspective* represents the internal structure of the system.

The first two perspectives model the needs of the environment, the other two model external behavior and internal structure; jointly, they cover the three system views described in chapter 2. For each perspective, a number of views are distinguished: goals, functions, data, processes, communication, control, organization, technical structure and distribution. This list can be expanded and/or contracted as necessary. Note that these views are not orthogonal.

Integrated methods. Several proposals for integrated requirements modeling methods have been made, that partly overlap with the proposal for an integrated ER-JSD-DF modeling method made here. The possibility to combine JSD modeling with ER modeling is briefly discussed by Sutcliffe [332] but is not worked out in detail. Carswell and Navathe [61] propose to integrate DF and ER models by making an ER model of each data *flow* and then joining these ER diagram fragments by view integration. The resulting diagram includes an ER diagram of data stores only, for the data flows entering and leaving data stores would by themselves yield that diagram. However, Carswell and Navathe's proposal leads to an ER model of nonpermanent data as well. The approach used in this chapter is the *de facto* standard in Structured Analysis and is presented by Yourdon [376].

Wrycza [372] combines the ISAC method with ER modeling by transforming the data manipulated in activities into entity types, and the flows between activities into relationships. Hanani and Shoval [136, 311] combine ISAC with NIAM, a modeling method with roughly the same power as ER modeling, by following ISAC until the specification of information systems, and using NIAM to define the structure of the data manipulated by information systems.

JSD and object-oriented requirements modeling. Booch [44] points out the usefulness of JSD as a requirements modeling method for object-oriented design. Similar remarks are made by Masiero and Hermano [219], Hull *et al.* [151], Birchenough and Cameron [33] and Sutcliffe [333]. Wieringa [363] compares JSD with object-oriented analysis and Structured Analysis. Sanden [301] shows how to integrate JSD with the Booch method.

An important difference between JSD and object-oriented modeling is the absence of taxonomic structures in JSD. Adding these structures to JSD would create the problem of how life cycles are inherited. This is still an open research problem. It is touched upon very briefly by Rumbaugh *et al.* [296]. More thorough discussions are given by Lopes and Costa [197], McGregor and Dyer [224] and Saake *et al.* [298].

Integration of Structured and Object-Oriented Analysis Bailin [19] proposes an object-oriented behavior specification method that defines objects in a way very close to the representation of the student objects in figure 13.18. These high-level objects are decomposed in Bailin's method into functional transformations as they are known from data flow modeling. Objects do not necessarily correspond to entity types in the ER diagram. According to Bailin, there are *passive* entities that do not appear as objects but as data flows in the high-level object-oriented diagram.

Ward [353] presents a similar way of representing objects by means of data flow diagrams. The basic heuristic recommended by Ward is to partition the behavior specification into specifications of objects first and in specifications of concurrent parts later. This means that data transformations in high-level DF diagrams correspond to objects in an object-oriented requirements model of the system, and that concurrent tasks will appear lower in the DF hierarchy. This contrasts with the heuristic given by Shumate [312] to partition the specification into specifications of concurrent tasks first and, within tasks, into object specifications. The difference is probably due to Shumate's orientation on distributed systems, in which the objects are nodes in a distributed network, and Ward's orientation on control systems, which are nondistributed systems that represent a UoD to be controlled. In Ward's approach, the UoD provides a useful partitioning criterion. This difference is related to the difference between decomposing a requirements specification into modules, while staying at the same level of aggregation, and decomposition the modeled system into subsystems. In the first decomposition, object identification is a good partitioning heuristic. In the second, concurrency gives a good partitioning heuristic.

Several authors propose preceding object-oriented system design with Structured Analysis [6, 305]. Jalote [164] proposes an interleaving between functional decomposition and object-oriented decomposition of a requirements specification, based upon a natural language analysis. Henderson-Sellers and Constantine [145] give a survey of the possibilities. A useful survey and comparison of object-oriented modeling and structured methods, both for analysis and design, is given by Fichman and Kemerer [101]. Their framework for comparison of analysis methods is similar to the one given in figure 13.4, but contains more concepts. Two interesting concepts that they add are large scale model partitioning and the ability to specify end-to-end processing sequences.

Reactive systems. The term "reactive system" was introduced by Manna and Pnueli [209]. McMenamin and Palmer [225] use the term "planned response system" but mean the same thing. Harel and Pnueli [140] contrast reactive systems with combinational systems (called *transformational* systems by them) that do not have a memory of past transactions. They argue that reactive systems are the hardest to specify, and that development of such systems will proceed by jointly decomposing a specification into more detailed specifications at the same level of aggregation, and decomposing the specified system into subsystems.

Quality Function Deployment. Useful references for quality function deployment are Hauser and Clausing [142], Brown [54] and West [359].

14

A Framework for Requirements Engineering II: Methods

14.1 Introduction

Finding a framework for methods to find requirements specifications is easy, since we have already encountered it: the rational problem solving cycle described in chapter 3. Combined with the hierarchy of aggregation levels identified in chapter 2, it gives us the framework for development methods presented in figure 3.9 (page 53). This is a framework for the *logical* tasks to be performed in requirements engineering; frameworks for the temporal ordering of tasks in the development process are given in chapter 15. We saw in chapter 3 that if the problem solving cycle is applied to the modeling of current systems, it turns into the *empirical cycle*, and if it is applied to the specification of a desired intervention, it turns into the *engineering cycle*. In system development, there are two cases where the empirical cycle is applied, in current system modeling and in UoD modeling (figure 14.1). Independently of this, in the case of data manipulation systems, the system under study can be the system itself or the UoD of the system. There are also two interventions of interest, the specification of required system behavior and the specification of a system decomposition. The specification of system decomposition is not the subject of this book, and we ignore it. As illustrated in figure 14.1, this gives us six applications of the problem solving cycle. In these six cases, applications of the problem solving cycle to current modeling take the form of the empirical cycle, and applications to planning a desired intervention take the form of

	Current	Desired
Observable UoD behavior	UoD modeling	
Observable system behavior	Current system modeling	Requirements specification
System decomposition		

Figure 14.1: Applications of the problem solving cycle.

	Current	Desired
Organization		ISAC Change Analysis, Information Strategy Planning
Business information supply system		ISAC Activity Study
Observable UoD behavior	ER modeling JSD modeling	
Software system	Essential system modeling (SA)	DF specification JSD function specification

Figure 14.2: Methods studied in this book.

Section	Empirical cycle	Engineering cycle
14.2 Starting points	Observation	Analysis
14.3 Finding a behavior specification	Induction	Synthesis
14.4 Evaluating a behavior specification	Deduction Test	Simulation Evaluation

Figure 14.3: Structure of this chapter.

the engineering cycle.

To multiply the number of applications of the problem solving cycle even more, the system in the figure may exist at any level in the aggregation hierarchy. For example, viewing an organization at least in part as a data manipulation system, we can be concerned with modeling the UoD of the organization, i.e. the part of the world of interest to it, or we may be concerned with performing an intervention to change this UoD into a desired state. We may also want to model the organization as it currently is, or plan an intervention to bring it into a desired state. Finally, we may study its decomposition into subsystems as it currently is, or we may plan an intervention to improve its decomposition into subsystems. Similar applications of the problem solving cycle can occur at the level of computer-based systems, software systems or at lower levels of the aggregation hierarchy.

Figure 14.2 shows the place of the methods reviewed in this book in the framework of figure 14.1. The business information supply system in figure 14.2 is a computer-based subsystem of the organization that may consist of many physically distributed information systems, some of which may be connected by networks. Only ISAC change analysis follows the logical problem solving cycle very clearly. However, for all methods, we found that the problem solving cycle provides a very useful framework to analyze the methods. In this chapter, we pull the results together under the headings shown in figure 14.3.

In section 14.2, we list possible starting points for problem solving: observations to be made of current systems or desires to be realized by future systems. In section 14.3, we discuss the road map of methods to find models of the UoD or specifications of system requirements. In section 14.4, we summarize the methods for evaluating the quality of the models or specifications found. Section 14.5 discusses alternative views of requirements specification, which seem to fall outside the framework for rational problem solving used in this book.

14.2   Starting Points

The possible starting points for finding a model of a current system or a specification of desired system behavior are independent of the kind of methods used to find the models. Many are even neutral with respect to modeling current or desired behavior; they can be used in either modeling activity. Below, a list of possible starting points is given. Section 14.8 gives some pointers to literature where these methods are described in more detail.

- If we are working on a requirements specification for a computer-based system, a **higher-level requirements specification** is a requirements specification for the organization, i.e. a business strategy. If we are working at the software system level, a higher-level requirements specification is a requirements specification for a computer-based system, e.g. an information strategy plan produced by ISP.

- **Participation** in the activity in the current UoD or the current system provides a lot of information useful for modeling and requirements specification. An example of participation is taking over the job of a circulation desk employee for a few weeks.

- Less time consuming than participation is **observation** of activity in the current UoD or the current system by walking around, talking with people, observing what happens, etc.

- The analyst can perform **experiments** to discover aspects of current system behavior not fully understood. These experiments may be very simple, such as pushing a button to see what happens, or they may require a complicated setup to obtain statistically significant statements about current system properties.

- The client often finds it easy to describe **scenarios** that the SuD will have to participate in. These are a rich source of material for the construction of behavior specifications and, at a later stage, for the validation of specifications as well as for acceptance testing of the product.

- **Forms** used in administrative systems give important clues as to what information is currently required. These forms may be implemented on paper, as part of a user-interface, or as reports produced by a system. Forms to be manipulated in the desired situation give important information about the desired system.

- **Record declarations** used in a current system can be analyzed to discover what information is currently stored. This may also give important clues about information to be stored in a desired system.

- **Quantitative documents** provide interesting information about data relevant to current or future systems. Examples of quantitative documents are status reports about inventory, sales, production, turnover, etc. Many of these reports are produced monthly, quarterly or yearly.

- **Qualitative documents** contain clues about information relevant for an organization in the current or desired state of affairs. Examples of qualitative documents are memos, bulletin boards, procedure manuals, policy handbooks, etc.

- The **company strategy** may be laid down in a qualitative document that contains important information for the writer of requirements specifications.

- **Product specifications** of hardware or software systems are essential reading for those who must model a current system, as well as for those who must specify a system that must interface with other products.

- **Interviews** with sponsors, customers, users, domain specialists and other stakeholders in a development process provide crucial information about current problems and requirements for the SuD.

- **Questionnaires** can be used to gather information from a larger population. Questionnaires do not make unexpected facts visible.

- **Reference models** are important sources of reusable information for the writer of requirements specifications. Reference models are example models of standard applications, that can be customized for a particular application. There are reference models of medical information systems, library information systems, production automation systems, etc.

With so many sources of information, the analyst must unavoidably make a choice for certain sources at the risk of missing important information available from another source. In other words, the analyst must *sample* data from a potentially very large collection. This can be done using statistical techniques but, as Gause and Weinberg [111] remark, it is easy to get lost here in the details of a sound statistical design of the sample. To get significant results, the most important thing is that the analyst is aware that he or she *is* sampling.

14.3   Finding a Behavior Specification

Figure 14.4 shows the road map of methods developed in part II, supplemented with the starting points listed above. An explanation of the placement of these starting points follows.

- A higher level requirements specification, strategy descriptions, or the written results of interviews or questionnaires provide a useful starting point for the definition of a function decomposition tree of a computer-based system or a software product. Because they contain text, they can also be the starting point for natural language analysis.

- Quantitative and qualitative documents are additional starting points for natural language analysis.

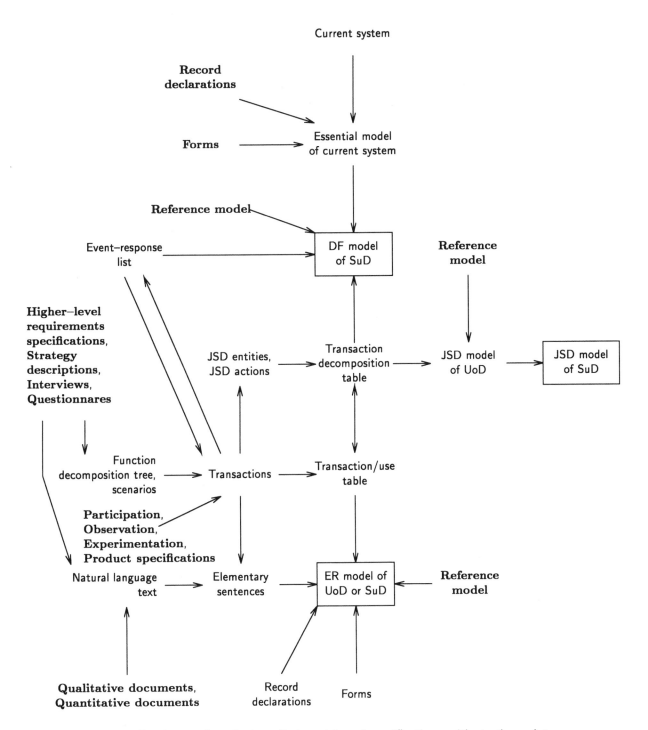

Figure 14.4: Road map of methods to find models and specifications, with starting points.

- Participation, observation and required scenarios give information about what trans-actions current systems perform, or what transactions would be desirable for a future system.

- Record declarations and forms are useful as a starting point for finding an ER model. Because the arrival of a filled-in form, or the update of a record, are events to which a system must react, they can also be used as starting points for DF modeling. As a matter of fact, a DF diagram can be viewed as a model of the flow of forms through an organization.

- Domain models can be useful starting points for ER modeling, DF modeling and JSD modeling, because they contain what can be generally expected to be relevant for a particular kind of application.

14.4   Evaluating a Behavior Specification

Figure 14.5 summarizes the evaluation methods of the reviewed modeling methods, classified according to the criteria for requirements specifications given in figure 4.4 (page 77). A motivation of this classification follows.

- **Communicability** is enhanced if we minimize the number of relationships in an ER model, and minimize the arity of each relationship. In a data flow model, it is enhanced if we minimize the interfaces between model components.

- **Truth** of an ER model of the UoD can be verified, partly, by checking whether the modeling constructs are used correctly. Thus, we check whether we properly distinguished entities, links and values and whether the *is_a* relationship in the model is a true representation of reality. Similar checks on the use of modeling constructs can be performed for JSD models.

  There are a number of validity checks that are independent of the modeling techniques and notations used. The elementary sentence check and population check were defined originally for the NIAM method [244] and were adapted in chapter 8 to the ER method.

- **Completeness** is enhanced if we check whether every entity is accessed by a transac-tion (horizontal balancing, data usage), in particular whether it is created or deleted in the model (creation/deletion check). We should also check whether the output of every data transformation has been specified completely in terms of its input (deter-minism). Building a model of one aspect of the system in different ways leads to more complete models (cross-checking), as does integration of models of different aspects (view integration).

- One aspect of **feasibility** is consistency. Consistency of the specification is enhanced if we follow several paths in our road map, possibly in reverse direction, and cross-check the results. In particular, we can check whether all queries can be answered (navigation check). In a data flow model, we should take care that the different parts of the model are mutually consistent (horizontal balancing) and that the different levels in a hierarchical DFD are consistent (vertical balancing). Cost-effectiveness of a specification can be verified by means of walkthroughs.

	ER	DFD	JSD
Communicability	• Derivable relationship check • Minimal arity check	• Minimality checks	
Truth	• Entity/value checks • Entity/link checks • Specialization check		• JSD entity checks • JSD action checks • Action allocation checks • Common action checks • Life cycle check
	• **Explanation**: Explain the model in natural language. This generalizes the **elementary sentence check** of ER modeling. • **Population check**: Show some possible states of the system to the domain specialist.		
Completeness	• Creation/deletion check • View integration • Cross-checking	• Determinism check • Horizontal balancing • Data usage	
Feasibility	• Cross-checking • Navigation check	• Horizontal balancing • Vertical balancing • Walkthrough	
General quality checks	• **Walkthrough**: Walk the domain specialist through the model. • **Inspection**: Verify that the model satisfies particular quality criteria. • **Requirements prototyping**: Specify requirements in an executable language, execute the specification, observe the result and evaluate it. In model **animation**, the result is shown graphically, using dynamic interfaces. A low-tech **mockup** of a system that would satisfy the requirements also falls under this category.		

Figure 14.5: Evaluation methods for requirements specifications.

- **General quality checks** can take the form of walkthroughs or inspections. **Executable specifications** can take a variety of forms, from high-tech execution of a formal specification, whose results are presented in a pleasing graphical form, to low-tech paper-based mockups of the system.

Looking at the requirements on requirements specifications listed in figure 4.4 (page 77), we remark that there are no checks on the verifiability and maintainability of a requirements specification. This can be explained by the fact that these are really properties of *notation systems and tool support* for requirements specifications, rather than for requirements specifications themselves. Traceability and modifiability, both aspects of maintainability, must for example be provided by tools for requirements specification languages, that should allow the writer of a specification to estimate the impact of a modification, to link parts of the requirements to system components, etc.

14.5   Requirements Engineering as Negotiation about Meanings

In this book the rational problem solving method is used as a framework for understanding requirements specification and current system modeling. It has been emphasized several times that the rational problem solving cycle is *not* a model for planning the requirements specification process. The relationship between the actual process and the rational problem solving method is the subject of the final two chapters of this book. However, even taking this caveat into account, there is a process in requirements engineering that seems to elude the framework of rational problem solving. This is the process of negotiation.

14.5.1   Negotiation in discovery and engineering

First, it must be remarked that negotiation occurs in the process of scientific discovery. In a simplistic view of the empirical cycle of discovery, we observe phenomena in the world, formulate hypotheses to explain them, and reject any hypothesis falsified by experiments. The reality of empirical research is not that simple. For example, we cannot observe phenomena without theories. If measuring instruments are used, then these instruments are built using theories that are assumed to be true and that are not under discussion when studying the facts observed with the help of those instruments. For example, observation of the behavior of distant galaxies requires sophisticated optical and electronic equipment, that exemplifies theories of optics and electronics not under discussion (at least not by astronomers). In addition, the observed phenomena can only be described by means of a number of general terms defined by scientific theories. Even a term like "galaxy" only has meaning if we assume a certain theory about the cosmos — it is meaningless if we assume that the stars are fallen angels. This means that if we make a prediction on the basis of a hypothesis, then there are numerous auxiliary hypotheses, drawn from other scientific theories, that are used in this inference; and if the prediction is falsified, any of these auxiliary hypotheses can be considered falsified. All of this shows that in the application of empirical cycle we need to make decisions about what to accept and what to doubt. Having made these decisions, we can proceed as if we follow the rational empirical cycle; but if we don't like the results, we return to the decisions and adjust them. This is not a solitary process but a *social* process, in which scientists weigh evidence, choose to maintain beliefs accepted as certain, and doubt other ideas. In many areas of science, scientists are divided into schools of thought that tend to make these decisions differently. The important thing to note is that this process is as much a negotiation about the meaning of theoretical terms as it is a rational process of problem solving.

Turning to engineering, we see negotiations going on as well. From a rational point of view, the engineer observes desires existing in the market or the client, translates these in objectives, writes a behavior specification, decomposes the product, and tells the builders how to implement it. However, as already remarked in chapter 3, the very act of finding out what the desires of clients are, may change those desires. This is the principle of requirements uncertainty. In addition, when a specification or implemented product does not satisfy the stated objectives, we may change the objectives or the product. This is a decision made by the sponsor, users, customers and the market and its outcome is not quite predictable. To compound the situation, the engineers, sponsors, users, customers and the marketing department may all have different objectives, and may be divided amongst themselves in competing factions. In such a situation, the result of evaluating a product specification or an implemented product may be just as much the result of negotiation as it is of rational problem solving. And much of this negotiation is about what the meaning of documents is: the meaning of a behavior specification, of a decomposition specification, of a statement of objectives, of a market analysis, of an interface specification, etc. is never as unambiguously determined as the meaning of a mathematical formula is — assuming that formulas are unambiguous.

The conclusion of these observations must not be that the rational problem solving cycle is useless, but simply that it does not describe the structure of the discovery and engineering processes. The rational problem solving cycle accurately describes the structure of a *rational reconstruction* of the process by which results are obtained in the discovery or engineering process. Even though the discovery and engineering processes do not follow the pattern of rational problem solving, the validity of the results obtained by these processes can and must be justified by reconstructing the process as if the rational cycle were followed. The role of rational reconstruction in system development is elaborated upon in chapter 15. Here, we note that the phenomenon of negotiation during discovery and engineering does not invalidate the usefulness of the rational problem solving cycle as a tool for the analysis of development methods, or as a tool for the justification of the results of development.

14.5.2 Implicit conceptual models and the ultimate communication breakdown

Software systems and computer-based systems are data-manipulation systems embedded in social systems. They often function as linguistic machines, answering queries, issuing commands and asking questions, and this makes the phenomenon of negotiation about meaning during their development even more important. The reason for this is that social systems are full of implicit meanings, while at the same time computer-based systems are devoid of any implicit meanings. Requirements engineering of a computer-based system must, at some point, make all relevant meanings of the data manipulated by the system totally explicit. To understand why this is a problem, consider first the extent to which meanings are implicit in social systems. The day-to-day affairs of people consist of *describing* to themselves and others what the world is in which they live, as well as *prescribing* to themselves and others what the world ought to be. During meetings, coffee breaks, lunch, gossip and business appointments, people talk about what happened, what ought to have happened, what will happen and what ought to happen. This everyday process took place before computer-based system development started, takes place during system development, and will continue to take place after development finishes. Let us call this **implicit conceptual modeling**, because it consists of producing and maintaining, by conversation with others, an **implicit conceptual model** of the universe of everyday discourse. Like all conceptual models, an implicit conceptual model is a set of *shared* concepts used by people in communicating about a UoD. What makes this conceptual modeling implicit is that it is not itself the subject of discussion but functions in the background of conversation, unnoticed by the speakers.

To get an impression of the contents of such an implicit conceptual model, consider what we know about the library and what is not specified in the explicit conceptual models of the library used in this book. An ER model just says that there is an entity type called *DOCUMENT*, that can be borrowed by entities of type *MEMBER*. Our implicit model of this contains, among others, the knowledge that documents can be read, that reading can be fun or can be boring, that some documents are rare, and that they may be valuable; it contains fond memories of some of our children's books as well as our opinion that there should be freedom of the press. If we think about this for a while, we realize that there is a sheer inexhaustible stock of everyday knowledge about books and documents that every normal member of our society knows but that no one cares to spell out in detail.

As another example of implicit conceptual models, take the following traffic violation data:

Day: May 28	*Time*: 5:00 p.m.	*Day of week:* Tuesday
Sex: Male	*Height:* 5' 2"	
Hair: Brown	*Weight:* 120	
Eyes: Blue	*Birthdate:* 12-7-11	

Violation(s): 21651 V.C. Divided highway driving to left of divided section; Driving W/B on wrong side of Shoreline Dr. against E/B traffic. Approximate speed: 20 mph.

To interpret this data, we need an implicit conceptual model that tells us what is norm, usual, expected, relevant, etc. This is illustrated by the interpretation of this data by an experienced traffic violation judge (Pollner [262, page 33]):

"See, here it says nineteen-eleven (1911) — he's an oldster. Now the fact that it says which traffic he was driving against and the time when he did it tells me its murderous — its thick traffic. No business address so the guy is probably retired. So he wasn't doing as if he were taking a chance. He just didn't know. He wasn't doing it intentionally. He was driving right into the sun. He probably didn't see or something. Now if it was an eighteen year old kid it's something else. There you have to search for what he was up to. The ticket tells you what he's like, what's he driving; does he work, anything about his occupation, where does he live, how old is he, can he pay, is he rich or poor. What was he driving? A fast car?"

Every member of a culture has an implicit conceptual model of things that can happen in everyday life. We can communicate with each other because much of our implicit conceptual models is shared and we need not talk about it. Similarly, we can interpret what people do in daily life because we have internalized a shared and implicit conceptual model that tells us what other people normally do in certain circumstances, and what we should normally do under certain circumstances. When we invite someone for lunch, we do not have to explain to him or her what lunch is, nor do we have to explain how you normally behave during lunch.

The shared part of implicit conceptual models functions as the background of normal conversation and action. Only if communication breaks down or if we are puzzled by someone's behavior, does it become necessary to reflect upon the contents of both our implicit conceptual models. This happens for example if we are transferred to a different culture. Eating habits, dress codes and etiquette may be different. Minor breakdowns also occur if we move to another job and we have to learn "how things are done around here".

When breakdown occurs, participants in the conversation can restore things to normal by a *negotiation* process in which they try to figure out what the other's implicit model of the state of affairs is, and by trying to influence the other's model and adjust their own model such that an agreement is reached about what is the case and about what ought to be done. This negotiation process is descriptive as well as prescriptive. As pointed out before, much of this negotiation is a negotiation about the meaning of words, e.g. about the meaning of "document", "book", "loan", etc. This negotiation is not only a process of linguistic analysis but also a negotiation about norms. For example, when we define "loan", we also state how a library member ought to behave.

Turning now to computer-based systems, the ultimate breakdown in communication occurs if we try to communicate a model of the universe of our discourse to a computer, for the computer by itself (without being programmed) understands nothing and has no conceptual model of anything. Yet, when the system is used, it functions as a linguistic machine that performs speech acts. It answers questions, poses questions, gives commands, obeys commands, etc. It thus functions as a linguistic actor without any knowledge of implicit meanings and it functions in a social environment that is full of implicit meanings. We are therefore forced to make whatever is relevant totally explicit in our specification of required product behavior, and we must make the explicit meaning understood and shared by all users. Success of these negotiations about meaning is a crucial factor in the success of the delivered result.

The upshot of the gap between our social world on the one hand, filled with an inexhaustible mass of implicit meanings, and computer-based systems on the other, devoid of any implicit meanings, is that negotiations about norms, problems, objectives, feasible solutions, shared interests and mutual conflicts can take very long, because the result must be totally explicit and unambiguous. If we were to try to make *everything* in an implicit conceptual model explicit, then we would discover that there is no end to this process. As Codd said, the task of capturing the meaning of data is a never-ending one [70]. On the other hand, if we leave too much implicit, then misunderstandings will arise when the system is used and this too degrades the quality of the system.

All of this does not invalidate the use of the rational problem solving method as framework for requirements specification. In the sometimes confusing network of implicit meanings and possibilities, it can be very useful to structure the negotiation by considering some facts as problems and others as non-problems, some options as feasible alternatives and others as out of bounds, and performing simulations which show us what the consequences of some of these alternatives are. However, the analyst must be prepared for the existence of a vast amount of unstated assumptions and norms and meanings, which, though invisible, have a pervasive influence on the requirements engineering process.

14.6   Summary

The rational problem solving method can be used as a framework to analyze methods for current systems modeling, UoD modeling and for behavior specification. The tasks recommended in a particular modeling or engineering method can be classified as belonging to one of the tasks in the rational problem solving method. The starting point of modeling is observation, and the starting point of engineering is analysis. There are numerous methods for observation and analysis, including analyzing a higher-level requirements specification, participation, observation, performing experiments, form analysis, record analysis, analyzing quantitative or qualitative documents, analyzing strategy statements, interviewing stakeholders, using questionnaires, analyzing interface specifications and analyzing domain models.

From these starting points, one can follow various roads through our road map (figure 14.4) of methods to find models or specifications. This corresponds to induction in the empirical cycle of modeling, and to synthesis in the requirements engineering cycle.

Having found a behavior model, one can evaluate it by deducing observable consequences and testing these; having found a behavior specification, it can be evaluated by simulating them and evaluating the results. There are a number of methods (figure 14.5) for evaluating the quality of a model or a specification. These evaluate different aspects, such as communicability, completeness, feasibility, and truth of the model or specification. We have found no checks for verifiability or maintainability, probably because these are characteristics for language and tool support rather than of a particular behavior model or behavior specification.

In practice, modeling and engineering often have the character of negotiation about meaning. This does not invalidate the usefulness of the rational problem solving cycle as a tool for analyzing methods and as a target for the rational reconstruction of the way in which the results were obtained, but it does point out that the process of obtaining these results may be very dynamic. In the case of requirements engineering of computer-based systems, the negotiations must lead to results that must be more explicit and unambiguous than is usual, because computer-based systems are devoid of any implicit meanings, but they will function in a world that assumes many implicit meanings.

14.7   Exercises

1. In the library case study, we followed all paths in the road map of figure 14.4. The transaction decomposition table is a central deliverable that can be produced on the way to a DF model as well as on the way to a JSD model of the system. Check whether the action allocation table of figure 12.4 corresponds to the transaction decomposition table given in figure 10.9. Explain any differences you find.

2. In the example of section 14.5, the judge used elements of her implicit conceptual model of traffic violations in interpreting the traffic violation data. Make a list of the elements she used.

BIBLIOGRAPHICAL REMARKS

14.8 Bibliographical Remarks

Starting points. A good introduction to sampling, interviewing and conducting questionnaires, with pointers to further literature, is given by Kendall and Kendall [174]. Byrd, Cossick and Zmud [55] give a useful survey of observation methods used for information systems and expert systems. Gutierrez [129] gives a survey of observation methods that can be used for information system development. Goguen and Linde [117] provide a critical analysis of several observation methods, including interviewing, protocol analysis and discourse analysis.

Finding a description. The bibliographical remarks in the chapters of part II give pointers to the literature on methods for finding models and specifications of systems. Not mentioned in those chapters are methods for *form and record analysis*. A practical and comprehensive introduction to form and record analysis for finding ER and DF models is given by Rock-Evans [281, 283]. A compressed version of this is presented in a shorter work [284]. Another useful introduction to form and record analysis is given by Batini, Ceri and Navathe [25].

Evaluating a description. Again, pointers to the literature on evaluation methods have been given in the chapters of part II. Not mentioned there are *inspections*, which were introduced in software development by Fagan [99, 100]. Walkthroughs are popular in Structured Analysis [375]. A survey of inspection and walkthrough techniques is given by Freedman and Weinberg [107]. A good introduction to verification and validation is given by Boehm [38]. Lindland, Sindre and Sølvberg [194] emphasize that requirements must be evaluated on their feasibility.

Requirements engineering as negotiation. Hirschheim and Klein [146] provide an introduction to alternative approaches to requirements engineering. According to what they call the objectivist position, the social world exists independently from its observers and can be described by causal models. According to the subjectivist position, the social world is a subjective construction, and only participation in a social system can create the social preconditions for understanding and interpreting it. Independently from the subjectivist-objectivist axis, Hirschheim and Klein sketch an opposition between those who view the social world as characterized by order and functional coordination and those who see it as characterized by change and conflict. Clearly, the requirements engineering methods discussed in this book take the objectivist-order position (with the possible exceptions of ISAC and ETHICS, which are closer to a subjectivist-order position). In my opinion, the UoD of data- or communication-intensive systems is a social construction that can be studied objectively. The analyst *must* distinguish his or her role as a participant and as external observer of the UoD. But because the analyst plays both roles, he or she must be able to switch between a subjectivist and an objectivist view of the social world. For example, as a subjectivist, the analyst understands that the social nature of a UoD and of the context of use of computer-based systems is an important source for requirements uncertainty (see subsection 3.3.3) and product evolution (figure 3.14). By being able to play both roles, the analyst becomes aware of the conflict between distance and engagement noted in subsection 3.5.3. The validity of the subjectivist view does not mean that we should *abandon* the search for objectively true statements. It just means that this search never ends.

Mangham [208] provides illustrations of how to use negotiation skills to direct a process of organizational change. Berger and Luckmann [29] is the classic source for how the interaction of people in a society results in the construction of a social reality. Negotiation plays a central role in this process. A classic source on the role of implicit knowledge in science and day-to-day affairs is Polanyi [260, 261]. Another interesting source for the role of implicit conceptual models is Garfinkel [109], who is the main driving source behind a method for investigating implicit models called *ethnomethodology*. A handy because brief introduction to these ideas is given by Agre [3]. Giddens [113] uses these and other ideas to argue for the duality of implicit models, which act at the same time as background to what we do and say, but which at the same time may be in the foreground, because our actions and statements are oriented at influencing each other's models. Winograd [368] gives a very insightful introduction to the role of implicit models and background knowledge in daily conversation, and to the role of breakdowns in conversation in explicating the contents of our background knowledge. Winograd and Flores [369] draw consequences from this for the design of computer-based systems. Giddens as well as Winograd draw upon Heidegger [143] for their ideas about the role of the background in normal speaking and doing, and for the disruptive effects of breakdowns on this role.

15

Development Strategies

15.1 Introduction

We now turn to the temporal ordering of tasks during the development process. Most of the methods discussed in part II concentrate on the *logical* tasks to be performed when developing a computer-based system. The framework of chapter 3 contains the dimensions of logic and aggregation level and therefore suffices to analyze these methods. We now add a third dimension, that of *time*, and ask how the problem solving tasks are to be ordered in time. This is the province of development planning, which itself is a part of process management.

In section 15.2, we give an overview of the different kinds of process management tasks. These are universal, because they appear in any process in which objectives must be achieved by the effort of others. Accordingly, many of the methods and techniques for process management are applicable in the management of a product development process. However, some tasks in the *software* product development process require special methods, or at least methods that are adapted to software product development. In these final two chapters of the book, we focus on one of these tasks, *strategy planning*. In the current chapter, we discuss a number of important software development strategies and in the the next chapter, we turn to methods to select the appropriate strategy for a development process.

In section 15.3 we discuss the *linear development strategy*, the *splashing waterfall strategy*, and the *V-strategy*. In section 15.4, these strategies are combined into a model of the concurrent development. In section 15.5, we describe *throw-away prototyping* as a way to reduce uncertainty before a product is constructed, and in section 15.6 we describe *phased delivery* as a strategy to reduce uncertainty based on early experience with a finished version of the product. In section 15.7, we return to our three-dimensional framework for development methods and argue that the relationship between the temporal and logical dimension of the framework is that the logical dimension provides a template for the rational reconstruction of what happened along the temporal dimension.

Figure 15.1 shows our classification of development tasks into product engineering and process management tasks. The **product engineering** task is further subclassified as follows:

- *Requirements engineering*, which produces a behavior specification of a product (at a certain aggregation level).

- *System decomposition*, which produces a specification of a decomposition of a system at a certain aggregation level into subsystems (at the next lower aggregation level).

- *System integration*, which produces a system as an assembly of subsystems.

- *System testing*, which applies tests to the system, observes the results, evaluates these and adjusts the system or its specifications if necessary.

Decomposition, integration and testing are part of the regulatory cycle as it is followed in product implementation. This is discussed in detail in section 15.3. The **process management tasks** are discussed in the next section. Figure 15.1 serves as a guideline for the rest of this chapter and also relates it to the methods discussed in part II.

15.2   Process Management

We follow Mackenzie [206] in his definition of **management** as the achievement of objectives through others. In order to achieve objectives by the effort of others, we must determine the objectives (plan), acquire resources, break down the work into manageable units (organize), motivate the workers (direct) and compare the results against the objectives (control). There is no temporal sequence in these activities: in general, management performs all of these tasks in parallel. Thayer [342, table 2.2] gives a more detailed breakdown of the tasks of management, reproduced in figure 15.2. A simplified version of this has already been given in figure 6.10. In Thayer's list, the acquisition of resources is viewed as staffing the development process. This ignores acquisition of other resources like hardware and software tools which aid in the performance of the development process and in the work breakdown of figure 15.1, we replaced staffing with acquisition. Note that even after this change, the list makes abundantly clear that management is a *people-oriented activity*. All management activities are concerned with what people must do, why they must do it, who should do it, what they should do it with, whether they like to do it, and whether they have done it.

Management tasks are *universal* in the sense that they occur in the management of any process in which results are achieved by the effort of others. This means that the logical problem solving methods for behavior specification and product decomposition are independent from methods for process management. This implies in turn that it is possible to eliminate any reference to process management from requirements engineering and product decomposition methods and vice versa. But if these references *can* be eliminated, they *should* be eliminated. One advantage of such an elimination is that this simplifies the presentation of the requirements engineering and product decomposition methods as well as of process management methods. A second advantage is that it makes the use of these methods more flexible, because requirements engineering and product decomposition methods can be combined as needed with process management methods. For example, a particular behavior specification method can be combined with different company standards for process management methods. Conversely, a development strategy like incremental development can be combined with structured as well as with object-oriented behavior specification methods.

A number of management tasks receive special attention in the management of software product development. Without being exhaustive, we list a number of them:

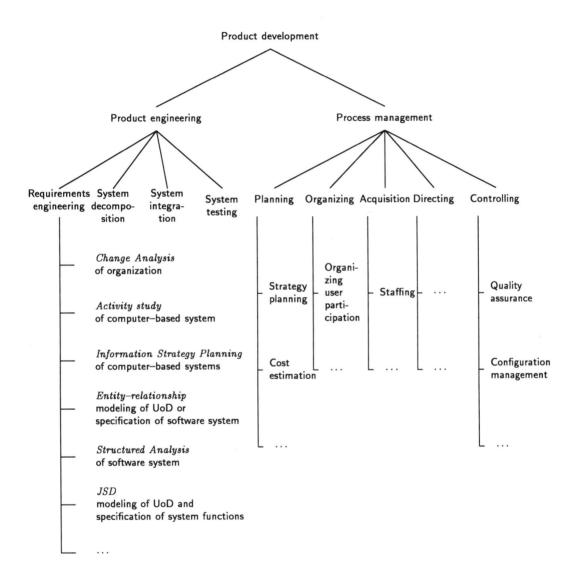

Figure 15.1: A classification of product development tasks into product engineering and process management tasks. Methods to perform tasks are written in italics.

- **Planning**: Predetermining a course of action for accomplishing organizational objectives.
  - Set objectives or goals.
  - Develop strategies.
  - Develop policies.
  - Determine courses of action.
  - Make decisions.
  - Set procedures and rules.
  - Develop programs.
  - Forecast future situations.
  - Prepare budgets.
  - Document project plans.
- **Organizing**: Arranging work, granting responsibility and authority.
  - Identify and group required tasks.
  - Select and establish organizational structures.
  - Create organizational positions.
  - Define responsibilities and authority.
  - Establish position qualifications.
  - Document organizational structures.
- **Staffing**: Selecting and training people for positions in the organization.
  - Fill organizational positions.
  - Assimilate newly assigned personnel.
  - Educate or train personnel.
  - Provide for general development.
  - Evaluate and appraise personnel.
  - Compensate.
  - Terminate assignments.
  - Document staffing decisions.
- **Directing**: Creating an atmosphere that will assist and motivate people to achieve desired end results.
  - Provide leadership.
  - Supervise personnel.
  - Delegate authority.
  - Motivate personnel.
  - Coordinate activities.
  - Facilitate communications.
  - Resolve conflicts.
  - Manage changes.
  - Document directing decisions.
- **Controlling**: Measuring and correcting performance of activities toward objectives according to plan.
  - Develop standards of performance.
  - Establish monitoring and reporting systems.
  - Measure results.
  - Initiate corrective actions.
  - Reward and discipline.
  - Document controlling methods.

Figure 15.2: Universal management activities [342]. Reproduced by permission of IEEE Computer Society Press, 1988.

- **Development strategy planning.** These determine the sequence of activities to perform during development. Selecting a development strategy is a part of the development *planning* task.

- **Cost estimation.** Estimating the cost of software is a difficult task, for which numerous methods have been proposed. Cost estimation is a part of the *planning* task.

- **Participation.** Users, customers, domain specialists and other interested parties may want to be involved in different degrees in the development process. There are several methods to do this and thereby increase the quality of the product or speed up the development process. Setting up a participatory structure is part of the *organizing* task.

- **Quality assurance.** During any product development process, procedures must be followed for assuring the quality of the delivered product. Quality assurance is part of the *controlling* task.

- **Configuration management.** During any development process, different versions of a product and its components may exist simultaneously. In addition, development resources are acquired, used and disposed. Configuration management methods deal with the proper management of all these items. Configuration management is part of the *organizing* task.

In the rest of this book, we focus on development strategy planning.

15.3 Top-down Development Strategies

The development strategies discussed in this section have been proposed primarily for client-oriented software product development. As explained in chapter 3, this means that product decomposition is also product implementation (because the product is software) and that there is no production process (because in client-oriented development there is only one instance of the product). Even for market-oriented software product development, we need not specify a complex production process in which many instances of a product type are produced in series. The real problem of market-oriented software production is the realization and maintenance of platform-independence. The strategies discussed here can easily be generalized to product development in general, software and non-software, client-oriented and market-oriented.

All strategies assume that there has been a development process in a social system, in which a solution to a need of the social system has been specified. Let us assume for the sake of the example that the social system is a business. The development process may have been a problem solving process (such as in ISAC change analysis) or a strategy development process (such as in Information Strategy Planning). This process produces a **charter** for a new development process and we assume that this charter assigns developers to the task of implementing a computer-based system as part of an implementation of the solution. For example, the charter may ask them to produce a customized information system in a client-oriented development process, or to select a software package that satisfies business needs.

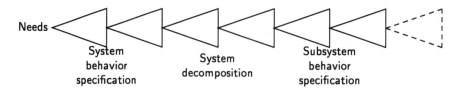

Figure 15.3: The linear development strategy, using a rational problem solving process.

15.3.1   The linear strategy

In the **linear system development strategy**, also called the **waterfall strategy**, we move top-down through the aggregation hierarchy and at each level of aggregation move linearly from initial needs analysis to behavior specification. Assuming that every task is performed in a rational problem solving way, we get the barbed wire process shown in figure 15.3. The process continues alternating between behavior specification and system decomposition until we reach a level of already existing and reusable components. At a very low level, these reusable components may be programming language statements. At a higher level, they may be modules taken from a library of reusable components, such as statistical routines or routines to draw graphics. At a still higher level the reusable components may be parametrized software packages, such as packages for order administration or cost calculation. The point where we reach reusable components is not important. The essential feature of the linear process is that the process never backtracks to an earlier task in the light of later experience.

Figure 15.4 shows another representation of the linear strategy, one that does not assume that the engineering cycle is used. It starts at the level of computer-based systems and takes the software engineer's point of view. Parallel developments for an information system or an EDI system invariably include adaptations to the organization, changes in administrative procedures and communication channels, possibly a restructuring of parts of the organization, etc. Parallel developments for a control system include the specification of hardware components and their interfaces.

Evaluation of the linear strategy

The advantage of the linear strategy is that it makes planning the development process easier than with any other strategy. For each stage of the linear process, the output products of the stage are defined, called the stage **deliverables**. In most development processes, stage deliverables are documents such as activity models, ER models, design specifications, user manuals, etc. The event that the deliverables of one stage are approved by the sponsor and developer is called a **milestone** of the development process. By this approval, the stage deliverables change their status because from that moment onwards, they function as a **baseline** for the rest of the process. Deliverables, milestones and baselines are important process management tools. The achievement of a milestone is observable, and one can therefore observe how far the process has progressed.

Unfortunately, a linear strategy is hard to follow in practice, for in any but the simplest development process, backtracking to earlier stages is necessary. For example, as stated in the principle of requirements uncertainty, clients may change their requirements *because of* the development process. As another example, we may have written an inconsistent

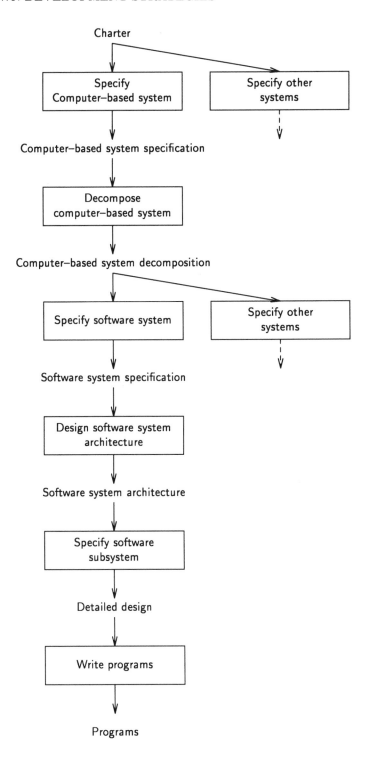

Figure 15.4: The linear client-oriented software product development process, starting at the level of computer-based systems, shown from the software engineer's point of view.

or incomplete system specification, or a specification that can only be implemented at a very high cost. These and many other reasons may cause us to backtrack to tasks already performed.

There are two kinds of feedback loops that can be added to the linear strategy, feedback to the previous stage and feedback from the evaluation of an implementation. We discuss these as two distinct extensions if the linear strategy. In practice, of course, both kinds of feedback can occur in one development process.

15.3.2   The splashing waterfall strategy

The **splashing waterfall strategy** is an extension of the linear strategy with feedback loops to the preceding stage of development, as shown in figure 15.5. It is left open how far backtracking goes, one or more stages back. The name "splashing waterfall strategy" is explained by the fact that this strategy allows "water" to flow against the flow of the development process.

Evaluation of the waterfall strategy

The splashing waterfall strategy is a designer's dream but a project manager's nightmare. It allows the designer unlimited freedom to backtrack to previous tasks. This means that what the designer delivers always has the proviso "this may possibly be revised later", which makes process planning impossible. When the process manager is asked how far the process has progressed, the answer can only be that the process is at all stages at the same time. The problem that the splashing strategy is intended to solve, the necessity to repair mistakes made earlier in the development process, is very real, but the solution offered by the splashing process is unmanageable.

15.3.3   The V-strategy

Client-oriented development is followed by an implementation of the specified product. If after the implementation we observe the behavior of the product, evaluate it, and take a next action, then we follow the regulatory cycle of action described in chapter 3. For example, we could extend the implementation of the charter for development to the following instance of the regulatory cycle:

- Define charter.

- Implement charter.

- Observe the behavior of the implementation.

- Evaluate the observations and respecify the charter if necessary.

In this cycle, the implementation task consists of the following subtasks:

- Decompose the system,

- specify the subsystems,

- implement the subsystems,

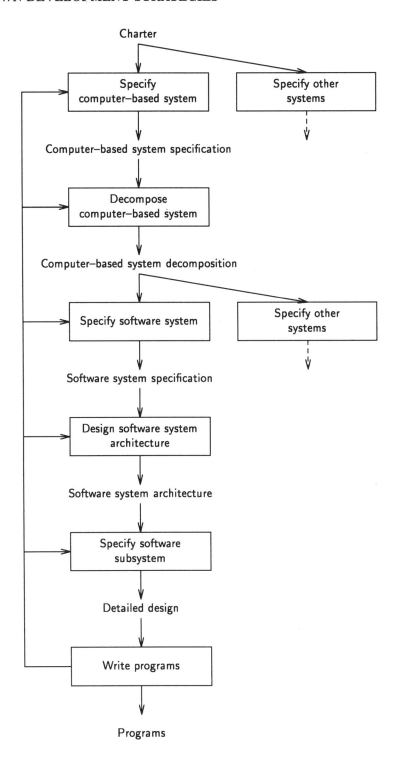

Figure 15.5: The splashing waterfall strategy for a client-oriented software product development process, starting at the level of computer-based systems, shown from the software engineer's point of view.

- Define charter
- Implement charter
    - Specify computer-based system
    - Decompose computer-based system
        - Specify software systems
        - Decompose software systems
            - Specify software subsystems
            - Implement software subsystems
            - Observe the behavior of the software subsystems (unit test)
            - Evaluate unit tests and go back to the specification of subsystems if necessary
        - Integrate software subsystems into software system
        - Observe the behavior of the integrated software system (integration test)
        - Evaluate the test and go back to software system specification if necessary.
    - Integrate software and other systems into computer-based system
    - Observe the behavior of the computer-based system (system test)
    - Evaluate system test and go back to the specification of the computer-based system if necessary
- Observe the behavior of the implementation of the charter (acceptance test)
- Evaluate the observations and respecify the charter if necessary

Figure 15.6: The tasks in the linear strategy performed according to the regulatory cycle.

- integrate the subsystems.

If we replace the implementation task by this process recursively, we get a nested structure. Figure 15.6 shows what we get if we expand the implementation of the charter, following the levels of the aggregation hierarchy top down. The picture has a more familiar form if we draw a box around every specification task and around every testing and evaluation task, and mirror the resulting diagram in one of the diagonals. Figure 15.7 shows the resulting V shape. This development (and implementation) strategy is called the **V-strategy**. We replaced the terms used in figure 15.6 by the commonly used terms in the V-strategy. We also assumed that all software components must be programmed. As mentioned before, the use of ready-made, reusable components can start at other levels. This does not affect the form of the V, although it does it make the descent less deep.

In the left leg of the V, we decompose the SuD and in the right leg, we integrate the components and evaluate the result. The evaluations in the right leg may lead us to redo part of previously performed tasks, and hence change the baselines produced by those tasks. After testing the computer-based system, the system must be handed over to the customer. The customer will perform an acceptance test of the computer-based system. After acceptance, the system is used and the needs of the client will evolve, leading eventually to a charter for a new development process.

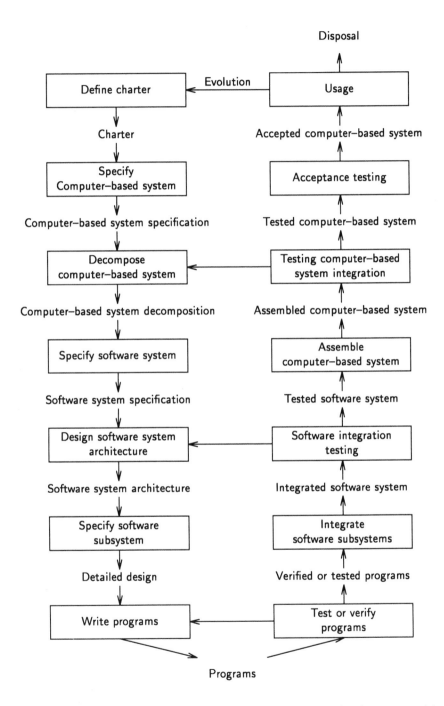

Figure 15.7: The V-strategy of client-oriented software product development and implementation.

Evaluation of the V-strategy

The V-strategy has the advantage that it allows the definition of weak milestones and baselines. Each stage deliverable in both legs of the V can turn into a baseline with the proviso that later testing may force us to improve or otherwise change the baseline. The disadvantage of the V-strategy is that the earlier an error is introduced, the later it is discovered. This can have devastating consequences. Empirical evidence suggests that the cost of repairing an error introduced in the system specification stage, but found in acceptance testing, can be 50 times as high as repairing that error in the system specification stage itself. Repairing the error during "adaptive maintenance" may even be 1000 times as expensive than the cost of repairing it in the system specification stage.

This disadvantage can be reduced if we perform every stage in the left leg of the V according to the engineering cycle. That is, before we commit the deliverables of the stage, we *simulate* the stage deliverables, *evaluate* the result of this simulation, and iterate over these tasks until the quality of the stage deliverables is believed to be high enough to warrant baselining them. The higher the quality of the simulations, the less frequent testing will cause us to revise a baseline. An important technique for simulation is throwaway prototyping, discussed later.

15.4   A Framework for Concurrent Development

There is an important shift of perspective as we moved from the linear strategy to the splashing waterfall and V-strategies. The boxes in the diagram of the linear strategy represent *stages* which occur sequentially in time. On the other hand, the boxes in the diagrams of the splashing waterfall and V-strategies represent *tasks*, to which we can backtrack if necessary. The feedback arrows in figures 15.5 and 15.7 do not represent time travel, but indicate a possible path through a collection of tasks. We can clarify the situation if we separate the *logical tasks* that have to be performed during development from the *temporal stages* of the development process. To do this, we return to the development framework of chapter 3, extended with the implementation, observation and evaluation tasks of the regulatory cycle (figure 15.8). Implementation of a software product consists of decomposing the specification until ready-made executable parts are encountered, and integrating these parts into a whole. Observation and evaluation are always lumped together under the term *testing*. Figure 15.8 thus shows a framework for product development and implementation, using the engineering cycle and regulatory cycle at each level of aggregation. This extended framework for product development and implementation still has two dimensions, aggregation and logic. We now turn it into the framework for concurrent engineering shown in figures 15.9 and 15.10 by adding the temporal dimension. To facilitate representation on a two-dimensional page, we merged the dimensions of aggregation and logic by stringing the cells together in the order in which they are numbered in figure 15.8. These numbers also appear in the vertical dimension of figures 15.9 and 15.10. The vertical dimension of figure 15.9 and 15.10 lists all logical product engineering tasks and the process management tasks already shown in figure 15.1. The horizontal dimension lists the progression of stages in time. To save space, we ignore the top layers of the aggregation hierarchy, and in order to agree with accepted terminology the cells in the bottom row of figure 15.8 that deal with programming are merged.

The tasks performed in the V-strategy lie on the diagonal of the upper half of figure 15.9.

	Requirements engineering	Decomposition	Integration	Testing
Social system				
Computer-based system				8
Software system	1	2	6	7
Software subsystem	3	4	4	5

Figure 15.8: A framework for development methods. The numbers are inserted for ease of reference.

Separating the temporal from the logical dimension frees us from the idea that we should perform all tasks in their logical order. At each stage of development, there is something to do in the entire column of tasks of that stage. To see how this works, imagine that we have created seven product development teams and a management team consisting of five managers. We assign a logical problem solving task in figure 15.9 to a different product development team, and assign the five management tasks to the five members of the management team. Now, each product development team and each manager has something to do in all stages of development. The requirements team will do most of its work in the requirements determination stage, but during all later stages it may have to improve its requirements based on feedback from the other teams and on changed requirements of the user of the software system. The programming team will do most of its work during the programming stage, but it will have to prepare its work already in the requirements stage by choosing a programming platform and tools. Figures 15.9 and 15.10 are thus a framework for **concurrent engineering**. Along the temporal dimension, management imposes a discipline of milestones and baselines. Along the vertical dimension, we achieve maximum concurrency by assigning logically different tasks to different development teams, who cooperate as best as they can in their effort to achieve the milestones.

Evaluation of the concurrent development framework

The framework for concurrent development makes clear that a high degree of concurrency between different development tasks is possible. This allows us to make feedback from other tasks available as early as possible and to avoid unnecessary delays by starting a task as early as possible, but it does not help in making the process more manageable. To make it manageable, we must impose a discipline of milestones and baselines, just as is done in the linear and V-strategies. The problem with the imposition of such a discipline is that it cannot deal with the correction of errors and mistakes made in a baseline product. The later these errors and mistakes are discovered, the more disruptive and costly their repair is. The only way to deal with this is to reduce the number of these errors. There are two ways to do this.

		Development stages						
		Software system requirements specification	Software system architecture design	Software subsystem specification	Programming	Software system integration	Software system acceptance	Usage
Product engineering tasks	1 Software requirements engineering							
	2 Software architecture design							
	3 Software subsystem specification							
	4, 5 Programming and program testing							
	6, 7 Software system integration and testing							
	8 Acceptance testing							

Figure 15.9: A framework for concurrent software product development and implementation — engineering tasks.

		Development stages						
		Software system requirements specification	Software system architecture design	Software subsystem specification	Programming	Software system integration	Software system acceptance	Usage
Process management tasks	Planning							
	Organizing							
	Acquiring resources							
	Directing							
	Controlling							

Figure 15.10: A framework for concurrent software product development and implementation — management tasks.

- Avoid errors and mistakes in a deliverable by producing the deliverable according to the engineering cycle. That is, simulate the effect of the deliverable until confidence is sufficiently high to permit commitment. Throw-away prototyping, discussed in the next section, is a major technique for simulating software deliverables.

- Make the deliverables as small as possible, but not smaller. The smaller they are, the less errors they can contain, even without simulation. This leads to the strategy of phased delivery, discussed in section 15.6.

15.5   Throw-away Prototyping

A product **prototype** is a system that displays some, but not all properties of the required product. **Throw-away prototyping** consists of producing a prototype of one of the alternatives in an iteration through the engineering cycle. Throw-away prototyping is part of the essence of engineering, because its aim is to simulate the effects of an alternative before the alternative is implemented. It is not a strategy to implement a product, but a technique to gain *knowledge* about a product alternative in order to decide whether the alternative will be implemented. The prototype need not be robust, well-structured, reliable or efficient as long as it allows us to learn more about how the alternative will behave before it is implemented. Any quick-and-dirty technique may be used, from Lisp programming to pencil and paper simulations of a user interface. After evaluation of the prototype, the results are used in evaluation of the prototyped alternative and the prototype is discarded. Because discarding the prototype is essential, we always talk of *throw-away* prototyping instead of just prototyping.

Throw-away prototyping can be used in any of the problem solving tasks in product development, from the determination of requirements to the coding of programs. If used at the early stages of development, a proof-of-concept prototype may be used to validate a product idea or to show the feasibility of a list of required product properties. In later stages, prototyping may be used to validate a product specification, to explore alternative system decompositions, to evaluate alternative user interfaces, to try out alternative algorithms, etc.

Evaluation of throw-away prototyping

Throw-away prototyping has a number of advantages:

- It increases certainty about the likely effects of an alternative before it is chosen. It can for example be used in the early stages of development to decrease requirements uncertainty, i.e. to increase certainty that the acceptance test will not lead to drastic revisions of the requirements.

- In client-oriented development, throw-away prototyping additionally helps reduce the customer's and user's uncertainty about what is possible and about what product they can expect. This has two beneficial consequences:

  - It makes it possible to reduce the number of changes in requirements after the requirements are committed.
  - In addition, it makes it possible to enhance user support for the final product.

If the product is developed for a market, then similar advantages exist with respect to the marketing department.

Prototyping also has its dangers:

- It may distract the attention of the developer, customer or user from important features. Presented with a prototyped user interface, for example, users may spend a lot of time evaluating the position of an icon on the screen but may ignore more important features such as the flow of the dialogue.

- It takes time to develop a prototype, so throw-away prototyping may increase development time. Some managers view time spent on coding a prototype as wasted time, because it is not spent on coding the final product. However, if used properly, time spent on throw-away prototyping is earned back by reduced backtracking later in the development process, and by a reduced need for corrective product maintenance. Of course, time spent on generating throw-away prototypes should be minimized by using program generators or other tools that allow fast production of software.

- The developer may become attached to the prototype, and start treating it as a portion of the end product. In client-oriented development, the customer or user too may become attached to prototypes. This is a danger because a throw-away prototype is usually produced *without* any attention to structure, safety, reliability, performance, etc. Software development managers should insist on discarding the prototype after use.

15.6   Strategies for Phased Development

The number of errors that creep through simulation can be further minimized by reducing the size of the system under development. This means that we turn to **phased development**, where we divide the system into portions to be developed successively. This is contrasted with a **monolithic development** process, where the entire system is developed in one shot. Any development process starts out as a monolithic process, in which a product idea is identified and product objectives are determined. However, at some point during the process, we can decide to select a portion of the product and develop that first, before developing other portions. Phased development strategies differ in the choice of the moment when they start dividing the product into portions. Some obvious possibilities are the following:

- Determine product objectives globally without baselining them, and then perform phased development. This is called **evolutionary development**. It is treated in subsection 15.6.2.

- Determine product objectives, baseline them, and then perform phased development. We don't treat this strategy here.

- Determine product objectives, specify external product behavior, and then perform phased development. This is called **incremental development**. It is treated in subsection 15.6.1.

- Determine product objectives, specify the product, decompose into subsystems, and then deliver the subsystems by means of phased development. This is part of the **cleanroom development strategy**, not treated here.

15.6.1 Incremental development

In **incremental development**, we determine system objectives and specify required system behavior, baseline these deliverables, and then select a portion of the required functionality that promises to yield the best cost/benefit ratio [115]. This functionality is then implemented according to a linear strategy, V-strategy or concurrent strategy. After acceptance testing of this portion of the product, another portion of the remaining functionality with the best expected cost/benefit ratio is selected, and this process iterates until the entire product is delivered. Each delivered portion of the product is called an *increment*.

Each increment is developed according to a traditional strategy. The tasks in the chosen strategy can be performed according to the engineering cycle, so that throw-away prototyping can be used at different stages in the development of an increment. The difference between incremental development and throw-away prototyping is that in incremental development a production-strength portion of a product is delivered, complete with error recovery procedures, input checking, exception-handling, required performance characteristics, hardware interface documentation, technical documentation, and user manuals. In throw-away prototyping, nothing is delivered, because the goal is the increase of knowledge about the requirements of the product.

Evaluation of incremental development

In incremental development, a version of the product is delivered early. This has a number of advantages:

- The results of *acceptance tests* will be available earlier than they would be using a monolithic development strategy. This means that errors in the product idea or requirements specification can be spotted earlier than in the case of monolithic development, and they will be cheaper to repair because the system is only delivered in small increments.

- A *working product* is delivered earlier than it would be using a monolithic development strategy. In client-oriented product development, this is reassuring for the customer as well as for the user, who can become accustomed to the product. Product acceptance is therefore enhanced.

Incremental development has two disadvantages:

- Errors introduced in the product objectives or requirements specification may not be discovered until very late in the development process, because some of these may only become apparent when the last increment of the product is delivered.

- Since the product architecture is defined incrementally, we may end up with no architecture at all. A bad product architecture leads to bad performance and bad maintainability of the product.

15.6.2 Evolutionary development

In **evolutionary development**, product objectives and behavior are specified globally first, without baselining them. One portion of the requirements is then selected for further development, following the V-strategy. After development, experience with the delivered portion of the product allows engineers and users to better understand the user needs and hence the product objectives, and to better understand feasible solutions to this needs and hence required product behavior. This is used to improve the objectives and the specification of required behavior, and to select the next portion of the aspect of the product to be developed and implemented.

There are two criteria that can be used to select a portion of the requirements to be developed:

- As in incremental development, the expected cost/benefit ratio can be used.

- Alternatively, the part of the requirements about which the most certainty exists can be chosen. This is a risk-avoidance strategy.

The difference between evolutionary and incremental development is that in evolutionary development a portion of the product is delivered before all required product behavior is specified. This means that the specification of external product behavior is written incrementally, as portions of the product are delivered. External product behavior is known with certainty only after the last increment has been specified. The difference with throw-away prototyping is, as before, that a production-strength portion of a product is delivered. In addition, in evolutionary prototyping, we may select the portion of the requirements to be developed about which the most *certainty* is experienced. By contrast, in throw-away prototyping, we select that portion about which the most *uncertainty* is experienced and about which we want to learn more.

Evaluation of evolutionary development

Evolutionary development has the same advantages as incremental development: early delivery of a portion of the product allows the developer to spot errors earlier and to repair spotted errors against lower cost than with monolithic development, and the user has a working product sooner than with monolithic development, which enhances acceptance. In addition, it has a number of advantages that arise from the fact that part of the requirements is specified after the first portion of the product is delivered.

- If only those requirements are selected for development about which most certainty is experienced, then there is a high confidence that there are few errors in the requirements.

- In client-oriented development, users have their hands on a version of the system early. In addition to increased user acceptance, this has two advantages:

  - Users can adapt their requirements to what is feasible. These changes in requirements are accommodated easily, because not all requirements are fixed at the start of the process.

- Conversely, developers can learn more about user's requirements, because experience with the delivered portions of the product are available earlier and the requirements can still be adapted.

In market-oriented development, these advantages exist with respect to the marketing department.

- Because requirements are kept global, conflicts over requirements are reduced. Furthermore, if the selected portions of the requirements are small enough, then they are too small to be worth battling over, and this reduces conflict as well. The result is reduced resistance to change. This advantage of the strategy is well-known in politics and is often called *salami tactics*, because change is implemented slice by slice.

Evolutionary development also has a number of important disadvantages:

- Since only global requirements are specified, the developer may not even have a consistent *product idea*. Again, this is a well-known phenomenon in politics: salami tactics may be a substitute for having a vision rather than a way to carefully implement a vision. Reacting to events like user dissatisfaction can be done with only short-term goals in mind and requires no vision.

- As with incremental development, the *system architecture* is specified incrementally. This may lead to a bad architecture and its concomitant maintenance and performance problems. Because the requirements specification is produced incrementally as well, coherence of this specification may be low as well, resulting in even less coherence of the product.

- It is not clear when to *stop* evolutionary development. When is development finished and does perfective maintenance start? The rule is that when the architecture of a system gets corrupted to the extent that maintenance becomes a problem, a new system must be developed. However, evolutionary development may result in a system with a bad architecture to begin with.

Figure 15.11 summarizes the properties of throw-away prototyping, incremental development and evolutionary development. Note that throw-away prototyping can be combined with either of the other two, but that incremental and evolutionary development are mutually exclusive.

15.6.3 Experimental development

In **experimental development**, a prototype is delivered for real use. Evaluation then may lead to an improvement of the delivered prototype or to an update of the requirements. The difference with throw-away prototyping is that the prototype is actually *used*. The difference with incremental and evolutionary development is that a *prototype* rather than a production-strength system is delivered.

Experimental development is a departure from the engineering cycle, because it drops the idea that an alternative must be evaluated *before* it is chosen. Experimental development is suitable only for research environments.

	Throw-away prototyping of requirements	Incremental development	Certainty-driven evolutionary development
Increases certainty of developers about requirements		Requirements errors spotted earlier	Requirements errors spotted earlier
	Prevents requirements errors		Avoid requirements errors
	Less product errors to repair	Product errors cheaper to repair	Product errors cheaper to repair
Increase certainty of clients or marketing about product	Prevent changes in requirements		Accommodate changes in requirements
	Enhance user support	Enhance user support	Enhance user support
Dangers	Possible attention to unimportant details	Errors in product specification discovered late	There may be no product idea
	Takes time		Development process may not terminate
	Prototype may be used as finished product	Possibly bad product architecture	Possibly bad product architecture

Figure 15.11: Properties of throw-away prototyping and two phased development strategies.

15.7   Rational Reconstruction of the Development Process

The framework for concurrent product development and implementation is really three-dimensional, the three dimensions being aggregation, logic and time. There is an important relationship between the logical and temporal dimensions. We have used the logical dimension to analyze requirements engineering methods in part II of this book. The logical dimension has a second use, viz. as a template for a rational *justification* of a result, after the result is produced. We give two illustrations of this.

- In the engineering cycle, we produce a justification for a design decision by listing the alternatives considered, their likely effects, and the evaluations of these effects against the product objectives. Estimation of the likely effects of an alternative can be backed up by a simulation in the form of a throw-away prototype, an informal argument, observation of similar systems elsewhere, etc.

- In the empirical cycle, we produce a justification of a modeling decision by listing the alternatives considered, their observable consequences, and the results of experiments in which these consequences are falsified or verified. The experiments may consist of simple observations, interviews with domain specialists, etc.

Obviously, one is in a very good position to produce these justifications if one actually followed the empirical and engineering cycles. However, the developer has more freedom than this. In order to produce these justifications after development, all that is required is that during development, a *record* of development is constructed that takes the form of these justifications. Development is then just as much the specification of a product as it is the construction of justifications for these specifications. We call this the **rational reconstruction** of the development process. As time goes by, we record the alternatives, their consequences and the evaluation of these consequences, independently from the order in which these were considered. The alternatives may have been considered at different points in time and after many backtrackings, but they appear on the record as if they were all considered during one iteration through the rational problem solving cycle.

Recording the considered alternatives not only helps us justify the result of development, but also helps us to accommodate changes in available technology, client needs, objectives or preferences. When alternatives and their simulations and evaluations have been recorded, then it will be easier to reconsider choices made in the light of the new situation. For example, if available technology drops in price and we remember that an otherwise promising alternative was rejected because it was estimated to be too expensive, then an opportunity arises to choose this previously rejected alternative. If we had not recorded the reasons for rejecting this alternative, this opportunity might not have become visible. Recording the alternatives considered and their simulations and evaluations is thus an important tool to realize *backward traceability* of specifications to the reasons why they were chosen over other specifications.

Summing up, rational problem solving now has four useful roles to play:

- As a tool to analyze development methods.

- As a tool for structuring the decision making process.

- As a tool for justifying the results of development.

- As a tool to allow us to reconsider of alternatives when circumstances change.

Rational reconstruction of a sometimes erratic real-world process occurs in many other areas where a historical process must be explained and justified in a rational way. The bibliographical remarks give some pointers to the literature.

15.8 Summary

There are two kinds of tasks in the development and implementation of a product, *product engineering tasks* and *process management tasks*. The product engineering tasks are requirements engineering, decomposition, integration and testing. The process management tasks are planning, organizing, acquisition, directing and controlling the development process.

An important class of methods for planning the development process is the class of methods to select a *development strategy* for the process. There are a number of different *top-down* strategies, in which we descend top-down in the aggregation hierarchy. In the *linear* or *waterfall* strategy, we descend top-down in the aggregation hierarchy without permitting backtracking. This is a developer's nightmare, because errors cannot be corrected, but a manager's dream, because a strict discipline of milestones and baselines is enforced. If we allow backtracking to the previous task, then we get the *splashing waterfall strategy*, which is a developer's dream but a manager's nightmare, because no stage deliverable is committed until all are committed. If we perform every task in the linear strategy according to the regulatory cycle, and allow backtracking if evaluation shows that the system contains an error, then we get the *V-strategy* of system development. The V-strategy allows a discipline of milestones and baselines, restricted by the possibility to renegotiate earlier baselines.

In the framework for *concurrent engineering*, tasks and stages of development have been separated, and all tasks are allowed to be performed in all stages. This freedom is limited by the choice of milestones by process management.

During any execution of the engineering cycle, at any level of aggregation, we may decide to simulate an alternative by building a *throw-away prototype*. Throw-away prototypes are not intended for real use. Rather, their purpose is to learn something about a decision alternative and after they have served this purpose, they are discarded. Throw-away prototyping has the advantage that it increases the certainty of the prediction of the effect of an alternative, that it involves users and therefore increases acceptance of the final product, and that it can be used in the requirements stage to achieve more certainty about requirements and let users formulate more realistic requirements. It has the disadvantages that it may distract the attention of users and developers from essential features, that it takes time and resources to develop a prototype, and that the developer or user may become attached to the prototype and starts using it as if it were a production-strength product.

Another strategy option, independent from the choice of top-down strategies and of throw-away prototyping, is whether or not to deliver a system in stages. In *incremental development*, the requirements specification is developed top down, and the system is then delivered incrementally with increasing functionality. Usually, the increments are selected using a cost/benefit criterion. In *evolutionary development*, the requirements are determined globally but not baselined, and portions of the requirements are then developed in stages. As a consequence, parts of the requirements are worked out further only after the first increment is delivered. Usually, the portion of the requirements developed further is the one about which the developers are most certain. The advantages and disadvantages of phased development are summarized in figure 15.11.

In *experimental development*, a prototype is delivered for real use and updated as required by experience. The difference with throw-away prototyping is that the prototype is not thrown away; the difference with incremental and evolutionary development is that a prototype is delivered rather than a production-strength product. Experimental development is a departure from the engineering cycle, because a product alternative is evaluated by using it, not before using it.

All these strategies allow a *rational reconstruction* of the development process as if the engineering cycle were followed. This allows the developer to justify the results of development. Maintaining a record of all alternatives considered and their simulations and evaluations also helps in accommodating changes that inevitably occur during or after development.

15.9 Exercises

1. Number the boxes in the V-strategy and write these numbers in the corresponding cells of figure 15.8.

2. (a) Change the V-strategy by generalizing it to software as well as non-software product development.

   (b) Change the V-strategy by turning it into a strategy for market-driven development.

3. Classify the following tasks by allocating them to one or more cells in figures 15.9 or 15.10. If necessary, add product development tasks or development stages to the table.

   (a) Determining a plan for acceptance testing of a software system.

   (b) Estimating the need for development resources and their cost.

   (c) Writing a user's manual.

   (d) Investigation of algorithms.

   (e) Documentation of programs.

   (f) Training system users.

   (g) Selection of a programming language and supporting tools.

   (h) Definition of interfaces between subsystems.

4. Enumerate as many ways to simulate a software product as you can imagine, in addition to throw-away prototyping.

5. In *The Wheelwright's Shop* (Cambridge University Press, 1923), George Sturt, a craftsman himself, describes nineteenth-century traditional wagon-making. The following description of this process is based on the summary by Jones [168, pages 15–20].

   Wagon craftsmen were very intimate with the peculiarities of the neighborhood, such as the nature of the soil in a farm, the gradient of a hill, or the type of horses used by a customer. The dimensions of a wagon, the timber used, the curves followed and many other details of a wagon were tailored to these conditions of use. Knowledge about the design of a wagon was not written down nor represented in drawings. It was spread out in a network of country prejudices and discussed over and over again in village workshops and farmyards. For centuries, these details were passed down from father to son. Most of it was a mystery. Because nobody knew the reasons for design decisions, changes to a design were only made locally, for example by choosing a slightly different "dish" (the angle with which a wheel slopes outward) or choosing a different kind of wood. Over the centuries, this trial-and-error process led to a well-balanced design and a close fit to user needs.

Compare this account with

(a) evolutionary development and

(b) experimental development.

6. Appendix C lists the stages and tasks of ETHICS. Although the lists have been ordered sequentially, not all methods recommend sequential performance of all these tasks. When we refer to "sequences" of tasks in what follows, this refers to sequences in the presentation of the methods, not necessarily in the performance of the methods. For each of the methods, do the following:

(a) Separate product development tasks from process management tasks.

(b) For the product development tasks, partition the method into groups of tasks such that each group is concerned with one level of aggregation in the aggregation hierarchy of figure 15.8.

(c) For each of the groups so identified, try if you can map the tasks in the group to particular tasks in the engineering cycle and/or to the regulatory cycle.

7. Answer the questions of exercise 6 for SSADM (appendix C). In part (b) look also for decomposition tasks that bring us to the next lower level of aggregation.

15.10   Bibliographical Remarks

Process management.   Useful introductions to process management are given by Southwell [322] and by Rook [288]. One of the best introductions to software process management is Rook [287]. Thayer [341] gather together an important collection of papers on software project management. Figure 15.2 is based on an overview paper by Thayer [342]. The concept of the universality of management is taken as point of departure in that paper. Thayer uses the breakdown of management tasks proposed by Mackenzie [206] and used, with a slight alteration, in figures 15.1 and 15.2. Boehm [40] gives a survey of management issues for software projects. Thayer and Pyster edited a special issue of the *IEEE Transactions on Software Engineering* on software project management [344]. Humphrey [152] gives well-rounded and influential view on managing the development process with a view to realizing continual improvement.

Top-down strategies. The regulatory cycle is a model of rational action taken from the field of social theory [329] and process consultancy [184]. It allows us to understand the relation between the V model of the software process and the engineering cycle. The V model was introduced by Jensen and Tonies [165]. It is used by Rook [287] and the STARTS Guide [240]. McDermid [222] contains an extensive treatment of the V model and its place in software process modeling. The classic source for the waterfall strategy is Royce [295], a paper that is still worth reading. It was popularized by Boehm [36] and used by Boehm [37] in his COCOMO model for estimating the cost of software products. A conveniently brief introduction to the waterfall strategy, with a summary of advantages and disadvantages, is given by Agresti [4]. Jones [168, page 75] lists all the strategies considered here in the context of industrial product engineering.

Framework for concurrent engineering. The matrix of stages against tasks of development is introduced by Rook [287]. Variations are given by McDermid [222] and by the STARTS Guide [240]. In all three sources, the cells of the matrix are filled in with the activities that a task generates during a stage. A very similar framework for the software engineering process is given by Peters and Tripp [258, 257]. As pointed out in the bibliographical remarks of chapter 3, the intellectual ancestor of these frameworks is a three-dimensional framework for the systems engineering process given by Hall [133]. In addition to the temporal and logical dimensions (stages and tasks), Hall used the aspect dimension mentioned in subsection 3.6.3 to represent the kind of knowledge that we use in system development.

A motivation for concurrent engineering in product development is given by Sprague, Singh and Wood [324]. Concurrent engineering is often combined with *integrated development*, also called *total product design*, in which marketing, engineering, design, manufacturing, sales and management personnel work together during the entire development process to develop a product specification. Concurrent engineering and integrated development are two important ingredients in Quality Function Deployment [54].

Empirical studies of the development process. In empirical studies done by Guindon [128] show that developers jump from task to task in an opportunistic way until the design is finished, i.e. until they have a requirements specification with a corresponding implementation. Empirical studies done by Zelkowitz [382] show that half of a system design is usually done after the formal design stage is finished, and that coding starts during design and continues until acceptance testing. A study by Visser [351] confirms these findings. These studies all concern the behavior of individual engineers; I am not aware of studies of task sequencing in project groups.

Parnas and Clements [255] give many reasons why a rational development process cannot be followed in practice. Among others, designers have limited time, preconceived ideas about how the product should be designed, make mistakes, have problems mastering the mountain of details involved in an engineering project, may be forced to reuse software that they cannot really use, etc. Swartout and Balzer [334] give an example that illustrates how the specification of a data structure may be influenced by implementation considerations.

Rational reconstruction. The concept of rational reconstruction has been introduced by Carnap [60] and was further developed by Reichenbach [277, 278]. Reichenbach remarks that logic governs the result of thinking, not the process of thinking itself. Once we have the result, we construct a chain of thoughts from the starting point to the point of arrival to explain and justify the result to others. It is this rational reconstruction that is governed by the laws of logic, not the process of thinking itself [278, page 2]. Accordingly, Reichenbach distinguishes the *context of discovery* from the *context of justification*. Transferring this argument to the development process, we can speak about the *context of development* and the *context of justification*. The selection of a development strategy is part of the context of development, rational problem solving and the rational engineering methods are part of the context of justification.

Suchman [330, 331] gives an interesting description of the role of rational reconstruction in office procedures. The actual course of events in an office is too unpredictable and chaotic to be captured by a procedure that takes care of all errors, like invoices received for the wrong amount, for missing orders, etc. Errors are left unstated in the formal office procedures. When an error occurs, office personnel engages in an activity in which they try to find out which sequence of events should have happened, and they then try to construct this history after the fact. They contact the sender of the invoice, they copy missing data from other departments, etc. This constructed history is a rational reconstruction of actual history, and it is the history they record in the books. This is not a falsification of history but a rational reconstruction of history as it would have taken place when the world would have been ideal. In this way, office employees take responsibility for what happened in the office, and it is the *only* way they can take responsibility for it [331, pages 326–327]. This does not mean that office workers "fake" the appearance of orderliness in the records. Rather, the construction of orderly records is the construction of evidence of action in accordance with the procedures. Computer scientists too easily look upon these procedures as if they were computer programs to be followed by office workers, just as they construe development methods as programs to be followed by themselves.

The difference between the logic of problem solving and the historical stages of a problem solving process is illustrated by management decision making too. As remarked in the bibliographical remarks of chapter 3, Mintzberg, Raisinghani and Théorêt [234] found that managers do not blindly follow through the rational problem solving process step by step, but choose a path through it that may skip tasks that are easy or for which there is no time, and that may iterate over tasks that are important for the problem at hand. In other words, the actual process usually differs from the rational process, but after the fact it can be rationally reconstructed as a number of iterations through the rational process.

Turning to software development, Parnas and Clements [255] advocate what they call "faking" a rational software development process by constructing a record of the development process as if it followed a rational procedures. From what has been said above, it should be clear that this is not faking in a bad sense. Rather, the construction of a record of a rational development process is the means by which software developers justify the result of development to others and take responsibility for it. The importance of justification of design decisions in software development has recently been pointed out by Potts and Bruns [265]. The importance of recording reasons of requirements for the reconsideration of design decisions when circumstances change is pointed out by Gause and Weinberg [111, page 271].

Rational reconstruction was a big issue in the philosophy of science in the beginning of the 1970s. Very roughly, where Popper [264] studied the logic of scientific discovery and Kuhn [186] studied the history of scientific discovery, Lakatos [187] saw the logical structure of scientific discovery as a rational reconstruction of its history. (Of course, philosophers would not be philosophers if they did not disagree about what the logic of discovery actually is.)

Throw-away prototyping.   Prototyping as an approach to software development was proposed at least as early as the mid-1970s. However, prototyping became popular only in the beginning of the 1980s; the *Software Engineering Notes* has a special issue on prototyping in December 1982 (volume 7, number 5). Carey and Mason [58] note that software professionals will frequently state that they have been working this way for ages — which is to be expected, because throw-away prototyping belongs to the essence of engineering. Another interesting observation made by Carey and Mason is that authors of papers on prototyping rarely quote each other, and that the origin of prototyping is either attributed to folklore or to the author's invention.

In the first half of the 1980s, throw-away prototyping and evolutionary development were not distinguished. The distinction is made very clear by Davis [78]. Gomaa [121] describes the effect of throw-away prototyping and evolutionary development on the system development process. Alavi [7] provides empirical evidence for the increase of user involvement and user satisfaction by means of throw-away prototyping. Alavi and Wetherbe [8] show in an experiment with students that throw-away prototyping preceded by data modeling yields better results in fewer iterations than throw-away prototyping not preceded by data modeling.

Useful surveys of prototyping are given by Agresti [5] and Ince [155]. Both authors argue that executable formal specification languages can be used to produce throw-away requirements prototypes. This argument confuses throw-away prototypes with evolutionary versions of the product. In a recent status report on prototyping, Luqi and Royce [205] correctly argue that a language for throw-away prototyping does not need to provide facilities for verifying correctness and completeness of a design or implementation, as a specification language does. Gordon and Bieman [123] provide a comprehensive survey of case studies of throw-away and evolutionary prototyping and their effects on software product quality and development process quality. Almost all case studies report that both forms of prototyping result in increased ease of use of the software product, a better match with user needs, reduced system development effort and increased user participation.

A short and interesting defense of the usefulness of throw-away prototyping is given by Andriole [10]. He argues that throw-away prototyping is always cost-effective and always improves specifications. Interestingly, he recommends using multiattribute evaluation techniques for evaluating throw-away prototypes, similar to the techniques used in evaluating alternative product designs in industrial development.

Incremental development.   An early reference to the incremental development strategy is Basili and Turner [24]. Distaso [88] attributes the idea of incremental development to Williams [367]. Dyer [93] gives an early report on its use at IBM is Incremental development was adopted by IBM as a software development strategy. Boehm [37, page 42] recommends it as an improvement on the monolithic application of the waterfall strategy. He points out that the major effect of incremental development on the software development process is a flattening of the distribution of labor over time.

Cleanroom development. One ingredient of cleanroom development is phased development, starting from an architecture of the system. The other ingredients of the cleanroom strategy are separation of programming and testing (programmers do not execute their programs), combined with formal correctness proofs of programs by their programmers [195], and statistical usage testing of programs by testers [73]. Cleanroom development is described by Linger [196] and Selby, Basili and Baker [306].

Evolutionary development. Evolutionary development is really an example of a well-known strategy known as "salami tactics" to politicians and "muddling through" to managers. The classic paper on muddling through is Lindblom [193], which should be mandatory reading for all software engineering students. The basic assumption of Lindblom is that administrators, politicians and managers must solve problems with a state space so large and of a complexity so vast that there is no reliable abstraction in terms of which they can analyze the situation and explore alternative solutions. And even if there were such a model, they do not have the time to commission a study to solve these problems and wait for its results. Consequently, instead of analyzing the situation, they try to remember a similar situation from the past and then do something that differs only marginally from what was done in that earlier situation. In evolutionary development too, developers deliver a new version of a product that differs only marginally from the current version and they do this for the same reason: they are not able to predict the consequences of any radical change to the current version. If they could, then they should practice engineering, i.e. simulate and evaluate product alternatives before they are implemented. The advantages and disadvantages of evolutionary development given in section 15.6 are all derived from Lindblom's paper.

In software engineering, evolutionary development is championed by Gilb [114, 115], who also calls it *design by objectives*. This is derived from the Lindblom's argument for "salami tactics" in the face of complex problems, as well as from the idea of *management by objectives* (MBO), introduced by Drucker [92].

Another important defense of the evolutionary strategy is given by McCracken and Jackson [221]. Their major argument against the linear development strategy is that the very process of developing a system will change the requirements; this is the principle of requirements uncertainty. Dearnley and Mayhew [83] give a brief introduction to the evolutionary strategy.

Boehm [43] provides empirical evidence for the relative advantages and disadvantages of waterfall development and evolutionary development with respect to each other. In a perceptive discussion of this result, Davis [77, page 348] remarks that the prototype produced in the experiment did not have any documentation and had no requirements specified for them. It is therefore more like a throw-away prototype than an evolutionary product.

Luqi and Royce [205] argue that evolutionary prototyping would benefit from software reuse, because that would allow faster production of a production-strength software system. They observe that, unfortunately, evolutionary development is needed most in those areas that are least understood. For these areas, it is likely that little reusable software is available.

16

Selecting a Development Strategy

16.1 Introduction

The previous chapter should have made it clear that no strategy is suitable for all types of development situations. In this chapter, we discuss two methods for selecting a development strategy for a particular development process, Boehm's spiral method (section 16.2) and the part of Euromethod that is concerned with selecting development strategies (section 16.3).

16.2 The Spiral Model for Software Development

The spiral model of software development proposed by Boehm [39, 42] is a method to adapt the development strategy dynamically to the changing pattern of risks that arise during the development process. According to Webster's [356], a **risk** is a possibility of loss or injury. In the context of product development, a risk is the possibility of not getting sufficient benefits from the product to justify the cost of developing it.

16.2.1 Structure

Boehm published several versions of his spiral model, the most recent of which is shown in figure 16.1 [35, 41]. The process iterates over four tasks. During each iteration, a portion of the product is developed. In the first task, the objectives of this portion of the product are determined, alternative strategies of developing it are generated, and constraints on these strategies are determined. In the second task, the alternative strategies are evaluated on the risk of developing a wrong product and the alternative is chosen with the greatest reduction of this risk. In the third task, the portion of the product is developed following the selected strategy. This takes us one or more steps further down the aggregation hierarchy and possibly yields a finished portion of the product. In the fourth task, the development is reported about and the next iteration through the spiral is planned.

The innovation of this process is the determination of the development strategy by means of an engineering cycle, in which risk is minimized. The spiral process is thus an

1. **Initialization**

   - Determine the objectives of the portion of the product to be elaborated in this iteration,
   - the alternative means of implementation of this portion of the product and
   - the constraints on the alternatives.

2. **Evaluation**

   - Evaluate alternatives with respect to objectives and constraints,
   - identify risks in each generated alternative and
   - choose a development process that minimizes the risks.

3. **Development**

   - Develop the next-level product according to the chosen development strategy and
   - verify it.

4. **Planning**

   - Determine process objectives, alternatives, constraints.
   - Evaluate process alternatives: identify process risks and resolve them.
   - Plan the next iteration through the spiral and
   - obtain commitment of all concerned parties to the plan.

Figure 16.1: Boehm's spiral method.

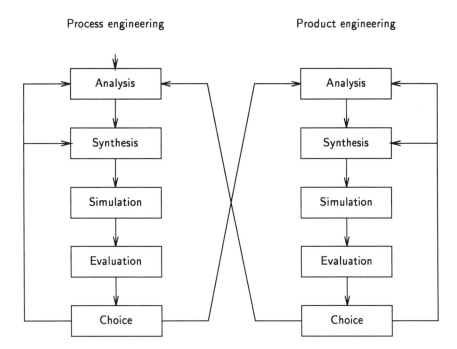

Figure 16.2: The logical structure of the spiral method.

interleaving of *process engineering* with *product engineering* tasks (figure 16.2). In an initial process engineering task, we select a strategy and then perform one iteration through the product engineering cycle. This reduces uncertainty about the product, for example by descending one level of the system aggregation hierarchy. This reduced uncertainty may cause us to redo the process engineering cycle, because the risk analysis in the new situation may differ from the previous risk analysis. The first task of the spiral method covers the analysis and synthesis tasks of process engineering. The second task covers simulation, evaluation and choice of strategy, and the third task consists of product development. The fourth task is a process management task (planning) and is not visible in figure 16.2.

Figure 16.2 makes clear that the spiral strategy is a generalization of all strategies discussed in chapter 15. In all these strategies, there is one initial process engineering task followed by a number of iterations over product engineering. In the spiral strategy, we may return to process engineering after every iteration over the product development process.

16.2.2 Strategies

During the process engineering stage, we generate a number of alternative development strategies. The following strategies are recognized by the spiral method.

- One of the simplest development strategies is to **buy** commercial off-the-shelf software, called COTS by Boehm. (The very simplest process is, of course, not to do development at all.)

- **Transformational development** is the development of a software product by successive transformation of a specification in such a way that the output of the final transformation is a program that implements the input of the first transformation.

- The standard (top-down) strategy discussed in the previous chapter is called by Boehm the **waterfall strategy**.

- Evolutionary delivery is called **evolutionary prototyping** by Boehm.

- The **capabilities-to-requirements** strategy determines the capabilities of available software (COTS, 4GL) and then adjusts the requirements as far as possible to these capabilities.

- **Risk reduction/waterfall** is a strategy in which the waterfall (i.e. standard) strategy is preceded by a few iterations through the spiral to reduce risks.

- In the **design-to-cost** strategy, priorities are assigned to the desired product capabilities and these are implemented starting with the highest priority capabilities. The development process stops when the budget is finished.

- In the **design-to-schedule** strategy, the same is done but now the process stops when there is no more time left for implementing more capabilities.

- **Incremental delivery** has been explained in the previous chapter, where it is called incremental devwelopment.

16.2.3   Strategy selection heuristics

Boehm [41] gives decision tables with heuristics to select a strategy, reproduced in figures 16.3 and 16.4. The spiral model is listed as one of the strategies which one can choose. The following situational factors are considered in the selection of a development strategy:

- The **growth envelope** of the development situation refers to the likely limits of the size of the product during its useful life and to the diversity of functions that it can be expected to provide. A limited growth envelope implies that we can use limited-domain approaches such as commercial off-the-shelf (COTS) software, fourth-generation languages, or transformational development, without incurring a large risk. For systems with a large growth envelope, these approaches would be very risky.

- A low **understanding of requirements** implies a high risk of developing the wrong software. This risk can be reduced by choosing an evolutionary development strategy.

- If the **robustness** of the product is required to be high, then an evolutionary strategy implies a high risk and a waterfall strategy would be more appropriate, possibly preceded by a risk reduction process to resolve uncertainty about requirements or product architecture.

- If the **available technology** includes commercial off-the-shelf software (COTS), fourth-generation languages or program transformation systems, and if these cover the growth envelope of the product, then these are the preferred implementation technology. Alternatively, a development strategy that adapts the requirements to

System objectives, constraints			Available product alternatives		Development strategy	Example
Growth envelope	Understanding of requirements	Robustness	Available technology	Architecture understanding		
Limited			COTS		Buy	Simple inventory control
Limited			4GL or transformational		Transformational or evolutionary development	Small business data processing application
Limited	Low	Low		Low	Evolutionary prototyping	Advanced pattern recognition
Limited to large	High	High		High	Waterfall	Rebuild of old product
	Low	High			Risk reduction followed by waterfall	Complex situation assessment
		High		Low	Risk reduction followed by waterfall	High performance avionics
Limited to medium	Low	Low to medium		High	Evolutionary development	New decision support system
Limited to large			Large reusable components	Medium to high	Capabilities-to-requirements	Electronic publishing
Very large					Risk reduction followed by waterfall	Air traffic control
Medium to large	Low	Medium	Partial COTS	Low to medium	Spiral	Software support environment

Figure 16.3: Decision table for development strategies [41]. Reproduced by permission of IEEE Computer Society Press, 1989.

Development situation	Development strategy
Fixed budget or schedule available	Design-to-cost or schedule
Early capability needed	
Limited staff or budget available	
Downstream requirements poorly understood	Incremental delivery
High-risk system nucleus	
Large to very large application	
Required phasing with product increments	

Figure 16.4: Additional decision table for orthogonal development strategy alternatives [41]. Only one of the conditions need be present for the incremental delivery strategy. Reproduced by permission of IEEE Computer Society Press, 1989.

the capabilities offered by the available implementation technology may also be appropriate.

- A low level of **architecture understanding** implies a high risk of following the waterfall strategy. Conversely, a high level of architecture understanding lowers the risk that the evolutionary strategy will result in radical revisions of the product architecture.

Example. Suppose that we must select a development strategy for a computerized administration for a library circulation desk, which currently has a manual administration. The development must be performed according to a strict budget and schedule and will be performed by a company specialized in library software systems. Looking at the spiral method heuristics, we note the following.

The growth envelope is limited, understanding of requirements can be assumed to be high. Desired robustness of the system can be assumed to be high, so that evolutionary prototyping is not an option. Depending upon available technology, buying or development by means of fourth-generation tools are possible options. However, due to the strict budget and schedule restrictions, design-to-cost, design-to schedule and incremental delivery are also options. Due to the high level of understanding of requirements, the pressure to follow the incremental delivery is low. We are left with a choice (or combination) of buying, 4GL development and design-to-cost or schedule.

16.2.4 Evaluation of the spiral model

The spiral model is an effort to combine the advantages of other development strategies. Like evolutionary delivery, it helps us to deal with changing requirements, and like incremental delivery, it allows us to deliver the most useful portions of the product first. Boehm mentions three disadvantages of the spiral model:

- It is hard to see how such a flexible development strategy could be used for external software projects, for which a contract with a customer is required. There is no clear process with milestones at which certain intermediary products are delivered.

- The spiral model heavily relies on the capability of the development manager to identify and manage development risks. This is however a difficult task which, if done wrong, directs the development process in the wrong direction.

- There is a danger that different participants in the development process have different, mutually inconsistent pictures of the development process. This makes the spiral process difficult to manage.

16.3   Euromethod

The Euromethod project was initiated by the Commission of the European Community in 1989, and delivered version 0 of its product in 1994, also called **Euromethod**. Euromethod is a method to regulate the interactions between suppliers and customers of information systems. It is intended to bridge the differences between development methods used by suppliers and customers in the European Community. This section is based on the documentation of version 0 of Euromethod [274, 270, 275, 271, 273, 266, 267, 268, 269, 272].

16.3.1   Structure

The core of Euromethod consists of two sets of guidelines:

- **Method bridging** guidelines, that can be used to describe the development methods of information system suppliers in a uniform terminology, so that they can be compared.

- **Delivery planning** guidelines, by which one can define a sequence of customer-supplier transactions during the development process.

Euromethod focuses on the **Information System (IS) adaptation** process, which is a process in which an information system is updated to reflect changed customer requirements. The term "adaptation" deliberately ignores the difference between initial development and perfective maintenance of an information system, because in both these cases there always is some initial information system. An information system may go through several adaptations after initial construction, and different adaptations may be performed by different suppliers.

Figure 16.5 shows a sequence of customer-supplier transactions envisaged by Euromethod for one IS adaptation process [267]. The sequence starts with a **tendering process** in which a customer selects a supplier to perform the adaptation. During the tendering process, the customer and potential suppliers negotiate about the nature of the adaptation to be performed, about the strategy to be followed by the adaptation and about the product development methods to be used during adaptation. The tendering process ends in the selection of a supplier that will perform the adaptation. This supplier is awarded the contract. The process then continues with a number of **customer-supplier transactions** as laid down in the contract. If the adaptation is successful, the transaction sequence is terminated by a **completion process**.

Part of the tendering process is the selection of the strategy to be followed in the IS adaptation. We focus on this part and leave other aspects, such as method bridging, out of consideration. Strategy selection starts with the determination of the number of adaptations that are required, given the initial state and final state of the desired information system adaptation. Figure 16.6 gives the Euromethod version 0 heuristics for this decision [270, page 34]. These are not decision rules, i.e. customer and supplier can deviate from them

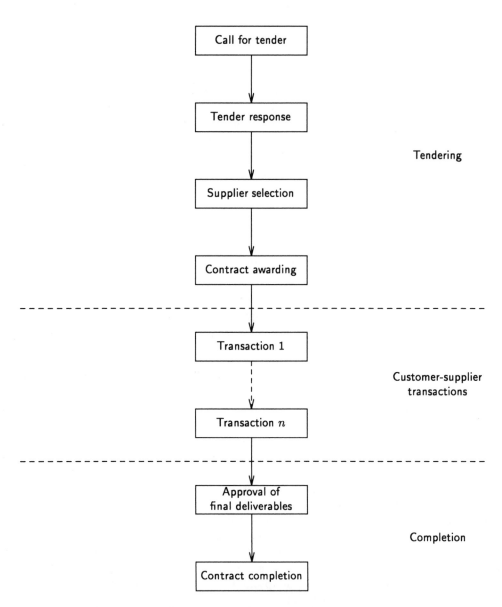

Figure 16.5: Customer-supplier transactions in Euromethod.

		Final state						
		Information system documentation	Information system change study	Computer system change study	Detailed business design	Detailed technical design	Tested information system	Installed information system
Initial state	Undocumented information system	x	x	x	!	!	!	!
	Documented information system	x	x	x	!	!	!	!
	Problem description	—	x	x	x	!	!	!
	Global design	—	x	x	x	x	!	!
	Detailed business design	—	—	—	x	x	x	x
	Detailed technical design	—	—	—	—	x	x	x
	Tested information system	—	—	—	—	—	x	x

Key: x   Performing a single IS adaptation usually suffices
      !   Split the adaptation process or plan for explicit contract change control
      —   Invalid combination

Figure 16.6: Heuristics for the determination of the number of required information system adaptations [270]. Reproduced by permission of the Euromethod Project, 1994.

when they find reason to do so. This observation holds for all heuristics provided by Euromethod.

16.3.2   Strategies

For each adaptation process, a situational analysis is performed to determine the strategy to be followed during the adaptation. The definition of a strategy results in the definition of a sequence of customer-supplier transactions that must be executed during the adaptation. In each transaction, deliverables are exchanged between supplier and customer and, possibly, the contract between supplier and customer is renegotiated.

Euromethod distinguishes four approaches for which a strategic option must be selected [269, pages 36–47]:

- The **system description** strategy options are to use an **analytical** mode of description, in which the developers write documents that specify system behavior, or else to use the **experimental** mode of description, in which developers perform experiments to learn about the system. Independently from this the developers have the option to follow an **expert-driven** cooperation mode, in which they produce descriptions of the system based on interviews and observations of system users, or to follow a **participatory** mode, in which users or their representatives are included in the development process.

- The **system construction** options are one-shot, incremental and evolutionary construction. The concepts are the same as those introduced in chapter 15 but with a slightly different terminology:

  - In **one-shot construction**, the system is constructed and tested as a whole.

  - In **incremental construction**, requirements of the system are determined first and the system is then constructed and tested incrementally.

  - In **evolutionary construction**, the system is constructed and tested in successive versions. Between two versions, the requirements can be changed after learning from system testing.

- The **system installation** options are linear, incremental and evolutionary installation.

  - In **one-shot installation**, the entire system is installed at once. The system may be *constructed* using a one-shot, incremental, or evolutionary strategy.

  - In **incremental installation**, the system is installed in portions. Requirements to the system are fixed before the first installation. This approach can be combined with one-shot construction as well as with incremental construction, and it can be combined with evolutionary construction if before the first installation, we evolve the requirements to the point where we can fix them.

  - In **evolutionary installation**, the system is installed in successive versions and the requirements to the system can change after the first installation and between successive installations. This approach can be combined with evolutionary construction but not with one-shot or incremental construction.

- **Project control**. There are three groups of choices to be made:

  - **Development control**. A choice can be made between frequent or infrequent customer-supplier transactions, between formal and informal control procedures, and between a high and a low degree of customer responsibility for development control.

  - **Quality control**. This consists of a choice of activities and techniques to be used for quality assurance.

  - **Configuration control**. This consists of a choice of activities and techniques for configuration management.

In this chapter, we focus on the heuristics given in Euromethod version 0 for the selection of a construction strategy.

16.3.3 Situational factors

Euromethod gives an extensive list of situational factors that are relevant in the selection of development strategies. The **problem situation** is the situation in which an organization has recognized the need for an information system adaptation and is seeking a supplier to perform the adaptation. Each problem situation is characterized by its uncertainty and complexity [269, page 16]:

- **Uncertainty** is defined as the lack of knowledge about the problem situation.

- **Complexity** is defined as the difficulty of handling available knowledge about the problem situation.

To determine the uncertainty and complexity of a problem situation, the Euromethod project has compiled a list of **situational factors** that characterize the problem situation, and provides a list of heuristics on how these factors influence uncertainty and complexity (figures 16.8 and 16.9). The uncertainty and complexity of the problem situation in turn determine the risk of not getting sufficient benefits from the IS adaptation process to justify the cost of the process. This risk also depends upon individual situational factors directly. Figure 16.7 [271] summarizes the relationships between situational factors, complexity, uncertainty and risks.

Figures 16.8 and 16.9 list all factors considered in Euromethod version 0 and their influence on the uncertainty and complexity of the problem situation [271, pages 30–31]. Attributes of the developed product are called **target domain factors** and are listed in figure 16.8. Attributes of the development process are called **project domain factors** and are listed in figure 16.9. The Euromethod list of situational factors was compiled after an extensive study of the literature on the situational approach to development, and can be considered as the state of the art of situational development. Precise descriptions of the meaning of the factors and references to the literature where they are proposed, are found in the Euromethod documentation [269].

Following the lines of influences in figure 16.7, complexity and uncertainty are major determinants of risk. Figure 16.10 lists the risks that may exist in a complex problem situation [271, pages 32–33] and figure 16.11 lists the risks that may exist in an uncertain problem situation. The uncertainty risks are ordered such that the later the risk occurs in

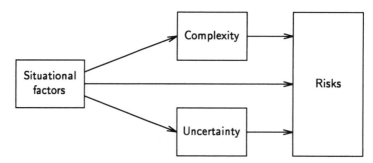

Figure 16.7: The relationships between situational factors, complexity, uncertainty and risks. The arrows indicate influence.

the list, the lower the probability that the danger identified by the risk materializes early in the development process.

As indicated in figure 16.7, the chance that a risk materializes may be increased by individual situational factors. For example, if the attitude of the actors in the information system is negative (situational factor), then there is a large danger that target domain actors do not participate in the adaptation process (risk) and that acceptance of the product is low (risk). The *Euromethod Delivery Planning Guide* [271] gives a detailed list of possible influences of situational factors on uncertainty risks.

16.3.4   Strategy selection heuristics

Based on an assessment of the problem situation, two groups of measures can be taken to reduce the risks of the adaptation process [271, pages 39–62] (figure 16.12):

- **Changes to the situational factors**. For example, when the attitude of the actors is negative, one can try to involve them or to explain the benefits of the system to them.

- **Selection of an IS adaptation strategy that will reduce risk**. This consists of three subgroups of measures:

  - Selection of the strategy options for description, construction, installation and project control. As an example, figure 16.13 gives the Euromethod heuristics for the selection of a construction strategy.

  - Selection of additional measures for reducing the uncertainty of the problem situation. For example, when there is a risk of infeasible requirements, one can decide to use a participatory adaptation approach, investigate similar information systems elsewhere, create a good understanding of the current system etc.

  - Selection of additional measures for reducing the complexity of the problem situation. For example, when the heterogeneity of the actors is high, one can adopt a participatory approach to system description, and one can explicitly define the customer's responsibility in reconciling the different interests of the actors.

The reason for selection of a particular construction strategy is that it reduces risks. For example, incremental construction may reduce the following risks [271, pages 48–49]:

Target domain	Complexity	Simple	Mode-rate	Complex	Uncertainty	Certain	Mode-rate	Uncer-tain
Information system	Heterogeneity of actors	Low	Medium	High	Attitude of actors	Positive	Neutral	Negative
	Size of target domain	Small	Medium	Large	Ability of actors	High	Medium	Low
	Size of distribution	Small	Medium	Large	Stability of environment	High	Medium	Low
	Complexity of information	Low	Medium	High	Formality of information	High	Medium	Low
	Complexity of business processes	Low	Medium	High	Formality of business processes	High	Medium	Low
					Stability of information and business processes	High	Medium	Low
					Specificity of information system	Low	Medium	High
					Understandability of existing system	High	Medium	Low
					Strategic importance	Low	Medium	High
					Importance of organizational changes	Low	Medium	High
					Availability, clarity and stability of the requirements	High	Medium	Low
					Quality of existing specifications	High	Medium	Low
Computer system	Complexity of data	Low	Medium	High	Importance of technological changes	Low	Medium	High
	Complexity of functions	Low	Medium	High				
	Complexity of nonfunctional requirements	Low	Medium	High				
	Number of replications of the computer system	One	Few	Many				
	Complexity of target technology	Low	Medium	High	Novelty of target technology	Low	Medium	High

Figure 16.8: Target domain factors and their influence on uncertainty and complexity [270]. Reproduced by permission of the Euromethod Project, 1994.

Project domain	Complexity	Simple	Mode-rate	Complex	Uncertainty	Certain	Mode-rate	Uncer-tain
Project task	Size of project	Small	Medium	Large	Novelty of IS application	Low	Medium	High
	Complexity of migration	Low	Medium	High	Adequacy of schedules	—	Normal	Tight
					Adequacy of budget	—	Normal	Tight
Project structure	Number of sub-contractors	None	Few	Many	Dependency on subcontractors	None	Low	High
	Number of interfaces to other IS adaptations	None	Few	Many	Dependency on other IS adaptations	None	Low	High
					Formality of customer-supplier context	High	Medium	Low
Project actors	Number of project actors	Small	Medium	Large	Capability of project actors	High	Medium	Low
Project technology	Complexity of development technology	Low	Medium	High	Novelty of development technology	Low	Medium	High
					Availability of appropriate development technology	High	Medium	Low

Figure 16.9: Project domain factors and their influence on uncertainty and complexity [270]. Reproduced by permission of the Euromethod Project, 1994.

- Loss of control of the project
- The information system is not working
- The information system is not capable of dealing with the complexity of its target domain (i.e. with the complexity of its UoD or of its immediate environment).

Figure 16.10: Complexity risks identified by Euromethod [270]. Reproduced by permission of the Euromethod Project, 1994.

- Uncertain or unfeasible requirements
- Uncertain interfaces to other systems
- Evolving requirements
- Unpredictable costs for the organization
- Unpredictable costs for the project
- Lack of target domain actor participation (e.g. lack of participation by users, domain specialists or customer representatives)
- Technical shortfalls in externally performed tasks
- Delays in the delivery of products.
- Poor quality of products
- Increased cost of the project
- Integration problems
- Shortfalls in nonfunctional properties
- Straining computer science capabilities
- Developing the wrong system or an unfeasible system
- The information system adaptation is not accepted by the IS-actors (e.g. by users or the customer)
- Business implications of project failure

Figure 16.11: Uncertainty risks identified by Euromethod [270]. Reproduced by permission of the Euromethod Project, 1994.

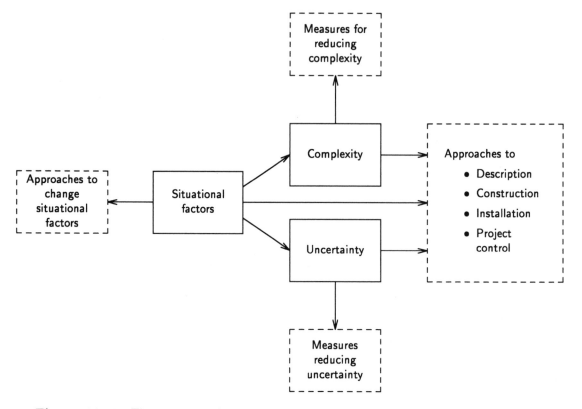

Figure 16.12: The measures that can be taken based on an assessment of the problem situation. The dashed boxes indicate decisions to be made by the developer.

- Evolutionary construction is suitable when the situation is uncertain.

- Incremental construction is suitable when the situation is complex but not uncertain.

- Incremental and evolutionary are suitable when the development schedule is tight.

- One-shot construction is suitable when the schedule is normal and the situation is not complex or uncertain.

Figure 16.13: Euromethod heuristics to select a construction strategy [270]. Reproduced by permission of the Euromethod Project, 1994.

- Loss of control of the project

- Unpredictable costs for the organization

- Unpredictable costs for the project

- Poor quality of products

- Increased cost of the project

- Integration problems

- Shortfalls in nonfunctional properties

Evolutionary construction may reduce the following risks:

- Uncertain or unfeasible requirements

- Uncertain interfaces to other systems

- Evolving requirements

- Unpredictable costs for the project

- Delays in the delivery of products

- Poor quality of products

- Increased cost of the project

- Integration problems

- Shortfalls in nonfunctional properties

- Straining computer science capabilities

- Developing the wrong system or an unfeasible system

Example. We take the same development situation as in the spiral method example, the development of a computerized administration for a library circulation desk, which currently has a manual administration. The development must be performed according to a strict budget and schedule and will be performed by a company specialized in library software systems. Looking at the Euromethod heuristics, we note the following.

The initial state is an undocumented information system and the final state is an installed information system. According to figure 16.6, this should be split into several adaptation processes. However, because the problem is well-understood (some software vendors specialize in library administration systems) and the customer can be expected to be able to state his requirements, a single adaptation process is decided.

Looking at the target domain factors, we see that the information system complexity factors all score on the simple side and that most information system uncertainty factors score on the certain side. However, the strategic importance of the system is high and the quality of existing specifications is low, which increases the uncertainty about the system. The complexity and uncertainty of the computer system are low. Project domain factors all tend towards low complexity and low uncertainty, except the adequacy of budget and schedules, which tends to high uncertainty. Due to the high level of experience of the software companies doing the development, a one-shot construction strategy is decided.

16.3.5   Evaluation of Euromethod

At the date of writing (1995), Euromethod is being evaluated by potential users of the method in the European Union and it is too early to collect any results. The results of these experiments will be incorporated in an improved version of the method.

Comparing Euromethod with the spiral method, we observe that Euromethod contains method bridging in addition to a process model for strategy selection. A comparison between the two methods must therefore be restricted to the strategy selection part.

The second observation to be made is that both methods recommend a repeated selection of a strategy. However, in Euromethod this takes place as part of contract negotiations for a series of IS adaptations. Renegotiation of the strategy requires renegotiation of the contract and will therefore be the exception rather than the rule. As a consequence, two of the three disadvantages of the spiral method noted at the end of section 16.2 are avoided:

- Euromethod can be used for external software projects, because it allows the definition of a clear development process with milestones and deliverables.

- Like the spiral method, it places a high premium on the ability of the project manager to assess the development situation. This responsibility is shared by the customer and supplier during the tendering process.

- Because of strict control of customer-supplier transactions, there is less danger than in the spiral method that different participants in the development process have different pictures of the process.

A third observation about the spiral method and Euromethod is that the space of strategies to choose from differs in both methods. We restricted ourselves to the selection of a construction strategy in Euromethod. There is a small number of mutually exclusive alternatives to be considered (one-shot, incremental and evolutionary). The same holds for the other choices to be made in Euromethod (system description, system installation and project control). By contrast, the spiral method uses a large space of strategies, which are not mutually exclusive. Choice between these options is therefore less structured than it is in Euromethod.

16.4   Summary

The *spiral method* consists of an iteration of process engineering, in which a development strategy is selected, and product engineering, in which part of the product is developed according to the selected strategy. The selection of the strategy is done on the basis of a risk analysis and may be redone whenever the changed development situation calls for this. Boehm gives a number of heuristics to select a strategy based on such situational factors as the growth envelope of the system, the understanding of the requirements, the required robustness of the system, understanding of the architecture.

Euromethod provides a framework in which a supplier and customer enter into a contract to perform one or more IS adaptations. One part of this contract is the selection of the development strategy that is to be followed during the adaptation. Euromethod distinguishes strategies for system description, system construction, system installation and project control. It gives heuristics for selecting among these based on a thorough analysis of situational factors. The situational factors are partitioned into target domain and project domain factors and include those identified by Boehm. Euromethod also gives heuristics to change these factors or to reduce the uncertainty and complexity that arises from these factors.

16.5   Exercises

1. Map the logical structure of the spiral method (figure 16.2) to the structure of the spiral method (figure 16.1).

2. Explain the strategy selection heuristics given by Boehm (figures 16.3 and 16.4).

3. Explain the construction strategy selection heuristics of Euromethod (figure 16.13).

4. Use the heuristics given in figure 16.13 to construct a decision table that recommends a construction strategy for each possible combination of values for the situational factors *schedule, complexity* and *certainty*. The possible values for each of these factors are *schedule* $\in$ {*normal, tight*}, *complexity* $\in$ {*simple, moderate, complex*} and *uncertainty* $\in$ {*certain, moderate, uncertain*}.

5. For each of the following situations, select a development strategy according to the spiral method heuristics and according to the Euromethod heuristics. In the case of Euromethod, recommend the number of IS adaptations to be performed. Motivate the choices you make and explain the differences between the selected strategies, if any.

   (a) The improvement of an elevator control system currently implemented in a system of electromagnetic switches, by a company that produces elevator systems. The system should be able to control several elevators such that they jointly give optimal service to the elevator users.

   (b) The development of an EDI system that connects the different local police departments in The Netherlands. In the past, each department has, independently from other departments, automatized some of its administrative tasks. The desired EDI network should allow uniform exchange of information about incidents (e.g. traffic accidents, burglaries) and persons (e.g. violators, criminals). Flexibility should be built in to allow smooth transition to integration into a European network, should such a network become mandatory in the future. The process to realize the national network shall take several years and there will be yearly reviews, at which budgets and schedules will be reconsidered.

16.6   Bibliographical Remarks

Strategy selection methods.   An early proposal for strategy selection is given by McFarlan [223]. Heuristics for strategy selection geared to the development of information systems are given by Shomenta *et al.* [310], Davis [81] and Naumann, Davis and McKeen [241]. These have all been used to produce the list of situational factors in Euromethod.

The spiral model. The spiral process was proposed by Boehm [39, 42]. Experience with the spiral model is reported in Belz [28] and Wolff [370]. In two later papers, Boehm [35, 41] added the explicit process engineering task and gave a decision table for choosing appropriate strategies. This table is given in figures 16.3 and 16.4.

As presented here, the essence of the spiral method is not the fact that the process by which we converge on a finished product can be represented by a spiral, but that during this process, we can adapt our development strategy to the changes in perceived risks. As stated in chapter 3, any problem-solving process can be represented by a spiral. Indeed, Hubka and Eder [150, page 35] represent the structure of the design process by a spiral process that converges on a finished product.

Euromethod The Euromethod documentation consists of ten short manuals, divided into four groups:

1. *Euromethod Overview* [274]

2. Euromethod Guides.

   - *Euromethod Customer Guide* [270]
   - *Euromethod Supplier Guide* [275]
   - *Euromethod Delivery Planning Guide* [271]
   - *Euromethod Method Bridging Guide* [273]
   - *Euromethod Case Study* [266]

3. Euromethod concept manuals.

   - *Euromethod Concepts Manual 1: Transaction Model* [267]
   - *Euromethod Concepts Manual 2: Deliverable Model* [268]
   - *Euromethod Concepts Manual 3: Strategy Model* [269]

4. *Euromethod Dictionary* [272]

The Euromethod Guides form the heart of the Euromethod documentation. The Customer and Supplier Guides are manuals to be used by the customer and supplier in the information system development process. The Method Bridging Guide explains how a method supplier can describe his method in the Euromethod terminology, so that customers can compare methods used by different suppliers in a tendering process. The Delivery Planning Guide explains the strategy selection process and shows how the sequence of customer-supplier transactions can be planned. The Case Study contains two examples of Euromethod application. The Concepts Manuals, finally, contain more detailed information about specific issues, such as the structure of customer-supplier transactions, the structure of deliverables, and the description of situational factors.

Appendix A

Answers to Selected Exercises

Chapter 2: Systems

1. (a) The function of the grinder for its users is to grind coffee beans. (b) The environment of the system consists of its users, the electrical power supply, and the surrounding air. The interface to the user consists of the following interactions: accept an on or off transaction from the switch, switch light on or off, accept a volume of coffee beans, produce a volume of ground coffee. The interface to the electrical power supply is to draw electrical energy from the power plug, and the interface to the surrounding air is to produce waste heat. (c) The system is hybrid.

2. At the highest level, the interface consists of the transaction *sell grocery*. This is the way a branch organization would look at the store: the only relevant thing the branch organization wants to know about the store is that it sells grocery. At the next lower level, we observe interactions like *sell bacon* and *sell cheese*. This is the way the customer looks at the store: he or she wants to know which grocery can be bought at the store. At the next lower level, we can observe transactions like *enter shop*, *walk to shelf*, *get packet of cheese*, etc. This is the way an operations researcher may look at the store, who is interested in finding out the optimal placement of the shelves, of the goods on the shelves, etc.

6. The two diagrams represent different behaviors, because in diagram (a), the action c is nondeterministic: it may lead to one out of a set of two possible next states. From one of these states, action b can occur, and from the other d can occur. In diagram (b), the action c is deterministic: it leads to exactly one state, from which a choice between b and d can be made. Thus, the moment of choice is different in the diagrams.

Chapter 3: Product Development

1. (a) The client is the aircraft vendor. If the software is market-produced, the sponsor is the vendor of the software and the customer is the aircraft building company; otherwise the sponsor and customer is the aircraft building company. The user is the pilot of the aircraft.

   (b) The sponsor is the DBMS vendor. The client of the development process and customer of the DBMS is the buyer of the DBMS, the user is the person who must install and maintain the DBMS.

(c) The client and customer is the buyer of the software. The sponsor is the software vendor and the user is the library employee at the circulation desk.

(d) The client, sponsor and customer is the government in the form of the ministry of defense. The users are the officials who query the database.

2. (a) (1) Informal reasoning by managers. (2) Pencil and paper sketches. (3) Informal reasoning, performed by the designer about the likely consequences of certain design options. (4) Building a prototype. (5) Performing a trial production.

(b) (1) Informal evaluation after discussion by managers. (2) Informal evaluation after discussion by designers and managers. (3) Comparison with required properties by designers. (4) Performing a consumer experiment. (5) The evaluation criteria are not mentioned in the case study. Examples of criteria are repeatability, reliability and economic feasibility of the process.

3. Because business concerns are transformed into software requirements, this framework applies to the level of computer-based systems. *Elicitation* is the fact-gathering part of needs analysis, *specification* consists of analyzing the gathered facts and of synthesizing it into a requirements specification, and *validation* consists of simulation, evaluation and choice.

6. The finite number of observations of the disturbances were used as evidence for a model of Neptune and its orbit. This orbit contains infinitely many points. The step from the observations to this model is the inductive jump.

7. The correspondence with rational problem solving is as follows: **Problem analysis** corresponds to *suggestions* and *intellectualization*. That is, the subject becomes aware that there are other ways of doing things, that the current way need not be taken for granted, and makes the transition from unreflective and unquestioning doing things the current way to a disengagement, distancing from the current way of doing things, which opens the possibility of reflective thinking; and the subject then starts to analyze the current situation. **Solution generation**: *hypothesis*. **Estimation of effects**: *reasoning*. **Evaluation of effects**: *testing* the hypothesis by action. It is not clear from the description in the exercise whether this action is an experiment or the real thing. **Solution choice** is not listed explicitly in Dewey's process. The process can be viewed as a prescription for reflective action in which we alternate between reflection upon the current situation and performing an action. After the first action is performed, reflection upon the current situation can be viewed as part of the regulatory cycle (observe and evaluate the effects) as well as of a rational problem solving process that prepares for the next action.

8. *Scouting* and *entry* are pre-development tasks that precede the engineering cycle. *Diagnosis* corresponds to **needs analysis**. *Planning* corresponds to **synthesis of product specifications** and **Simulation of specified products**. Kolb and Frohman do not mention **evaluation of effects of simulations** or **choice of specification** explicitly, but these can be viewed as part if their *action* task. Their *evaluation* task is really part of the regulatory cycle. *Termination* is a post-development task that follows the engineering cycle as well as any applications of the regulatory cycle.

Chapter 4: Requirements Specifications

2. (a) In the first iteration, the documented objective was to preserve TANA market share. The alternatives considered were to search new markets for existing products, to develop new products for the same market, and to adjust the marketing mix. The likely effects of these alternatives were simulated and evaluated with respect to the objective by management. The discussion is likely to have been recorded in the form of minutes of a management meeting.

(b) The alternatives considered are listed in figure 3.7. The simulations were their own documentation, because they are paper and pencil sketches. Their evaluations are probably recorded as minutes taken at a meeting in which management evaluated the sketches against the marketing objectives.

Chapter 5: ISAC Change Analysis and Activity Study

2. Figure A.1 gives a solution. The activities are systems with local memory, which resemble the objects of object-oriented modeling. The arrows indicate messages sent by one object to another. This model is simpler than the one in figure 5.8, because it contains less interaction, and the interaction that it contains is essential for the functioning of the system. It has the disadvantage that data are distributed over different activities, whereas in fact they are located in one place (a paper or automated database). The diagram thus has less resemblance than figure 5.8 to the way that work is currently done in the circulation system.

4. Alternative 2 of the library case study (section 5.2.8, the store room alternative), has the same activity model as the current situation.

Chapter 6: Information Strategy Planning

4. See figure A.2 for an example. This is not the only solution; in fact, the tree may differ for different travel agencies.

5. See figure A.3 for one possible solution. A segment is characterized by a point of departure and a point of arrival. A scheduled segment in addition has particular departure and arrival dates and times, which are not represented in the diagram because they are attributes and not entity types. It is not clear from the exercise whether the segments of one flight must be consecutive in space and/or time. A reservation can profit from the price arrangements by reserving a number of segments such that a Saturday night falls in the time between departure from the starting point and departure from the destination. A complex reservation consists of a reservation for several segments. Each complex reservation is a reservation for one person. A complex reservation has a price that depends upon the departure and arrival dates of some of its segments. The price is not shown, because it is an attribute of complex reservation. Return flights have not been modeled explicitly. They can be defined as a view on *FLIGHT* instances, defined by the predicate that the sequence of segments of the flight starts and ends in the same airport.

6. Example subject areas and entity types that belong to those areas are:

   - *CUSTOMERS*: *PERSON*
   - *FLIGHTS*: *AIRPORT, FLIGHT, SEGMENT, SCHEDULED_SEGMENT*
   - *SALES*: *COMPLEX_RESERVATION*

   The *FLIGHTS* subject area corresponds to the products subject area of figure 6.14. Note that there is no reason to stick to the list of example subject areas of figure 6.14. Any partitioning in subject areas that the client agrees with, suffices.

7. See figure A.4. The matrix covers only two of the business areas of the travel agency, Sales and part of the Acquisition business area.

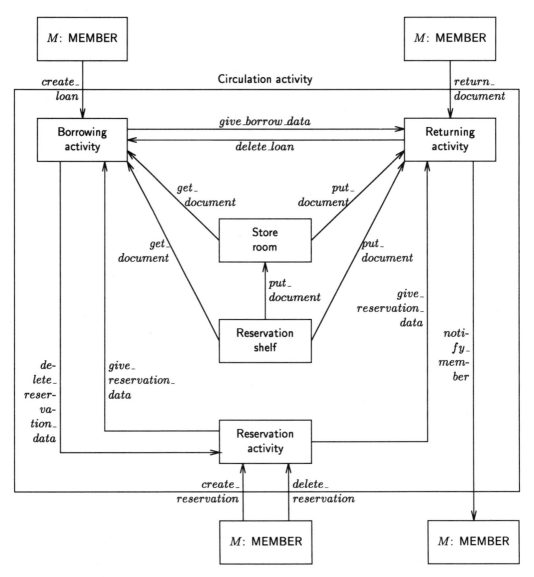

Figure A.1: An activity model of the circulation system that encapsulates memory in the activities.

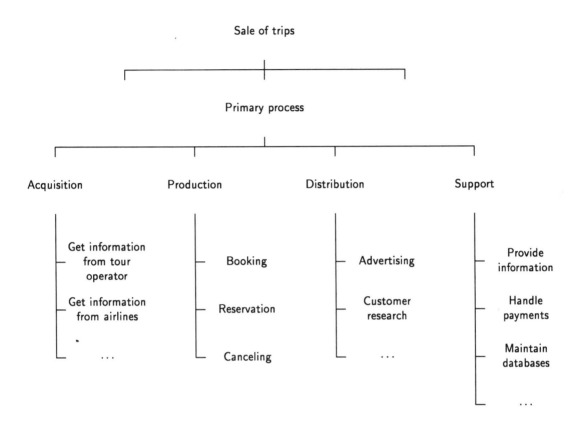

Figure A.2: A function decomposition tree of the primary process of a travel agency.

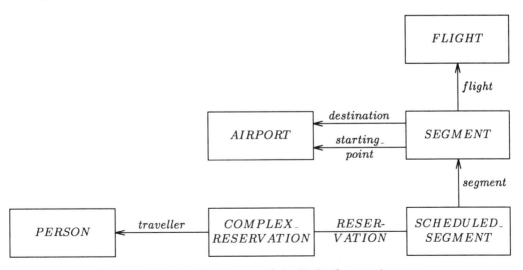

Figure A.3: An ER diagram of the UoD of a travel agency.

Get information from tour operators					
Get information from airlines					
Canceling					
Reservation					
Booking					
PERSON	CR	CR			
COMPLEX_RESERVATION		C	D		
BOOKING	C		D		
FLIGHT		R	R	CUD	
SEGMENT		R	R	CUD	
SCHEDULED_SEGMENT		R	R	CUD	
AIRPORT		R	R	CUD	
......					

Figure A.4: Fragment of a function/entity matrix for a travel agency.

Chapter 7: The Entity-Relationship Approach I: Models

2. In the UoD, each existing airline has at least one existing flight. There exist cities without airports, addresses without people having that address, and flights and people without reservations. The only visible constraint is thus ≥ 1 at the *FLIGHT* side of *airline*.

   In the system, each existing airline has at least one existing flight. We want to represent cities without airports, but we do not want to represent addresses without people. The other cardinalities are the same as in the UoD. Thus, we have ≥ 1 at the *FLIGHT* side of *airline* and ≥ 1 at the *PERSON* side of *address*.

4. The second one cannot be represented, because a cardinality constraint at the root of the arrow *supplier* says how many links can occur in which a single supplier s can occur. It does not and cannot say anything about the number of links in which s and a part p occur.

5. If attribute a is not applicable to some instances of entity type E_1, remove a from the definition of E_1 and define a specialization E_2 of E_1 for which this attribute is defined.

6. Replace a partial function by a relationship in diamond notation.

7. Define a relation *TRANSPORTED_DELIVERY* with components *COMPANY* (playing role *transport_company*) and *DELIVERY*, which itself is a relation with components *COMPANY* (playing role *supplier*), *PART* and *PROJECT*.

8. Turn *LOAN* into an entity type. It then has its own identity and there can be arbitrarily many *LOAN* instances with the same member and document. The cardinality constraints that one member borrows at most 20 documents, and one document is borrowed by at most one member, are not expressible anymore in the diagram.

9. The referential integrity constraint allows the referring key to be *null*. A component of a relationship must never be *null*.

10. If a many-many relationship is transformed into one relational schema, it is not in the fourth normal form. A relationship not in fourth normal form contains two independently varying multi-valued facts. See also Kent [175].

11.   • Less then 100 students follow course CS101 every year. This can be a descriptive regularity in the UoD. Treating this as a constraint on the system, we get a system

that cannot be used in a situation where more than 100 students enroll for CS101. We should only turn this sentence into a system constraint if we can be absolutely sure that the UoD regularity expressed by the sentence will never be falsified.

- Course CS100 is a prerequisite for course CS101. This may or may not be an official rule. If it is not an official rule, it is a descriptive sentence that expresses an observation made of the UoD. If we were to turn this into a system constraint, we would turn this observation into a UoD regularity that will never be falsified; which is a risky decision. If the rule is a UoD constraint and we want to enforce this by means of the system, we should turn it into a system constraint. Exceptions cannot be recorded. If the rule changes, we must then change the system specification.

- Students always follow CS100 before they follow CS101. This may be a consequence of a rule or a consequence of a habit of the students; which habit may follow from the fact that CS100 really is a prerequisite of CS101, even if the rules don't say so. The same considerations as above apply.

Chapter 8: The Entity-Relationship Approach II: Methods

1. The first one can be represented by adding the cardinality ≥ 1 at the root of the arrow $SALE \rightarrow CLIENT$. The other constraint says that the multivalued function $CLIENT \times SHOP \rightarrow\rightarrow PRODUCT$ defined by $SALE$ assigns at most two products to any particular $\langle c, s \rangle$ and this cannot be represented in the diagram.

4. - This is a car: Instance-type relationship.

   - A Ford is a car: is_a relationship.

   - A Ford is a type of car: Instance-type relationship, since "Ford" is now treated as the name of an individual.

   - A teacher is a member of staff: is_a relationship.

5. Add relationships $RECEIVE\_MARK\_FOR\_TEST$ and $FINISH\_TEST$ that represent the events of obtaining a result. The relationships $PRACTICAL\_REG$ and $TEST\_REG$ represent the events of registering for a practical and a test, respectively, and allocation of a $result$ attribute to these events is a type error.

7. The key of the relational schema corresponding to a relationship can now have components that are themselves compound, and referential keys may now also be compound.

Chapter 9: Structured Analysis I: Models

3. (a) Material stores have only two operations: remove and add. Removal is a destructive read and corresponds to the effect of a read and delete operation on a data store. Addition corresponds to a creation operation on a data store. Data stores have non-destructive reads and additionally have an update operation, which is absent from material stores. Material flows move material items just like data flows move data items. However, if masses are manipulated (like water), then the flow is continuous and we need an additional notation to distinguish these from discrete flows. Material manipulations are physical processes that must be specified by means of notations from physics, chemistry, biology, etc. They can be discrete or continuous.

   (b) There is no difference with material manipulation. The dashed line is therefore superfluous and can be replaced by whatever notation is used for material flows.

Event	Response	Transaction
Member requests title reservation	Reserve title	Reserve title
Member requests cancellation of title reservation	Cancel title reservation	Cancel title reservation
Member requests to borrow a document	Lend document	Borrow document
Member requests to extend a document loan	Extend loan	Extend loan
Member returns a document	Accept document return	Return document
Document loan is overdue	Send reminder	Send reminder
Member loses document	Register document loss	Lose document

Figure A.5: Event list for the ciculation administration.

Chapter 10: Structured Analysis II: Methods

1. When a document borrow request is received, the administration must check whether it has been reserved (read access) and if so, whether the borrower is the reserver; if the borrower is not the reserver, the document cannot be borrowed, otherwise a reservation record must be deleted (write access). This is one data store access in which records may be read and updated at the same time.

3. See figure A.5.

4. 1. Feasibility study is a behavior specification process at the level of computer-based systems.

    2.(a)–(c) Structured analysis is a behavior specification process at the level of computer-based systems that makes the result of feasibility study more explicit.

    2.(d)–(i) This is a decomposition process that follows the engineering cycle. A computer-based system is decomposed into manual tasks and software systems. The observable behavior of the software systems is specified.

    3. Structured design is a decomposition process that decomposes software systems into modules.

    4. Structured programming is a decomposition process that decomposes software modules into executable parts.

5. 1. This is a behavior specification process at the level of computer-based systems. Needs analysis is already assumed to have taken place, as this task begins with understanding system objectives that are already previously identified.

    2. Building a processor environment model is a decomposition task as well as a behavior specification task for the units into which the system is decomposed.

    3. Specifying the human-computer interface is a behavior specification task at the level of software systems.

    4. Specifying a software environment model is a decomposition and behavior specification task, in which each unit is decomposed into software subsystems called tasks and the behavior of these tasks is specified.

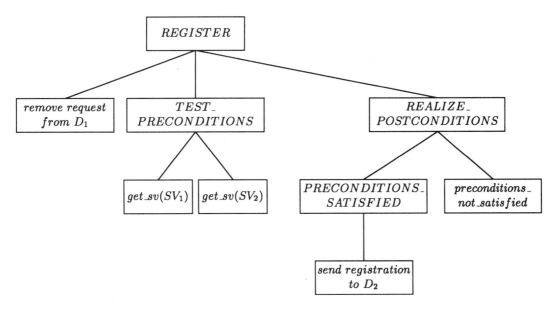

Figure A.6: Outline of a PSD for the $REGISTER$ function.

    5. Structured design is a decomposition of tasks into units of code.

Modern structured development decomposes software systems into tasks, and tasks into modules, where classical structured development decomposes software systems into software modules immediately.

Chapter 11: Jackson System Development I: Models

1. Input: A registration request of student s for test t.
   Precondition: s and t exist and the *register* action can occur in the life of t.
   Postcondition: The registration request has been removed from D_1 and a registration record has been sent to D_3.

   Precondition: s or t do not exist or the *register* action can occur in the life of t.
   Postcondition: The registration request has been removed from D_1 and a refusal has been sent to D_2.

   Figure A.6 gives an outline of the $REGISTER$ PSD.

2. The $REPORT$ subtree of the $LATE$ PSD is a short-running version of $LATE$. The connection cardinality must be changed so that the ≥ 0 cardinality is on the $LATE$ side.

   To turn $ACCT\_HISTORY$ into a long-running function, make the short-running function one iteration in a process that is triggered by the arrival of a *historical_query*. The connection cardinality changes so that one $ACCT\_HISTORY$ instance is connected to many $ACCOUNT$ instances.

3. This requires addition of a JSD entity $REGISTRATION$. In ER terms, this is a relationship between the ER entity type $STUDENT$ and the ER entity type $TEST$. The *register* action is the creation action for this relationship. The $REGISTER$ function of figure 11.21 is a function process that performs the input transactions in which this creation action is executed. The PSD of $REGISTRATION$ is trivial and consists of a sequence *register*;

perform; *mark*. We should add the *perform* action to the *TEST* life cycle as well. The *REGISTRATION* life cycle then shares all its actions with the *TEST* life cycle but enforces an ordering per test–student pair.

4. What is required is that allocation must be a synchronous communication between *ROOM* and *ALLOCATE* instances. Turn the data stream D_2 into a controlled data stream that locks a *ROOM* instance, observes the state of the instance, and then updates the *ROOM* instance.

Chapter 12: Jackson System Development II: Methods

1. This requires a periodic function process that scans all outstanding reservation processes and cancels those that are past their final date. The connection with the reservation processes must be by controlled data stream, because the deletion is conditional upon the state of the deleted processes.

2. The structure of *D_RESERVATION* is the same as that for *T_RESERVATION*. There are now two *res_borrow* actions, *t_res_borrow* and *d_res_borrow*, and the normal *borrow* action has an extended precondition that tests that none of these other cases is true.

3. The *FINE* life cycle now starts with a *lose* action and continues with an iteration over *lose* and *pay* actions. A fine is only created upon the first document loss.

4. This is a historical query that is periodically triggered by a temporal event. It is therefore a long-running function. Because it is a historical query, we cannot scan model processes on their current state using a state vector connection, but we must keep a log of the relevant action occurrences in a data stream. In addition, the function process will take input from the clock, to be able to notice the end of a week. The system network and a possible process structure for the periodic borrowing report function are shown in figure A.7. This process assumes that there is always at least one borrowing in a week. If this assumption cannot be made, a provision for a null report must be added, similar to the *null* action of F1. The *LOAN* process must be extended with the action *add borrow to borrow_stream* immediately after the *borrow(* and *borrow_res* actions (figure 12.7).

Chapter 13: A Framework for Requirements Engineering I: Models

1. (a) There is not enough information to put any other constraint in the model than $n \geq 0$.

    (b) A possible subject area *PRODUCT_OBJECTIVE* is the tree whose root is *GOAL*. The rest is then part of the subject area *PRODUCT_ENVIRONMENT*.

2. Figure A.8 gives a possible trace of a model containing one student s, one course c and one test t. Each column shows a history of an object, with the earliest action occurrences at the top. Synchronization by common actions is indicated by horizontal lines. Actions in the history of different objects not connected by a horizontal line may occur in any order (compatible with the synchronization points). The student receives a mark twice, without doing a test in between. This possibility remains when there are many students, many courses and many tests.

4. (a) Figure A.9 shows part of a specification of a simulation of a data stream. The connected processes are represented by external entities. The data store contains records labeled by a sequence number, that indicates the sequence in which they were put in. It

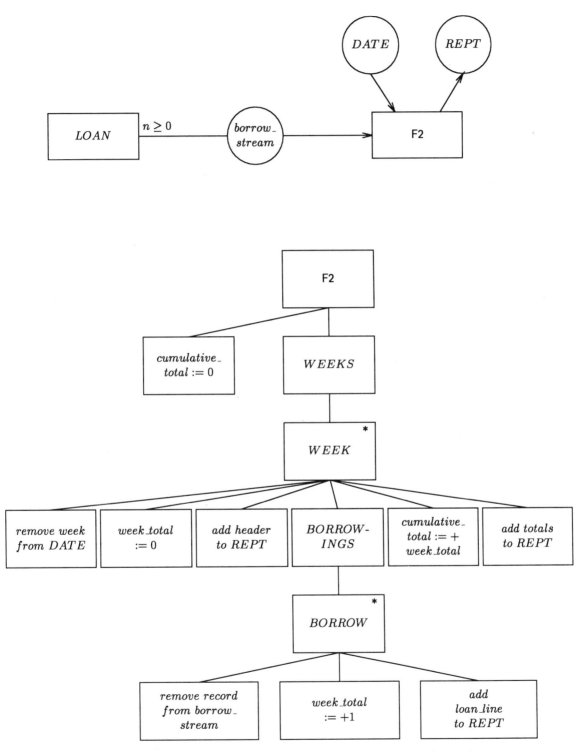

Figure A.7: System network and process structure for the periodic borrowing report.

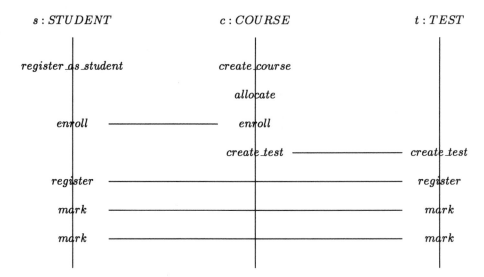

Figure A.8: A possible history of the student administration.

starts with the next sequence number to be given out and then contains the set of records written to it but not yet removed. This model cannot simulate the case where records are not stored but passed immediately, because addition and removal are then one atomic action. In the DF simulation, they are two atomic activities (functional primitives) performed in sequence. Moreover, The DF simulation cannot adequately represent the cardinality of the data stream connection.

(b) Figure A.10 shows a simulation of a controlled data stream. Records are passed immediately, depending upon the current state of the receiver. The conditional update is a functional primitive and is therefore atomic. (Just like the controlled data stream connection in JSD, it may have to wait till the observed process sends it its state vector.) However, it cannot represent the cardinality of the connection.

5. (a) Each JSD entity type corresponds to a JSD entity type or to a relationship. To complete it, we should check whether there are relevant actions in the remaining ER entity types and relationships.

(b) Each functional primitive corresponds to a JSD action in the UoD model. There are some minor differences in naming, due to the difference in perspectives of JSD and DF modeling, that can be easily resolved.

(c) Figure A.11 contains the DF diagram and the minispecs. The minispecs use pseudocode that is sufficiently clear for a programmer to code the functions.

Chapter 14: A Framework for Requirements Engineering II: Methods

1. As explained in subsection 12.2.1, the action allocation table omits all R's because these represent the testing of preconditions. As indicated by the action allocation heuristics in

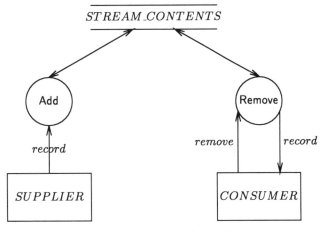

$STREAM\_CONTENTS = next\_sequence\_nr + 0\{record\}next\_sequence\_nr - 1$
$next\_sequence\_nr = NATURAL$
$record = sequence\_nr + \cdots$
$trigger = $ "Remove record"

Add
Read *record* from $SUPPLIER$,
read value of $next\_sequence\_nr$ from $STREAM\_CONTENTS$,
write value of $next\_sequence\_nr + record$ to $STREAM\_CONTENTS$
increase $next\_sequence\_nr$ by 1 and
write it to $STREAM\_CONTENTS$.

Remove
Read *trigger*,
Read *record* with highest $sequence\_nr$ from $STREAM\_CONTENTS$,
Remove this *record*,
Write it to $CONSUMER$.

Figure A.9: A DF simulation of a data stream.

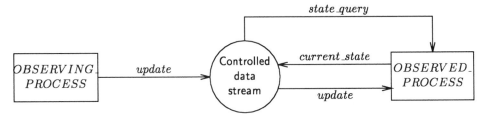

Conditional update:
Read *update* from $OBSERVING\_PROCESS$,
write *state_query* to $OBSERVED\_PROCESS$,
read *current_state* from $OBSERVED\_PROCESS$,
if *current_state* satisfies the update condition of the controlled data stream
then write *update* to $OBSERVED\_PROCESS$.

Figure A.10: A DF simulation of a controlled data stream.

F1:
Each day at 9:00 do:
search $LOANS$ for records with $date\_last\_reminded \le today - 6\ weeks,$
for each of these,
        read $pass\_nr$ of member from the record,
        write $suspend$ to this member in $MEMBERS.$

Figure A.11: DF diagrams and minispecs of F1.

figure 12.3, testing the state vector of an entity type is not sufficient reason for allocating the action to that entity.

Chapter 15: Development Strategies

2. (a) To generalize to arbitrary client-driven development, replace the programming task by the construction task.

     (b) To change it into a market-driven strategy, the acceptance test is performed by the marketing department. Often, this is followed by β testing at selected customer sites, after which a release follows.

3. (a) Specification of required properties, performed during the initial stages of development.

     (b) Planning, performed during the initial stage of development.

     (c) Producing a user's manual is part of product development when the product to be delivered consists not only of executable software but is an installed system. It is performed during the implementation stages, starting from architectural design.

     (d) This is part of architectural design, as a preparation for the selection of algorithms in the next stage.

     (e) This is part of the programming task.

     (f) This is a task belonging to organizational implementation of the developed product.

     (g) This is part of the coding task, performed during the initial stage of development.

     (h) This is part of architecture design and performed during the corresponding stage.

5. Just like evolutionary development, the craftsman changes his design (1) in small steps and (2) in response to a mismatch between the product and user requirements that is experienced in actual use. However, (3) in evolutionary development, the product is then changed to reduce this mismatch. Wagons are not so easily changed as software is, and in general the learning experience led to an incrementally changed design for the *next* wagon to be built. In this respect, wagon-making is more truly evolutionary than evolutionary software development. Evolution is the property that *populations* adapt themselves to their ecological niche. As a metaphor, this is more accurate for traditional wagon-making than it is for software development. (4) A second difference is that there is no global product idea, part of this is then worked out. At any point in time, there are already wagons in use. (5) A third difference is that no global design of the wagon is ever made. This means that no global change to the design can be planned, nor can the likely effects of such a change be estimated.

Changes must be local and only incrementally different from designs that are known to work from experience.

The difference with experimental development is (6) that the customer requires a robust product. The livelihood of the customer depends in part on the quality of the product, so the customer doesn't want any surprises. This is another explanation for the incremental nature of design changes.

6. (a) ETHICS only contains product development tasks.

(b) The entire ETHICS method deals with the social system level. The two questions that it tries to answer are: 1. How can the efficiency and job satisfaction needs of the organization unit be met? and 2. How do we decompose the organization unit into social and technical subsystems so that these needs are met?

(c) ETHICS contains an exact match with the engineering cycle: tasks 1 to 9 correspond to **needs analysis**. Tasks 10 and 11 correspond to **synthesis, simulation** and **evaluation**. Task 12 corresponds to **choice**. This ends the correspondence with the engineering cycle. In terms of our development framework, task 13 is a decomposition task that brings us to a lower level of aggregation.

Task 14 implements the design and task 15 evaluates the implementation. Thus, tasks 13, 14 and 15 correspond to the regulatory cycle.

7. (a) All tasks that say which documents must be written and whom to consult at which point in time are process management tasks. In particular, the *assemble report* tasks are process management tasks.

(b) **Social system level**: feasibility study and requirements analysis. **Software system level**: requirements specification. **Decomposition of software system**: investigate technical system options (410, 420). **Software subsystem level**: specify logical design. **Software subsystem decomposition**: physical design.

(c) Feasibility study and requirements analysis are two iterations through the engineering cycle at the social system level. After the preliminary cycle (feasibility study), requirements analysis performs a thorough needs analysis (investigate current environment), generates solutions, simulates and evaluates these (cost/benefit analysis and impact analysis in task 210) and chooses one.

Requirements specification does not match to the engineering cycle. It can be viewed as a conceptual modeling task, in which a vaguely specified solution is modeled more explicitly. This is a descriptive activity; the normative questions have been dealt with in requirements analysis (task 2).

Task 4 (investigate technical system options) is a decomposition that follows the rational problem solving cycle.

Task 5 (specify logical design) is a conceptual modeling task at the level of software subsystems.

Chapter 16: Selecting a Development Strategy

5. (a) *Spiral method.* The growth envelope is limited, understanding of the requirements is high and robustness of the system must be very high. Depending upon available product alternatives, transformational development or waterfall development are possible options.

Euromethod. Although this is an embedded system and not an information system, it is nevertheless illuminating to apply the Euromethod heuristics. The initial state is that there exist requirements for the current generation of control systems. These are well-understood and the project aims at reimplementing these systems using new technology. According to figure 16.6, this should be performed in several adaptations. Due to the high safety requirements and the strategic importance of of the system, risk must be reduced to a minimum. It is decided to perform two adaptations, one in which a global system design is produced and a second one in which this design is implemented.

In both adaptations, the complexity of the manipulated information is low; however, the target domain factor more suitable to this domain is the complexity of the control structure of the system, and this is complex. Furthermore, the strategic importance of the system is high, which increases the uncertainty about the system. Complexity and uncertainty are further increased because the complexity of the target technology is high and the technology is novel. Uncertainty arises in the project domain as well, because the *development* technology is complex and relatively unknown: the company's engineers have little experience with computer technology. All of this leads to the selection of an incremental construction strategy: Requirements are known but will be implemented incrementally for each of the two adaptation processes. Note that the second adaptation process (from global design to implementation) can start as soon as the first process delivered its first increment of the global design and that from that point onwards, there will be two parallel adaptation processes until the global design is finished.

In this example, Euromethod leads to a more conservative advise than the spiral method. This is mainly due to the larger number of factors considered by Euromethod, which leads to a sharper focus on the project risks and thus to more risk-avoidance.

(b) *Spiral method.* The growth envelope is large and the understanding of requirements is low. Robustness of the system must be high and there is, at the higher levels of network technology, no technology of reusable components. (At the lower levels, standard network software is available on the market.) Architecture understanding is low. The spiral method heuristics lead to risk reduction followed by waterfall as one possible strategy, and the full spiral method as another. Due to the high robustness desired of the system, risk reduction followed by waterfall is chosen.

Euromethod The difference between initial and final state leads to a decision to perform more than one adaptation. One possible sequence would be the production of an information system change study first, the production of a global design next, the production of a tested system next, and finally the production of an installed system. For any of these adaptations, the information system complexity factors all score on the high side; the information system uncertainty factors all score on the uncertain side. Due to the many different systems in operation, the complexity of the computer system is high. The uncertainty about the computer system is medium to low, for all computer technology to be used in the project is commercially available. The complexity of the project task is high and the uncertainty of the project is medium to high. The number of interfaces is potentially high. Project uncertainty is also increased by the potential dependency on subcontractors and on other IS adaptations. Given the complexity and uncertainty about the target domain as well as about the project, the project manager would do well to keep the complexity and novelty of the development technology low. In the face of all of this uncertainty, the Euromethod heuristics recommend evolutionary construction.

The difference with the spiral method recommendation can be explained by the fact that risk reduction, recommended by the spiral method, is *always* recommended by Euromethod (we did not treat risk reduction in chapter 16). Furthermore, the sequential nature of the waterfall process is also present in the Euromethod advice to perform several adaptations in sequence. The Euromethod advice can be viewed as a refinement of the spiral method advice by recommending evolutionary construction.

Appendix B

Cases

B.1   The Teaching Administration

A teaching administration maintains data about courses, practicals, tests, examinations and students. Each course and each practical is given regularly and there are one or more tests for each course. An examination consists of a number of tests. The examination is done by doing these tests. Examinations are done once every month and consist of a ceremony in which students receive proof of having passed the examination. When a student hands over proof of having done these tests with sufficient result, he or she has the right to participate in the ceremony.

To be able to do a test for a course, a student must register for the test. Each test has two or more supervisors, who check that the test participants are registered for the test. Students must register for a test at the teaching administration. One day before the test is conducted, the teaching administration produces a list of test participants, and this is given to the supervisors. When students come to a test unregistered, they are sent by the test supervisor to the teaching administration to register. The student receives a late registration slip from the administration, which he or she can show to the supervisor as proof of registration.

There are members of staff, called counselors, whose task it is to monitor student progress and help students when there are problems with their progress. Every six months, the results of all students are aggregated in a report and discussed by student counselors. Students whose progress is too slow, are called to their counselor for advice. In addition, each student receives an advise about study continuation after his or her first year of study. Every year, each student receives a report about his or her results so far.

B.2   The University Library

The functions of the Free University Library are (1) to acquire documents containing information that is of use for scientific research and education, (2) to catalog these documents, (3) make them available, (4) preserve them, and (5) to act as custodian of the documents it acquired. The collection is made available not only for the Free University but for any scientific research or education at all. Other universities and colleges have the right to use the library, and as a matter of fact do so. The only prerequisite for getting registered as a library user is showing a valid proof of identity, so private individuals can use the library as well. However, most users are students or staff at the Free University.

The library is divided into departments that more or less reflect the structure of the university in departments. Thus, there is the Biology library for the faculty of Biology, the Mathematics and Computer Science library for the Faculty of Mathematics and Computer Science, etc. Department libraries are located close to the Faculty they serve. Department libraries are grouped together into Scientific Area libraries. For example, there are α, β and γ areas. Libraries in one scientific area have a common administration.

A user is someone who has a reader's pass. Any student or employee can acquire a pass, as well as citizens who are not otherwise related to the university. A group of employees can also acquire a pass, called a "group pass". There should be one person accountable for the actions of this group, but any member of the group can borrow a book.

The library acquires a wide diversity of items, such as books, journals, series (e.g. the Springer Lecture Notes in Computer Science), Proceedings, internal reports from their own or from other universities, unpublished reports from research laboratories, Ph.D. theses, maps, microfiches, videotapes, old manuscripts, newspapers, microfilms, etc. Some of these are acquired for students (often several copies), most of these are for research purposes. Books themselves can come into a great variety of forms, such as multivolume works, multi-edition works, and even works that appear as one volume in one edition and as several volumes in the next — after which only volume 1 goes through successive editions.

Most books can be lent to users, but some can only be read in special rooms. Similarly, old volumes of journals, when bound, can be borrowed, but loose issues cannot be borrowed. Borrowable items receive a unique code so that they can be traced to a borrower.

A user can borrow a book for three weeks. Researchers can in addition borrow it for three months. At the end of the allowed lending period, a user should return the book or else renew the borrowing. Renewal can only be done when there is no reservation for the book. If a user does not return of book or does not renew the lending period, action is only taken after 1 extra week, by sending him or her (or them) a reminder. So a user is reminded of his obligation to return the book 4 weeks after it was borrowed. If it is not yet returned or renewed, a second reminder is sent after 7 weeks. After the second reminder, the user has still one week to respond. If one week after the second reminder there is no message from the user, he or she must pay a fine of Dfl 70 and is not allowed to borrow any more books until the book is returned and the fine is paid.

Any user can reserve books that are currently borrowed by someone else. He or she will receive a message when the book is available and the library will hold the book for ten days so that this user can borrow the book. If the book is not fetched after ten days, the book is returned to the shelf. There can be at most one reserver for a book.

If a user loses a book, he or she has to report this to the administration, who will issue an invoice for the price of the book. If a user loses a pass, the pass is registered as lost and the library will issue a new pass at no cost. If the lost pass is found, the user has to return it to the library. Journal issues can be lost as well. Since issues are not lent to users, this cannot be attributed to any particular reader.

For some years now, the library experiences problems that cause increasing hindrance to library staff as well as users and that hinder the library in the realization of its primary function, making scientific documents available to its users. An unknown number of books and journal issues is lost or stolen, and often it is not known which of the two is the case.

Sometimes, a book registered as present cannot be found on its shelf and there is no record of it being borrowed to anyone. On the other hand, a book registered as borrowed or even as stolen may be found on a shelf. There are no reliable statistics of the use of documents and of their availability, such as the ratio between reservations and borrowings. Availability of documents is further decreased because some users, especially University staff, lend books for months or even years without bothering to return them.

These problems have budgetary consequences, for lost or stolen documents must be replaced and the costs of this are added to the normal costs of paying for journal subscriptions and the acquisition of books. In the coming years, the library budget for the university is not likely to increase, to put it mildly. In view of cuts in university funding by the government, the budget will probably decrease in the next few years. At the same time, scientific publishers start new journals almost every month, and tend to double the subscription rate every few years. Most subscriptions are in US dollars, and due to fluctuations in the dollar rate, this price increase may pass unnoticed in some years and hit extra hard in other years.

Some faculties chronically overspend their budget by simply refusing to terminate subscriptions. Especially faculties of "old" sciences such as Chemistry, Physics and Mathematics have some very expensive reference journals and in addition a wide assortment of subscriptions that cover some specialities within their science very well. However, those faculties argue that they have a minimal subscription portfolio already, and that termination of more subscriptions would endanger the quality of their scientific research, which is of a high level. All faculties, young and old, argue that they only have subscriptions to a fraction of the available journals, and that it would be irresponsible to terminate even one of them. For some of the older faculties, some of these subscriptions were started in the nineteenth century and the library and faculties all agree that it would be a shame to terminate such a subscription. However, they disagree on whether this implies that these subscriptions therefore should not be terminated, no matter what the budgetary consequences.

There are no competitors which aim at the same part of the market, and the library is a non-profit organization, so performance cannot be measured in terms of profit. The long-term objective of the library is to improve the level of service currently provided to the user, and to look for possibilities to provide new services. As part of the realization of the first objective, organizational measures are taken that aim at making more efficient use of the financial means at the disposal of the library than is done now. These measures are described below.

As part of the realization of the second objective, the possibilities for providing new services are being studied. There is a national EDI network for university libraries and public libraries of which the library is not yet a part. Access to this network would allow the users to find literature fast and request it from the appropriate library anywhere in The Netherlands. Possibilities for extending this kind of service by connecting to a European network are also considered. In addition, the library catalogue should be made available online to users, and there are plans to provide entry into the catalogue by terminals installed at the library itself, through a modem connection, and through the local area network of the university.

To eliminate some problems experienced by the library, and reduce others, the library is reorganized. To spend the library budget more efficiently, all double subscriptions to journals should be terminated, so that for each journal, there is at most one subscription owned by the University. Similarly, books already present in the University library in one department should not be bought by another, unless there is good reason to do so.

Journals cannot be borrowed anymore, neither in single issues nor in bound volumes. All library departments get photocopiers so that papers from journals can be copied without borrowing them.

To reduce theft, documents that can be borrowed are marked in an indelible way, and ports with sensors are installed at the entry of each library.

An IS should be installed that supports library staff in the stricter enforcement of library rules. For example, the borrowing limit of three weeks will be strictly maintained, and to support this enforcement, a report should be produced each week on documents who are borrowed for longer than their allowed lending period, together with a standard letter that is sent to the user. In addition, once every year, all users are to be sent a list of lost or stolen books, so that they become aware of the problem.

Appendix C

An outline of some development methods

C.1 ETHICS

ETHICS (Effective Technical and Human Implementation of Computer-Based Systems) is a sociotechnical system development method, developed by Enid Mumford of the Manchester Business School in the late 1970s and early 1980s [237, 235]. A **sociotechnical** development method is a method to develop a system that consists of of a human subsystem and a technical subsystem. Sociotechnical development is oriented to developing both subsystems in an integrated way, so that the integrated system functions in an optimal way. This development strategy has its background in studies done in the 1950s on the relationship between social structure and technology in organizations [347]. Emery and Trist [95] give a brief introduction to sociotechnical development. Bostrom and Heinen [47] give an introduction to sociotechnical ideas for system developers and apply these ideas to an analysis of success and failure factors of information system development. ETHICS is a sociotechnical development method oriented towards information systems at the operational level of an organization. Pava [256] shows how sociotechnical ideas can be applied to the development of strategic information systems.

ETHICS can best be viewed as a development method for organization units, with equal emphasis on the job satisfaction aspect, the workflow aspect and the information aspect of the unit. Most of the method is spent in requirements determination, which follows a rational choice cycle. Work design and implementation involves designing and implementing a (new or renovated) information system, but there is no specific advice of ETHICS about this.

ETHICS is a participative method that follows the consensus model. The efficiency needs and job satisfaction needs are collected and diagnosed by means of questionnaires given to all people who work in the organization unit. Decisions are made by involving all workers in the unit, who should all support the decisions. The decision about the change option should be verified with the appropriate management authorities.

An outline of the ETHICS method is given in figure C.1.

419

1. Determine the reasons for change.

2. Determine the boundaries of the organization unit to be developed.

3. Describe the organization unit as it currently is.

4. Define the key objectives of the unit.

5. Define the key tasks performed in the unit.

6. Determine the *information needs* of these tasks.

7. Collect the accidental problems with the current organization of work in the unit, i.e. problems that are due to the way the workflow in the unit is currently implemented. Diagnose these problems. The underlying problems are called *efficiency needs*.

8. Collect information on job satisfaction problems in the current organization of work. Diagnose these, and call the underlying problems *job satisfaction needs*.

9. Use the information needs, efficiency needs and job satisfaction needs to determine the change objectives of the development process.

10. Generate and evaluate organizational change options.

11. Generate and evaluate technical change options.

12. Merge the technical and organizational options and choose one.

13. Make a detailed work design for the chosen option.

14. Implement the work design.

15. Evaluate the new situation.

Figure C.1: Outline of the ETHICS method.

1. **Feasibility study.** Find out if the development of a computer-based system would provide benefits that justify the cost of the development process.

2. **Classical structured analysis.**

   (a) Specify the current system, allowing physical details.

   (b) Specify the current essential system by eliminating all physical details.

   (c) Transform this into an essential model of the desired situation.

   (d) Generate alternative physical implementations of the new system.

   (e) Quantify each alternative by a cost/benefit analysis.

   (f) Choose an option.

   (g) Propose a budget for the chosen option.

   (h) Plan the rest of the project.

   (i) Package the resulting documents into a structured specification.

3. **Structured design.**

   (a) Derive structure charts for the design and add control.

   (b) Design the module structure of the system.

   (c) Package the resulting documents into a structured design specification.

4. **Structured implementation.**

Figure C.2: Outline of classical structured development.

C.2 Structured Development

There are several versions of structured development that can be classified as **classical structured development** and **modern structured development**. In classical development, the current system is reverse engineered to retrieve an essential system model, which is then re-engineered to a model of the desired system. In modern developmemt, the desired system is modeled using event partitioning, without assuming that a current system has been modeled first. Figure C.2 gives an outline of the classical method as proposed by DeMarco [84]. Figure C.3 gives an overview of the modern structured analysis as described by Goldsmith [118].

C.3 SSADM

SSADM (Structured Systems Analysis and Design Method) is the standard method prescribed by the UK government for carrying out development projects for computer-based systems [14, 91, 98]. It assumes that there is a strategic information plan for the business and gives a number of steps that lead from a global information strategy to an implemented information system. SSADM uses structured techniques from a number of other methods, including Entity-Relationship modeling, Structured Analysis and Jackson System

1. Build an essential model of the desired system.

  1.1 Build a context diagram.

    (a) Understand the purpose of the system.

    (b) Identify the external entities.

    (c) Define the data flows entering and leaving the system.

    (d) Check the context diagram.

  1.2 Build an event list.

  1.3 Build a behavioral model.

    (a) Build a DFD, an ER diagram, and state transition diagrams (not treated in this volume).

    (b) Integrate the diagrams.

    (c) Divide the diagrams into levels.

    (d) Complete the data dictionary.

    (e) Add implementation constraints.

2. Build a processor environment model.

  2.1 Allocate data transformations and data stores to available processors.

  2.2 Document the allocation by means of allocation tables.

3. Specify the human-computer interface.
4. Build a software environment model.

  4.1 For each processor, allocate behavior to standard software already available on the processor.

  4.2 Allocate remaining behavior to execution units.

  4.3 Document the allocation by means of allocation tables.

5. Build a code organization model.

  5.1 Translate each DFD into a structure chart.

  5.2 Complete the traceability tables that show allocation of transformations to modules.

Figure C.3: Outline of modern structured development.

Development. SSADM assumes that there is a project board which monitors the information strategy of the business and to which the project team executing the SSADM process reports. Every step in the feasibility study is verified with the project board.

SSADM consists of 5 tasks, called *modules*, each of which is divided into one or more tasks called *stages*, which themselves are devided into a sequence of *steps*. Figures C.4 and C.5 give an outline of SSADM. The construction, test and operation tasks are not part of SSADM.

Feasibility study

0. Feasibility

010 *Prepare feasibility study.* Define scope of the project, identify stakeholders and problem areas, create a high level model of data and activities.

020 *Define the problem.* Identify the activities and information necessary for the business unit to meet its objectives, identify those aspects of current operations where improvement is required, identify new features of the system, identify nonfunctional requirements.

030 *Identify feasibility options.* Draw up a list of minimum requirements, to be met by all options. make a list of up to six business system options and up to six technical system options. Combine, trim down to about three, document these and do a cost/benefit analysis and impact analysis of these. Identify preferred option and assist project board and users in selection.

040 *Assemble feasibility report.*

Requirements analysis

1. Investigate current environment.

110 *Establish analysis framework.* Review output from feasibility study, identify target users, plan the project.

120 *Investigate and define requirements.* Investigate current system operation, including frequencies, volumes, etc. Identify intended users and identify opportunities for improving current system, as well as desired functions and data not currently provided.

130 *Investigate current processing.* Create a data flow diagram of current processing. Identify shortcomings of current processing with users and add to requirements.

140 *Investigate current data.* Create an entity model of current data. Identify shortcomings of current data with users and add to requirements.

150 *Derive logical view of current services.* Make logical model of current processing and data.

160 *Assemble investigation results.*

2. Investigate business system options.

210 *Define business system options.* Make a list of requirements, define up to six business solutions, cut down to three with user, describe each of these and do a cost/benefit analysis and an impact analysis.

220 *Select business system option.* Present to project board, record choice made and complete description of this choice.

Figure C.4: Feasibility study and requirements analysis in SSADM.

Requirements specification.

3. Specify requirements.

    310 *Define required system processing.* Transform logical model of current processing to agree with selected option. Define user roles and correlate role with new processing model.

    320 *Develop required data model.* Transform logical model of current data to agree with selected option and with new processing model.

    330 *Derive system functions.* Identify update and enquiry functions, specify I/O interface of each function, cross-reference with user roles and identify critical dialogues.

    340 *Enhance required data model.* Normalize data of selected functions and verify the result with logical data model.

    350 *Develop specification prototyping.* Create prototypes of dialogues, reports, screens and access paths for selected functions. Test with users and iterate if necessary.

    360 *Develop process specification.* Identify for each entity in the logical data model which events create, update or delete it and define a life cycle of events for the entity. Include parallelism, interaction and abnormal termination. Specify all entities affected by an event and define enquiry access paths.

    370 *Confirm system objectives.* Ensure that all functional requirements are met and that all non-functional requirements are defined.

    380 *Assemble requirements specification.*

Logical system specification

4. Investigate technical system options.

    410 *Define technical system options.* Identify ways to implement requirements.

    420 *Select technical system option.*

5. Specify logical design.

    510 *Design user dialogues.*

    520 *Define update processing model.*

    530 *Define enquiry processing model.*

    540 *Assemble logical design.*

Physical design

6. Specify physical design

    610-... (Details omitted)

Figure C.5: Requirements specification, logical system specification and physical design in SSADM.

Bibliography

[1] R.J. Abbott. Program design by informal English descriptions. *Communications of the ACM*, 26:882–894, 1983.

[2] ACM. ACM code of professional conduct. *Communications of the ACM*, 16:262–269, 1973.

[3] P.E. Agre. Book review of Lucy A. Suchman, *Plans and Situated Actions: The Problem of Human-Machine Communication. Artificial Intelligence*, 43:369–384, 1990.

[4] W.W. Agresti. The conventional software life-cycle model: its evolution and assumptions. In W.W. Agresti, editor, *New Paradigms for Software Development*, pages 2–5. Computer Society Press, 1986.

[5] W.W. Agresti, editor. *New Paradigms for Software Development*. Computer Society Press, 1986.

[6] B. Alabiso. Transformation of data flow analysis models to object oriented design. In N. Meyrowitz, editor, *Object-Oriented Programming Systems, Languages and Applications, Conference Proceedings*, pages 335–353. ACM Press, 1988. SIGPLAN Notices, volume 23.

[7] M. Alavi. An assessment of the prototyping approach to information systems development. *Communications of the ACM*, 27:556–563, 1984.

[8] M. Alavi and J.C. Wetherbe. Mixing prototyping and data modeling for information system design. *IEEE Software*, 11(5):86–91, May 1991.

[9] R.E. Anderson, D.G. Johnson, D. Gotterbarn, and J. Perrolle. Using the new ACM code of ethics in decision making. *Communications of the ACM*, 36(2):98–105, February 1993.

[10] S.J. Andriole. Fast, cheap requirements: prototype, or else! *IEEE Software*, 14(3):85–87, March 1994.

[11] L.B. Archer. *Technological Innovation — A Methodology*. Inforlink, on behalf of the Science Policy Foundation, 1971.

[12] L.B. Archer. Whatever became of design methodology? *Design Studies*, 1(1):17–18, July 1971.

[13] L.B. Archer. Systematic method for designers. In N. Cross, editor, *Developments in Design Methodology*, pages 57–82. Wiley, 1984. Originally published by *The Design Council*, 1965.

[14] C. Ashworth and M. Goodland. *SSADM: A Practical Approach*. McGraw-Hill, 1990.

[15] M. Asimov. *Introduction to Design*. Prentice-Hall, 1962.

[16] D.E. Avison and A.T. Wood-Harper. *Multiview: An Exploration in Information Systems Development*. Blackwell, 1990.

[17] R.L. Baber. "software engineering" vs. software *engineering. Computer*, 22(5):81, 1989.

[18] J.C.M. Baeten and W.P. Weijland. *Process Algebra*. Cambridge Tracts in Theoretical Computer Science 18. Cambridge University Press, 1990.

[19] S.C. Bailin. An object-oriented requirements specification method. *Communications of the ACM*, 32:608–623, 1989.

[20] J.P. Bansler and K. Bødker. A reappraisal of structured analysis: Design in an organizational context. *ACM Transactions on Information Systems*, 11(2):165–193, April 1993.

[21] R. Barker. *Case*Method: Entity Relationship Modelling*. Addison-Wesley, 1990.

[22] R. Barker. *Case*Method: Tasks and Deliverables*. Addison-Wesley, 1990.

[23] R. Barker and C. Longman. *Case*Method: Function and Process Modelling*. Addison-Wesley, 1992.

[24] V.R. Basili and A.J. Turner. Iterative enhancement: a practical technique for software development. *IEEE Transactions on Software Engineering*, SE-1(4):390–396, December 1975.

[25] C. Batini, S. Ceri, and S.B. Navathe. *Conceptual Database Design: An Entity-Relationship Approach*. Benjamin/Cummings, 1992.

[26] C. Batini and M. Lenzerini. A methodology for data schema integration in the entity relationship model. *IEEE Transactions on Software Engineering*, SE-10:650–664, 1984.

[27] C. Batini, M. Lenzerini, and S.B. Navathe. A comparative analysis of methodologies for database schema integration. *ACM Computing Surveys*, 18(4):323–364, December 1986.

[28] F.C. Belz. Applying the spiral model: observations on developing system software in ADA. In *Proceedings of the 4th Annual Conference on Ada Technology*, pages 57–66, 1986.

[29] P.L. Berger and T. Luckmann. *The Social Construction of Reality: A Treatise in the Sociology of Knowledge*. Anchor Books, 1984. First edition 1966.

[30] D.M. Berry. Academic legitimacy of the software engineering discipline. Technical report, Software Engineering Institute, Carnegie Mellon University, Pittsburgh, Pennsylvania 15213, November 1992. Available through anonymous ftp from ftp.sei.cmu.edu (128.237.2.179).

[31] G. Berry and I. Cosserat. The ESTEREL synchronous programming language and its mathematical semantics. In S. Brookes and G. Winskel, editors, *Seminar on Concurrency*, pages 389–448, 1985. Lecture Notes in Computer Science 197.

[32] L. von Bertalannfy. *General Systems Theory*. Penguin, 1968.

[33] A. Birchenough and J.R. Cameron. JSD and object-oriented design. In J. Cameron, editor, *JSP & JSD - The Jackson Approach to Software Development*, pages 292–304. IEEE Computer Science Press, second edition, 1989.

[34] B.I. Blum. A taxonomy of software development methods. *Communications of the ACM*, 37(11):82–94, November 1994.

[35] B. Boehm and F. Belz. Applying process programming to the spiral model. In *Proceedings of the 4th International Software Process Workshop*, pages 46–56, 1988.

[36] B.W. Boehm. Software engineering. *IEEE Transactions on Computers*, C-25:1226–1241, 1976.

[37] B.W. Boehm. *Software Engineering Economics*. Prentice-Hall, 1981.

[38] B.W. Boehm. Verifying and validating software requirements and design specifications. *IEEE Software*, pages 75–88, January 1984.

[39] B.W. Boehm. A spiral model of development and enhancement. *Software Engineering Notes*, 11(4):14–24, 1986. (Proceedings of International Workshop on Software Process and Software Environments, March 1985).

[40] B.W. Boehm. Improving software productivity. *Computer*, pages 43–57, September 1987.

[41] B.W. Boehm. Implementing risk management. In B. Boehm, editor, *Software Risk Management*, pages 433–440. IEEE Computer Society Press, 1989.

[42] B.W. Boehm. A spiral model of software development and enhancement. *Computer*, pages 61–72, may 1988.

[43] B.W. Boehm, T.E. Gray, and T. Seewalt. Prototyping versus specifying: A multiproject experiment. *IEEE Transactions on Software Engineering*, SE-10:290–302, 1984.

[44] G. Booch. Object-oriented development. *IEEE Transactions on Software Engineering*, SE-12:211–221, 1986.

[45] G. Booch. *Object-Oriented Design with Applications, Second edition*. Benjamin/Cummings, 1994.

[46] A. Borgida, J. Mylopoulos, and H.K.T. Wong. Generalization/specialization as a basis for software specification. In M.L. Brodie, J. Mylopoulos, and J.W. Schmidt, editors, *On Conceptual Modelling*, pages 87–114. Springer, 1984.

[47] R.P. Bostrom and J.S. Heinen. MIS problems and failures: A sociotechnical perspective. Part I: The causes. *MIS Quarterly*, pages 17–32, September 1977.

[48] J.M. Bots, E. van Heck, V. van Swede, and J.L. Simons. *Bestuurlijke Informatiekunde*. Cap Gemini Publishing/Pandata B.V., 1990.

[49] K.E. Boulding. General systems theory — the skeleton of science. *General Systems*, 1:11–17, 1956.

[50] J.W. Brackett. Software requirements: SEI Curriculum Module SEI-CM-19-1.2. Technical report, Software Engineering Institute, Carnegie Mellon University, Pittsburgh, Pennsylvania 15213, January 1990. Available through anonymous ftp from ftp.sei.cmu.edu (128.237.2.179).

[51] M.L. Brodie, J. Mylopoulos, and J.W. Schmidt, editors. *On Conceptual Modelling*. Springer, 1984.

[52] M.L. Brodie and E. Silva. Active and passive component modelling: ACM/PCM. In T.W. Olle, H.G. Sol, and A.A. Verrijn-Stuart, editors, *Information Systems design Methodologies: A Comparitive Review*, pages 41–91. North-Holland, 1982.

[53] F. Brooks. No silver bullet: essence and accidents of software engineering. *Computer*, 20(4):10–19, April 1987.

[54] P.G. Brown. QFD: echoing the voice of the customer. *AT&T Technical Journal*, pages 18–32, March/April 1991.

[55] T.A. Byrd, K.L. Cossick, and R.W. Zmud. A synthesis of research on requirements analysis and knowledge acquisition techniques. *MIS Quarterly*, pages 117–138, March 1992.

[56] J. Cameron, editor. *JSP & JSD - The Jackson Approach to Software Development*. IEEE Computer Science Press, second edition, 1989.

[57] J.R. Cameron. An overview of JSD. *IEEE Transactions on Software Engineering*, SE-12:222–240, 1986.

[58] T.T. Carey and R.E.A. Mason. Information system prototyping: techniques, tools, and methodologies. In B. Boehm, editor, *Software Risk Management*, pages 349–359. IEEE Computer Society Press, 1989. Appeared in *INFOR — The Canadian Journal of Operational Research and Information Processing*, 21(3), 1983, pages 177–191.

[59] E. Carmel, R.D. Whitaker, and J.F. George. PD and Joint Application Design: a transatlantic comparison. *Communications of the ACM*, 36(6):40–48, June 1993.

[60] R. Carnap. *Der logische Aufbau der Welt*. Felix Meiner verlag, 1928.

[61] J.L. Carswell and A.B. Navathe. SA–ER: a methodology that links structured analysis and entity–relationship modeling for database systems. In S. Spaccapietra, editor, *Entity–Relationship Approach*, pages 381–396. North–Holland, 1987.

[62] P. Checkland and J. Scholes. *Soft Systems Methodology in Action*. Wiley, 1990.

[63] P.B. Checkland. *Systems Thinking, Systems Practice*. Wiley, 1981.

[64] P. Chen, editor. *Proceedings of the 1st International Conference on the Entity-Relationship Approach to Systems Analysis and Design*. North-Holland, 1980.

[65] P.P.-S. Chen. The entity-relationship model – Toward a unified view of data. *ACM Transactions on Database Systems*, 1:9–36, 1976.

[66] P.P.-S. Chen. English sentence structure and Entity-Relationship diagrams. *Information Sciences*, 29:127–149, 1983.

[67] C.W. Churchman. *The Systems Approach and Its Enemies*. Basic Books, 1979.

[68] P. Coad and E. Yourdon. *Object-Oriented Analysis*. Yourdon Press/Prentice-Hall, 1990.

[69] E.F. Codd. A relational model of data for large shared data banks. *Communications of the ACM*, 13:377–387, 1970.

[70] E.F. Codd. Extending the database relational model to capture more meaning. *ACM Transactions on Database Systems*, 4:397–434, 1979.

[71] D. Coleman, P. Arnold, S. Bodoff, C. Dollin, H. Gilchrist, F. Hayes, and P. Jeremaes. *Object-Oriented Development: The FUSION Method*. Prentice-Hall, 1994.

[72] Arthur Young & Company. *The Arthur Young Practical Guide to Information Engineering*. Wiley, 1987.

[73] P.A. Currit, M. Dyer, and H.D. Mills. Certifying the reliability of software. *IEEE Transactions on Software Engineering*, SE-12(1):3–31, 1986.

[74] B. Curtis, H. Krasner, and N. Iscoe. A field study of the software design process for large systems. *Communications of the ACM*, 31(11):1268–1287, November 1988.

[75] O.-J. Dahl, E.W. Dijkstra, and C.A.R. Hoare. *Structured Programming*. Academic Press, 1972.

[76] A.M. Davis. A taxonomy for the early stages of the software development life cycle. *The Journal of Systems and Software*, 8:297–311, 1988.

[77] A.M. Davis. *Software Requirements: Objects, Functions, States*. Prentice-Hall, 1993.

[78] A.M. Davis, E.H. Bersoff, and E.R. Comer. A strategy for comparing alternative software development life cycle models. *IEEE Transactions on Software Engineering*, 14:1453–1461, 1988.

[79] A.M. Davis and P.A. Freeman. Guest editor's introduction: Requirements engineering. *IEEE Transactions on Software Engineering*, 17(3):210–211, March 1991.

[80] A.M. Davis and P. Hsia. Giving voice to requirements engineering. *IEEE Software*, 10(6):12–16, March 1994.

[81] G.B. Davis. Strategies for information requirements determination. *IBM Systems Journal*, 21:4–30, 1982.

[82] G.B. Davis and M.H. Olson. *Management Information Systems: Conceptual Foundations, Structure, and Development*. McGraw-Hill, 2nd edition, 1985.

[83] P.A. Dearnley and P.J. Mayhew. In favour of system prototypes and their integration into the system development life cycle. *The Computer Journal*, 26:36–42, 1983.

[84] T. DeMarco. *Structured Analysis and System Specification*. Yourdon Press/Prentice-Hall, 1978.

[85] R. Descartes. Rules for the direction of the mind. In J. Cottingham, R. Stoothoff, and D. Murdoch, editors, *The Philosophical Writings of Descartes*, volume 1. Cambridge University Press, 1985. Trans. D. Murdoch.

[86] J. Dewey. *How We Think: a restatement of the relation of reflective thinking to the educative process*. D.C. Heath and Company, 1933.

[87] E.W. Dijkstra. Notes on structured programming. In *Structured Programming*, pages 1–82. Academic Press, 1972.

[88] J.R. Distaso. Software management — a survey of the practice in 1980s. *Proceedings of the IEEE*, 68(9):1103–1119, September 1980.

[89] M. Dorfman. System and software requirements engineering. In R. Thayer and M. Dorfman, editors, *System and Software Requirements Engineering*, pages 4–16. IEEE Computer Science Press, 1990.

[90] M. Dorfman and R.H. Thayer, editors. *Standards, Guidelines, and Examples on System and Software Requirements Engineering*. Computer Science Press, 1990.

[91] E. Downs, P. Clare, and I. Coe. *Structured Systems Analysis and Design Method: Application and Context*. Prentice-Hall, second edition, 1992.

[92] P. Drucker. *The Practice of Management*. William Heinemann, 1955.

[93] M. Dyer. The management of software engineering part IV: software development practices. *IBM Systems Journal*, 19(4):451–465, 1980.

[94] R. Elmasri and S.B. Navathe. *Fundamentals of Database Systems*. Benjamin/Cummings, 1989.

[95] F.E. Emery and E.L. Trist. Socio-technical systems. In C.W. Churchman and M. Verhulst, editors, *Management Science, Models and Techniques* Vol. 2, pages 83–97. Pergamon, 1960.

[96] M.D. Ermann, M.B. Williams, and C. Gutierrez, editors. *Compuers, Ethics, and Society*. Oxford University Press, 1990.

[97] G. Ernst and A. Newell. *GPS: A Case Study in Generality and Problem Solving*. Academic Press, 1969.

[98] M. Eva. *SSADM Version 4: A User's guide*. McGraw-Hill, 1992.

[99] M.E. Fagan. Design and code inspections to reduce errors in program development. *IBM Systems Journal*, 15:182–211, 1976.

[100] M.E. Fagan. Advances in software inspections. *IEEE Transactions on Software Engineering*, SE-12:744–751, 1986.

[101] R.G. Fichman and C.F. Kemerer. Object-oriented and conventional analysis and design methodologies: Comparison and critique. *Computer*, 25:22–39, October 1992.

[102] S. Fickas and A. Finkelstein, editors. *International Symposium on Requirements Engineering*. IEEE Computer Science Press, 1993.

[103] C. Finkelstein. *An Introduction to Information Engineering*. Addison-Wesley, 1989.

[104] G. Fitzgerald, N. Stokes, and J.R.G. Wood. Feature analysis of contemporary information systems methodologies. *The Computer Journal*, 28:223–230, 1985.

[105] M. Flavin. *Fundamental Concepts of Information Modeling*. Yourdon Press, 1981.

[106] T. Forester and P. Morrison. *Computer Ethics: Cautionary Tales and Ethical Dilemmas in Computing. 2nd edition*. The MIT Press, 1994.

[107] D.P. Freedman and G.M. Weinberg. *Handbook of Walkthroughs, Inspections, and Technical Reviews*. Dorset House, 1990.

[108] C. Gane and T. Sarson. *Structured Systems Analysis: Tools and Techniques*. Prentice-Hall, 1979.

[109] H. Garfinkel. *Studies in Ethnomethodology*. Prentice-Hall, 1967.

[110] O. Gatto. Autosate. *Communications of the ACM*, 7(7):425–432, July 1964.

[111] D.C. Gause and G.M. Weinberg. *Exploring Requirements: Quality Before Design*. Dorset House Publishing, 1989.

[112] D.C. Gause and G.M. Weinberg. *Are Your Lights On?* Dorset House, 1990.

[113] A. Giddens. *Central Problems in Social Theory*. MacMillan, 1979.

[114] T. Gilb. Evolutionary delivery versus the "waterfall model". *ACM Sigsoft Software Engineering Notes*, 10(3):49–61, July 1985.

[115] T. Gilb. *Principles of Software Engineering Management*. Addison-Wesley, 1988.

[116] G.R. Gladden. Stop the life-cycle, I want to get off! *Software Engineering Notes*, 7(2):35–39, April 1982.

[117] J.A. Goguen. Social issues in requirements engineering. In S. Fickas and A. Finkelstein, editors, *International Symposium on Requirements Engineering*, pages 194–195. IEEE Computer Science Press, 1993.

[118] S. Goldsmith. *Real-Time Systems Development*. Prentice-Hall, 1993.

[119] H. Gomaa. A software design method for real-time systems. *Communications of the ACM*, 27(9):938–949, September 1984.

[120] H. Gomaa. Software development of real-time systems. *Communications of the ACM*, 29(7):657–668, July 1986.

[121] H. Gomaa. The impact of prototyping on software system engineering. In R. Thayer and M. Dorfman, editors, *System and Software Requirements Engineering*, pages 543–552. IEEE Computer Science Press, 1990.

[122] H. Gomaa. *Software Design Methods for Concurrent and Real-Time Systems*. Addison-Wesley, 1993.

[123] V.S. Gordon and J.M. Bieman. Rapid prototyping: lessons learned. *IEEE Software*, 12(1):85–94, January 1995.

[124] O. Gotel and A. Finkelstein. Contribution structures. In *Second IEEE International Symposium on Requirements Engineering*. IEEE Computer Society Press, 1995.

[125] F. de Graaf and J.M.A. Berkvens, editors. *Hoofdstukken Informaticarecht*. Samsom H.D. Tjeenk Willink, 1991.

[126] J. Gray. The transaction concept: virtues and limitations. In C. Zaniolo and C. Delobel, editors, *Proceedings of the Seventh International Conference on Very Large Databases*, pages 144–154, Cannes, France, September 9–11 1981.

[127] J.J. van Griethuysen (ed.). Concepts and terminology for the conceptual schema and the information base. Technical Report TC97/SC5/WG3, International Organization of Standards, 1982.

[128] R. Guindon. Designing the design process: exploiting opportunistic thoughts. *Human-Computer Interaction*, 5:304–344, 1990.

[129] O. Gutierrrez. Experimental techniques for information requirements analysis. *Information & Management*, 16:31–43, 1989.

[130] R.D. Hackathorn and J. Karimi. A framework for comparing information engineering methods. *MIS Quarterly*, 12(1):203–220, June 1988.

[131] A.D. Hall. *A Methodology for Systems Engineering*. Van Nostrand, 1962.

[132] A.D. Hall. Three-dimensional morphology of systems engineering. *IEEE Transactions on System Science and Cybernetics*, SSC-5(2):156–160, 1969.

[133] A.D. Hall and R.E. Hagen. Definition of system. In J.A. Litterer, editor, *Organizations: Volume 1, Structure and Behavior*, pages 31–43. Wiley, second edition, 1969.

[134] P. Hall, J. Owlett, and S. Todd. Relations and entities. In G.M. Nijssen, editor, *Modelling in Database Management Systems*, pages 201–220. North-Holland, 1976.

[135] M. Hammer and D. McLeod. Database description with SDM: A semantic database model. *ACM Transactions on Database Systems*, 6:351–386, 1981.

[136] M.Z. Hanani and P. Shoval. A combined methodology for information systems analysis and design based on ISAC and NIAM. *Information Systems*, 11(3):245–253, 1986.

[137] D. Harel. Statecharts: a visual formalism for complex systems. *Science of Computer Programming*, 8:231–274, 1987.

[138] D. Harel. Biting the silver bullet. *Computer*, 25(1):8–20, Jan?uray 1992.

[139] D. Harel, H. Lachover, A. Naamad, A. Pnueli, M. Politi, R. Sherman, A. Shtull-Trauring, and M. Trakhtenbrot. STATEMATE: a working environment for the development of complex reactive systems. *IEEE Transactions on Software Engineering*, 16:403–414, April 1990.

[140] D. Harel and A. Pnueli. On the development of reactive systems. In K. Apt, editor, *Logics and Models of Concurrent Systems*, pages 477–498. Springer, 1985. NATO ASI Series.

[141] D. Hatley and I. Pirbhai. *Strategies for Real-Time System Specification*. Dorset House, 1987.

[142] J.R. Hauser and D. Clausing. The house of quality. *Harvard Business review*, 66(3):63–73, May–June 1988.

[143] M. Heidegger. *Sein und Zeit*. Max Niemeyer Verlag, 15th edition, 1979. First edition 1927.

[144] S.J. Heims. *John von Neumann and Norbert Wiener: From Mathematics to the Technologies of Life and death*. MIT Press, 1980.

[145] B. Henderson-Sellers and L.L. Constantine. Object-oriented development and functional decomposition. *Journal of Object-Oriented Programming*, pages 11–16, January 1991.

[146] R. Hirschheim and H.K. Klein. Four paradigms of information systems development. *Communications of the ACM*, 32(10):1199–1216, October 1989.

[147] N.R. Howes. On using the users' manual as the requirements specification. In R.H. Thayer, editor, *Software Engineering Project Management*, pages 172–177. IEEE Computer Science Press, 1988.

[148] N.R. Howes. On using the users' manual as the requirements specification II. In R. Thayer and M. Dorfman, editors, *System and Software Requirements Engineering*, pages 164–169. IEEE Computer Science Press, 1990.

[149] P. Hsia, A. Davis, and D. Kung. Status report: requirements engineering. *IEEE Software*, 10(6):75–79, November 1993.

[150] V. Hubka. *Principles of Engineering Design*. Butterworth, 1982. Translated and edited by W.E. Eder.

[151] M.E.C. Hull, A. Zarea-Aliabadi, and D.A. Guthrie. Object-oriented design, Jackson system development (JSD) specifications and concurrency. *Software Engineering Journal*, pages 79–86, March 1989.

[152] W.S. Humphrey. *Managing the Software Process*. Addison-Wesley, 1989.

[153] i Logix. The Languages of STATEMATE. Technical report, i-Logix Inc., 22 Third Avenue, Burlington, Mass. 01803, U.S.A., January 1991.

[154] IEEE. IEEE code of ethics. Technical report, The Institute of Electrical and Electronic Engineers, Inc., 345 East 47th Street, New York, NY 10017-2394, U.S.A., 1979.

[155] D. Ince. Prototyping. In J.A. McDermid, editor, *Software Engineer's Reference Book*, pages 40/1–40/12. Butterworth/Heinemann, 1992.

[156] The Institute of Electrical and Electronic Engineers, Inc., 345 East 47th Street, New York, NY 10017, USA. *Software Engineering Standards*, 1987.

[157] M. Jackson. *Principles of Program Design*. Academic Press, 1975.

[158] M. Jackson. *System Development*. Prentice-Hall, 1983.

[159] M. Jackson. Some complexities in computer-based systems and their implications for system development. In *Proceedings of the 1990 IEEE International Conference on Computer Systems and Software Engineering — COMPEURO'90*, pages 344–351, Tel-Aviv, Israel, 8–10 May 1990. IEEE Computer Society Press.

[160] M. Jackson. Problems, methods and specialization. *IEEE Software*, 11(6):57–62, November 1994.

[161] M. Jackson and P. Zave. Domain descriptions. In S. Fickas and A. Finkelstein, editors, *International Symposium on Requirements Engineering*, pages 56–64. IEEE Computer Science Press, 1993.

[162] M.A. Jackson. Constructive methods in program design. In P. Freeman and A.I. Wasserman, editors, *IEEE Tutorial on Software Design Techniques*, pages 514–532. IEEE Computer Society Press, 1983. Reprinted with permission from *Proceedings of the First Conference of the European Cooperation in Informatics*, vol. 44, 1976, pages 236–262.

[163] I. Jacobson, M. Christerson, P. Johnsson, and G. Övergaard. *Object-Oriented Software Engineering: A Use Case Driven Approach*. Prentice-Hall, 1992.

[164] P. Jalote. Functional refinement and nested objects for object–oriented design. *IEEE Transactions on Software Engineering*, 15(3):264–270, March 1989.

[165] R.W. Jensen and C.C. Tonies. *Software Engineering*. Prentice-Hall, 1979.

[166] JMA. Information Engineering Methodology/Facility (IEM/IEF) Overview Seminar, 1990. Course notes.

[167] D.G. Johnson. *Computer Ethics*. Prentice-Hall, 1985.

[168] J.C. Jones. *Design Methods: Seeds of Human Futures*. Wiley, 1970.

[169] J.C. Jones. A method for systematic design. In N. Cross, editor, *Developments in Design Methodology*, pages 9–31. Wiley, 1984. Originally published in J.C. Jones, D. Thornley (eds.), *Conference on Design Methods*, Pergamon, 1963.

[170] D. Katz and R.L. Kahn. *The Social Psychology of Organizations*. Wiley, 1978. Second edition.

[171] P.G.W. Keen and M.S. Scott Morton. *Decision Support Systems: An Organizational Perspective*. Addison-Wesley, 1978.

[172] S.E. Keller, L.G. Kahn, and R.B. Panara. Specifying software quality requirements with metrics. In R. Thayer and M. Dorfman, editors, *System and Software Requirements Engineering*, pages 145–163. IEEE Computer Science Press, 1990.

[173] J.G. Kemeny. *A Philosopher Looks at Science*. Van Nostrand, 1959.

[174] K.E. Kendall and J.E. Kendall. *Systems Analysis and Design*. Prentice-Hall, 1992. Second edition.

[175] W. Kent. A simple guide to five normal forms in relational database theory. *Communications of the ACM*, 26(2):120–125, 1983.

[176] W. Kent. The breakdown of the information model in MDBs. *Sigmod record*, 20(4):10–15, December 1991.

[177] W. Kent. A rigorous model of object reference, identity, and existence. *Journal of Object-Oriented Programming*, 4(3):28–36, June 1991.

[178] S.N. Khoshafian and G.P. Copeland. Object identity. In *Object-Oriented Programming Systems, Languages and Applications*, pages 406–416, 1986. SIGPLAN Notices 22 (12).

[179] R. King and D. McLeod. A unified model and methodology for conceptual database design. In M.L. Brodie, J. Mylopoulos, and J.W. Schmidt, editors, *On Conceptual Modelling*, pages 313–327. Springer, 1984.

[180] R. King and D. McLeod. Semantic data models. In S. Yao, editor, *Principles of Database Design*, pages 115–150. Prentice-Hall, 1985.

[181] W. Kneale and M. Kneale. *The Development of Logic*. Clarendon Press, 1962.

[182] B.V. Koen. Toward a definition of the engineering method. *Engineering Education*, 75:150–155, December 1984.

[183] B.V. Koen. Definition of the engineering method. 1985.

[184] D.A. Kolb and A.L. Frohman. An organization development approach to consulting. *Sloan Management review*, 12(1):51–65, Fall 1970.

[185] J.A. Kowal. *Analyzing Systems*. Prentice-Hall, 1988.

[186] T. Kuhn. *The Structure of Scientific Revolutions*. University of Chicago Press, second, enlarged edition edition, 1970.

[187] I. Lakatos. Falsification and the methodology of scientific research programmes. In I. Lakatos and A. Musgrave, editors, *Criticism and the Growth of Knowledge*, pages 91–196. Cambridge University Press, 1970.

[188] F. Land and R. Hirschheim. Participative systems design: Rationale, tools and techniques. *Journal of Applied Systems Analysis*, 10:91–107, 1983.

[189] J.Z. Lavi, A. Agrawala, R. Buhr, K. Jackson, M. Jackson, and B. Lang. Computer based systems engineering workshop. In J.E. Tomayko, editor, *Software Engineering Education*, pages 149–163. Springer, 1990. Lecture Notes in Computer Science 536.

[190] H.W. Lawson. Philosophies for engineering computer–based systems. *Computer*, 23(12):52–63, December 1990.

[191] M.M. Lehman. Software engineering, the software process and their support. *Software Engineering Journal*, 5(6):243–258, September 1991.

[192] S.W. Liddle, D.W. Embley, and A.N. Woodfield. Cardinality constraints in semantic data models. *Data and Knowledge Engineering*, 11:235–270, 1993.

[193] G.E. Lindblom. The science of 'muddling through'. *Public Administration Review*, 19:79–88, 1959.

[194] O.I. Lindland, G. Sindre, and A. Sølvberg. Understanding quality in conceptual modeling. *IEEE Software*, 11(2):42–49, March 1994.

[195] R.C. Linger. The management of software engineeering part III: Software design practices. *IBM Systems Journal*, 19(4):432–450, 1980.

[196] R.C. Linger. Cleanroom process model. *IEEE Software*, 11:50–58, March 1994.

[197] A. Lopes and F. Costa. Rewriting for reuse. In *Proceedings ERCIM Workshop, Nancy, November 2-4*, pages 43–55. INRIA, 1993.

[198] P. Loucopoulos and V. Karakostas. *System Requirements Engineering*. McGraw-Hill, 1995.

[199] M. Lubars, C. Potts, and C. Richter. A review of the state of the practice in requirements modeling. In S. Fickas and A. Finkelstein, editors, *International Symposium on Requirements Engineering*, pages 2–14. IEEE Computer Science Press, 1993.

[200] M. Lundeberg. The ISAC approach to specification of information systems and its application to the organization of an IFIP working conference. In T.W. Olle, H.G. Sol, and A.A. Verrijn-Stuart, editors, *Information Systems Design Methodologies: A Comparative Review*, pages 173–234. North-Holland, 1982.

[201] M. Lundeberg. An approach for involving the users in the specification of information systems. In P. Freeman and A.I. Wasserman, editors, *IEEE Tutorial on Software Design Techniques*, pages 133–155. IEEE Computer Society Press, 1983. Reprinted with permission from *Formal Models and Practical Tools for Information Systems Design*, H.-J. Schneider (ed.), North-Holland 1979.

[202] M. Lundeberg, G. Goldkuhl, and A. Nilsson. A systematic approach to information systems development - I. Introduction. *Information Systems*, 4:1–12, 1979.

[203] M. Lundeberg, G. Goldkuhl, and A. Nilsson. A systematic approach to information systems development - II. Problem and data oriented methodology. *Information Systems*, 4:93–118, 1979.

[204] M. Lundeberg, G. Goldkuhl, and A. Nilsson. *Information Systems Development — A Systematic Approach*. Prentice-Hall, 1981.

[205] Luqi and W. Royce. Status report: computer-aided prototyping. *Computer*, pages 77–81, November 1992.

[206] R.A. MacKenzie. The management process in 3–D. In R.H. Thayer, editor, *Software Engineering Project Management*, pages 11–14. IEEE Computer Science Press, 1988. First appeared in *Harvard Business Review*, November/December 1969.

[207] B.J. MacLennan. Values and objects in programming languages. *Sigplan Notices*, 17(12):70–79, December 1982.

[208] I. Mangham. *The Politics of Organizational Change*. Associated Business Press, 1979.

[209] Z. Manna and A. Pnueli. *The Temporal Logic of Reactive and Concurrent System Specification*. Springer, 1992.

[210] D.A. Marca and C.L. Gowan. *SADT: Structured Analysis and Design Technique*. McGraw-Hill, 1988.

[211] J.G. March and R. Weissinger-Baylon, editors. *Ambiguity and Command: Organizational Perspectives on Military decision Making*. Pitman, 1986.

[212] J. Martin. *Strategic Data-Planning Methodologies*. Prentice-Hall, 1982.

[213] J. Martin. *Information Engineering*. Prentice-Hall, 1989. Three volumes.

[214] J. Martin. *Information Engineering, Book I: Introduction*. Prentice-Hall, 1989.

[215] J. Martin. *Information Engineering, Book II: Planning and analysis*. Prentice-Hall, 1989.

[216] J. Martin. *Information Engineering, Book III: Design and construction*. Prentice-Hall, 1989.

[217] J. Martin and C. Finkelstein. *Information Engineering*. Savant Institute, 2 New Street, Carnforth, Lancashire, LA5 9BX, England, 1981. Two volumes.

[218] J. Martin and J.J. Odell. *Object-Oriented Analysis and Design.* Prentice-Hall, 1992.

[219] P.C. Masiero and F.S.R. Germano. JSD as object oriented design method. *Software Engineering Notes,* 13(3):22–23, July 1988.

[220] J.A. McCall, P.K. Richards, and G.F. Walters. Factors in software quality assurance. Technical Report RADC-TR-77-369, Rome Air Development Center, 1977.

[221] D.D. McCracken and M.A. Jackson. A minority dissenting position. In W.W. Cotterman, J.D. Couger, B.L. Enger, and F. Harold, editors, *Systems Analysis and Design — A Foundation for the 1980's,* pages 551–553. Elsevier - North-Holland, 1981.

[222] J. McDermid and P. Rook. Software development process models. In J.A. McDermid, editor, *Software Engineer's Reference Book,* pages 15/1–15/36. Butterworth/Heinemann, 1992.

[223] F.W. McFarlan. Portfolio approach to information systems. In B. Boehm, editor, *Software Risk Management,* pages 17–25. IEEE Computer Society Press, 1989. Appeared in *Harvard Business review,* January/February 1974.

[224] J.D. McGregor and D.M. Dyer. Inheritance and state machines. *Software Engineering Notes,* 18(4):61–69, 1993.

[225] S.M. McMenamin and J.F. Palmer. *Essential Systems Analysis.* Yourdon Press/Prentice Hall, 1984.

[226] A.T. McNeille. Jackson system development (JSD). In T.W. Olle, H.G. Sol, and A.A. Verrijn-Stuart, editors, *Information Systems Design Methodologies: Improving the Practice.* North-Holland, 1986.

[227] S.J. Mellor and P.T. Ward. *Structured Development for Real-Time Systems.* Prentice-Hall/Yourdon Press, 1985. Volume 3: Implementation Modeling Techniques.

[228] Michael Jackson Limited. *JSD Course Notes,* 1986.

[229] G.A. Miller. The magical number seven, plus or minus two: Some limits on our capacity for processing information. *The Psychological Review,* 63:81–97, March 1956.

[230] J.C. Miller. Conceptual models for determining information requirements. In *AFIPS Conference proceedings,* volume 25, pages 609–620, 1964. Spring Joint Conference.

[231] R. Milner. *A Calculus of Communicating Systems.* Springer, 1980. Lecture Notes in Computer Science 92.

[232] R. Milner. *Communication and Concurrency.* Prentice-Hall, 1989.

[233] M.L. Minsky. *Computation: Finite and Infinite Machines.* Prentice-Hall, 1967.

[234] H. Mintzberg, D. Raisinghani, and A. Théorêt. The structure of "unstructured" decision processes. *Administrative Science Quarterly,* 21, June 1976.

[235] E. Mumford. *Designing Human Systems for New Technology: The ETHICS Method.* Manchester Business School, 1983.

[236] E. Mumford. Participation from Aristotle to today. In Th. Bemelmans, editor, *Beyond Productivity: Information Systems Development for Organizational Effectiveness,* pages 95–105. North-Holland, 1984.

[237] E. Mumford and M. Weir. *Computer Systems in Work Design – The ETHICS Method.* Associated Business Press, 1979.

[238] G. Nadler. An investigation of design methodology. *Management Science,* 13(10):B–642–B–655, June 1967.

[239] E. Nagel. *The Structure of Science.* Routledge and Kegan Paul, 1961.

[240] National Computing Center, Oxford road, Manchester, M1 7ED, U.K. *The STARTS Guide: A Guide to Methods and Software Tools for the Construction of Large Real-Time Systems*, 1987. Prepared by industry with the support of the DTI and NCC.

[241] J.D. Naumann, G.B. Davis, and J.D. McKeen. Determining information requirements: a contingency method for selection of a requirements assurance strategy. *Journal of System and Software Sciences*, 1:273–281, 1980.

[242] S. Navathe, R. Elmasri, and J. Larson. Integrating user views in database design. *Computer*, pages 50–62, January 1986.

[243] G.M. Nijssen, editor. *Modelling in Database Management Systems*. North-Holland, 1976.

[244] G.M. Nijssen and T.A. Halpin. *Conceptual Schema and Relational Database Design*. Prentice-Hall, 1989.

[245] H. Obbink. Systems engineering environments of ATMOSPHERE. In A. Endres and H. Webers, editors, *Software Development Environments and CASE Technology*, pages 1–17. Springer, 1991. Lecture Notes in Computer Science 509.

[246] T.W. Olle, J. Hagelstein, I.G. Macdonald, C. Rolland, H.G. Sol, F.J.M. van Assche, and A.A. Verrijn-Stuart. *Information Systems Methodologies: A Framework for Understanding*. Addison-Wesley, 1988.

[247] T.W. Olle, H.G. Sol, and C.J. Tully, editors. *Information Systems Design Methodologies: A Feature Analysis*. North-Holland, 1983.

[248] T.W. Olle, H.G. Sol, and A.A. Verrijn-Stuart, editors. *Information System Design Methodologies: A Comparative Review*. North-Holland, 1982.

[249] T.W. Olle, H.G. Sol, and A.A. Verrijn-Stuart, editors. *Information Systems Design Methodologies: Improving the Practice*. North-Holland, 1986.

[250] M.A. Ould. Quality control and assurance. In J.A. McDermid, editor, *Software Engineer's Reference Book*, pages 29/1–29/12. Butterworth/Heinemann, 1992.

[251] M. Page-Jones. *The Practical Guide to Structured Systems Design*. Prentice-Hall, 2nd edition, 1988.

[252] M. Page-Jones. Comparing techniques by means of encapsulation and connascance. *Communications of the ACM*, 35(9):147–151, September 1990.

[253] D.L. Parnas. On the criteria to be used in decomposing systems into modules. *Communications of the ACM*, 5:1053–1058, 1972.

[254] D.L. Parnas. Software aspects of strategic defense systems. *Communications of the ACM*, 28(12):1326–1335, December 1985.

[255] D.L. Parnas and P.C. Clements. A rational design process: How and why to fake it. *IEEE Transactions on Software Engineering*, SE-12:251–257, 1986.

[256] C. Pava. *Managing New Office Technology: An Organizational Strategy*. The Free Press, 1983.

[257] L.J. Peters. *Software Design: Methods and Techniques*. Prentice-Hall, 1981.

[258] L.J. Peters and L.L. Tripp. A model of software engineering. In *Third International Conference on Software Engineering*, pages 63–70. IEEE Computer Science Press, 1978.

[259] K. Pohl. The three dimensions of requirements engineering: a framework and its applications. *Information Systems*, 19(3):243–258, 1994.

[260] M. Polanyi. *Personal Knowledge*. Chicago University Press, 1958.

[261] M. Polanyi. *The Tacit Dimension*. Routledge and Kegan Paul, 1966.

[262] M. Pollner. *Mundane Reason: Reality in Everyday and Sociological Discourse.* Cambridge University Press, 1987.

[263] G. Polya. *How to Solve it. A New Aspect of Mathematical Method.* Princeton University Press, second edition, 1985. First edition 1945.

[264] K.R. Popper. *The Logic of Scientific Discovery.* Hutchinson, 1959.

[265] C. Potts and G. Bruns. Recording the reasons for design decisions. In *10th International Conference on Software Engineering*, pages 418–427, 1988.

[266] Euromethod project. Euromethod case study. Technical Report EM-2.5-CS, Euromethod project, 1994.

[267] Euromethod project. Euromethod concepts manual 1: Transaction model. Technical Report EM-3.1-TM, Euromethod project, 1994.

[268] Euromethod project. Euromethod concepts manual 2: Deliverable model. Technical Report EM-3.2-DM, Euromethod project, 1994.

[269] Euromethod project. Euromethod concepts manual 3: Strategy model. Technical Report EM-3.3-SM, Euromethod project, 1994.

[270] Euromethod project. Euromethod customer guide. Technical Report EM-2.1-CG, Euromethod project, 1994.

[271] Euromethod project. Euromethod delivery planning guide. Technical Report EM-2.3-DPG, Euromethod project, 1994.

[272] Euromethod project. Euromethod dictionary. Technical Report EM-4-ED, Euromethod project, 1994.

[273] Euromethod project. Euromethod method bridging guide. Technical Report EM-2.4-MBG, Euromethod project, 1994.

[274] Euromethod project. Euromethod overview. Technical Report EM-1-EO, Euromethod project, c/o Sema Group, 16, rue Barbès, 92126 Montrouge Cedex, France, 1994.

[275] Euromethod project. Euromethod supplier guide. Technical Report EM-2.2-SG, Euromethod project, 1994.

[276] S. Pugh. *Integrated Product Engineering.* Addison-Wesley, 1991.

[277] H. Reichenbach. *Experience and Prediction.* University of Chicago press, 1938.

[278] H. Reichenbach. *Elements of Symbolic Logic.* The Free Press/Collier-MacMillan, 1947.

[279] H.W.J. Rittel and M.M. Webber. Planning problems are wicked problems. In N. Cross, editor, *Developments in Design Methodology*, pages 135–144. Wiley, 1984. Originally published as part of "Dilemmas in a general theory of planning" in *Policy Sciences*, 4 (1973), 155–169.

[280] R. Rock-Evans. *Analysis within the Systems Development Life Cycle*, volume 1: Data Analysis —The Deliverables. Pergamon Infotech, 1987.

[281] R. Rock-Evans. *Analysis within the Systems Development Life Cycle*, volume 2: Data Analysis —The Methods. Pergamon Infotech, 1987.

[282] R. Rock-Evans. *Analysis within the Systems Development Life Cycle*, volume 3: Activity Analysis —The Deliverables. Pergamon Infotech, 1987.

[283] R. Rock-Evans. *Analysis within the Systems Development Life Cycle*, volume 4: Activity Analysis —The Methods. Pergamon Infotech, 1987.

[284] R. Rock-Evans. *A Simple Introduction to Data and Activity Analysis.* Computer Weekly Publications, 1989.

[285] J.F. Rockart. Chief executives define their own data needs. *Harvard Business Review*, 57(2):81–93, April/May 1979.

[286] G.-C Roman, M.J. Stucki, W.E. Ball, and W.D. Gillett. A total system design framework. *Computer*, 17(5):15–26, May 1984.

[287] P. Rook. Controlling software projects. In R.H. Thayer, editor, *Software Engineering Project Management*, pages 108–117. IEEE Computer Science Press, 1988. Appeared in the *Software Engineering Journal*, January 1986.

[288] P. Rook. Project planning and control. In J.A. McDermid, editor, *Software Engineer's Reference Book*, pages 27/1–27/36. Butterworth/Heinemann, 1992.

[289] N.F.M. Roozenburg and J. Eekels. *Productontwerpen, Struktuur en Methoden*. Lemma B.V., 1991.

[290] D.T. Ross. Douglass Ross talks about structured analysis. *Computer*, 18(7):80–88, July 1085.

[291] D.T. Ross. Structured analysis (SA): A language for communicating ideas. *IEEE Transactions on Software Engineering*, SE-3(1):16–34, January 1977.

[292] D.T. Ross. Applications and extensions of SADT. *Computer*, 18(4):25–34, April 1985.

[293] D.T. Ross and J.W. Brackett. An approach to structured analysis. *Computer Decisions*, 8(9):40–44, September 1976.

[294] D.T. Ross and K.E. Schoman. Structured analysis for requirements definition. *IEEE Transactions on Software Engineering*, SE-3(5):6–15, January 1977.

[295] W.W. Royce. Managing the development of large software systems. In R.H. Thayer, editor, *Software Engineering Project Management*, pages 118–127. IEEE Computer Science Press, 1988. Appeared in *Proceedings of IEEE WESCON* 1970, IEEE, pp. 1–9.

[296] J. Rumbaugh, M. Blaha, W. Premerlani, F. Eddy, and W. Lorensen. *Object-oriented modeling and design*. Prentice-Hall, 1991.

[297] H.D. Ruys. *ISAC voor docenten*. Moret Ernst & Young, 1990.

[298] G. Saake, P. Hartel, R. Jungclaus, R.J. Wieringa, and R.B. Feenstra. Inheritance conditions for object life cycle diagrams. In U.W. Lipeck and G. Vossen, editors, *Formale Grundlagen für den Entwurf von Informationsystemen*, pages 79–88. Institut für Informatik, Universität Hannover, Postfach 6009, D-30060, Hannover, May 1994. Informatik-Berichte Nr. 03/94.

[299] M. Saeki, H. Horai, and H. Enomoto. Software development process from natural language specification. In *11th International Conference on Software Engineering*, pages 64–73. IEEE Computer Society press, May 15–18 1989.

[300] B. Sanden. Systems programming with JSP: example — a VDU controller. *Communications of the ACM*, 28(10):1059–1067, October 1985. See also the exchange in the *Communications of the ACM*, 29(2), February 1986, 89–90.

[301] B. Sanden. The case for eclectic design of real-time software. *IEEE Transactions on Software Engineering*, 15(3), March 1989.

[302] B. Sanden. An entity-life modeling approach to the design of concurrent software. *Communications of the ACM*, 32(3):330–343, March 1989.

[303] B. Sanden. *Software Systems Construction with Examples in ADA*. Prentice-Hall, 1994.

[304] E. Seidewitz. General object-oriented software development: Background and experience. *The Journal of Systems and Software*, 9:95–108, 1989.

[305] E. Seidewitz and M. Stark. Toward a general object-oriented software development methodology. *ADA Letters*, 7(4):54–67, july/august 1987.

[306] R.W. Selby, V.R. Basili, and F.T. Baker. Cleanroom software development: an empirical evaluation. *IEEE Transactions on Software Engineering*, SE-13(9):1027–1037, September 1987.

[307] B. Selic, G. Gullekson, and P.T. Ward. *Real-Time Object-Oriented Modeling*. Wiley, 1994.

[308] S. Shlaer and S.J. Mellor. *Object-Oriented Systems Analysis: Modeling the World in Data*. Prentice-Hall, 1988.

[309] S. Shlaer and S.J. Mellor. *Object Lifecycles: Modeling the World in States*. Prentice-Hall, 1992.

[310] J. Shomenta, G. Kamp, B. Hanson, and B. Simpson. The application approach worksheet: an evaluative tool for matching new development methods with appropriate applications. *MIS Quarterly*, 7(4):1–10, 1983.

[311] P. Shoval. An integrated methodology for functional analysis, process design and database design. *Information Systems*, 16(1):49–64, 1991.

[312] K. Shumate. Structured analysis and object–oriented design are compatible. *Ada Letters*, 11(4):78–90, May/June 1991.

[313] K. Shumate and M. Keller. *Software Specification and Design: A Disciplined Approach for Real-Time Systems*. Wiley, 1992.

[314] H. Simon. The architecture of complexity. *Proceedings of the Aristotelian Society*, 106:467–482, 1962. Reprinted in H. Simon, *The Sciences of the Artificial*, Second edition, MIT Press, 1961.

[315] H.A. Simon. A behavioral model of rational choice. *Quarterly Journal of Economics*, 69:99–118, 1955.

[316] H.A. Simon. *The New Science of Management Decision*. Harper and Row, 1960.

[317] H.A. Simon. On the concept of organizational goal. *Administrative Science Quarterly*, 9:1–22, 1964.

[318] H.A. Simon. *The Sciences of the Artificial*. MIT Press, 1969.

[319] J.L. Simons and G.M.A. Verheijen. *Informatiestrategie als Managementsopgave: Planning, Ontwikkeling en Beheer van de Informatieverzorging op Basis van Information Engineering*. Kluwer Bedrijfswetenschappen, 1991.

[320] J. M. Smith and D.C.P. Smith. Database abstractions: Aggregation and generalization. *ACM Transactions on Database Systems*, 2:105–133, 1977.

[321] J.M. Smith and D.C.P. Smith. Database abstractions: Aggregation. *Communications of the ACM*, 20:405–413, June 1977.

[322] K. Southwell. Managing software engineering teams. In J.A. McDermid, editor, *Software Engineer's Reference Book*, page Chapter 32. Butterworth/Heinemann, 1992.

[323] J.F. Sowa and J.A. Zachman. Extending and formalizing the framework for information systems architecture. *IBM Systems Journal*, 31(3):590–616, 1992.

[324] R.A. Sprague, K.J. Singh, and R.T. Wood. Concurrent engineering in product development. *IEEE Design and Test of Computers*, 8(1):6–13, March 1991.

[325] W. Stevens, G. Myers, and L. Constantine. Structured design. *IBM Systems Journal*, 13:115–139, 1974.

[326] D.A. Stokes. Requirements analysis. In J.A. McDermid, editor, *Software Engineer's Reference Book*, pages 16/1–16/21. Butterworth/Heinemann, 1992.

[327] V.C. Storey. Relational database design based on the Entity-Relationship model. *Data and Knowledge Engineering*, 7(1):47–83, June 1991.

[328] V.C. Storey and R.C. Goldstein. A methodology for creating user views in database designs. *ACM Transactions on Database Systems*, 13(3):305–338, September 1988.

[329] P.J. van Strien. *Praktijk als Wetenschap. Methodologie van het Sociaal-Wetenschappelijk Handelen*. Van Gorcum, 1986.

[330] L. Suchman and E. Wynn. Procedures and problems in the office. *Office: Technology and People*, 2:135–154, 1984.

[331] L.A. Suchman. Office procedures as practical action: Models of work and system design. *ACM Transactions on Office Information Systems*, 1:320–328, 1983.

[332] A. Sutcliffe. *Jackson System Development*. Prentice-Hall, 1988.

[333] A.G. Sutcliffe. Object-oriented systems development: survey of structured methods. *Information and Software technology*, 33(6):433–442, August 1991.

[334] W. Swartout and R. Balzer. On the inevitable intertwining of specification and implementation. *Communications of the ACM*, 25:438–440, 1982.

[335] V. van Swede and J.C. van Vliet. A flexible framework for contingent information system modelling. *Information and Software Technology*, 35(9):530–548, September 1993.

[336] W.M. Taggart, Jr. and M.O. Tharp. A survey of information requirements analysis techniques. *ACM Computing Surveys*, 9:273–290, 1977.

[337] A.S. Tanenbaum. *Structured Computer Organization*. Prentice-Hall, 3rd edition, 1990.

[338] T.J. Teory. *Database Modeling and Design: The Entity-Relationship Approach*. Morgan Kaufmann, 1990.

[339] T.J. Teory, D. Yang, and J.P. Fry. A logical design methodology for relational databases using the extended entity-relationship model. *ACM Computing Surveys*, 18:197–222, 1986.

[340] B. Thalheim. Fundamentals of cardinality constraints. In G. Pernul and A.M. Tjoa, editors, *Entity-Relationship Approach –ER'92*, pages 7–23. Springer, 1992. Lecture Notes in Computer Science 645.

[341] R.H. Thayer, editor. *Software Engineering Project Management*. IEEE Computer Science Press, 1988.

[342] R.H. Thayer. Software engineering project management: A top-down view. In R.H. Thayer, editor, *Software Engineering Project Management*, pages 15–53. IEEE Computer Science Press, 1988.

[343] R.H. Thayer and M. Dorfman, editors. *System and Software Requirements Engineering*. IEEE Computer Science Press, 1990.

[344] R.H. Thayer and A.B. Pyster. Guest editorial: software engineering project management. *IEEE Transactions on Software Engineering*, SE-10(1):2–3, January 1984.

[345] B. Thomé, editor. *Systems Engineering: Principles and Practice of Computer-Based Systems Engineering*. Wiley, 1993.

[346] B. Thomeé. Definition and scope of systems engineering. In B. Thomé, editor, *Systems Engineering: Principles and Practice of Computer-Based Systems Engineering*, pages 1–23. Wiley, 1993.

[347] E.L. Trist and K.W. Bamforth. Some social and psychological consequences of the Longwall method of coal-getting. *Human Relations*, 4:3–38, 1951.

[348] C. Tully. System development activity. In B. Thomé, editor, *Systems Engineering: Principles and Practice of Computer-Based Systems Engineering*, pages 45–80. Wiley, 1993.

[349] J. in't Veld. *Analyse van Organisatieproblemen: Een Toepassing van Denken in Systemen en Processen*, vijfde druk. Stenfert Kroese, 1988.

[350] J. Vincent, A. Waters, and J. Sinclair. *Software Quality Assurance. Volume 1: Practice and Implementation*. Prentice-Hall, 1988.

[351] W. Visser. More or less following a plan during design: opportunistic deviations in specification. *International Journal of Man–Machine Studies*, 33:247–278, 1990.

[352] P.T. Ward. The transformation schema: An extension of the data flow diagram to represent control and timing. *IEEE Transactions on Software Engineering*, SE-12:198–210, 1986.

[353] P.T. Ward. How to integrate object orientation with structured analysis and design. *Computer*, pages 74–82, March 1989.

[354] P.T. Ward and S.J. Mellor. *Structured Development for Real-Time Systems*. Prentice-Hall/Yourdon Press, 1985. Volume 1: Introduction and Tools.

[355] P.T. Ward and S.J. Mellor. *Structured Development for Real-Time Systems*. Prentice-Hall/Yourdon Press, 1985. Volume 2: Essential Modeling Techniques.

[356] *Webster's Dictionary of English Usage*, 1989.

[357] G.M. Weinberg. *An Introduction to General Systems Thinking*. Wiley, 1975.

[358] V. Weinberg. *Structured Analysis*. Yourdon Press, 1978.

[359] M. West. Quality function deployment. In *Colloquium on Tools and Techniques for Maintaining Traceability During Design*, Savoy Place, London WC2R OBL, U.K., 2 December 1991.

[360] S. White, M. Alford, J. Holtzman, S. Kuehl, B. McCay, D. Oliver, D. Owens, C. Tully, and A. Willey. Systems engineering of computer-based systems. *Computer*, 26(11):54–65, November 1993.

[361] N. Wiener. *Cybernetics*. MIT Press, 1965.

[362] R.J. Wieringa. Three roles of conceptual models in information system design and use. In E.D. Falkenberg P. Lindgreen, editor, *Information System Concepts: An In-Depth Analysis*, pages 31–51. North-Holland, 1989.

[363] R.J. Wieringa. Object-oriented analysis, structured analysis, and Jackson System Development. In F. van Assche, B. Moulin, and C. Rolland, editors, *Object Oriented Approach in Information Systems*, pages 1–21. North-Holland, 1991.

[364] R.J. Wieringa. Combining static and dynamic modeling methods: a comparison of four methods. *The Computer Journal*, 38(1):17–30, 1995.

[365] R.J. Wieringa and W. de Jonge. Object identifiers, keys, and surrogates. *Theory and Practice of Object Systems*, 1(2):101–114, 1995.

[366] R.J. Wieringa, J.-J. Ch. Meyer, and H. Weigand. Specifying dynamic and deontic integrity constraints. *Data and Knowledge Engineering*, 4:157–189, 1989.

[367] R.D. Williams. Managing the development of reliable software. In *Proceedings of the 1975 International Conference on Reliable Software*, pages 3–8, April 1975.

[368] T. Winograd. What does it mean to understand a language? In D.A. Norman, editor, *Perspectives on Cognitive Science*, pages 231–263. Ablex, 1981.

[369] T. Winograd and F. Flores. *Understanding Computers and Cognition: A New Foundation for Design*. Ablex, 1986.

[370] J.G. Wolff. The management of the spiral model: 'Project SP' and the 'new spiral model'. In B. Boehm, editor, *Software Risk Management*, pages 481–491. IEEE Computer Society Press, 1989. Appeared in *Software Engineering Journal*, May 1989.

[371] D.P. Wood and W.G. Wood. Comparative evaluations of specification methods for real-time systems. Technical Report CMU/SEI-89-TR-36 ADA219187, Software Engineering Institute, Carnegie Mellon University Pittsburgh, PA 15213-3890, 1989.

[372] S. Wrycza. The ISAC-driven transition between requirements analysis and ER conceptual modeling. *Information Systems*, 15(6):603–614, 1990.

[373] R.T. Yeh and P.A. Ng. Software requirements — a management perspective. In R. Thayer and M. Dorfman, editors, *System and Software Requirements Engineering*, pages 450–641. IEEE Computer Science Press, 1990.

[374] R.T. Yeh, P. Zave, A.P. Conn, and G.E. Cole. Software requirements: new directions and perspectives. In C.R. Vick and C.V. Ramamoorthy, editors, *Handbook of Software Engineering*, pages 519–543. Van Nostrand Reinhold Company, 1984.

[375] E. Yourdon. *Structured Walkthroughs*. Prentice-Hall, 1985.

[376] E. Yourdon. *Modern Structured Analysis*. Prentice-Hall, 1989.

[377] E. Yourdon. *Object-Oriented Systems Design: An Integrated Approach*. Prentice-Hall, 1994.

[378] E. Yourdon and L.L. Constantine. *Structured Design: Fundamentals of a Discipline of Computer Program and Systems Design*. Prentice-Hall, 1979.

[379] J.A. Zachman. A framework for information systems architecture. *IBM Systems Journal*, pages 276–292, 1987.

[380] P. Zave and D. Jackson. Practical specification techniques for control-oriented systems. In G.X. Ritter, editor, *Information Processing 89*, pages 83–88. North-Holland, 1989.

[381] P. Zave and M. Jackson. Conjunction as composition. *ACM Transactions on Software Engineering and Methodology*, 2(4):379–411, October 1993.

[382] M.V. Zelkowitz. Resource utilization during software development. *Journal of Systems and Software*, 8(4):331–336, 1988.

Index